Herbert Read Reassessed

Herbert Read, about 1950 (photo, Vernon Richards)

HERBERT READ REASSESSED

Edited by David Goodway

LIVERPOOL UNIVERSITY PRESS

First published 1998 by
LIVERPOOL UNIVERSITY PRESS
Liverpool L69 3BX

British Library Cataloguing-in-Publication Data
A British Library CIP record is available

ISBN 0-85323-862-6 (hardback)
ISBN 0-85323-872-3 (paperback)

Typeset in 12/13pt Perpetua by
XL Publishing Services, Lurley, Tiverton
Printed by Henry Ling Limited, Dorchester

Contents

List of Illustrations

Acknowledgements

We are grateful to the following for permission to reproduce the extracts listed:

Balkin Agency Inc. from *The Way of Man* by Martin Buber.
Oxford University Press from *The Principles of Art* by R. G. Collingwood, 1938.
Macmillan USA from *Educating Artistic Vision* by Elliott Eisner, 1972.
Liveright Publishing Corporation from *Introductory Lectures on Psycho-Analysis* by Sigmund Freud, translated by James Strachey. Translation © 1965, 1964, 1963 by James Strachey.
Sigmund Freud Copyrights, the Institute of Psycho-Analysis and the Hogarth Press for quotations from *The Standard Edition of the Complete Psychological Works of Sigmund Freud* translated and edited by James Strachey.
Mrs Virginia Rowan for Louis Adeane's poem 'The Night Loves Us'.
Weidenfeld and Nicolson Ltd from *The Last Modern* by James King, 1990.
Yale University Press from *Towards Social Architecture* by Andrew Saint, © 1987 by Yale University Press.

We are especially grateful for the permission of the Read Archive, University of Victoria, to quote from its manuscript holdings; to Ben Read and the Read Discretionary Trust for permission to quote from the published and unpublished writings of Herbert Read; and to David Higham Associates for permission to quote from the published works of Herbert Read.

Introduction

DAVID GOODWAY

THE interest, as well as the importance, of Herbert Read lies in his high achievement in a considerable number of diverse activities: as a poet, as a literary critic, as an anarchist, as an educationalist, as an art critic, as a philosopher of art, as an historian of and, perhaps above all, as a propagandist for modern art and design. In addition, he was responsible for some of the best writing to come out of the First World War, produced a series of remarkable autobiographies, and wrote one greatly admired novel. The interest of his œuvre, difficult though it is for one person, especially in an era of narrow specialization, to comprehend in its entirety, resides further in its interconnectedness and essential unity. This volume reassesses each area of Read's principal attainment.

Herbert Read was born on 4 December 1893 at Muscoates Grange, a farm near Kirkbymoorside and Helmsley in North Yorkshire. When his father died in 1903, the family, being tenants, had to leave the farm – and the arcadian life that Read was to describe in *The Innocent Eye* – and he was sent to an orphanage in a very different part of Yorkshire: Crossley's School, Halifax. He left school in 1908, aged fifteen, went to Leeds and worked at the Leeds, Skyrac and Morley Savings Bank. In 1912, having borrowed some money from an uncle, he enrolled at the University of Leeds, where he studied a diversity of subjects, although economics was possibly the only one, he later recalled, in which he ever received 'what pedagogues would call a "thorough grounding"'.[1] He left university before finishing his degree to join the army (he was an eager volunteer) and in 1915 was commissioned as a Second Lieutenant in the Yorkshire Regiment, 'the Green Howards'. The same year saw the publication of his first book, *Songs of Chaos,* a volume of poetry. Read had a good war – he was awarded the Military Cross for conducting a raid and capturing an enemy officer, and the Distinguished Service Order for leading a retreat during the Germans' massive offensive of spring 1918 – and he seriously considered pursuing a military career.

In the event he went to work at the new Ministry of Labour and then the Treasury in 1919 and was able in 1922 to transfer, within the Civil Service, to the Department of Ceramics at the Victoria and Albert Museum. This provided the springboard for his highly influential involvement for the rest of his life with the plastic arts. Books soon appeared on *English Pottery* (1924), *English Stained Glass* (1926) and *Staffordshire Pottery Figures* (1929). A long and prolific association began in 1929 with Read

1

contributing art criticism to the *Listener;* and his widely-read *The Meaning of Art* (1931), one of the very few of his books to have remained in print, was adapted from some of these articles.

He left the V&A in 1931 to become Watson Gordon Professor of Fine Art at the University of Edinburgh, but was obliged to resign the following year on account of personal scandal. Already married, he had met Margaret Ludwig ('Ludo'), a Lecturer in Music, who was to become his second wife. Back in London he established close friendships with the members of the most experimental group of artists working in England – Henry Moore, Ben Nicholson, Barbara Hepworth, Paul Nash, soon to be joined by Naum Gabo – and earned a living partly by becoming editor of the art-historical (and establishment) *Burlington Magazine* from 1933 until 1939.

Read was by now the foremost British advocate of modern art. He was the author of *Art Now* (1933), of the first book on his lifelong intimate, Henry Moore (1934), and of a seminal work on industrial design, *Art and Industry* (1934). His avant-gardism led to a close association with the International Surrealist Exhibition of 1936 and he edited the collective statement, *Surrealism,* in the same year; but his fundamental, persistent advocacy was for abstraction. *Art and Society* (1937), originally delivered as the Sydney Jones Lectures at the University of Liverpool, was a pioneering contribution to the sociology of art.

Parallel to these important activities in the world of art was an equally distinguished and productive literary output. Read became a regular contributor from its first issue in 1923 to the *Criterion*, the periodical edited by another lifelong friend, T. S. Eliot. He wrote also for the *Times Literary Supplement* (from 1925) and the *Nation and Athenaeum* (from 1927). Particularly noteworthy was 'Psycho-analysis and the Critic', a *Criterion* article of 1925, which introduced Read as the anglophone pioneer of the application of psychoanalytical theory to literary and art criticism. There were also *Phases of English Poetry* (1928) and *Form in Modern Poetry* (1932). Collections of his literary essays appeared as *Reason and Romanticism* (1926), *The Sense of Glory* (1929), *In Defence of Shelley and Other Essays* (1936) and a large *Collected Essays in Literary Criticism* (1938). In 1929 he delivered the Clark Lectures at Trinity College, Cambridge, and these were published as *Wordsworth* (1930); and his deep engagement with the Romantic poets continued with 'In Defence of Shelley' and the later writings collected as *The True Voice of Feeling* (1953).

The booklets, *In Retreat* (1925) and *Ambush* (1930), were prose treatments of war experiences; *Naked Warriors* (1919) and *The End of a War* (1933) constituted his war poetry. Other volumes of poems were *Eclogues* (1919), *Mutations of the Phoenix* (1923) and, during the renewed European civil war, *A World within a War* (1944). An initial volume of *Collected Poems* was published as early as 1926. The lucid *English Prose Style* came out in 1928. *The Innocent Eye*, the memoir of his childhood and a small masterpiece, followed in 1932 (it was to be incorporated in *Annals of Innocence and Experience* (1940)), and *The Green Child*, a mysterious utopian work and his only novel, in 1934.

2

A series of successful anthologies was launched in 1931 with *The London Book of English Prose* (co-edited with Bonamy Dobrée), to be followed by *The English Vision* (1933), *The Knapsack* (1939), *The London Book of English Verse* (also jointly with Dobrée, 1949) and *This Way Delight* (1956).

In total, when Read declared in 1937 for the unconventional doctrine of anarchism he was already a figure of considerable cultural authority, at the height of a dual career in literature and writing about the visual arts. An eloquent manifesto, *Poetry and Anarchism,* appeared the next year; and his fifteen-year-long collaboration with Freedom Press, only broken by his paradoxical acceptance of a knighthood in 1953, produced *The Philosophy of Anarchism* (1940), a selection of Kropotkin's writings (1942), *The Education of Free Men* (1944) and *Existentialism, Marxism and Anarchism* (1949). His political writings were largely gathered as *Anarchy and Order* (1954); but publications linking politics, society and art included *To Hell with Culture* (1941), *The Politics of the Unpolitical* (1943) and *The Grass Roots of Art* (1947). And he remained a committed anarchist for the remainder of his life.

In 1939 Read resigned his editorship of the stuffy *Burlington Magazine* and became a director of George Routledge and Sons (Routledge and Kegan Paul from 1947) – a position he retained until obliged to retire in 1963. At Routledge (for whom he had acted as a reader since 1937) he introduced Samuel Beckett's *Murphy*, Georges Simenon and such libertarian theorists as Simone Weil, Martin Buber and Leopold Kohr, as well as a poetry list that was to include Sidney Keyes, John Heath-Stubbs, Alex Comfort, Norman MacCaig, Geoffrey Grigson and E. J. Scovell. He edited the 'English Master Painters' series (1939–60), and was responsible for the initiation, jointly with the Bollingen Foundation, of the collected works not only of Jung but also of Coleridge and Valéry.[2]

From around 1930 Read had been interested in both art education and children's art. Then, in 1940, he was invited by the newly established British Council to select drawings by British schoolchildren to form exhibitions for touring overseas in wartime. This experience was to prove overwhelming and enabled him to make the link between his writings on the visual arts and his anarchist politics. During 1940–42 he held the Leon Fellowship at the University of London and researched the weighty book which was published as *Education through Art* as early as 1943. In 1947 he became President of the Society for Education in Art (the Society for Education through Art from 1953), an office he held until his death; and following the sponsorship by UNESCO of an International Society for Education through Art, he gave the opening address in 1954 to its first general assembly. *Education for Peace* (1949), a collection of papers on his educational theory, was reissued towards the end of this life as *The Redemption of the Robot* (1966).

Read's involvement with industrial design, which had been signalled by *Art and Industry* in 1934, was continued by the foundation of the Design Research Unit in 1943; and for the two years down to 1945 he was, as Director, in sole charge of its running. Its most spectacular, although abortive, project was a design by Gabo for Jowett Cars. *The Practice of Design* (1946) was edited, as well as introduced, by Read.

Towards the end of the war Read began work on a series of monographs – lavishly produced by Lund Humphries, and which he either edited or contributed to – on the artists closest to him: Moore (1944), Nicholson (1948), Nash (1948), Hepworth (1952) and Gabo (1957). During these years he also became the champion of the next generation of British sculptors: Kenneth Armitage, Reg Butler, Lynn Chadwick and others. *Contemporary British Art* (1951) was stimulated by the Festival of Britain; and *The Philosophy of Modern Art* (1952) was a major collection of art criticism written over more than fifteen years. He had played a leading role in the foundation in London of the Institute of Contemporary Arts in 1947 and was the automatic choice as its first president.

In the 1930s Read's influence had been exerted primarily in Britain; after 1945 it spread worldwide and he travelled endlessly, lecturing throughout Europe and the United States (which he had not visited before 1946). Seminar lectures at Princeton in 1951 became Part One of *The True Voice of Feeling* (1953); the Charles Eliot Norton Lectures at Harvard in 1953–54 were published as *Icon and Idea* (1955); and the A. W. Mellon Lectures at the National Gallery of Art, Washington, DC, in 1954, appeared as *The Art of Sculpture* (1956).

Art and the Evolution of Man, a lecture in 1951, announced a new direction for Read – the exploration of the origins of art and its function in evolutionary development – and this was continued in *Icon and Idea* and the work he considered his most assured, *The Forms of Things Unknown* (1960). Initially influenced by the American theorist, Susanne Langer, Read's philosophy of art became increasingly indebted to Carl Gustav Jung, whose annual conference, the Eranos Tagung, at Ascona, Switzerland, he had begun to attend from 1946.

The best-selling *A Concise History of Modern Painting* (1959), one of the earliest volumes in Thames and Hudson's 'World of Art' series, was followed by *A Concise History of Modern Sculpture* (1964), *Henry Moore: A Study of His Life and Work* (1965) and *Arp* (1968), all in the same series.

Over the decades an essential feature of Read's production could be found in the collections of articles and papers, frequently mingling writings on both art and literature. So far unmentioned are *A Coat of Many Colours* (1945), *The Tenth Muse* (1957), *A Letter to a Young Painter* (1962), *To Hell with Culture and Other Essays on Art and Society* (1963; and a revision of *The Politics of the Unpolitical* of 1943), *The Origins of Form in Art* (1965), *Art and Alienation* (1967), *Poetry and Experience* (also 1967), and the posthumously published *The Cult of Sincerity* (1968). *Truth is More Sacred* (1961) was a selection of the critical correspondence between him and the American writer, Edward Dahlberg.

Just at the time that his reputation was taking off on to a global level, Read had moved in 1949 from the Home Counties back to his origins in North Yorkshire:

Stonegrave was only some three miles from his birthplace. The locality nurtured the poetry of *Moon's Farm* (1955) and final gathering of autobiographies, *The Contrary Experience* (1961). The definitive *Collected Poems* followed in 1966. He himself chose the *Selected Writings* (1963), the contents of which, extracts from *The Green Child* and the autobiographical works being intentionally omitted, are revealing: 36 per cent of space devoted to literary criticism, 23 per cent to art criticism, 16 per cent to poetry, 14 per cent to 'social criticism', 11 per cent to education. Herbert Read died at Stonegrave on 12 June 1968; and was buried nearby at St Gregory's Minster, Kirkdale, close to his parents and other relatives.[3]

This remarkable career and formidable output have generated a surprisingly limited critical and biographical literature, in terms of both quantity and quality. Only two books were published about Read during his lifetime. First came Henry Treece (ed.), *Herbert Read: An Introduction to His Work by Various Hands* (London: Faber and Faber, 1944). Edited by a fervent disciple of Read and one of the prime movers of the New Apocalypse (whose second collection, *The White Horseman,* Read had published at Routledge in 1941), this volume continues to be a useful starting-point.[4] This was succeeded by Francis Berry, *Herbert Read* (London: Longmans, Green, 1953 and, 2nd edn, 1961), a booklet in the 'Writers and Their Work' series, published for the British Council and the National Book League, and in which Read's own *Byron* had appeared two years before. Insightful though Berry can be, he is limited by his emphasis on Read as primarily a poet and, in any case, the restrictions of a literary series.

Hard on Read's death in June 1968 came a special issue of the *Malahat Review* (January 1969), which was then republished as Robin Skelton (ed.), *Herbert Read: A Memorial Symposium* (London: Methuen, 1970). Despite the generosity of impulse and extremely distinguished contributors, the transition to hard covers seems unjustified – it is noticeable how very few of those participating in the present volume make reference to the Skelton symposium – although all serious writers on Read are indebted to the checklist of the Read Archive at the University of Victoria, including the most useful bibliography of his books to have been published, which it contains. The death of Read also occasioned George Woodcock, *Herbert Read: The Stream and the Source* (London: Faber and Faber, 1972). Woodcock was an anarchist writer who had been a friend of Read for a 'quarter of a century' and his book has the great merit of being both sympathetic and attempting to see Read as a whole. But it is not, as he explains, 'a Life of Herbert Read', rather 'an intellectual biography' – in effect, a comprehensive study of the published works.[5]

The only biography to date, and drawing on all the relevant manuscript sources, is James King, *The Last Modern: A Life of Herbert Read* (London: Weidenfeld and Nicolson, 1990). Its utility is indicated by the extent to which the contributors to the current collection draw upon it. Its demerits are the failure to take the politics seriously and the absence of that empathy necessary for the best biography: King seems always to be trying to cut Read down to size and crowing over his occasional pratfalls. In contrast stands David Thistlewood, not only the most prolific writer on Read (whom he knew), but also the most erudite, and the author of the two chapters below. His *Herbert Read: Formlessness and Form: An Introduction to His Aesthetics* (London: Routledge and Kegan Paul, 1984), is a critical biography, limited to the aesthetics, but ranging over Read's entire life and output.

Finally there are two catalogues. *A Tribute to Herbert Read, 1893–1968* (Bradford Art Galleries and Museums) is the catalogue of an exhibition, held at The Manor House, Ilkley, which was part of the 1975 Ilkley Literature Festival. It contains the indispensable 'Herbert Read: His Life and Work' by Benedict Read, an essay by Robert Parrington Jackson on 'Herbert Read: The Yorkshire Background', and some unpublished documents. Benedict Read and David Thistlewood (eds), *Herbert Read: A British Vision of World Art* (Leeds City Art Galleries in association with The Henry Moore Foundation and Lund Humphries) is the catalogue of the major exhibition held at Leeds City Art Gallery in 1993–94 to commemorate the centenary of the birth of Read. Among its contents are important essays and reprinted documents, as well as an exceedingly useful chronology of Read's life and select bibliography.

The starting-point of this volume was a weekend conference I organized in December 1993 at the (then) Department of Adult Continuing Education, University of Leeds, in association with the Institute for the Humanities, Simon Fraser University, British Columbia, to mark the centenary of Read's birth. The contributions by Hugh Cecil, Robin Kinross, myself, David Thistlewood and Jerald Zaslove had their first airing on this occasion (and Kieron Winn and John R. Doheny were among those who attended). Other contributions have been commissioned in order to survey and re-evaluate all of Read's major activities.

In his study of the poetry Kieron Winn convincingly shows how Read's instinctive romanticism, submerged by his wartime experiences and repressed by the classicism of Anglo-American modernism, began to reassert itself from the mid-1920s – as he increasingly attempted to distance himself from the objectives of his admired friend, Eliot. He concludes that Read's poetry, although currently underrated, is a considerable achievement. Hugh Cecil's contribution, making use of the records of the Green Howards, is a longer, more detailed, version of the chapter on Read in his acclaimed *The Flower of Battle: British Fiction Writers of the First World War*[6] (although personally, in spite of the short stories of *Ambush*, I consider it very misleading to classify Read as a writer of fiction). Read's military service in the Great War is second only to his upbringing on – and expulsion from – a Yorkshire farm as the formative influence in his life. Cecil believes *In Retreat* to be 'one of the best pieces of writing to come out of the war', a judgement shared by, for example, D. J. Enright, who includes Read with Blunden, Graves and Sassoon as the authors

6

of the 'first-class' prose works to deal with the war.[7]

John R. Doheny continues by discussing the literary critic. He is of the opinion that *Wordsworth* is Read's best work of literary criticism, but rates 'Surrealism and the Romantic Principle' almost as highly, preferring the more direct, assertive and confrontational aspects of Read's œuvre in contrast to the polite, tolerant and overly cautious literary essays. He suggests that Read needed psychoanalysis to distinguish himself from the narrow criticism practised in the 1920s by his friends and contemporaries, particularly Eliot and Richards. Embedded within Doheny's vast first draft was a lengthy digression on Read's use of Freud. This was much too valuable to lose completely and I encouraged him to remove it and extend it as a separate chapter. In his first chapter Doheny points out how Read read eclectically in order to find support for his own ideas; his second is a case study of how Read distorted Freud's ideas in order to find such support.

In his chapters Doheny speculates concerning Read's own psychology and attitude to sexuality. The former is a theme taken up compellingly in the incisive discussion of the autobiographies by Peter Abbs, who points out how much of Read's work is, in some way, autobiographical. While he regards *The Innocent Eye* as 'a unique prose-poem', ultimately he sees it as limited, and the remaining constituents of *The Contrary Experience*, which equally dispense with human relationships, as largely unremarkable (in literary, if not psychological, terms).[8] Consideration of Read's literary output concludes with Bob Barker's chapter on *The Green Child*. This is not a reassessment of the novel, but rather a highly illuminating analysis of Read's heterogeneous, sometimes virtually plagiarized, sources: literary, historical, philosophical, artistic.

Barker emphasizes the correspondence between the work of Read's 'nest of gentle artists' in 1930s Hampstead and the crystalline world of the Green People. Andrew Causey continues by tracing Read's art criticism from its initiation in 1929 through to the early 1950s. He regards as central Read's membership of the Hampstead group, Unit One, which included 'some of the most adventurous artists anywhere at that time': Moore, Nicholson, Hepworth, Nash. Causey makes the important point that, after the Second World War, in the impressive monographs on these friends, in his reception of the new, 'geometry of fear' sculptors and in other writings, Read's two roles, as the critic of contemporary art and the historian of world art, coexist uneasily.

Robin Kinross, although he rightly recognizes that *Art and Industry* became one of the gospels of design in Britain, is savagely dismissive of the book, from Read's content through to Herbert Bayer's design. His cogent critique proceeds to lambast the Design Research Unit, what he calls 'the British design establishment' – and the conservatism that pervades English life. This is the paper Kinross gave at the Leeds conference in 1993. Soon afterwards he sent a copy to Norman Potter, one of the sticks he uses to beat Read with and himself the designer who has been described as 'the English Rietveld' (the reference is to the great Dutch furniture-maker and archi-tect, Gerrit Rietveld). Potter fired back two angry, remarkable letters. Kinross and I thought it would be ideal to elicit a similar short and informal riposte for this book. Potter took some convincing and needed considerable coaxing before he produced his differently conceived, much longer, but splendid chapter, a second, unrevised draft of which I received shortly before his death on 22 November 1995.[9]

In my own discussion of Read's politics I contend that his anarchism needs to be taken seriously. (Read is an un-English writer, with much more in common with the radical intellectuals of continental Europe – for example, Camus, Sartre and Breton – than with such contemporaries as Roger Fry, F. R. Leavis or Robert Graves.) I stress that the route from Read's youthful to his post-1937 libertarianism was not unfailingly consistent; that the political theory of his mature anarchism was deriva-tive; and that there was inconsistency – at least, until late in his life – between his politics and his professional concerns with the visual arts. On the other hand, I regard his educational vision as innovative and an inspiring revolutionary strategy. In contrast, the limitations of *Education through Art* and Read's other writings on educa-tion are ably exposed by Malcolm Ross. Ross, whose fiftieth-anniversary reflections on *Education through Art* were considerably more favourable,[10] has in the course of this longer treatment realized two things. The first is that Read was writing as a committed anarchist and seeking to transform society by educational change – it is this, of course, that I applaud. The second is that he imposes his psychological data and curricular prescriptions in an arbitrary, pseudo-scientific way and to this – it is reminiscent of Rudolf Steiner's pedagogy – I am as resistant as Ross.[11] Yet Ross ends by praising the 'zest' of Read.

David Thistlewood in his two chapters displays his customary mastery of Read's writings, both published and manuscript. In the first chapter he traces the develop-ment of Read's organicist aesthetic from the end of the First World War to the gathering for publication of the essays of *The Philosophy of Modern Art*. Thistlewood here moves beyond his earlier work in a sub-theme concerning Read's desire to distance himself from Alfred Barr and what was going on at the Museum of Modern Art in New York. Until 1932 Read was proposing the ultimate authority of Bauhaus values, which he then played down when he began to argue the prominence of the British avant-garde, substantially because he believed in it but also because it had become obvious that Kandinsky and Klee had been 'adopted' by Barr. In the following chapter Thistlewood discusses the new course in Read's aesthetics from *Art and the Evolution of Man* down to his death. The new thinking here resides in the identification of an American–European duality in Read's discourse. The discourse to American audiences, with Jung only slightly in evidence, was ruled by Read's head and only eventually abandoned when he found it difficult to sustain Gabo's sculp-ture as representing the most advanced state of aesthetic consciousness. In contrast, the European discourse, in which Jungian theory was paramount, was ruled by his heart and fully vindicated by an emergent generation of British sculptors whose work was genuinely interpretable as 'archetypal'. It was in defence of this second discourse that Read was to assault pop art (in its American phase) and downgrade the significance of abstract expressionism.

Paul Street takes the book by Read which is now best known to the student and general reader alike and subjects *A Concise History of Modern Painting* to a perceptive analysis, although he is bemused why such 'an unsatisfactory primer of modern painting', moulded by the perspective Read had acquired in the late 1920s and the 1930s, should continue to be so successful. Street surprises himself, though, in finding that 'the pope of modern art' finally ceased to adopt the latest artistic innovation and spoke out vehemently against the nihilism and decadence of the contemporary world (characteristics even more pronounced as the millennium approaches).

The final two contributions are different in approach from what has preceded. Kevin Davey and Jerald Zaslove explore themes running throughout Read's work and the concerns of both are informed by current debates and perspectives. Davey shows that, although Read's work challenged key components of the dominant English identity of the early twentieth century and attempted to open up the English visual aesthetic to European modernism, he at the same time constructed and celebrated an Englishness. Davey draws attention to an important article on 'English Art' as well as the previously overlooked anthology, *The English Vision*, but he draws impressively from Read's complete œuvre. Along with Thistlewood and Street, he concludes with Read's rejection of Americanization and of the nihilism of abstract expressionism and pop art. Zaslove seeks to rescue Read from the enormous condescension of such contemporary writers on twentieth-century culture as Charles Harrison, to claim Read as the British manifestation of German theory (with an especially close correspondence to the Frankfurt School) as against his own dismissal of the contemporary rise of cultural studies, and in general to instate him as the exemplar of 'essential modernism', literary and artistic. He ends his chapter with a provocative comparison between Read and Raymond Williams.

A different set of contributors would doubtless have arrived at a different series of reassessments; but what is clear from the chapters that follow is the very considerable relevance and vitality of much, if not all, of Read's work. With such a figure it is imperative not to concentrate on any single activity to the exclusion of the rest. As Read remarked of William Morris: 'It is customary to consider Morris in his threefold aspect as poet, craftsman, and socialist. In this way we break down the fundamental unity of the man.'[12] Exactly the same applies to Read himself. To understand any one of his activities that activity needs to be considered in the context of the totality; to assess the stature of the man each of his individual achievements have to be added together (and the total is greater than the sum of the parts); and, I repeat, the anarchist politics should be seen, not as an embarrassing aberration, but as a central, integrating component. (To continue the analogy, studies of Morris that seek to ignore, or to minimize, his revolutionary socialism are intellectually impoverished.)

After reading George Woodcock's *The Crystal Spirit*, in 1966 Read wrote to him in terms that reveal as much, if not more, about himself as they do about Orwell:

> I haven't re-read any of Orwell's books recently, but they have always remained in my mind, and his personality, which remains so vivid after all these years, often rises like some ghost to admonish me. I suppose I have felt nearer to him than to any other English writer of our time, and though there were some aspects of his personality that irritated me – his proletarian pose in dress, his insensitivity to his physical environment, his comparatively narrow range of interests – yet who was, in general, nearer in ideals & even in eccentricities? You bring out his contradictions very well, & justify them. They didn't trouble me much, except when it came to the war – but by then he was a sick man & I saw little of him... If only he had lived a little longer he would have got rid of those 'monumental imperfections' & would have become as great as any of the authors of the past he admired so much.[13]

Read also had 'monumental imperfections' which, in my view, prevented his very great gifts from being manifested, ultimately, in work of the first order. What are the 'imperfections' that I am thinking of? He wrote too much and spread himself over too many fields (although this is one of the very things that makes him so stimulating!). He attempted to accommodate himself to classicism when he was inherently a romantic; and he subordinated himself to the influence of Eliot (an influence I consider to have been malign for Read in particular and for English culture in general). He accepted a knighthood, which was at odds with both his revolutionary politics and his championing of avant-garde art and artists. He lived the life of a member of the landed gentry,[14] and this produced (along with the need to pay alimony to his first wife) the financial desperation of his final years, necessitating lecture series and tours – and because he did not enjoy lecturing he was a poor performer – and the 'hack work' of the 1960s: recycling already-existing publications, retitling second editions, and generally serving his reputation ill.[15]

And yet he was a marvellous writer. There are things I come back to time and again from throughout his career, although his best work is concentrated in the 1930s and 1940s as he struggled to forge his own romantic persona. His historical importance as the principal conduit for the reception of visual modernism in conservative Britain cannot be gainsaid. But, continuing to write in a personal capacity, I believe he will survive as the author of the autobiographies, the poetry, *The Green Child*, the political and social essays, and some of the literary criticism.[16] He wrote 'some of the finest prose of our time', as Eliot said. At least I assume that it was Eliot who was responsible for the publisher's blurb on the dust-jacket of *The Contrary Experience*:

> Readers of *Annals* [*of Innocence and Experience*] and that strange romance *The Green Child* know that Sir Herbert Read has written some of the finest prose of our time; readers of *Moon's Farm* know that he has written some of the most moving poetry. And those who have read all these three books know that he is always inspired when he writes of his native Yorkshire.[17]

Notes

1   Herbert Read, *Annals of Innocence and Experience* (London: Faber and Faber, 2nd edn, 1946), p.127.

2   *150 Years of Great Publishing* (London: Routledge and Kegan Paul, 1986), pp.19–20.

3   The foregoing biographical summary is heavily dependent on the authoritative 'Herbert Read: His Life and Work' (by Benedict Read) in *A Tribute to Herbert Read, 1893–1968* (Bradford Art Galleries and Museums: catalogue of exhibition at The Manor House, Ilkley, 1975). It has been supplemented at points by *The Contrary Experience: Autobiographies* (London: Faber and Faber, 1963), Read's collected autobiographical writings; George Woodcock, *Herbert Read: The Stream and the Source* (London: Faber and Faber, 1972), chapter 1; James King, *The Last Modern: A Life of Herbert Read* (London: Weidenfeld and Nicolson, 1990); Terry Friedman and David Thistlewood, 'Herbert Read 1893–1968: The Turbulent Years of "The Pope of Modern Art": A Chronology and Select Bibliography', in Benedict Read and David Thistlewood (eds), *Herbert Read: A British Vision of World Art* (Leeds and London: Leeds City Art Galleries in association with The Henry Moore Foundation and Lund Humphries, 1993).

4   The extensive correspondence from Treece to Read, 1940–43, containing much on the genesis of this book, survives in the Read Archive, University of Victoria Library, British Columbia, Canada.

5   Woodcock, *Herbert Read*, p.11. For Woodcock's final comments on Read, see his 'Herbert Read: Contradictions and Consistencies', *Drunken Boat* (New York and Seattle, no. 2, 1994).

6   London: Secker & Warburg, 1995.

7   D. J. Enright, 'The Literature of the First World War', in Boris Ford (ed.), *The Pelican Guide to English Literature, vol 7: The Modern Age* (Harmondsworth: Penguin Books, 1961), pp. 168–69.

8   For an earlier, abbreviated discussion of *The Contrary Experience*, see Peter Abbs, 'Autobiography: Quest for Identity', in Boris Ford (ed.), *The New Pelican Guide to English Literature, vol. 8*: *The Present* (Harmondsworth: Penguin Books, 1983), pp. 515–17.

9   Obituaries appeared in the *Guardian*, 29 November 1995; *Independent*, 2 December 1995; *Freedom*, 16 December 1995. I am much indebted to Robin Kinross for his assistance in preparing Norman Potter's chapter for publication.

10   'In the Picture', *Times Educational Supplement,* 2 April 1993; and extended as 'Living There: Herbert Read's *Education through Art* Fifty Years On', *Journal of Art and Design Education*, XII (1993).

11   Cf. the cool and significantly brief comment of Stuart Macdonald, *The History and Philosophy of Art Education* (London: University of London Press, 1970), pp. 372–73.

12   Herbert Read, *Art and Industry: The Principles of Industrial Design* (London: Faber and Faber, 1934), p. 29, and repeated in Herbert Read, *A Coat of Many Colours: Occasional Essays* (London: George Routledge, 1945), p. 77.

13   Read Archive, letter from Read to Woodcock, 3 August 1966 (reprinted in part in Woodcock, *Herbert Read*, p.239). For Orwell's very penetrating assessment of Read, see his review of *A Coat of Many Colours*, which I quote, p. 186 below.

14 See the very interesting observations by George Woodcock, *Beyond the Blue Mountains: An Autobiography* (Markham, Ontario: Fitzhenry & Whiteside, 1987), chapter 23: 'A Yorkshire Knight'.

15 King, *The Last Modern*, pp. 174, 307, 310; Piers Paul Read, 'Herbert Read', in *Homage to Herbert Read* (Kent County Council Education Committee: catalogue of exhibition at Canterbury College of Art, 1984), p. 2.

16 I find myself, unusually, in considerable agreement with Graham Greene. See his 'Herbert Read', *Horizon*, vol. 3, no. 15 (March 1941), and 'A Personal Foreword' to Herbert Read, *The Contrary Experience: Autobiographies* (London: Secker & Warburg, 1973).

17 Eliot, though, quite rightly considered that, ironically, Read's unrelenting opponent, Wyndham Lewis, was 'the greatest prose master of my generation – perhaps the only one to have invented a new style' (King, *The Last Modern*, p. 279).

The Poetry of Herbert Read

KIERON WINN

READ always thought himself primarily a poet, despite his range of interests, and his poetry was widely praised during his lifetime: in the *Listener* in 1935, Michael Roberts, who the following year gave him a number of pages in his influential *Faber Book of Modern Verse,* said that his work represented 'the expression of a body of metaphysical thought more fully developed than that of any English romantic poet since Wordsworth'.[1] But Read's poetry, along with the bulk of his work, has fallen victim to a curious form of cultural memory loss.

It may be wise to gloss the use of certain terms in this chapter. By 'romanticism' I mean the idea that a continuum exists between mankind and an ultimately benevolent natural world; in this system of belief, the individual's emotions and experiences are of paramount value. By 'modernism', applied to poetry roughly from 1910 to 1925, I mean the attempt to curb the worst sentimental excesses of degenerate romanticism, and the desire for a language which would be 'austere, direct, free from emotional slither'.[2] Modernist poets attempted, often using shock tactics, to incorporate contemporary realities: urban squalor; the world's increasing mechanization; the horror of the First World War. With its goals of concision and formal tightness, and of a cool, impersonal tone, modernist poetry was considered by its contemporary adherents to be 'classical'.

It is difficult to categorize Read. He marched under the modernist banner all his life, yet is recognizably an English romantic. Essentially, he is an integrator, not only of different literary traditions, but also of mankind and the cosmos – 'or nature as we more politely call it'[3] – from which modernist literature is typically so estranged. Read began his career as a supporter of the classical-modernist ideals of T. S. Eliot, and throughout this chapter, I will draw comparisons between the work of the two men, who first met in 1917, and were close friends for nearly half a century. In 1925 Eliot wrote to Read that it meant a great deal to him to have Read's name associated in any way with his own;[4] and despite Read's increasing adherence to romantic beliefs which Eliot found antipathetic (even heretical), a sense of alliance endured.

This chapter attempts to show that Read's instincts are romantic, but that after his initial contact with modernist art, and his experiences in the trenches, these instincts are suppressed. They are recovered in the mid-1920s, from which time Read develops his romanticism with increasing confidence.

Read's first, romantic inclinations are born of his memories of a 'Fair seed-time'[5] on his father's farm in Yorkshire, which he thinks of as an age of innocence. He was

13

expelled from paradise in 1903, following the death of his father, and sent to school in the industrial town of Halifax. In 1908 he left school, and went to live with his mother in Leeds. Here, in 1911, he met a tailor, William Prior Read (no relation), who unofficially adopted him, and introduced him to the work of such writers as Tennyson, Browning, Dostoevsky, Turgenev, Ibsen, Chekhov, Yeats, and, above all, William Blake, whose poems astounded the young man. The following year he entered Leeds University, became a member of the Leeds Arts Club – a society which, among other activities, promoted the avant-garde – and obtained access to the private art collection of the Vice-Chancellor, Michael Sadler. This contained works by, among others, Gauguin and Kandinsky, and at the time was one of the finest collections of modern art in the country.

Read's early poems were dominated by the romantic influence of Blake, Yeats and Ralph Hodgson, but it was not long before he became attracted to the imagism of Ezra Pound. His first book of poems, *Songs of Chaos*, was published in 1915 by Elkin Mathews, whom Read approached because he was Pound's publisher.

The opening poem is a long narrative, 'The Song of the Lark' (1915).[6] It is certainly chaotic, and the source appears to be hormonal, as the poem's concern, though not directly stated, is the unwilling loss of innocence in the face of growing sexual feelings. Some important elements of Read's later work are present: in particular, there is a strong sense that a continuum exists between man and nature. Although the poem has occasional successful touches, the overriding impression is of immaturity. At one point, the moon's light is described, not as silver, but as golden, which suggests the extent to which the poem is derivative of hackneyed poetic language. Such a blunder is particularly striking in view of the mature Read's emphasis on the redemptive power of living through the senses, and above all the visual sense.

The other poems in the book are short lyrics, frequently concerned with breakage and dissatisfaction. Although Read certainly had experience of these, having lost his childhood Eden, the poems are derivative. 'The Daisy' (1915), for example, draws off Blake and Hodgson and a literary sexuality:

> A daisy on a green grave grows –
>   A message from the dead;
> And all its slender petals seem
>   Besmeared with something red.
>
> Oh, is there any daisy glows
>   Just quite as red as this?
> For underneath a maiden sleeps
>   Forspent ere passion's bliss.[7]

What set out to be songs of experience are songs, not even of innocence, but of naïvety.

Read had to pay for the publication of *Songs of Chaos* himself. Showing the poems to Elkin Mathews was virtually his last act before entering the army. While a soldier, he wrote both war and pastoral poems, published, up to three years after they were written, as *Naked Warriors* and *Eclogues* (both 1919).

These titles imply a neat, if not schizophrenic, segregation of pastoral and war themes, but this is not in fact the case, as the subtitle of *Eclogues* suggests: '1914–18'. A poem such as 'Champ de Manœuvres' (1919) reveals the tensions clearly, as it also reveals those between the romantic and the avant-gardist in Read at this time. The title's military term is redeployed to allow the manœuvres to be those of a soul through various phases of a sunset. In the first line, a hill 'indents' the soul, in a hard, physical metaphor which Pound would have approved. However, the 'silver mist' to which he compares himself in this state is a regression to the language of nineteenth-century romanticism. 'I dwell / in the golden setting of the sun' clearly recalls Wordsworth's 'Tintern Abbey' ('a sense sublime / Of something far more deeply interfused, / Whose dwelling is the light of setting suns'). However, the mists then 'invade' the trees, and the melting light is felt to 'assail' the hill. These are hard, vigorous words of the avant-garde; in particular, of course, they are further redeployments of war terms.

The implication of this poem, as war inexorably infiltrates the language of pastoral, is a tension between the need for action and duty, and the desire for private reverie. There is an analogous sense of the wartime tension between public and private in 'Liedholz' (1919), based on Read's capture of a German officer:

> When I captured Liedholz
> I had a blacken'd face
> like a nigger's
> and my teeth like white mosaics shone.
>
> We met in the night at half-past one
> between the lines.
> Liedholz shot at me
> and I at him;
> in the ensuing tumult he surrendered to me.
>
> Before we reached our wire
> he told me he had a wife and three children.
> In the dug-out we gave him a whisky.
> Going to the Brigade with my prisoner at dawn
> the early sun made the land delightful
> and the larks rose singing from the plain.
>
> In broken French we discussed
> Beethoven, Nietzsche and the International.

He was a professor
Living at Spandau
and not too intelligible.

But my black face and nigger's teeth
amused him.

'Liedholz' has none of the bizarre surrealism of Owen's 'Strange Meeting', which
also tells of the encounter of enemies. Instead, it emphasizes gentle absurdities: the
ridiculous-looking camouflaged face; discussing famous Germans with a German in
broken French; the not uncommon unintelligibility of professors. The two men
'met', aptly suggesting a social engagement. It is the supposed enemy who speaks
first, initiating the return to humanity, and crossing the barriers of language as well
as those of formal hostility. Small, human details are emphasized: that the prisoner
has a wife and three children; the gift of a glass of whisky. Typically, a lyrical, pastoral
moment is salvaged from the war, as the sun rises and larks are heard. 'Liedholz'
aims to create anti-war feelings in the reader by ironically, comically leading us to
share in a recognition of the incivility of war, which disrupts our natural brother-
hood. It is a daring enterprise to write a gently absurd comedy, with a touch of
pastoral lyricism, about the First World War, and in its quiet way, 'Liedholz' is a
revolutionary poem. In implying an unmartial, benevolent instinct, it contains a
principle of the anarchism which Read would later promulgate. The poem's integration and tolerance are characteristically Readian virtues, although, as we shall see,
his poetry loses them in the years following the war, as it tries to bring itself into
line with the work of writers such as Eliot and Pound, who drew their strength from
intolerance and a sense of fragmentation.

In part 2 of his 'Ode', written at the time of Dunkirk (1940), Read looks back
on his First World War poetry and says that he had resolved 'to tell the truth without
rhetoric' about 'the indignities of war', phrases which suit 'Liedholz'. This determination to speak plainly is signalled again and again in the war poems. Read must
have been glad to receive the *Daily Herald*'s review of *Naked Warriors*, the following
extract from which appeared as an advertisement for the book in several numbers
of the journal *Art and Letters*, with which Read was closely involved:

> *Naked Warriors* is not propaganda; it is the horrid truth. The whole thing is relent-
> less and quite convincing.... I wish his poems could be filmed: they would serve
> as an effective antidote to the emotional thrills of supreme sacrifices and military
> pageants.[8]

It is interesting to consider the origin, in Read's case, of this style. It appears to come
simultaneously from two sources: the manifesto of plain speaking set out in
Wordsworth's Preface to *Lyrical Ballads*; but also from Pound's insistence that verse
needs the same hard, clear virtues conventionally seen as attributes of good prose.

16

Later, Read would construct heretical theories of modernism,[9] in which the free verse of Eliot and Pound, and their goal of a determinedly 'unpoetic' diction based on contemporary speech, is seen as directly inherited from romantic notions of organic form and the need for unornamented, purely emotional poetic language. This connection is already exemplified in his war poems: 'Liedholz' reads like a lyrical ballad written by an imagist.

Read's anger and disillusion after the war were in part caused by his experience of the despoliation of nature, which he associated with innocence. His resentment is visible in a passage from 'Killed in Action' (1919), described as a chapter from an unfinished novel, which concludes *Naked Warriors*. It is a relentlessly bitter and nihilistic story, revealing the motives leading to the suicide of an officer, whose death would have been reported to his family in the bland elision of the title:

> Devil's Wood was a naked congregation of shattered trunks, like an old broken comb against the skyline. An emotion – a sudden realisation and anger – flushed his brain. This was his earth, earth of green slopes, earth of lithe green trees, earth of vigorous sap and delicate growth.[10]

In the years following the war, Read's poems register his bitterness with a barbed, satirical tone. This has much to do with his contact, from 1917–18 onwards, with Pound, Eliot and Wyndham Lewis, who often wrote in a similar style, castigating Victorian complacencies. That a number of poems in this vein were, unusually, never collected in book form, suggests how quickly Read became dissatisfied with the style. One of these, 'Smoker' (1919), is a description of a dance-hall in which 'Three elaborate coons / Intone a melody'. The dancers are described with a disgust which is extraordinary given the mature Read's acceptance and celebration of the physical:

> The oily bright faces of the audience
> Grimace and sing.
> Moved in some current of laughter,
> Their elastic cheeks
> Oscillate from a rock of skulls
> Like sea-anemones.[11]

There is clearly a similarity to Eliot's 'Preludes' and 'Whispers of Immortality'.[12]

Read's Preface to *Naked Warriors* is, perhaps, the clearest indicator of his anger after the war. It includes such phrases as: 'From the sickness of life revealed let us turn with glad hearts to the serenity of some disinterested beauty'.[13] The desire for such beauty is clear in the metaphysical poems of Read's next collection, *Mutations of the Phoenix* (1923). In 'The Nature of Metaphysical Poetry', an essay published that year in the *Criterion*, Read effectively characterizes the unromantic tone of his book: 'Metaphysical poetry is determined logically: its emotion is a joy that comes with the triumph of the reason, and is not a simple instinctive ecstasy'.[14] Despite this, the title poem, 'Mutations of the Phoenix' (1923), contains the essence of Read's mature, romantic philosophy: the need to stay within the realm of the senses, the stress on universal flux. It is the language which is so strikingly different to the later poems, with its attempt at neo-scientific objectivity. There are many occasions in *Mutations of the Phoenix* when a romantic note is audible, though somewhat stifled by the diction. In 'The Analysis of Love' (1923), passion, indubitably romantic in its nature, is analysed in tight, logical terms:

> The teas'd fibrils of reason
> Weave vainly to dam
> Some bank against the giant flood
> Of this emotion.
>
> Waves' and winds' erosion
> Crumbles granitic cliffs,
> Æonly obliterating
> The earth's known visage.

Here, the teas'd fibrils of rational poetic diction weave vainly to dam the irrational romantic passion which is the poem's concern, and which Read will increasingly see as the source of poetry.

For several years after the war, Read was a supporter of Eliot and the classical-modernist ideals of the *Criterion*. In the mid-1920s, however, partly due to a growing interest in Freud and the light he shed on the relationship of the artist's personality to his work, Read came to feel that Eliot's goals of impersonality and objectivity in art were specious. The effective end of his satirical and metaphysical phases, and the beginning of his mature romanticism, can be marked by the revisions to his poem about Huskisson, a farmer. As it appeared in 1919, with the title 'Huskisson Sacred and Profane',[15] it relates, in a satirically modernist scenario, how Huskisson moves to the city, becomes dissatisfied with bourgeois life, and flees to an exotic existence on the savannas of South America. In all subsequent appearances of the poem, beginning with that in *Collected Poems 1913–25* (1926),[16] only the first section is retained, with the title 'Huskisson in Arcadia', and at the end of this Huskisson is still content on the farm.

The poem begins with an evocation of a classical Arcadia:

> Early dawn and the nymphs are gliding
> in an elusive sequence
> of gold light along the woodland's edge;
> and the songs
> of rousèd birds are making
> dawn vocal in leafy domes.

The next line appears, at this stage, to invite mockery: 'Huskisson is yet sleeping'.

By the time he eventually opens his 'puffy lids', the nymphs 'have taken to their far recesses / and birds are busy on their wings'. This appears to satirize Huskisson, but the substitution of the brazen world for the golden is not so simple, as is signalled by the next word: 'But soon he takes his whittled stick'. This 'But' is the central hinge of the poem, and signals the start of Huskisson's redemption. He goes to urge the 'mournful milky cattle' down to the garth-pen. Here milkmaids, holding bright pails, meet them, and as they milk 'lean their pretty heads / against a cow's roan glossy flank'. Huskisson, meanwhile, is in the meadows, calling to the lambs. The poem's conclusion shows him contentedly at work:

> He lifts the old ewes' feet to scrape the rot
> and scatters fresh swedes for them to eat.
>
> The peewits cry, the sun climbs high
> Huskisson is gay in the meadows.

In this version of the poem, we leave him there. He does not go on to be satirized, ironized, or subjected to urban squalor and routine. In fact, his way of life is entirely vindicated. In scraping the rot from the old ewes' feet, he is doing no more than a kindly service: the word 'rot' has no overtones of mortality, as it may have in the total context of the longer version, and as it would certainly have in a poem by Eliot. The fresh swedes are similarly to be taken at face value, in contrast to Eliot's use of 'tubers' to suggest pejoratively vegetative human life in the opening lines of *The Waste Land*. That the nymphs have departed is neither here nor there to Huskisson: such literary abstractions simply do not enter his comely, organic world. It is this ease with the organic processes of life, an ease instinctively felt in his childhood and recovered after the trauma of the war, which is Read's mature keynote as a poet. It is what distinguishes him most from Eliot, who ultimately regards the body as disgusting, and nature, to use a phrase from the first part of 'East Coker', as a matter of 'Dung and death'. The original, longer version of Read's poem shows him trying to be scathing about the merely organic in the Eliot manner; his subsequent removal of all but the first part suggests an admission of the inauthenticity of this position, as he finds it impossible not to accept and celebrate his childhood world.

That man's contentment rests in nature is from the later 1920s established as an absolute in Read's poetry. Other central areas of his mature poetic philosophy will now be examined: the supremacy of the senses in understanding the world; the universal condition of flux; the glimpses of pattern within that flux.

For Read, the most important way of remaining in close touch with the natural world, of not drifting off into 'the transcendental inane' as he calls it in the radio play *Moon's Farm* (1955),[17] is trusting the five senses. The idea that the senses are the paramount measure of our place in the world is implicit in Read's conception of innocence, the ideal state, which in his poem 'The Innocent Eye' (1932) is a matter of 'senseful surfeit', a phrase incorporating the idea of the knowledge, of the sense in sense. The same matrix defines innocence in part 7 of 'Daphne' (1962). Although the arborified Daphne is rooted, 'her senses / did not decay',

> but in the waving wilderness
> found their surfeit
> voices of innocence to celebrate
> the god's defeat[.]

The importance of the senses is emphasized as early as 'Kneeshaw Goes to War' (1918). At the start of the poem Kneeshaw is growing 'In the forest of his dreams', like a woodland flower with 'anæmic petals', unattached to his senses or his sexuality. The outside world appears 'a far perspective / Of high black columns'. When Kneeshaw reaches the front, he witnesses horrors. On one occasion, while digging in, he finds a skull, and at that moment is hurled by an explosion into a coma which is 'beautiful' because it allows him to return to his original state, where he was effectively unconscious. The final section of the poem contains the song that the disabled Kneeshaw sings on his return to his native land. It includes these lines:

> *I stand on this hill and accept*
> *The pleasure my flesh dictates*
> *I count not kisses nor take*
> *Too serious a view of tobacco .[. . .]*
>
> *I stand on this hill and accept*
> *The flowers at my feet and the deep*
> *Beauty of the still tarn;*
> *Chance that gave me a crutch and a view*
> *Gave me these.*

What Kneeshaw has learnt is the importance of attachment to the world of present perception, in the knowledge of its fragility.

Read is often conscious of himself as the 'senser', the perceiver of the world. In part 3 of his Dunkirk 'Ode' he writes of:

> eye's eagerness, lickerous tongue
> ear's selection, finger's fine division
> all senses single and combin'd
> construing the living scene [.]

In part 2 of this poem he is conscious of the means by which he becomes aware of the wider world. As he listens to faint echoes of fighting on the shores of France, he is aware that his knowledge of the war is hardly dependent at all on his own senses, or on the words of a friend; instead, he is conscious of it by the indirect, possibly propagandist media of radio and the press, which are described in an alienated manner suggestive of their potential untrustworthiness:

> Unreal war! No single friend
> links me with its immediacy.
> It is a voice out of a cabinet
> a printed sheet, and these faint reverberations
> selected in the silence
> by my attentive ear.

This acute awareness of the division of private and public is a further manifestation of the tension in 'Champ de Manœuvres' and 'Liedholz'. The belief in the self-sufficiency of the private, romantically subjective individual has political implications which lead directly into Read's anarchist principles.

The main characteristic of the sensing, perceiving self, and of the cosmos of which it is a part, is a permanent state of flux. In 'Legend' and the second part of 'The End of a War' (both 1933), Read uses an unusual and precise term, 'labile', an adjective meaning prone to chemical change, to suggest our condition. (That Read should choose a scientific word is characteristic: he is convinced of the need for reconciliation between what C. P. Snow called the two cultures, art and science. This is a further instance of his integrative temper.) The autobiographical Second Voice of *Moon's Farm* speaks of his chameleon-like ability to empathize with all sides,[18] which suggests an accusation often levelled at Read's poetry, that it lacks a recognizable and distinctive voice. Beyond Read's mature poetry is the philosopher of flux, Heraclitus, whose ideas are woven into *Moon's Farm*,[19] and who makes a fleeting personal appearance in the lyric 'Live and Love' (1953). Instinctively Read accepts flux as a condition of the natural world in which he feels at home.

Yet amongst the flux, pattern is discernible. The place of the sensing, labile self in the world is suggested by what Read calls his favourite symbol, the Tree of Life:

> The human race is the trunk and branches of this tree, and individual men are the leaves which appear one season, flourish for a summer, and then die. I am like a leaf of this tree, and one day I shall be torn off by a storm or simply decay and fall, and become a pinch of compost about its roots. But meanwhile I am conscious of the tree's flowing sap and steadfast strength. Deep down in my consciousness is the consciousness of a collective life, a life of which I am a part and to which I contribute a minute but unique extension. When I die and fall, the tree remains, nourished to some small degree by my brief manifestation of life. Millions of leaves have preceded me and millions will follow me; the tree itself grows and endures.[20]

A version of this symbol is used as early as a lament for the poet's brother, 'Auguries of Life and Death' (1919). A similar pattern of human life appears in *Moon's Farm*. Millions of people are spinning out the thread of their destiny, and form the pattern 'we call history. / A crazy pattern / but the only one that exists'. When the thread of an individual life is cut,

> Why, then the pattern changes
> but so infinitely little
> it makes no difference.[21]

Perhaps the passivity of Read's attitude is related to the loss of life he witnessed during the war. His belief is very different from that of Eliot, who is alarmed rather than comforted by the thought of himself as one among many (as when, in the first part of *The Waste Land*, he sees the crowds undone by death, flowing over London Bridge), and who is anxious to redeem his own guilty soul in a realm beyond nature. Read's attitude is essentially Wordsworthian, recalling that poet's understanding, in the last of the 'Lucy' poems, of why the girl had to be reclaimed by nature, to be rolled round 'With rocks, and stones, and trees'.

Just as he is concerned with the relationship of the individual leaf to the Tree of Life, Read is keen to see patterns in the microcosm which suggest the plan of the macrocosm. This, too, is an essentially romantic vision, like Blake's in 'Auguries of Innocence' when he sees 'a World in a Grain of Sand / And a Heaven in a Wild Flower'. As the Second Voice says in *Moon's Farm*:

> Our very consciousness expands when we discover
> some corner of the pattern of the universe
> realize its endless implications
> and know ourselves
> to be part of that intricate design.[22]

In part 3 of 'A World within a War' (1943), Read finds sermons in stones:

> The best of life is sparely spent
> In contemplation of those laws
> Illustrious in leaves, in tiny webs
> Spun by the ground-spider: in snailshells
> And mushroom gills: in acorns and gourds –
> The design everywhere evident
> The purpose still obscure [.]

Life and art are ultimately a question of discovering 'The pattern in the bone, in branching veins' and imitating 'in acts that beauty'.

Such matters naturally lead to questions of God, the original creator of pattern in the universe. As a young man, Read was a disciple of Nietzsche, and would doubtless have agreed with his mentor A. R. Orage when he said that 'Blake is Nietzsche in English'.[23] Yet there is a tension in the early poems between the Superman and the fellow man. In the last part of the war poem 'My Company' (1919), for example,

Read talks of his ability to assume

> a giant attitude and godlike mood
> and then detachedly regard
> all riots, conflicts and collisions.

Ultimately, however, he bows his head to join the men under his command, assumes 'human docility' and prepares to 'share their doom'. His last poem on the First World War, 'The End of a War', amounts to a debate between a Nietzschian and a Christian within Read. The speaker of the first part, a dying German officer, is an imperialist who believes that God is to be created 'in the end of action, not in dreams': the deity is invented by man in his own image as a supernatural, cosmic sanction on the natural ties of friendship, confederacy and nationhood. The speaker of the final section, an English officer waking on the first morning of peace, looks forward to relinquishing his will to that of God, and living a life of meekness. While Read never approaches becoming a Christian, it is arguable that this poem does effectively see the final banishment of Nietzsche from his thought. Certainly there are no more suggestions of the Superman, or exaltations of the will; and in general terms, the mature Read's characteristic gentleness, tolerance and pacifism are much closer to Christ than to Nietzsche. What Read retains from his earlier leanings, as explored in the first part of 'The End of a War', is a belief in the necessity of living with one's feet firmly in the world we know, and not drifting off into the 'transcendental inane'. In *Moon's Farm*, the Second Voice says that it would be 'a great relief' to give one's soul to God, 'to feel utterly empty'; but that it is 'an illusion, of course', though 'one of the desirable illusions'.[24] Read's sensible, rather distinctively English attitude, again contrasts with Eliot's, whose goal is exactly the erasure of self in submission to the will of God.

In *Moon's Farm* the Second Voice takes us through the stages of our ancestors' belief in God. Initially, they worshipped 'the cosmos of which they were a part', but in time this became 'the idea of the cosmos which they could separate from themselves as a word / and make absolute as an idea'. Recently, mankind reached the stage where

> The idea of God
> had not risen from man's experience of the world
> but had been an original intuition of the mind
> an idea divinely inspired
> a glimpse of some transcendental realm of being
> where time does not exist.[25]

One manifestation of this idea is Eliot's notion of the timeless realm in *Four Quartets*. For Read, though, God is equated with nature. In *Moon's Farm* he must be 'staring us in the face':

23

> His face is the sky
> His eyes are red berries in yon hedge
>   or the glittering quartz in this stone. [...]
> What sort of God would play hide-and-seek?[26]

Read has a version of religious inspiration in what he calls 'the sense of glory'.[27] In part 4 of 'A World within a War', it will lead to the creation of a new age, to the building of 'A crystal city in the age of peace'. Such expressions of humanist hope can sound a little hollow, as Read himself knows in the fifth part of the Dunkirk 'Ode', where those who can relieve suffering with prayer are happy,

> But we who have put our faith
> in the goodness of man
> and now see man's image debas'd
> lower than the wolf or the hog –
> Where can we turn for consolation?

Towards the end of 'The Gold Disc' (1955), Read proclaims, in one of his most memorable poetic statements:

> in the end I have put all in doubt
> God, man; earth, heaven: I live on in alert suspense.
>
> I believe in my unbelief – would not force
> One fibre of my being to bend in the wind
> Of determinate doctrine.

At the other extreme from the reliance on finely-tuned senses, from the labile world of nature, from the sense of glory inspiring the building of new cities, are moments of purity in which the detail of the world dissolves. The same stanza of 'The Gold Disc' continues with a celebration of stillness, not what Eliot, in the second part of 'Burnt Norton', calls 'the still point of the turning world', but endless, over-whelming outer space:

> In doubt there is stillness
> The stillness that elsewhere we may find
> In the sky above us where the fix'd stars
> Mete out infinity [.]

Elsewhere, for instance in 'Night's Negation' (1935) and 'Gala' (1955), the stillness is also reached through the night sky. In 'September Fires' (1934), bonfires stand for 'a world burning its dross'; their smoke rises against 'hills blue and clear / but featureless'. There are related areas of calm: in part 3 of 'A World within a War', Read writes of rest

24

> Above the beating heart: the body
> Settles round its axis: mind simulates
> The crystal in the cooling rock
> The theorem in the beetle's eye –
> After the day's mutations
> Finds the silver node of sleep....

This peace is a principle inherent within the body. Eliot's moments of release are different: the 'awful daring of a moment's surrender' in the final part of *The Waste Land* is an unexpected existential crisis, and the epiphanies in *Four Quartets* point us far away from the world of the flesh, which is merely dust in sunlight in the epiphanic moment at the end of 'Burnt Norton'.

Underlying Read's mature philosophy, as we have noted, is the effect of the new psychology. The influence of Freud, and then Jung, is increasingly felt in his work. One of his first explicit, deliberate attempts to harness the unconscious to the creation of poetry is represented by the poems 'A Dream' and 'Love and Death', which were first published in the essay 'Myth, Dream and Poem', in *Collected Essays in Literary Criticism* (1938).[28] Both poems are based on dreams; the second, Read says, was written virtually in a trance.[29] Such material and methods become more and more a part of Read's poetry (though they never entirely displace a more rational, discursive voice, which remains heard in other poems, such as 'The Gold Disc'). Characteristic of Read's dreamlike poetry is 'Constellation' (1955):

> There was a fall as from the sky
> It might have been a burning star
> We walked like mortals in a street
> And up a marble stair. Restless water
> Everywhere. Sharp shadows wove
> A portent of some change: broke up
> The unreal world. There was a bell
> A barge of yellow fruit: and at the end
> A garden wall: a door which she unlatch'd
> To show a room its white walls hung
> With trophies from the labyrinth.
> And she was there and I was there
> And there a bull for sacrifice.

This is a long way from the austerity of *Naked Warriors*. Essentially, the development is from a classical to a romantic language. Read's ultimate aspiration in his later work, his idea of pure poetry, is suggested by his exhortation to his daughter in the uncollected poem 'For My Daughter's Second Birthday' (1942): 'Oh, long may you babble like the crystal beck / and leave learning to the owl'.[30] The goal is Wordsworthian:

that poetry should be a spontaneous overflow of feeling, or, more accurately in Read's case, of the unconscious. This is not to imply that Read turns his back on modernism. In part 2 of 'A World within a War' he talks of his desire to produce poems 'Crisp as medals, bright but cool', and even in his most dreamlike poems there is a brightness and coolness of image which has its roots in his early allegiance to Pound and the belief that poems should be 'austere, direct, free from emotional slither'.

In *Moon's Farm*, the Second Voice says:

> In the beginning was the word
> and in the end are many words
> nets to catch the butterfly truth.[31]

This seems especially suited to the last section in the final *Collected Poems* of 1966, 'vocal avowals'. (Some of these poems were first published in 1959.[32]) The following piece, 'silk wrist', is typical of their extraordinary strategy and technique:

> gross funicular gilt
> waste icicle gun lea
> hurtle glass low linger
> so delicate call clasp
> cast finger cool column
> no drum clam drastic
> hollow coronal all ice
> false fire cloud o' maul
> memory now milk

In his essay 'What is a Poem?', appended to the 1966 *Collected Poems*, Read eventually answers his own question by saying that it is an unbroken unit of rhythm and sound, and that 'a verifiable meaning, an intellectual or moral or social communication',[33] is ultimately irrelevant to a poem's worth as pure poetry. In 'vocal avowals' he wishes to test this theory to the utmost. The poems take their cue from various human actions or states. One is baby-talk, as implied in the title 'cradle song'. Another is the deterioration of logic while falling asleep, and in this, they are reminiscent of the end of the Anna Livia Plurabelle section of *Finnegans Wake*. The poems have a further psychological root in sexual pleasure or post-coital ease, as hinted at, for example, in 'asp', with its 'breast pastures' and 'sovereign silk waterfall'.

In 1962, Eliot rejected 'vocal avowals', saying that they did not fit into the Faber category.[34] The poems aspire to a pure, supremely subjective romanticism, an unimpeded outpouring of the unconscious, to which Eliot could not respond.

The only other poems of Read's which resemble the 'avowals' are two written around the same time, 'Fertile Feathers' and 'Bower Bird' (both 1963). The opening of 'Fertile Feathers' is typical of the tone and movement of both poems:

Feather & weather & the fertile zone
feature forever the mind of God
grace & gristle butcher-bird & bat
distribute the seed by splitting the pod[.]

As these lines suggest, both poems celebrate the harmonious energy and fecundity of nature, too fleeting to be registered except by the movement, rhythm and sounds of a poem: the joy must be caught as it flies. A similar sense of the plenitude, variety and vigour of the world lies behind the 'avowals'. We are far away from the satirical detachment of the author of 'Smoker', or from Kneeshaw, vegetating in the forest of his dreams, unaware of anything or anyone around him. A character called Kneeshaw also appears in Read's only novel, *The Green Child* (1935), where he is a brute tormenting the Green Child, a symbol of nature and innocence. Here, he must be killed before Olivero, the clearly autobiographical hero, can continue his spiritual quest. Just as Kneeshaw has had to be destroyed, so has the related, elitist detachment represented by Nietzsche. The similarity of their names is no coincidence (although Kneeshaw is a name actually found in Read's area of Yorkshire, not merely a coinage). They represent isolation from the daily round of human life and the diurnal course of nature. Ultimately, we arrive at a celebratory attachment to and involvement in the natural world which takes us full circle, back to Read's childhood and innocence.

What, in the final analysis, are Read's strengths as a poet? *Songs of Chaos* are naïve; *Eclogues*, with some exceptions, rather still and dull. The poems of *Naked Warriors*, though, are mostly striking and memorable, distinguished by their resolutely unpropagandist approach, and their implicit defence of the right to lead a civil, gentle life. The metaphysical poems of *Mutations of the Phoenix* now seem, on the whole, unsatisfactory. Eliot said of one, 'John Donne Declines a Benefice', that it contained unassimilated Browning;[35] and there is unassimilated matter of some kind in most of the other poems of *Mutations*, primarily the logical-metaphysical style itself, which, as we have seen with 'The Analysis of Love', was ultimately uncongenial to Read's temperament. It is with some of the poems first collected in *Collected Poems 1913–25* that the characteristic romantic note starts to be heard. 'Huskisson in Arcadia', as we have seen, is one of these; so is 'The White Isle of Leuce' (1926), an enthusiastic celebration of a sacred isle, sex, revelry, beauty and battle, which reads like a graph of the heartbeat of romanticism. With these romantic notes established, from the mid-1920s Read produces a large number of fine lyrics, and memorable longer poems, such as the Dunkirk 'Ode', 'A World within a War', 'Daphne' and *Moon's Farm*. These deserve a better fate than oblivion.

Even great poets have blind spots. Eliot cannot accept or understand the delights of physicality;[36] Yeats has a poor understanding of man as a social creature. Read was criticized by Stephen Spender for having an insufficient awareness of the reality of evil, and this does seem to be his Achilles heel: he puts too much faith, romantically, in the essential goodness of man.[37] In particular, his hopeful, humanist declarations, in the Dunkirk 'Ode' and 'A World within a War', that a new kind of mighty city will be built in the age of peace sound empty and flailing. But amongst those who confront fragmentation and despair, it is good to have a poet who has nevertheless retained a vision of innocence.

Above all, Read is an integrator, and his reconciliation of disparate twentieth-century elements is a considerable, and greatly underrated, achievement. It leads to a salutary brand of modernism which is refreshing and regenerative. His poetry encompasses the First World War, and goes on to incorporate the new interest in psychology and the unconscious. It exhibits a modernist freedom from romantic emotional excess, while at the same time exemplifying and continuing the distinctively English romantic tradition of attachment to nature. Read emerges as that rare creature, a modernist not exiled, like Pound and Eliot, but in touch with his native and ancestral soil.[38]

Notes

1   Quoted on the inside dust-jacket of *Collected Poems* (London: Faber and Faber, 1946), from a review of *Poems 1914–1934*.

2   Ezra Pound, 'A Retrospect' in T. S. Eliot (ed.), *Literary Essays of Ezra Pound* (London: Faber and Faber, 1954), p. 12.

3   Herbert Read, *Moon's Farm, Collected Poems* (London: Faber and Faber, 1966), p. 209. Unless otherwise stated, all quotations from Read's poetry are from this, final, edition. (Sinclair-Stevenson reprinted the book in 1992, although the only year of publication recorded in the volume is 1966. Bizarrely, while the cover bears the eccentric title of *Selected Poetry*, the title page retains *Collected Poems*.) The date in parentheses after the first mention of the poem is that of its first publication, whether in a periodical or a book. In the single case of references to the lengthy and undivided verse play *Moon's Farm*, endnotes give the page number for the 1966 *Collected Poems*.

4   Read Archive, University of Victoria Library, British Columbia, Canada, Lot 48, Item 32, MS HR/TSE 45.

5   William Wordsworth, *The Prelude* (1805), Book First, line 305.

6   Herbert Read, 'The Song of the Lark', *Songs of Chaos* (London: Elkin Mathews, 1915), pp. 11–22.

7   Herbert Read, 'The Daisy', *Songs of Chaos*, p. 33.

8   The first appearance is in *Art and Letters*, vol. 2, no. 2 (Spring 1919), p. ii.

9   See especially Herbert Read, *The True Voice of Feeling* (London: Faber and Faber, 1953).

10 Herbert Read, 'Killed in Action', *Naked Warriors* (London: Art and Letters, 1919), pp. 55–56.

11 Herbert Read, 'Smoker', *Coterie*, no. 2 (September 1919), p. 17.

12 All Eliot poems referred to in this chapter are found in T. S. Eliot, *The Complete Poems and Plays* (London: Faber and Faber, 1969).

13 The Preface is included in Herbert Read, *Collected Poems* (1966 edition), pp. 277–78.

14 Herbert Read, 'The Nature of Metaphysical Poetry', *Criterion*, vol. 1, no. 3 (April 1923), p. 264.

15 Herbert Read, 'Huskisson Sacred and Profane', *Coterie*, no. 3 (December 1919), pp. 81–85.

16 Herbert Read, *Collected Poems 1913–25* (London: Faber and Gwyer, 1926).

17 Herbert Read, *Moon's Farm*, *Collected Poems* (1966 edition), p. 220. The play was broadcast by the BBC on 21 January 1951.

18 See ibid., pp. 206–07.

19 E.g., ibid., p. 225: 'And the way up and the way down are the same'. Cf. Herbert Read on Heraclitus in *The Cult of Sincerity* (London: Faber and Faber, 1968), pp. 55–56.

20 Herbert Read, *The Contrary Experience* (London: Faber and Faber, 1963), pp. 184–85.

21 Herbert Read, *Moon's Farm*, *Collected Poems* (1966 edition), p. 212.

22 Ibid., p. 215.

23 Quoted in James King, *The Last Modern: A Life of Herbert Read* (London: Weidenfeld and Nicolson, 1990), p. 28.

24 Herbert Read, *Moon's Farm*, *Collected Poems* (1966 edition), p. 221.

25 Ibid., pp. 209–10.

26 Ibid., p. 204.

27 The phrase gave the title to a collection of Read's essays: *The Sense of Glory* (Cambridge: Cambridge University Press, 1929). In the poetry, the phrase occurs in part 4 of the Dunkirk 'Ode' and part 4 of 'A World within a War'.

28 See Herbert Read, *Collected Essays in Literary Criticism* (London: Faber and Faber, 1938), pp. 105–07, 111–15. 'A Dream' has no title until the final *Collected Poems* of 1966.

29 Clearly, this emphasis on the artistic value of material from dreams links in with Read's commitment to the surrealist movement. He was much involved with the 1936 International Surrealist Exhibition, and edited *Surrealism* (London: Faber and Faber, 1936).

30 Herbert Read, 'For My Daughter's Second Birthday', *Kingdom Come*, vol. 3, no. 11 (Winter 1942), p. 19.

31 Herbert Read, *Moon's Farm*, *Collected Poems* (1966 edition), p. 210.

32 Herbert Read, 'Vocal Avowals', *Encounter*, vol. 12, no. 3 (March 1959), pp. 42–43.

33 Herbert Read, 'What is a Poem?', *Collected Poems* (1966 edition), p. 274.

34 The letter in which Eliot rejects the poems is Read Archive, Lot 48, Item 32, MS HR/TSE 219. A volume did appear: *vocal avowals* (St Gallen: Tschudy Verlag, 1962). The poems were included as the last set in the 1966 *Collected Poems*, by which time Eliot had died.

35 Read Archive, Lot 48, Item 32, MS HR/TSE 15.

36 This is true except in Eliot's last poem, 'A Dedication to My Wife', *The Complete Poems and Plays*, p. 206.

37 See King, *The Last Modern*, p. 192.

38 I would like to thank my supervisor at Oxford, Dr Lyndall Gordon, for her valuable help. I am also grateful to Dr David Goodway, Miss Amanda Holton, Mr Bernard O'Donoghue and Professor Jon Stallworthy for their remarks.

Herbert Read and the Great War

HUGH CECIL

ERBERT Read came out of the First World War haunted by what he had witnessed, but hoping to play a part with other former servicemen in the creation of a co-operative, unselfish society. He wanted also, as he later put it, to tell, without rhetoric, the truth about the war and the men who fought it.[1] Much that he said was positive and the fact that, though a pacifist by inclination, his post-war reflections on the war are so different in tone from those other writers regarded generally as 'anti-war', bears witness to the general truth that every participant in the war had their own particular vision and was not primarily swayed in their accounts, as is often assumed, by prevailing contemporary trends. Read was a man preoccupied with public issues all his life and, some have said, over-anxious to keep up with the main trends in art. Yet he put a high value on the intimate personal memories and thoughts that make up the individual's inner landscape.

His war writing, over a lifetime, is to be found in his poetry, short stories, personal memories and wartime letters to his future wife, which appeared, among other places, in his various autobiographies; the war pervades his mysterious novel, *The Green Child*. War, with its twenty years' intermission, cast its shadow even over described moments of innocent happiness with his children:

> They came running over the perilous sands
> Children with their golden eyes
> Crying: *Look! We have found samphire*
> Holding out their bone-ridden hands.
>
> It might have been the spittle of wrens
> Or the silver nest of the squirrel
> For I was invested with the darkness
> Of an ancient quarrel whose omens
> Lay scatter'd on the silted beach.
> The children came running toward me
>
> But I saw only the waves behind them
> Cold, salt and disastrous
> Lift their black banners and break
> Endlessly, without resurrection.[2]

What makes Read's contribution to Great War literature of special interest is his combination of an intense vision and philosophical turn of mind with an actual battle-field heroism, matched in this respect by only Siegfried Sassoon in England and Ernst Jünger in Germany. Particularly striking is the detached authority with which he later recalled battle memories, in this contrasting with the less heroic viewpoints of writers such as Remarque and also with the fierce, ironical tone of many of Read's own wartime poems.[3]

Read was more complex than most warriors. In 1914, although his commitment to revolutionary ideas was not sufficiently formulated to stop him going to war, he was a theoretical pacifist, a socialist and an admirer of Georges Sorel and syndicalism; he was also an aesthete, and even in wartime a contributor to radical political and cultural journals. In later life his anarchist views were well-known.

Wiry and energetic, however, nature and inheritance contributed to his excellence as a soldier. His happy early years near Kirkbymoorside gave him a faith in life too strong to be uprooted by later turmoil.[4] A Yorkshire yeoman by birth, his profound sense of identity with a locality and its people built an inner confidence to succeed as an officer. When his father died, the family left their farm for an insecure existence in Leeds.[5] His mother died in December 1914, shortly after he had left Leeds University and had joined the army. Already mature for his years, intellectually, Read was freed by the loss of his parents from family ties in a way that probably made him a more effective soldier. In 'The Raid', where he recalled his state of mind before a dangerous military operation, he described 'P—', a timid fellow-officer. Like the pathetic boy-soldier, Howells, in Henry Williamson's novel about the 1916 Somme battle, *The Golden Virgin* ('It's fatal to imagine your mother in everything from home', wrote Williamson), 'P—' had become a coward partly because of his inability to cut loose from his home:

> He had a mother and a sweetheart, and he spent a lot of time writing letters. He never got free from his home thoughts; he was still bound in some sort of personal dependence to these ties. His mind, at any rate, was not free to lead its own existence. I think that is why he was a coward.[6]

Read himself had a fiancée, Evelyn Roff, whom he had met at the university.[7] Whilst the relationship gave him confidence, he was not, however, so dependent on her as to sap his fighting spirit. Possibly he mistook for attachment his as yet unfulfilled desire for sexual experience. His letters to her were often didactic and impersonal in tone, even allowing for the probability that expressions of intimacy may have been expunged before publication (the originals have been destroyed).[8]

Whilst Christianity, which he had renounced, played no part in sustaining his morale, its images were deeply planted in his consciousness and he often used them when writing of his men's suffering and stoical endurance. Rather, however, it was the ideas of the philosopher Nietzsche to which he turned. This played a part in his seeing his war career as a kind of test and a sign for him, after he had come through it, that he was destined to achieve greater things.

Read's pre-war membership of the Leeds University Officers' Training Corps was not a sign of militarism but typical at the time of young men of all political persuasions, seeking discipline in their lives and outdoor adventure in reaction to a citified existence.[9] Moreover, although he hoped that the threatened war – to him simply the product of commercial and imperial rivalry – would be stopped at once by a general strike in every country, he was no different from most Edwardians and late Victorians in accepting a romanticized view of soldiering from newspapers and literature. Doubtless, too, some remnant of the patriotic loyalties he had grown up with still affected him subconsciously. Finally, though ambitious, he was uncertain about his future. 'The War meant a decision: a crystallisation of vague projects: an immediate acceptance of the challenge of life. I did not hesitate.'[10]

In January 1915 he was commissioned in the Yorkshire Regiment – 'the Green Howards'.[11] In November, he joined his battalion, the Seventh Green Howards, in the area between Ypres and Hooge. It was a relatively 'quiet' month with few casualties, despite intense artillery and aeroplane activity, but mud and rain – and later snow – hampered trench work. The rest billets at Busselboom were a quagmire.[12] In Ypres where Read was later billetted with his company, 'B', in cellars near the ramparts, conditions were drier, but here he came to realize the price the army paid for clinging on to the Ypres salient, the sacred symbol of defiance against the German invasion. 'It was not justified in a strategic sense. It was a blind impulse, to which hundreds of thousands of lives were sacrificed.'[13] Quick to disappear were any notions of war as glorious and dignified:

> War through my soul has driven
> Its jagged blades:
> The riven
> Dream fades –
> So you'd better grieve, heart, in the gathering night,
> Grieve heart in the loud twilight.[14]

He and his platoon, during their four-day periods in the trenches, were worked to the extreme of fatigue by the endless night patrols, wiring and revetment of trenches – and he was unprepared for the tedious periods of inaction or the ugliness of war: spades driven through the skulls of buried men; soldiers urinating in their breeches with fear; shot men sniggering blood; shattered villages.[15]

In December, after a period of training 'as far as climate and circumstance would permit', they were back in trenches near Hooge, vacating these each morning for four days while British howitzers pounded ineffectually at the tough thickets of wire on the enemy side.[16] Gas from an unsuccessful German attack on 17 December reached the Seventh Green Howards as they waited in support. Following a period of rest after Christmas they faced more German assaults near Vormezeele. Now wearing the short length of green braid on each sleeve associated with their eighteenth-century battle honours,[17] which tradition dictated but supply problems had prevented earlier, the Seventh Green Howards proved their mettle in dismal and harrowing circumstances, when for weeks the Germans hurled every kind of projectile at their opponents. Facing Saxon soldiers of the 123rd regiment in late February the Yorkshiremen gave as good as they got, despite snow and frost: 'After we had thrown our bombs', recorded the battalion diary, 'the enemy asked, "Are you the Guards?" The sentry replied "Yes".'[18]

In March 1916, Read was badly lacerated by barbed wire and was sent back to England. It had been an ordeal, but he had found he could endure the experience of war, even at its worst, better than some of those who, seeing him reading poetry at Wareham training camp, had doubted his soldierliness: 'This is far from claiming I was fearless: the first days in the trenches, the first bombardment or attack, was a draining sickness of the spirit. But I presently recovered, as from a plunge into a cold sea.' With growing confidence he came to see that personality was more important than the habit of superiority conferred by an élite background.[19]

In June 1916, after convalescence, Read joined the Eleventh Green Howards, training recruits at Rugeley Park in Staffordshire. There he found time for contributing to journals such as the *New Age*, and embellishing his room with sketches by Watteau and Whistler, and some of his own very interesting war sketches, in the vorticist vein.[20] Surprisingly, his long absence from war, and this development of his artistic interests, seem not to have affected his military spirit. Even now, he told Evelyn, he felt the desire of Rupert Brooke possess him – 'to turn, as swimmers into cleanness leaping' – which shows how wrong it is to generalize about that mood evaporating after a few months of war. Though in no way chauvinistic, he continued to see war as the ultimate test, the purging of the soul through courage and duty.[21]

In April 1917, transferred to the Tenth Green Howards, he returned to the front and, after intense fighting, trained with his battalion at Hendecourt for a projected raid of considerable importance near Fontaine-les-Croisilles, south of the Arras–Cambrai road, in June. Read and a senior officer of recognized courage, Lieutenant J. L. Smith, MC, were selected to lead it.[22] He professed himself glad of this first chance to prove his leadership and for it to be recognized 'that I'm of the clan who don't give a damn for anything'.[23]

As Read, Smith and their men crawled laboriously across no-man's-land, they were surprised to encounter a strongly protected German wiring party and decided immediately to go on the defensive. However, since the Germans were coming very close to where Read lay, he realized it was vital to attack first. Leaping to his feet he ordered them to put up their hands, to which they replied with rifle fire. During the ensuing mêlée, Read seized a prisoner – the object of the raid – and, covered by his companions, hurried back with his prize to Brigade. He claimed to Evelyn that he and his prisoner, a cultivated officer, formed a close, instantaneous, friendship, though afterwards he remembered his brief acquaintance with the German soldier more ironically in his poem, 'Liedholz'.[24] On 18 August he was decorated with the Military Cross, and subsequently promoted to full lieutenant. Thus he had encountered his first great test and won.[25]

It was the comradeship, he told Evelyn earlier, which enabled him to face such danger, and which alone made the army tolerable to him: 'To create a bond between yourself and a body of men and a bond that will hold at the critical moment, that is work worthy of any man and when done an achievement to be proud of'.[26] For the men in his charge, Read's feelings acquired an intensity familiar to soldiers.[27]

Both from his accounts and from battalion diaries, it is clear that the morale of Tenth Battalion, the Green Howards (and the Second which he later joined) was excellent – in the Fontaine-les-Croisilles raid, out of a possible sixty, forty-seven men had volunteered. A large proportion of the officers or other ranks were rural Yorkshiremen with a strong collective identity.[28] What the companionship gave Read was a deep conviction that human goodness and love, his belief in which had been reinforced, throve best in small units. Survival, as he said elsewhere, came through the members of a community being *with* each other in real communion. This lay at the root of his anarchism, and was why he always so much valued his experience at that time.[29] His concern to show courage was not just so as to prove himself, but because that quality was essential for the survival and success of the whole group.

Read was obsessively determined not to betray his own men through cowardice.[30] In his poem 'Kneeshaw Goes to War', his crippled protagonist Kneeshaw returns home tortured by his experiences and guilt about a moment of failing nerve, mercifully just at the moment of being wounded, so that this spiritual desertion remains unknown.[31] It was not that Read could not sympathize deeply with a man like Cornelius Vane, his protagonist in another poem, who allows terror to take possession.[32] Read long concealed from Evelyn how frightened he had been about the raid, in case it might upset her and unman him. He had observed how natural physical fearlessness, the source of many heroic acts, could be destroyed by shock. He therefore relied on a balanced outlook on life and death to sustain his will to fight. Cowards had not the will-power, or 'decency of thought',[33] to make themselves overcome fear. He himself had learned to find comfort in an image of all humanity springing from a tree of life, growing continually, while individual lives were like leaves which were shed when they had had their time. This made his own life, and sometimes the lives of others, seem less precious to himself, though it did not protect him from the worst grief, as when his brother was killed.[34]

On leave in September 1917, he missed some of the dreadful Third Battle of Ypres which his battalion endured in the autumn of 1917. Returning to the front in October, he wrote to Evelyn: 'Life has never seemed quite so cheap nor nature so mutilated'.[35] He evoked the horror of that muddy hell in 'Kneeshaw Goes to War'.[36]

Yet he still could feel satisfaction from his responsibilities. 'I got four Military Medals today out of seven for the Battalion', he wrote to Evelyn: 'And damned proud of it we are.'[37]

In February 1918, the Tenth Battalion, like many others whose strength had been depleted in the previous months, was finally disbanded. Dreary winter weather, monotony and high casualties earlier, leading to the break-up of battalions with their sense of identity, contributed to a widespread mood of war-weariness. Read shared it; now in the crack Second Battalion, he told Evelyn: 'there has been... an immense growth of pacifist opinion'.[38]

Yet it is clear that the British Army's spirit was subdued rather than crushed when it faced its toughest test. On 21 March, along a forty-mile front, the German Army, reinforced by divisions released from the fighting in Russia, attacked sparsely-manned British lines and those of the exhausted French. For Read himself, it was the moment when his original decision to volunteer was justified by the heroic conduct he now displayed. *In Retreat*, his account of the episode, is one of the best pieces of writing to come out of the war.[39] While sharing much of their beauty of language, it contrasts in tone with the anger of his war poems, which appeared as a volume, *Naked Warriors*, in the same year, 1919, as he was writing this account of the fateful days of March 1918.

When the German assault began, the Second Green Howards and other units, part of General Gough's Fifth Army, were hastily moved up to defend their redoubt at Roupy, in the third line of defence. Read took Thoreau's *Walden* with him to read, confident in the solid strength of the fort and power of its machine-gun fire, and anticipating no more than two or three weary days of passive defence, not the ordeal which was to come.

Heavy mist shrouded the battlefield, giving cover for an unseen foe. Anxiety mounted; by ten o'clock that morning, 'our hearts were like taut drum skins beaten reverberantly by every little incident'.[40] By eleven o'clock the Germans had penetrated the front line ahead of them.

During the ferocious two-day siege that followed, the enemy attacked repeatedly, undeterred by a heroic counter-attack by one of the Green Howards' companies. Read was told how the company commander with a dozen men reached a trench held by the Germans and in the hand-to-hand fighting that lasted a few minutes, like some hero in a Henry Newbolt poem, 'was last seen cursing, pinned to a trench wall by a little mob of Germans, in one hand his empty smoking revolver'.[41]

Meanwhile the British artillery was firing short, smashing their own defences and hitting the Second Green Howards in the redoubt, while German field guns, hauled up with speed, had been brought to bear on it. Shortly after midday on the second day the enemy reached the inner ring of the redoubt.

To avoid being trapped, he, and the colonel commanding, established new headquarters at an old gun pit further back. There they were pounded by a British gun whose crew believed, mistakenly, that Roupy had been evacuated, and Colonel Edwards had to retire, wounded, to a dressing station, leaving Read, now the senior officer, to lead the survivors out of the redoubt. The Yorkshiremen burst out into the open, ignoring German cries of '*Halt Englisch!*' and rushed through a storm of bullets, which cut them down in swathes, to a line of trenches three hundred yards behind – only to find no reinforcing troops to give covering fire and that what looked like entrenchments was no more than a shallow depression where the sods had been removed.

This terrible moment proved to be the pattern for the week that ensued: to find their way to defensive positions, then to be quickly outflanked and forced to escape. He and his men had repeatedly to move after only an hour or two of snatched sleep, and were ordered to take defensive action when they were at the end of their energies; indeed it was only their sheer exhaustion, he felt, which stopped his men rebelling against such orders. At Esmery Hallon they were commanded – much against his will, for he felt too much had been asked of his men – to defend that village, which stood on a detached conical hill, overlooking a surrounding plain. After co-ordinating with a small group of Inniskillings on their left, there was a moment of blessed quiet. His account of feeding the soldiers reads like that of the sacred moment of union at a eucharist – a scene worthy of a mural by Stanley Spencer:

> there was any amount of wine, but I was afraid to distribute it among the men for fear lest on fasting stomachs it should make them drunk. So S. and I each took a wine glass, and starting at different points, we began to go a round of the men. Each man lay curled up in his shallow pit, resting. To each we gave a glass of wine and a few biscuits. They took it thankfully. There was a lull in the distant fighting: I don't remember any noise of fire during that hour. The sun was warm and seemed to cast a golden peace on the scene. A feeling of unity with the men about me suddenly suffused my mind.[42]

Just after dark they were ordered to relieve soldiers of the Royal Engineers in front of the village, leaving the security of the heights. Despite this they were buoyed up with wild hope by a message that a French reinforcement was on its way. The following morning, however, they saw, fleeing towards them through the same 'fateful mist', stragglers from a retreating British force. The enemy were soon upon them. After momentary panic caused by German machine-gun fire and British shrapnel falling short, Read and his companions withdrew across the plain, joining a British force at Ramecourt. With fifteen of his men, he was ordered to dig in on the bank of the Nesle-Noyon canal. Dispirited and exhausted, Read later maintained that it was only because he was shamed into action by his men's dogged endurance that he forced himself to work: 'I seemed to be lifting utterly impossible burdens.

My flesh seemed to move uneasily through iron bands; my leaden lids drooped smartingly upon my eyes.'[43] A depth of three feet was all they could manage, but it was effective. In the morning German infantry advanced in open order, across the exposed plain, and he and his fifteen companions began to 'pot' them 'like a rifle-gallery entertainment at a fair'.[44] He was confident that the Germans would be stopped, but once again British artillery came to the Germans' rescue, raining down shells on to their own lines.

He led his men at break-neck speed up on to a large crescent-shaped mound fifty yards behind, which commanded the plain. There he was ready to hold the position with a few British troops already up there, under a colonel, but soon found his own group deserted, and saw French troops retreating on his right, so dashed out of the trap and crossed a stream behind the mound with his fifteen men, recalling as he did so a childhood memory of water-rats plunging at dusk into the mill-dam near his home.

They ran, until they could do no more than stroll, across the open plain, enemy shrapnel bursting too high to do them damage, and finally reached a sign pointing them in the direction of a 'Stragglers Post'. 'So I was a straggler', he wrote. 'I felt very bitter and full of despair.'[45]

Eventually they came to a divisional headquarters at Roye, where their spirits were revived by foraging French bread, butter, honey, hot milky coffee and champagne, after days with almost nothing to eat: 'We cried out with wonder. We almost wept. We shared the precious stuff out, eating and drinking with inexpressible zest.'[46] They were not yet out of the fight, however, and were sent back to Folies to hold an entrenched position. Read's own exceptional efforts had worn him out completely, and he was ordered out of the line, but his protests that his men were also exhausted were ignored. On 26 March he galloped, dazed, on a borrowed horse back to La Neuville, where he slept for more than twelve hours. Only after that was he reunited with his battalion, who had been sent out of the line at last.

He had revealed himself as a resourceful tactician as well as steadily courageous. As he freely admitted, it would have been impossible had it not been for the determination of his men, though exhausted to the limit of their powers. Subsequently promoted to Captain, he later received the DSO, which, in that war, junior officers were only awarded for exceptional bravery which did not quite fulfil the stringent requirements for a VC.

The situation was such that no soldier could long be relieved from the fighting. In April and May the Second Green Howards were defending Ypres at the Dickebusch Lake where exceptionally heavy bombardments from gas and high-explosive shells caused many casualties and reduced their trenches to rubble pits. On 8 May, the enemy penetrated the line they were holding and took prisoners, including Read's close friend, Captain Colin Davidson.[47]

On 16 June, Read left his battalion and returned to England. He had applied for transfer to the RAF and had to face a medical board for entry. Sick of the war, he was increasingly distressed by what he saw as the wanton slaughter of German and English youth to further the lust of politicians and states for domination, glory and commercial wealth. In such a revulsion against the large all-powerful nation-state can be seen yet another source of his anarchism.[48]

Fortunately for Read he was rejected for the RAF, which while it might have satisfied a Nietzschean hero's desire to soar, would, in 1918, have been no escape from intense nervous strain. In order to bomb enemy positions, pilots were often required to fly over them in a straight line at five hundred feet or below, 'Giving the Huns machine-gun practice'.[49]

He did not return to the front. When peace came, for a while, like the Liberal journalist and wartime press officer, C. E. Montague, author of *Disenchantment* (1922), he expected to see the marvellous wartime spirit of the veterans being turned to challenging the old deceitful order. In the manner of the vorticist journal *Blast*, he issued a statement, prefacing his collection of war poems, in which he called on his generation to 'be resolved to live with a cleaner and more direct realisation of natural values'.[50] For him it was unbearable that these tragic events should not have some constructive function in founding a fair and creative society with a new morality expressed through the arts – by which he did not mean 'the falsely artistic prettifying of life'. The poems accompanying this statement are some of the finest to come out of the war.

Despite this gesture against the established order, he finally took the 'bourgeois path' of marriage and salaried jobs in the Ministry of Labour and the Treasury, though still writing literary and cultural criticism and, sometimes, creatively.[51] His transfer, in 1922, to the Victoria and Albert Museum, where he became personal assistant to the Museum's Director, laid the foundation of his future position as the most influential English art critic of the century.

The war, however, was deep in his thought throughout his life. It saddened him to see the companionship of the trenches dissolving. 'O beautiful men, O men I loved, / O whither are you gone, my company?' he had written in *Naked Warriors*, anticipating such a painful parting.[52] For a time he, like others, stuck to friends for whom army service was a bond, because neither he nor they could yet let the war go. One of these was the ebullient imagist poet, Richard Aldington.[53]

Aldington's service experiences had left him embittered against England and the avant-garde establishment, which he believed had squeezed him out while he was at the front, but he remained an enthusiastic promoter of those whose work, such as Read's imagist verse and war prose works, he admired.[54] However, despite their shared dislike of post-war bourgeois England, by the 1930s a gulf began to open between them.[55] A 'modern' poet in 1914, Aldington was not truly part of the modern movement which Read came so passionately to champion. He also rejected the idea of any new political order as the solution to mankind's troubles and looked back for inspiration and solace to Europe's long tradition of civilization.[56] Although Read was to find an exception in Henry Moore, it had dawned on him that the inspiration of most of Britain's war veterans was exhausted and they were not going to be the creative force of the future, in the way that both Joyce or Eliot – neither of them ex-servicemen – now presented to the world. Among the exhausted he numbered Aldington, who had quarrelled with Eliot and who feared that he was now moving Read away from creative work and a romantic imagination into a sterile world of criticism. Read denied this: his success in war, reinforcing the heritage of his background, gave him confidence about being able to educate and influence. He was indeed one of the few members of the war servicemen's generation – one might add John Reith and F. R. Leavis – who by the mid-1930s took up a central position of cultural authority for the nation.

Nor had his interest in creative writing really diminished, though it is true that the short war stories that were published as *Ambush*, in 1930, had mostly been written some time before. This interesting collection included 'The Raid', described earlier. 'Killed in Action' was to have been part of a never-finished novel and had originally been the last item in *Naked Warriors*; influenced by the vorticists, it is uncharacteristically brutalistic. 'First Blood' evokes the first horrific days at Ypres; and 'Man, Melodion, Snowflakes', a moment on a march in winter. The delicately-handled 'Cloud-Form', owing something to D. H. Lawrence, is about a young schoolteacher, whose pent-up turmoil about bad news from the front releases itself, as she lies gazing at a cloud, in an involuntary orgasm, mysterious and overwhelming, like a visitation of Zeus. 'Cupid's Everlasting Honeymoon' is a satirical (and disturbing) fantastical picture of a grand hotel in wartime, full of soldiers and classical gods. These highly original pieces represent, from their different angles, many faces of the war – fear and horror, aesthetic intensity, emotional disturbance, the war machine and the mythologizing of the experience – making up a powerful collective picture.[57]

In his own emotional life, Read's relationship with Evelyn Roff was fated to be a long-delayed casualty of the war. His early ardour for her, unnaturally heightened in wartime, had died down with their marriage in 1919. Still emotionally stunned by his experiences,[58] Read, though kind-hearted, was not a comfortable partner in the decade after the war. Evelyn, for whom too the war had been a strain, with a child now, and pining for Yorkshire, felt isolated. When Read took the chair of art history at Edinburgh, his new love for the young violinist, Margaret Ludwig, who was to be his second wife, spelt the end of the marriage. After that happened, Evelyn's mental health, already poor, deteriorated.[59]

Read returned to important creative work in the 1930s. One of his finest poems, *The End of a War*,[60] was published in 1933. In his preface to it, Read tells the true story of how, at the very end of the war, an unnamed British force is about to attack a French town, which they think to be still occupied by the retreating enemy. On the outskirts, however, they are deceived by a dying German officer into believing that his regiment has just withdrawn. Entering the town, the British troops are ambushed and over a hundred of them killed, before the place is cleared. Some of them return to bayonet the German officer. Later the mutilated corpse of a French girl, possibly murdered for spying for the Allies, is found in a house. Read must have heard the story from his fellow Green Howards, but about a unit other than his own, for although the Second Green Howards were involved in just this sort of fighting throughout October and November 1918 in the same part of France as described in the poem, their battalion diary does not tally in detail with his account.[61]

Given the time when it was written, it seems likely that through the poem Read found expression partly for his tortured feelings about the end of the relationship with his first wife, which had been part of the war and through which the war had lived on unhappily. The three protagonists – the courageous, ruthless German officer; the English officer, grateful only to be alive to enjoy a world without war; and the body and soul of the girl destroyed by the conflict – these stood in some measure for two sides of Read and for the broken woman whose bond with him, tied so closely in an atmosphere of war, was now irreparably cut.

But the poem has a wider significance. The corpse of the French girl speaks for the innocent human body, sacrificed brutally to ideas of honour and domination. The heroic, destructive German represents the logical conclusion of total commitment to war, and the sterility and evil of war itself. The English officer, released from its toils and rejoicing in life, voices the hope against hope that something can be drawn from the experience of war:

> ... our savage fate
> a fire to burn our dross
> to temper us to finer stock
> man emerging in some inconceived span
> as something more than remnant of a dream.[62]

Much of Read's writing – such as 'The Raid', dealing with mastery of fear – was preoccupied with the theme of achieving self-understanding in battle and, with it, power over circumstances. Whatever the overall significance of *The Green Child*,[63] it seems probable that at one level the book reflects symbolically Read's awareness of the dramatic break with his past that the war had caused, and the testing of the spirit in a hazardous real world, comparable with the war. At first too ineffective to defend his ideals, Oliver, the young schoolmaster, acquires power to rescue the delicate Green Child, the incarnation of an ideal aesthetic, from the brutal, destructive miller Kneeshaw, representing all 'negation and inhumanity', of which war is the worst example. Then, through her world, Oliver eventually takes the pure way of beauty. As Read had written sixteen years before in his preface to *Naked Warriors*: 'From the sickness of life revealed let us turn with gladness to the serenity of some disinterested beauty'.[64]

After his own war experiences, Read felt, like Oliver, a resolute self-possession. His sense of destiny, as it appears in his war writing, leaves a very different impression from the confused reactions of most other *English* First World War authors. However, there are more than a few affinities between Read and the German man of letters, Ernst Jünger, the author of *The Storm of Steel (In Stahlgewittern)*,[65] a vivid chronicle of the élite *Stosstruppen*, who were responsible for softening up enemy positions in the first wave of a major offensive, such as that of 21 March 1918. Jünger earned the *Pour le Mérite*, the highest German decoration for valour. To him the war was the supreme test. As young officers, Read and Jünger shared a philosophical bent and also a cultural dandyism. Jünger's protagonist in one of his novels, *Sturm*,[66] has a dug-out adorned with frescoes, and a collection of eighteenth-century leather-bound books on classical erotica. In *In Stahlgewittern* Jünger describes his appreciation of a collection of fine china and 'lovely old leather bindings' in a deserted house at Combles,[67] while in *Das Abenteuerliche Herz*, he wrote of his absorbed reading of *Tristram Shandy*, during the fighting around Bapaume and in hospital afterwards.[68] Such passages recall Read embellishing his room in Rugeley Camp and carrying Thoreau's *Walden* through the March 1918 retreat.

Jünger had none of Read's pacifism, and Aldington, an anti-war writer *par excellence* (who prided himself on never having taken a German life), regarded him as 'an almost unrivalled fanatic in the idolatry of destruction'.[69] Yet Jünger was always too sophisticated to be an unthinking jingo, and like Read his interest in war was as a test of the individual, though he went far further in justifying it than Read could ever do.

It is striking also that both writers wrote notable symbolic 'fantasy' works in the 1930s, both oblique in their message, but the resemblance cannot be stretched too far: for if Jünger's *On The Marble Cliffs* (1939) was connected to any real war, it was to the war which was to come, or to the Spanish Civil War, and to tyrannical leaders of his period who endangered peace, such as Stalin and Goering (he avoided evoking Hitler); whereas the development of Read's protagonist in *The Green Child* was related to ordeals through which he had passed, and derived from Read's conclusions about what the 1914–18 war had done to him.[70]

Ultimately, too, Read's pacifist views were more important to him after the war than any pride he may have felt in his war career; this is why we find him praising unreservedly Remarque's fervent, but shallow, anti-war novel, *All Quiet on the Western Front*, which shared no common ground, in tone or accuracy, with his own dignified and subtle writings. In the *Nation and Athenaeum*, he commented: 'This is the greatest of all war books... It is the first completely satisfactory exposition in literature of the greatest event of our time.' Yet though agreeing wholeheartedly with Remarque's view that the war had 'withered something in the war generation that should have come to full growth', he distilled from the novel his own truth, one greater, he rightly added, than any that Remarque had voiced: 'that although modern war is totally devoid of glory, the glory of the human spirit is indestructible, and nowhere was this more evident than in the brutal and degrading experiences of those four terrible years'.[71]

Having, as he said in one poem, 'no visible wounds to lick',[72] Read cannot be classed as a 'disenchanted' writer on the war. There was initially anger and always sadness in his view of it, but he was not embittered. There is nothing in *In Retreat* of the resentful, mocking quality of his friend Richard Aldington's novel, *Death of a Hero*, a work angrily attacking British society and lampooning the contemporary literary scene – notably T. S. Eliot, whom Read respected. From what Read wrote of Aldington as a poet and as 'an outstanding novelist', after his death in 1962, it is clear that he felt his friend's poems on love and war had given the world more 'intuition of the inalterable gods' than had any of his ephemeral and tempestuous fiction.[73]

On the other hand, Read's work differed greatly from the more 'optimistic' and crudely patriotic British interpretations of the war as being an unalloyed force for good, such as Gilbert Frankau's *Peter Jackson, Cigar Merchant*, by a former Royal Artilleryman who had no doubts about the righteousness of his country's cause against 'the Beast in Grey'. Frankau's book, like many in this genre, was sentimental although authentic and even critical, about the army life and battle conditions.[74]

No British writer, not even Siegfried Sassoon, was more a soldier than Herbert Read. His combination of confidence and efficiency with a forceful intellect and idealism give his war writings – particularly his post-war prose – a controlled power rare among English literary contemporaries. We must look outside England for his real equivalent in war literature. *In Retreat*, less than forty pages long, is as great a classic of war writings as Jünger's *In Stahlgewittern*. Yet the profound difference between Read and Jünger was that from the start, Read had a profound sense of the tragedy of war, and could not feel like the German that it had been a 'gift' to his generation, even though Read himself derived valuable lessons from it. For him, by 1940, the war that had ended in 1918 had been in vain: 'The world was not renewed'. Never again, he declared, must 'an army of young men marching / Into the unknown' do so believing that such a renewal was possible, or a hero's crown of glory achievable, through the destructive cruelty of war. Once again the world was swept up into death and darkness and despair; and only unillusioned understanding, and faith in the inner essence of man, could redeem the warrior:

> ... if you can go
> Knowing that there is no reward, no certain use
> In all your sacrifice, then honour is reprieved.
>
> To fight without hope is to fight with grace,
> The self reconstructed, the false heart repaired.[75]

Here, conflicting with Read's rationalism, was a conviction of mystery at the core of being which is convincing because we are aware that he knew what he knew from *experience*. At the end of his life he was still defending his views against the charge that it is only literary men who 'agonize' about war. To him , 'honest silence' might have been appropriate in the ancient world, but it seemed an inadequate reaction to a conflict on an unprecedented scale involving also genocide and attacks on women and children. One must either, he maintained, dignify the event and call it tragic, or despair and call it absurd. Read's belief in love and his respect for humanity – as well as his strong romanticism – left him in no doubt which choice he should take.[76]

Notes

1 Herbert Read 'Ode II', *A World within a War* (London: Faber and Faber, 1944), p. 11.

2 Herbert Read, '1945', *Collected Poems* (London: Faber and Faber, 1946), p. 197.

3 Herbert Read, *Naked Warriors* (London: Art and Letters, 1919).

4 Herbert Read, *Annals of Innocence and Experience* (London: Faber and Faber, 1946 edn), p. 26.

5 See James King, *The Last Modern: A Life of Herbert Read* (London: Weidenfeld and Nicolson, 1990); and Michael Paraskos, 'Herbert Read and Leeds', in Benedict Read and David Thistlewood (eds), *Herbert Read: A British Vision of World Art* (Leeds: Leeds City Art Galleries, 1993).

6 Henry Williamson, *The Golden Virgin* (London: Macdonald, 1954), p. 279; Herbert Read, 'The Raid', in *Annals of Innocence and Experience*, chapter 6.

7 King, *The Last Modern*, chapter 4.

8 The letters were published as 'A War Diary', in Herbert Read, *The Contrary Experience: Autobiographies* (London: Faber and Faber, 1963). I am grateful to Terry Tuey of the Special Collections, Read Archive, University of Victoria Library, British Columbia, Canada, for assistance.

9 See, for example, Henry Woodd Nevinson, *The Fire of Life* (London: Gollancz, 1935) pp. 37–38. Nevinson was a radical journalist; the Liberal writer R. H. Mottram took an equitation course at the local barracks before the war; Henry Williamson, the apolitical, rebellious son of a Conservative father, joined a territorial regiment and had been in the Boy Scouts. Rifle practice was compulsory at public schools and many grammar schools.

10 Read, *Annals of Innocence and Experience*, p. 138.

11 For details of battalions in which Read served, see Col. H. C. Wylly, *The Green Howards in the Great War 1914–1919* (Richmond, Yorkshire: privately published, 1926), chapters 6, 11, 17, 18.

12 See P[ublic] R[ecord] O[ffice], WO 95/2004, W[ar] D[iary of] 7th Btn [the] Yorkshire Reg[imen]t, November 1915.

13 Herbert Read, 'First Blood', in *Ambush*, Criterion Miscellany no. 16 (London: Faber and Faber, 1930), p. 9.

14 Read, 'Parody of a Forgotten Beauty', *Naked Warriors*, p. 4.

15 Ibid., pp. 17, 23, 57, 59.

16 PRO, WO 95/2004, WD 7 Btn Yorkshire Regt, 15–17 December 1915.

17 Ibid., 18 January 1916.

18 Ibid., 21/22 February 1916.

19 Read, *Annals of Innocence and Experience*, pp. 140–41.

20 Read, 'A War Diary', p. 80.

21 Ibid., p. 89.

22 PRO, WO 95/2156, WD 10 Yorkshire Regt, April–June 1917; and Read, *Annals of Innocence and Experience*, 'The Raid'.

23 Read, 'A War Diary', p. 99.

24 PRO, WO 95/2156, WD 10 Yorkshire Regt, 31 July 1917; Read, 'A War Diary', pp. 99–102; and Read, 'Liedholz', *Naked Warriors*, p. 27.

25 PRO, WO 95/2156, WD 10 Yorkshire Regt, 9 and 14 August, 9 September 1917.

26 Read, 'A War Diary', p. 113.

27 Read, *Naked Warriors*, pp. 31, 34.

28 See Wylly, *The Green Howards in the Great War, 1914–1919*.

29 Read's anarchism: J. B. Pick to author, August 1996. The writer John Pick took an interest in Read's anarchism during the 1940s and heard him speak publicly on the topic.

30 Read, 'Fear', *Naked Warriors*, p. 25.

31 Read, *Naked Warriors*, p. 9.

32 'The Execution of Cornelius Vane', ibid., p. 46.

33 Read, 'A War Diary', p. 97.

34 Read, *Annals of Innocence and Experience*, pp. 108 and 148.

35 Read, 'A War Diary', p. 112.

36 Read, *Naked Warriors*, pp. 15–16.

37 Read, 'A War Diary', p. 113.

38 Ibid., p. 117.

39 Herbert Read, *In Retreat*, Criterion Miscellany no. 8 (London: Faber and Faber, 1930 [originally issued by the Hogarth Press, 1925, and also reprinted in *Annals of Innocence and Experience*, pp. 159–88, and *The Contrary Experience*, pp. 228–54]). See also PRO, WO 95/2329, WD 2 Yorkshire Regt, March–April 1918, and see Aldington's comments on *In Retreat*, in David S. Thatcher (ed.), 'Richard Aldington's Letters to Herbert Read', *Malahat Review*, no. 15 (July 1970), pp. 5–44.

40 Read, *In Retreat*, p. 17.

41 Ibid., p. 22.

42 Ibid., p. 34; see also 'My Company', in Read, *Naked Warriors*, pp. 31–32.

43 Read, *In Retreat*, p. 37.

44 Ibid., p. 38.

45 Ibid., p. 41.

46 Ibid., p. 43.

47 PRO, WO 95/2329, WD 2 Yorkshire Regt, May 1918.

48 Read, 'A War Diary', pp. 123–33.

49 See V. M. Yeates, *Winged Victory* (St Albans: Mayflower Books, 1974), p. 97 [1st edn London: Cape, 1934].

50 Read, *Naked Warriors*, p. 5.

51 Read, *Annals of Innocence and Experience*, chapter 8.

52 Read, 'My Company', *Naked Warriors*, p. 32.

53 Read, 'A War Diary', pp. 143–44.

54 Thatcher, 'Richard Aldington's Letters to Herbert Read', p. 44.

55 King, *The Last Modern*, pp. 70, 81–82; see also letter from Aldington to H.D., 14 April 1929, in Caroline Zilboorg (ed.), *Richard Aldington and H.D.: The Later Years in Letters* (Manchester: Manchester University Press, 1995), p. 25.

56 See Richard Aldington, *All Men Are Enemies: A Romance* (London: Chatto and Windus, 1933).

57 Read, *Ambush*.

58 King, *The Last Modern*, p. 76.

59 Ibid., chapter 7.

60 Herbert Read, *The End of a War* (London: Faber and Faber, 1933).

61 See PRO, WO 95/1809, WD 2 Yorkshire Regt, May 1918–February 1919.

62 Read, *The End of a War*, p. 28.

63 Herbert Read, *The Green Child: A Romance* (London: Heinemann, 1935).

64 Read, *Naked Warriors*, p. 5.

65 Ernst Jünger, Lieutenant, 73rd Hanoverian Fusilier Regiment, *The Storm of Steel: From the Diary of a German Storm-Trooper on the Western Front* (London: Chatto and Windus, trans. Basil Creighton, Phoenix Library edn, 1930).

66 Ernst Jünger, *Lieutenant Sturm* [first published in *Hannoverischer Kurier* as serial, beginning April 1923, forgotten and 'discovered' in 1963, published Stuttgart: Ernst Klett Verlag, 1978], French trans. Philippe Giraudon (Mayenne, France: Editions Viviane Hamy, 1991), p. 25.

67 Jünger, *Storm of Steel*, p. 105.

68 See French translation, by Henri Thomas: *Le coeur aventureux*, (Paris: Gallimard, 1969 [2nd edn]), pp. 22–24.

69 Richard Aldington, 'Junger [sic] Junker?', review of Jünger's *Copse 125*, in *Sunday Referee*, 20 April 1930, p. 6; and see Tom Nevin, 'Whipping Thersites out of Camp', in Alain Blayac and Caroline Zilboorg (eds), *Richard Aldington: Essays in Honour of his Birth* (Montpellier: Université Paul Valéry, 1994).

70 For insights on *On the Marble Cliffs* and Jünger, generally, up to the end of the Second World War, see Tom Nevin's pioneering study of Jünger: *Ernst Jünger and Germany: Into the Abyss 1914–1945* (London: Constable, 1997).

71 Herbert Read, review of *All Quiet on the Western Front*, *Nation & Athenaeum*, 27 April 1929.

72 Read, 'Ode II', *A World Within a War*, p. 11.

73 See Richard Aldington, *Death of a Hero* (London: Chatto and Windus, 1929); Herbert Read, 'Richard Aldington', in *The Cult of Sincerity* (London: Faber and Faber, 1968), pp. 152, 156–59; Zilboorg, *Richard Aldington and H.D.*, pp. 44–45.

74 Gilbert Frankau, *Peter Jackson, Cigar Merchant: A Romance of Married Life* (London: Hutchinson, 1920).

75 Read, 'To a Conscript of 1940', *A World Within a War*, p. 22–23.

76 See foreword by Herbert Read to George Panichas (ed.), *Promise of Greatness: The War of 1914–18* (London: Cassell, 1968).

Herbert Read as Literary Critic

JOHN R. DOHENY

THE necessary incompleteness of focusing on only a part of Herbert Read's broad range of interests can be compensated for by concentrating on certain works in order to discover, and to discuss in concrete detail, some of his achievements as well as his failures as a literary critic.[1]

Read's most sustained and, in my view, his best work of literary criticism is *Wordsworth*.[2] The book also demonstrates Read's quiet independence as a critic: he is seldom a confrontational literary critic, but his independence is important. At a time when T. S. Eliot was promoting tradition, reason, and even religion in his criticism, and I. A. Richards and others were arguing for a focus on individual poems and interpretation, laying the groundwork for a school of criticism which gained a dominance of sorts especially in universities in the USA, Read was creating his own independent position and area. The Wordsworth book is an example of this process, for in nearly every statement Read is going against the grain, beginning in the first two paragraphs:

> In the lives of some poets... the works... are in themselves simple events: the facts explain the art... In the lives of others, the works of art stand out in severe relief: no events explain them; they have no background, no gradations towards experience, no transitions to events. Then biography becomes an analysis... only when we have established some causal relationship between the character of the poet and his poetry, have we begun to understand that poetry.[3]

The Prelude, Read asserts, is a great poem whose greatness does not rest on its biographical veracity; it is, rather, an idealization of the poet's life, a 'mask'. There were, he says, two Wordsworths, and 'by way of baldly announcing my theme, I might say that these two Wordsworths were Man and Mask – not Youth and Age, not Energy and Decay, but rather Reality and Myth'.[4] That is, there were two Wordsworths even during his lifetime: a man and a legend. Read sets out to unmask the legend in order to reach a deeper understanding of the poetry, and he does this in opposition to those critics who take the mask for the whole and thereby miss the greatness of the poetry. Read has in mind mainly Matthew Arnold and Leslie Stephen. In spite of James King and the anonymous reviewer from whom he quotes,[5] I think Read accomplishes this task brilliantly.

Read takes a phrase from John Stuart Mill's comments on his experience of reading Wordsworth ('the very culture of the feelings') as his own 'text':

Poetry *is* the culture of the feelings; not the *cultivation* of the feelings – not their rank growth nor yet their forced bloom; but their education, their growth to fullness and perfection, to harmonious life and rhythm. This is, under the aspect of poetry, merely the process of all art, and it is as an artist that Wordsworth must be freely praised.[6]

Wordsworth did not develop a philosophy in the usual sense in which it is impersonal and formulated in universal terms; instead he moved away from formulation, towards individuality: '... his philosophy is a projection of his personal psychology... it is impossible to say where the philosophy ends and the poetry begins'.[7] According to Read, this allows Wordsworth to create a poetic theory of the growth of the poet's mind in *The Prelude*. Wordsworth's philosophy disappears into the poet who transmutes, in his poetry, his human passion of sexual love into a general connection with nature, an act which involves 'universalization of individual experience' rather than accurate biographical information.

Read sets out on the dual task of sifting out the significant events of Wordsworth's life from the poetry, from letters, from Dorothy's journals and other sources and demonstrating the greatness of his poetry for that brief ten-year period between 1797 and 1807. Both are complex processes, and Read carries them out brilliantly, so brilliantly, in fact, that no one has ever surpassed his work. Perhaps that is one of the reasons that it is now nearly forgotten history, but the most obvious reason that the book received little direct attention (and still fails to receive it) is that Read presents a Wordsworth which went against the grain of scholars and critics.

One of those disturbing elements occurs when Read demonstrates that Wordsworth's passionate intensity and his feeling for nature – not found in his earliest poetry – occurred as 'an issue from the emotional storm that descended upon him in France'.

As that storm subsided, the outraged feelings sought compensation in memories; and then, at first slowly, then riotously, the treasury of his unconscious mind, so richly stored in childhood, was opened and given forth in the poetry of one wonderful decade... Wordsworth was a [supreme] poet for a limited period of about ten years. This period does not emerge gradually out of his youth or adolescence. It begins almost suddenly at the age of twenty-seven; it comes to an end, just as suddenly, at the age of thirty-seven.[8]

During his second visit to France between 30 November 1791 and late December 1792, Wordsworth fell passionately in love with Annette Vallon and became deeply sympathetic to the revolution, probably on the side of Brissot and the Girondists. By the time Annette gave birth to their daughter, whose birth was registered as Anne Caroline Wordsodsth (sic) on 15 December 1793, Wordsworth had fled to Paris because, Read believes, he might have been in danger due to his revolutionary sympathies, and he went back to England after he heard the news of his daughter's birth. 'It transformed his being', Read writes. 'I think that this passion and all its melancholy aftermath was the deepest experience of Wordsworth's life – the emotional complex from which all his subsequent career flows in its intricacy and uncertainty. It was this experience which Wordsworth saw fit to hide – to bury in the most complete secrecy and mask with a long-sustained hypocrisy.' Read's conclusion is that 'Wordsworth, as a character and as a poet, is inexplicable without this key to his emotional development. With this key he becomes, not indeed, a rational being, but a man whose thwarted emotions found an external and objective compensation in his poetry.'[9]

Read also believes that Wordsworth returned to England to publish his poems and to seek the money he needed to return to France to Annette and Caroline, but, unfortunately, that return was made impossible when France declared war on England in February 1793. Wordsworth lived a restless and frustrated life for a time, and then three momentous events helped him to direct his frustrated passion into his greatest poetry.

A small legacy from William Calvert in 1795 gave him some financial security. This allowed him to set up house with his sister Dorothy whom he had seen very little since their mother's death in 1778. Dorothy became his closest companion and confidante, and she remained so even after his marriage to Mary Hutchinson in 1802. The third event was his meeting with Coleridge. Coleridge's friendship and his admiration for Wordsworth's poetry, which Coleridge expressed not only to Wordsworth but to everyone else he spoke or wrote to, fed Wordsworth's vanity and helped to bring forth his best poetry. Read's contention is that in this period of about ten years Wordsworth wrote his greatest poetry with the inspiring influence of Dorothy as companion and collaborator and Coleridge as admirer and fellow poet. After 1802, Wordsworth wrote with more difficulty, perhaps also with more anxious despair combined with a narrow morality, exhibited, for example, in 'Ode to Duty' in 1805. Finally, establishing a conventional idealized sense of self, he became more and more conservative, defensively self-absorbed and reclusive. For Read he became a lesser poet with only occasional flashes of his old passionate and brilliant poetry. He wrote less and less and eventually not at all. This is, in summary, Read's position.

The other aspects of Read's practical criticism in this book are more difficult to summarize. The two main versions of *The Prelude* are a constant in the book both as great poetry and as indirect source material for biographical information, but Read examines many other poems, both good and bad, in great detail. This criticism is also well integrated into his larger view of Wordsworth as a poet, and the complex detailing of his position *vis-à-vis* the view held of him by other critics is supremely worked out. His argument can be summarized as follows. Wordsworth as a poet of nature is not a sentimental poet who idealizes nature both as beauty and as a moral agent for the prevailing social values; he does not identify himself with nature nor nature with himself. Wordsworth was able to develop a view in both poetry and prose of nature and himself as separate but related entities, parts of a larger wholeness.[10]

Read also demonstrates a Wordsworthian theory which is not only essential to Wordsworth but also to himself throughout his life. He finds in *The Prelude* and other poems a three-staged conception of the development of the poet: the stage of early sensation in which everything is experienced for the first time, the age of childhood; then the age of youth which is the age of simple ideas; and finally, the age of complex ideas, the age of maturity.[11] Read argues that Wordsworth's poetry involves feeling, synthesis, and reflection. He believes that the 'distinguishing mark of the poet, as opposed to the philosopher', is that he strives 'to express [his] attitude immediately, intensively... In the process of poetic composition, words spring into consciousness as isolated objective things of a definite emotional equivalence.'[12]

I have been bringing out only some of the highlights of the book, and its well-integrated development of complex ideas and revelations suffer in the process. The whole book is its own test and needs to be read carefully in full. In a radio broadcast in 1944[13] Read summarizes his own position, but I choose to quote the concluding paragraph of the book to indicate Read's position on Wordsworth because it is also a version of his own critical values throughout his criticism, often expressed in different terminology but always with the same root beliefs. He has just quoted lines 269–86 from Book 12 of the 1850 version of *The Prelude*:

> In these lines we have not only the poetic faith of Wordsworth, but also an exact statement of the essential doctrine of poetry. That doctrine affirms the primacy of feeling... Wordsworth qualifies the *kind* of feeling. Diversity of strength attends the poet *if once he has been strong*. The poet must give, or else never can receive. Power resides in a hiding-place, which we can penetrate only at rare intervals; perhaps not at all as we grow old. Armed with this power of penetration, which he has in exceptional degree, the poet opens up these reservoirs of feeling, and with this reawakened power, gives substance and life to his thought. This is the doctrine which Wordsworth inculcates, not only here, and not only in his poems generally, but explicitly in the theory of poetry which he developed in his prose essays. His own genuine poetry is the most evident sanction which his theory ever received. But I think that the main tradition of English poetry illustrates it equally well. In Chaucer and in Spenser, in Shakespeare and in Milton, wherever we are overwhelmed by the apocalyptic presence of beauty, we know that the mystery proceeds from a depth which is the intense emotional experience of a human being, and that the beauty of the word and of thought is only there in virtue of this fund of personal feeling.[14]

The reference to prose works needs some comment, for in the 1800 and 1802 prefaces to the *Lyrical Ballads* Read finds an explanation of the composition of poetry which is not only essential to Wordsworth's poetry; it is also a concept which Read held and used in its various forms manifested through his uses of psychoanalysis and other theories for the rest of his life. He also believes that it is generally misunderstood, so he intends to make it clear in its four stages. Wordsworth wrote, says Read, that

> Poetry *takes its origin* from emotion recollected in tranquillity... next 'the emotion is contemplated till by a species of reaction the tranquillity gradually disappears, and an emotion, kindred to that which was before the subject of contemplation, is gradually produced, and does itself actually exist in the mind. In this mood successful composition generally begins, and in a mood similar to this it is carried on.' The process, therefore, has four stages: recollection, contemplation, recrudescence, and composition.[15]

Wordsworth illustrates for me both Read's strengths as a literary critic and his weaknesses. Unless one begins with prejudices so firmly fixed against his methods and conclusions, Read is a compelling and convincing writer. He argues in detail with abundant textual analysis, and he is clear in his judgements and conclusions. He makes a very complex argument forcefully and clearly, and he is demonstrating new and significant insights into the poetry of Wordsworth with directions for finding the same importance in other poetry. He is also taken in, I think, by matters which soar above concrete human experience. His search for 'wholeness', for the poet as bearer of a culture, or a key to culture, beyond the broken and diseased society of humans in the present – for poets as unacknowledged leaders towards a better future for humanity – fails him, and the inevitable disappointment for Read is registered in *The Cult of Sincerity* essays.

Poets and critics of poetry often wish for poetry to rise above the concrete experience of humans, both social and psychological, which novels present so well: D. H. Lawrence's novels are a good example. The wish is for poetry to present us with some ultimate and whole truth, as Read suggests so often, especially in his most ardent Jungian days.[16] I don't mean by this that poetry doesn't concern itself with concrete human experience, social and psychological, for it often does that, as I will show later in a consideration of Coleridge's 'Dejection: An Ode'. And like great novels, great poetry often produces new and significant insights into human experience. I mean that critics and poets *wish* for a higher truth, an emotional release from frustration and misery which voices itself in, as Read says, 'beauty'.

It may seem a contradiction to say that in spite of the importance of Read's book I'm not convinced that Wordsworth is the great poet Read believes him to be, but it isn't. Instead, I think it is a further indication of the strength of Read's book, a strength which is too much for the conventional readers of the poetry of Wordsworth because it undercuts the conventional view so effectively that it isn't possible to go on reading him in the old comfortable way. But Wordsworth himself insists too much in his poetry on the salvation to be found for his troubled psyche in various external sources, mainly in nature.

Reaching the edge of despair, Wordsworth tries to throw it off as a momentary sensation of unhappiness, putting all his lyrical efforts into proving to himself and to his readers or listeners that despair is a weakness of character to be unlearned in the contemplation of 'nature' or natural man. It is an act of turning a blind eye to misery and using such lines as 'The still sad music of humanity', 'The stings of viperous remorse' or, as in 'Intimations of Immortality from Recollections of Early Child-hood', 'But yet I know, where'er I go, / That there hath past away a glory from the earth' and 'Whither is fled the visionary gleam? / Where is it now, the glory and the dream?' merely as springboards for pursuing some answer which evades the question by dismissing the feeling. Herbert Read sees this as a positive step toward the philosophy of beauty which makes Wordsworth so important for him and leads him to value 'Intimations of Immortality' above Coleridge's 'Dejection: An Ode', but it still seems an unenlightening escape to me.

It makes a difference to know that during the time of the composition of the first four stanzas of his poem, Wordsworth was arranging to marry Mary Hutchinson after his planned trip (accompanied by Dorothy) to meet with Annette and his daughter Caroline, now about nine years old, at Calais in order to explain his plans to them, plans which meant that any possible family relationship for the three of them had now become impossible. It is also important to know that Coleridge wrote his own 'Dejection: An Ode' in response to these four stanzas. However, there are no hints of this anywhere in the poem itself, hints which would make it possible for Wordsworth to produce some powerful insight into this dilemma. Instead, the poem becomes more a matter of passive self-encouragement. The power of despair and guilt which, as Read demonstrates, must be behind the poetry and which is so painful that it generates the lyrical escape through the insistence that nature, by means of its natural presence, helps the poet to cure himself of his unexplored despair. In this larger sense the failure or refusal to face the despair is revealing in its own way; it requires a different kind of attention than the remaining seven stanzas of the poem which were composed a couple of years after the marriage, a recognition of the poet clutching for consolation and not quite managing it:

> We will grieve not, rather find
> Strength in what remains behind;
> In the primal sympathy
> Which having been must ever be;
> In the soothing thoughts that spring
> Out of human suffering;
> In the faith that looks through death,
> In years that bring the philosophic mind.

51

Wordsworth doesn't quite manage this escape because this is not the last stanza of the poem; the eleventh and last stanza demonstrates that the philosophic mind can't rise above or get outside the human unhappiness. It ends: 'To me the meanest flower that blows can give / Thoughts that do often lie too deep for tears'. This last stanza does, however, save the poem from sentimentality.

As I have suggested, the failure to escape is nearly as revealing in its own way as a full disclosure of the dilemma would have been, and Read has supplied this awareness even though he does so only indirectly. No critic before him had been able to do so for Wordsworth. Read broke new ground in his criticism by insisting that it is essential to understand the emotional condition of the artist in order to reach a full understanding of his work.

The charge that Read identifies Wordsworth with himself and, therefore, writes more about himself than Wordsworth is, as I see it, a false charge designed to deny the deep insights which Read provides.[17] He did feel an affinity for Wordsworth as with a kindred spirit, and it makes Read sensitive to the human dilemma of the poet, thereby allowing him to recognize and to appreciate the importance of the poetry as products of the creative imagination. Identification would mean that the critic could consciously understand no more than the poet, whereas affinity or empathy makes it possible to understand more fully the psychological condition leading to the poetry itself as an expression of the whole person, the artist. This latter is Read's position.

In his literary criticism of individual writers Read always followed this procedure of taking into account the emotional and social conditions of the writer as a means to an understanding and appreciation of the work, and it was clearly against the grain of the developing New Criticism of his day where interpretation became the activity of criticism, leading to moral messages and attitudes, and anything from outside the poem was rejected. Read was conscious of treading a separate path in criticism and took up the argument in favour of his method. Such an approach led him naturally to his interest in psychoanalysis:

> Even before I read Freud, I tended to probe beneath the surface of the work of art, my conviction being that the work of art is either an objective phenomenon which we accept integrally and sensuously and therefore without intellectual understanding; or that alternatively it demands for its understanding, not merely a measured view of its external aspects, but also a complete analysis of the circumstances in which it came into existence. This latter type of criticism I have called genetic, and it may, if so desired, be separated from aesthetic criticism. But an adequate criticism must include both methods.[18]

Read's interest in the various claimants to psychoanalysis, including Freud, was lifelong, but it is clear that he never saw it as a means to understanding himself more fully and clearly. James King quotes a letter of 1937 which provides us with an important reason why Read chose not to undergo analysis himself as well as an important clue to his character. He writes that he could have profited from psychoanalysis 'about 1925' but he suggests that it is, in 1937, too late. However, he confesses, 'it is due to a certain caution – to a feeling that I must not wade too deep into these waters or I shall drown'.[19]

At first glance this seems a very strange anxiety for someone who values psychoanalysis so highly; it suggests that his own idea of his character is so fragile in its fixity that he can imagine some new and conscious knowledge of himself as a destructive force. Read's own life experience and his own view of it as he expressed it, especially in his autobiographical works, is crucial here. The death of his father in 1903, just two months after Read's ninth birthday, was traumatic. It transformed him, as he described it, into an orphan, and it transplanted him (as well as his brother, William) from the family farm to a strict and 'monastic' school for poor boys in a city (Halifax) while his mother and the youngest brother, Charles, lived apart from them. The mother found work and struggled to keep the family together.

Read blocked off that early childhood, recreated it as a mythical ideal, and it is possible to argue that it touched every idea he had: the notion of the innocence of childhood became a cornerstone of his discussion of Wordsworth as well as his theories of poetic composition and the origins of poetic 'inspiration'. It helped to create his evaluative criteria for poetry as celebration of the beauty of life, and his ideas about regionalism. It allowed him to believe that his passion for reading in boyhood, for example, was an inborn passion rather than a compensation for loneliness, frustration, jealousy, competition, indirect or direct response to his own sexual instincts, or any of the other possibilities he might have thought of. Even much later in life when he read and quoted E. G. Schachtel's 'On Memory and Childhood Amnesia', he distorted or ignored Schachtel's arguments about the myth of the happy childhood and childhood sexuality, both to avoid recognition about his own childhood and to support his own theory about the unconscious source of artistic inspiration. I believe that these two purposes are closely enough related to be interdependent.[20]

No real-life childhood can be like the one Read created for himself. Even the language in which it is described is idealistic, mythical, and ritualistic. Read's brother, William, apparently remembered a more ordinary and down-to-earth life. He told James King that Herbert never learned to milk a cow, and the younger brothers teased him unmercifully about it.[21] Clearly, the loss of his father at a crucial age is a contributing factor to Read's developing character, but he was not, in fact, an orphan nor entirely alone even though his brothers have only minor roles to play in his autobiographical writings. Neither was death a new event in his immediate family. His young sister died a bit less than a year before his father, just before her second birthday, but it was his father's death which changed his material circumstances and his expectations in very dramatic ways. Read's response to the trauma is significant for an understanding of him as a man. Not only did he idealize his early

53

childhood, he also saw himself fighting his adolescent battles for independence alone against school authorities and later against his mother. He stubbornly sticks to his view that his passion for reading and later for writing were innate passions even while acknowledging that writing gained him admiration and prizes in school. His fiercely independent, reserved self-reliance, so obvious all his life, he often attributed to his Yorkshire heritage rather that seeing it as a psychological defence growing out of his personal traumas.

The death of his mother just before his enlistment in the army, his experiences in the First World War trenches, and the death of his youngest brother in battle just before the end of the war all contributed to his strong sense of self-reliance and his inability (or unwillingness) to belong to groups where his actions, decisions, and thoughts might be compromised. His contemporaries and friends were intellectual enemies or at least competitors from whom he had to separate himself intellectually while retaining their friendship. He seldom compromised and never ungrudgingly.

This explains, at least in part, the independent and original thinker Read was. It also explains why he had no confrères. His ideas developed from his character (not always consciously) and his eclecticism in his reading was nearly always a search to find added support for his own developing ideas. For example, in his preface to the 1965 edition of *Icon and Idea*, he writes: 'In the interval [between the 1953 lectures and this edition of the book] I have had ample opportunity to test this theory against the criticism it received and to seek further support for it in the works of other writers'.[22]

Psychoanalysis was part of that support, and, as he says, he chose material from many sources to suit his needs. But Jung was always his most congenial source even though he sometimes quietly went against him. Jung's ideas more comfortably suited Read's ideals than the more concrete, reality-focused, ideas of Freud did, and Read often distorted Freud's ideas not only to suit his own but also to coincide with or at least reflect Jung's.

Herbert Read was one of the pioneers in his various ways of relating psycho-analysis to literature and the other arts, though he was by no means the first. Psychoanalysis was in the air: not in Eliot's air or Pound's or Dobrée's or Aldington's or Lewis's air, but that must have made it all the more attractive to Read's desire for independence. Read's use of psychoanalysis was unique and different from the many, mainly in the USA, who came to use psychoanalysis, often superficially, as interpretive tools for literature.

Five years before the Wordsworth book, in January 1925, Read had published an essay on 'Psycho-analysis and the Critic'. This essay was reprinted in *Reason and Romanticism* in 1926 where it was called 'Psycho-analysis and Criticism', and for his *Collected Essays in Literary Criticism* in 1938 the essay was revised, expanded and published as 'The Nature of Criticism'.[23] In this essay Read announces his intention to describe a 'science' of literary criticism in order to raise it 'above the vague level of emotional appreciation' and to supply 'a corrective to the narrowness of criticism' of his day. 'The critic, in approaching psychology, will not be altogether disinterested: he will merely raid it in the interest of what he conceives to be another science, literary criticism.' Read sees himself 'as a mere expropriator... I take the liberty to lift my material from whichever quarter suits me best'.[24] These are big ambitions which never work out and which are probably inappropriate since literary criticism can never be a science, as D. H. Lawrence says, because 'it is much too personal' and because the 'touchstone is emotion, not reason'.[25]

The truth is that Read's expropriation is not so much extrapolation as it is a rewriting in order to make the various psychoanalysts' work fit his own ideas, many of which he held before he discovered them in the psychoanalysts' work. David Cohen notes 'Read's eclectic attitude towards psychoanalysis, and his ability to select and adapt those theories which accord with his own system'.[26] Eclecticism and heterodoxy it may also be but, most importantly, it is distortion which has a personal purpose whether Read is always consciously aware of it or not.

I believe that Read needed something like psychoanalysis in order to separate himself off from what he rightly saw as a narrow brand of literary criticism practised by his contemporaries, particularly T. S. Eliot whose stance as an arbiter of taste was merely a thinly disguised Christianity which usually ended by discovering that literature was in support of a hierarchical system of society either directly or indirectly, a position expressed clearly in *After Strange Gods: A Primer of Modern Heresy* (1934), and I. A. Richards whose *Practical Criticism* (1929) worked in much the same way. As Read says, psychoanalysis gave him scientific support for the views he held.

His psychoanalysis was of his own making. When he tried to remain faithful to some of Jung's notions of archetype or primordial images and racial memory, he ran into great difficulty. The desire for certainty as well as an ideal of an autonomous yet mystical source in a collective unconscious makes Read forget or refuse to recognize that it is *never* true that everyone understands works of art in the same way, that it is *never* true that everyone judges a particular work of art as good or great – there is always disagreement – and that *never* is it true that works of art appeal to everyone even in a particular society. Not even 'education through art' will make poets, painters, sculptors, and designers the bearers of culture to everyone.[27] Read's anarchism, his suspicion of monolithic systems and leaders, makes him draw back in several ways. One way is to say that the individual artist finds his own form for the wellings-up of material from the unconscious, even when he is ready to insist that the unconscious is universally and eternally the same. Even his attempt to maintain his nicely created triumvirate of the Id, the Ego and the Superego sometimes needed to be revised.

Many of these manœuvres are merely digressive traps, and I think that Read's position, expressed in many ways throughout his life, is as follows. The inspiration of the artist wells up from the unconscious. The ego, as Read defines it for himself, both unconsciously and consciously gives these deep intuitions form which is pleasing to an audience and which expresses not the ideals or spiritual aspirations of an existing society but the ideals and aspirations of a higher, more humane and egalitarian society, an ideal society for which this audience longs. The great artists, then, are the bearers of an idea of a higher culture, and they lead us indirectly to desire that higher culture. It can only be indirect because the greatest artists never reach the reader or viewer or user through the conscious mind but through the senses.

I recognize that in this summary I may be reworking Read's position in order to arrive at one which I can accept as worth considering even when I sometimes disagree with what he writes about literature in general and with his comments on individual writers. But I have tried to be objective enough to understand his position, and I believe that I have done so; therefore, if the summary is in error, it is more likely to be the consequence of what I see as Read's inexplicitness than of my own prejudice. I share Read's view that psychoanalysis can make us more sensitive to the well-springs of life in the psyche and in the society, and I share his idea that it is important to focus on the artist's life, his emotional and social condition, as a means of understanding the work's full expression. I also agree with the focus on the artist's tendency to be as open in experiencing life as a child is; that is, the artist feels experience intensely as if for the first time and communicates the full impact of it in effective form which grows out of the particular needs of the work, this form being, therefore, organic. But I disagree sometimes with Read's version of this idea, as I noted earlier, in 'The Problem of Pornography', 'The Cult of Sincerity', and what he believes he has found in Schachtel's 'On Memory and Childhood Amnesia'.[28]

It also seems to me to be a serious flaw in his reading of Wordsworth's 'Intimations of Immortality from Recollections of Early Childhood' when he fails to notice that Wordsworth's epigraph which is part of a stanza from his earlier 'My Heart Leaps Up' is a contradiction of one poem or the other. They take opposite stands. The fifth stanza of 'Intimations of Immortality' describing the child coming into the world trailing clouds of glory means that he comes from somewhere else before birth and is not, therefore, illustrative of the view which Read assumes it to be, which he summarizes in 'The Cult of Sincerity': 'The Youth still is "Nature's Priest"…'.[29] It is also a serious flaw, though this one he shares with others, that Read fails to notice in the parts of the poem written after Wordsworth's marriage and after Coleridge's 'Dejection: An Ode', where Wordsworth is struggling for a positive and happy view of his own life by appealing to nature around him, that he is clearly trying too hard and insisting too much to be believed; the effect of the poem is despairing in spite of the author.

Furthermore, in those essays where Read deliberately sets about putting his psychoanalytic criticism to work, such as in his long 'In Defence of Shelley' and in his treatment of Coleridge's 'Dejection: An Ode', I find his results mixed. For the most part I think he succeeds with Shelley even though the psychoanalysis contributes little, and in the two treatments of Coleridge's poem I find myself objecting that, in the very act of explaining, Read is misreading and flattening out the moving quality of the work by making it overbearingly cerebral.[30]

Just as he did with Wordsworth, Read believes that it is necessary to understand Shelley the man in order to appreciate his poetry fully. 'The particular quality of Shelley's poetry [is] directly related to the nature of his personality... Understanding the personality, we may more easily, more openly, appreciate the poetry.'[31] The use of Trigant Burrow was probably new and exciting for Read at the time, but looking back from the present, it seems like excess baggage. Read could have done for Shelley what he did for Wordsworth without resorting to his scientific cover. However, the discussion of Shelley's poetry is, I think, very good as far as it goes. Read's disputes with Coleridge, Arnold, Eliot, Dowden, and Richards are effectively used to establish his own analysis of and praise for particular works. Had he carried the work through to book length, I think he would have produced the same sort of original and significant insights into Shelley's work as he did for Wordsworth's. He would, I'm sure, have taken the time to convince, through textual analysis, his own and Shelley's detractors that *Prometheus Unbound* is indeed

> an epic, the greatest expression ever given to humanity's desire for intellectual light and spiritual liberty. The hundred years since it was written is but a very short time in the history of that long effort, and the day may yet come when this poem will take its commanding place in a literature of freedom of which we have yet no conception.[32]

One of the gems of the essay for me is the drubbing he gives T. S. Eliot's dismissal of Shelley, for Eliot represents the sort of criticism which was posing as authority in Read's day. It is probably one of the earliest Eliot ever received; it is certainly the most thorough and effective. Here is its high point: Read insists that

> Shelley's ideas were no more shabby and incoherent than those of Plato who was their chief inspiration; and that in so far as they were unplatonic, they showed a close parallel to the ideas of Lucretius, whom Mr. Eliot accepts. Retracing the steps of his inference, we must come to the conclusion that Mr. Eliot's objection to Shelley's poetry is irrelevant prejudice (for 'a simple blind spot' would not excite abhorrence); and such, I would suggest, is the kind of poetic approach of all who believe, with Mr. Eliot, that 'literary criticism should be completed by criticism from a definite ethical and theological standpoint.' I do not deny that such criticism may have its interest; but the only kind of criticism which is basic, and therefore complementary not only to literary but also to ethical, theological and every other kind of ideological criticism, is ontogenetic criticism, by which I mean criticism which traces the origins of the work of art in the psychology of the individual and in the economic structure of society.[33]

It is fair to argue that Read's study of psychoanalysis gradually made him more sensitive to the fullness of human experience, at least to its possibilities, and that this led him to greater insight than he otherwise would have found. And we could do this by comparing his earlier work, collected in *The Sense of Glory*, with later work, but this would be too neat. While I see those nine essays and the four he added to them later as more symptomatic of Read's character (idealism, regionalism, and the wish to beat the conventional critics on their own ground) than they are momentous as significantly insightful critical essays, Read did republish them more than once and thought highly of them. [34]

I can't read the Swift essay for profit since I've already read Warren Tallman's 'Swift's Fool: A Comment upon Satire in *Gulliver's Travels*' and Norman O. Brown's discussion in *Life Against Death*. [35] I can't take seriously an essay on Sterne which sets out to dismiss his 'licentiousness' with Coleridge's condemnation and analysis of it because what they are calling, in effect, dirty jokes are the indicators and often the content of the anxieties about sexuality, injury, and death which produce the great insights of the novel. To dismiss all this in favour of Locke and all the great thinkers of the world can only lead (as it does in this essay) to the dismissal of Mrs Shandy's most serious question about the winding of the clock. [36] Sterne tells us that Tristram's father was 'one of the most regular men in everything he did'. One of those things was 'on the first *Sunday night* of every month' he wound the clock and 'gradually brought some other family concernments to the same period... to get them all out of the way at one time, and be no more plagued and pester'd with them the rest of the month'. It so fell out at length, Tristram tells us, his 'poor mother could never hear the said clock wound up, – but the thoughts of some other things unavoidably popp'd into her head, – & *vice versa*'. [37] It is the *vice versa* which makes all the difference, and since the clock is wound only once a month, there must be thousands of descendants of Mrs Shandy who would say, if they had the fine rhetoric of a Sterne character, 'Damn Mr Locke, just wind the clock and get into bed'.

I can't take Read's idealized view of Cervantes's character, Don Quixote, seriously after reading *Don Quixote and the Dulcineated World* by Arthur Efron and *The Panzaic Principle* by Wayne Burns; and Burns's essay on 'The Critical Relevance of Freudianism' puts Read's essay on the Brontës in the background for me. Read's extended praise of form, of structure, in Henry James is overshadowed by Philip Rahv's 'Fiction and the Criticism of Fiction'. [38]

I don't believe that my lack of interest in the 'Particular Studies' section of the *Collected Essays in Literary Criticism* is a flaw in my critical judgement, but the admission that neither my patience nor my interest are enough to carry me through serious and attentive reading of most of the essays in *The True Voice of Feeling* is a limitation of my critical interests. I feel competent to discuss only the revised version of 'In Defence of Shelley' and 'The Notion of Organic Form: Coleridge'. Read writes 'as a poet, I am aware that my criticism suffers from the suspicion of being written in self-defence'.[39] My own self-defence is that I am not a poet; I am not interested in how poems are or should be made.

Read's preoccupation with his version of psychoanalysis and with his own theories about inspiration and form are debilitating to his criticism of some individual works. As I have argued for the Shelley essay, I think his use of psychoanalysis, anybody's, is more a digression than an aid. I believe he could have found the sources of Shelley's peculiar genius in the same way he found Wordsworth's. However, it is possible that Trigant Burrow honed Read's sensibilities to Shelley and produced sensitivity to the poems, for the sensitivity is clearly there. In such a case, psychoanalysis would not be a digression. But in the two essays in which he writes about Coleridge's 'Dejection: An Ode' where, in each essay, he is using the poem to prove a theoretical point, Read is, in my view, so concerned with his theory that he is insensitive to the poem. In other words, he is not a sensitive reader engaged with the expressed feeling of the poem; rather, he is a distant observer with the tenets of his theory taking precedence over sensual participation and understanding. This condition occurs most clearly in his lecture for the Eranos Tagung where Jung's spirit and presence seemed to overwhelm Read.

This lecture, delivered in 1959, was later published as 'The Creative Experience', chapter eight of *The Forms of Things Unknown*. In order to describe 'authentic experiences of poetic creation', Read takes as an example for analysis Coleridge's 'Dejection: An Ode'.[40]

If we read and engage the poem rather than the critics – Read included – I don't see how we can miss the sense of deep, complete, inescapable despair brought on by external obstacles to the consummation of love, returned love, with a woman, addressed only as 'O Lady!' In the first, unpublished version of the poem (as Read notes) the lady is named. She is Sara Hutchinson, and Coleridge was hopelessly in love with her. She was also the sister of Mary Hutchinson, Wordsworth's future wife. Coleridge was already married, though unhappily, and a father, and he could not, therefore, fulfil his love for Sara. It is extremely likely that Coleridge also had heard or read the first four stanzas of Wordsworth's 'Intimations of Immortality from Recollections of Early Childhood'. Responding sympathetically to Wordsworth's dilemma (which was complicated by his French lover and their child), Coleridge wrote of his own sorrow. By the time that Wordsworth wrote the remaining seven stanzas of his poem, I believe he was not only trying to assure himself that he was happy and unchanged in that happiness but that assurance required also an answer to Coleridge.[41]

Read is so concerned with his own and Coleridge's idea in *Biographia Literaria* ('The best poetry is *objective*, as we say – it is *aloof*') that his own reading is completely devoid of sensitive understanding. The poem is forced to fit the concept of 'depersonalization' and becomes in Read's mind an argument for a celebration of creative poetic utterance: 'The great passages of the poem', Read asserts, are to be seen as a 'sudden flash of transcendental feeling'.[42] This seems to me to be a complete misrepresentation of the poem. Unremitting misery, that is the poem's content, but Herbert Read is determined by his theories. Perhaps he would dismiss my view as another case of interest in the 'theme', the 'process', rather than in the product, the language, the imagery, the symbol, and all those devices which go to make up the poet's art, as he dismissed the focus of psychoanalysis on 'process'.[43] But his own argument, then, makes the emotional content of the poem meaningless or at least secondary to the poetic devices, which in turn makes the devices devoid of emotional content and, therefore, merely mechanical construction, a version of what Read objects to in the classical view.

The poem begins in despondency, the poet noting the 'coming-on of rain and squally blast' and hoping that, as it had in the past, the blast 'might startle this dull pain, and make it move and live'. In stanza two he describes his condition:

> A grief without a pang, void, dark, and drear,
> A stifled, drowsy, unimpassioned grief,
> Which finds no natural outlet, no relief,
> In word, or sigh, or tear –

Gazing all evening 'on the western sky… with how blank an eye!', the clouds, the stars, and the moon, he ends the stanza with:

> I see them all so excellently fair,
> I see, *not feel*, how beautiful they are! [my italics]

All this parallels Wordsworth's four stanzas of 'Intimations of Immortality' written in early 1802. But Wordsworth cannot express his despair so openly, deeply, and painfully as Coleridge does. A case can be made that Coleridge's next three stanzas are an argument against Wordsworth's position. Coleridge's own argument is that outward nature is only important in what the poet makes of it:

> I may not hope from outward forms to win
> The passion and the life, whose fountains are within.

Wordsworth's stanzas three and four are an unsuccessful attempt to make the joy he sees in nature, people, and animals soak into himself so that he may feel it also. Coleridge, on the other hands, insists:

> And in our life alone does Nature live:
> Ours is her wedding garment, ours her shroud!

His answer is that joy can only come from inside, from love and from hope in life, life flowering, issuing forth:

> Which wedding Nature to us gives in dower

60

> A new Earth and new Heaven
> Undreamt of by the sensual and the proud –
> Joy is the sweet voice, Joy the luminous cloud –
>   We in ourselves rejoice!
> And thence flows all that charms or ear or sight,
>   All melodies the echoes of that voice,
> All colours a suffusion from that light.

In his youth, stanza six tells us, distress meant nothing to him because he had hope for the future. He could be open, honest, spontaneous. But now he has no hope and can only indirectly, circumspectly reveal his feelings.

> But now afflictions bow me down to earth:
> Nor care I that they rob me of my mirth;
>   But oh! each visitation
> Suspends what nature gave me at my birth,
>   My shaping spirit of Imagination.
> For not to think of what I needs must feel,
>   But to be still and patient, all I can;
> And haply by abstruse research to steal
>   From my own nature all the natural man –
>   This was my sole resource, my only plan:
> Till that which suits a part infects the whole,
> And now is almost grown the habit of my soul.

Stanza seven carries the horror further and number eight presents the only consolation, the hope that 'Dear Lady' will not suffer such despair.

More serious, and perhaps more revealing, than his misreading of the meaning in the poem is Read's response, which is an escape from the deep despair of the poem.

> Coleridge proceeds to identify that sweet and potent voice, this beautiful and beauty-making power, with joy, with the celebration and utterance of a feeling of spiritual identity with the creative forces of nature.
>
> The poem, we see, proceeds quite directly from a conflict in Coleridge's mind, a moral and emotional embarrassment caused by his passion for a woman not his wife. This personal conflict is seen by Coleridge as parallel to a conflict between metaphysical speculation and poetic expression. The emotional conflict creates a tension which is relieved by the act of poetic utterance... There supervenes in this emotional conflict an intellectual conflict, a fear that he... may be deprived of the capacity for poetic utterance by an indulgence in 'abstruse research', spontaneity may be endangered by reflection.[44]

Something more than simple misreading is needed to explain this response; it must

61

indicate a deeper form of self-protection than even a case of being blinded by theory explains, but I don't know what it is. It is clear in this essay that Read needs a 'reconciliation' device of some sort in the poem to fit his wish as well as his theory. The reconciliation of the conflict, as Read see it, between 'social morality' and Coleridge's 'defiant love of Sara' is 'the relief of poetic utterance, of a projection of the conflict into the objective form of poetry. The relief is all the greater the more objective that projection can be made. We also call the process sublimation.'[45]

A bit later Read writes that Coleridge defined poetry in the line from the poem, 'This light, this glory, this fair luminous mist' and concludes for himself, 'we cannot find more precise words to describe the experience of poetry'.[46] Coleridge is making indirect reference here to the source of poetry rather than to poetry itself, but, more importantly, his emphasis is on the pain of its absence in himself at this time, probably never to return because he can't resolve his dilemma. Read's emphasis is on the power of poetry to rise out of despair through its own utterance. 'The hidden self, in tragic renunciation, submits to Fate, or Truth, or God – by whatever name we designate the collective wisdom of the race or group.'[47] It is the renunciation of joy, of love, of full life, which Coleridge so clearly protests against in the poem, as all great romantics do. It must be left to someone else to explain why Read must run away from this, his own greatest insight about the Romantics expressed both directly and indirectly in *Wordsworth*, 'In Defence of Shelley', and in 'Surrealism and the Romantic Principle'.

The idea that art is protest is not a new one. It has been around for a very long time. An argument could be made that it is inherent in Plato and even in a meliorist version in the notion of catharsis derived from Socrates. In our time Alex Comfort presents it at length in *Art and Social Responsibility* (which he dedicates to Herbert Read) where he also connects romanticism with anarchism. Herbert Marcuse connects it with Freud in *Eros and Civilization*, and it is often, in these two works and others, expressed as the main social function of art.[48] My own argument is that the invitation of great novels for the reader to participate vicariously in the experience of the characters leads us to new and significant insights into human experience which may or may not become ideas; more importantly, however, they change our outlook on life. In other words, works of great literature, particularly novels, teach us how not to live more often than the reverse, by providing us with new awareness of the human dilemma. That awareness is, as Comfort argues, a form of 'inchoate protest' which may, in turn, lead us to know how to live our lives more fully.[49] Such is the intention of great literature, both its formal and emotional intention, whether the artist consciously knows it or not. Freud provides a clue to this process in one of the essays used by Herbert Read: 'The psychological novel in general no doubt owes its special nature to the inclination of the modern writer to split up his ego, by self-observation, into many part-egos, and, in consequence, to personify the conflicting currents in his own mental life in several heroes'.[50]

Herbert Read, however, looks to create a more uplifting view of art and, in doing so, he must raise it above the down-to-earth sexuality (in its broadest sense) and ordinary sensual reality which concerns Sigmund Freud and which would destroy Read's idealism if taken fully into account. It goes against Read's developing idea that art is

> the *exercise* of an expanding consciousness… An increasing apprehension of the nature of reality, or of being, is about as near as we can get to a definition of its purpose… Without the creative arts there would have been no advance in myth or ritual, in language or meaning, in morality or metaphysics.[51]

Near the end of 'The Nature of Criticism', Read asks himself if psychoanalysis modifies 'in any way our conception of the critic's function'. His answer is that it doesn't amount to anything 'more precise than a general admonition to tolerance'.[52] But there are clues here in the essay which indicate the importance of psychoanalysis for Read as literary critic. He discusses Ernest Jones's psychoanalytic criticism of *Hamlet* and quotes Jones's assertion that 'in writing *Hamlet* Shakespeare was giving expression to a conflict passing through his own mind'. Read believes that this work by Jones shows 'the possibilities of this new approach to the problems of literature'.[53] Of course, it is a position which Read himself was to take both in practical criticism and in theory: 'criticism must concern itself, not only with the work of art itself, but also with the process of writing, and with the writer's state of mind when inspired…'[54]

Early in 'The Nature of Criticism', in a footnote, Read writes that psychology can 'quicken our general sensibility'.[55] This is important because so much of psychoanalytic criticism which developed over the years engaged in the act of smothering the work itself under psychoanalytic terms without producing insight into anything, in much the same way Read notes in the 'unprofitable task' of translating 'into crude terms of sexual phantasy a poem like William Blake's "I saw a Chapel all of Gold"'.[56]

Over thirty years after 'Psycho-analysis and the Critic', in an important essay now also forgotten, Wayne Burns took up these issues in more detail.[57] Burns is also critical of those critics who 'deny the uniqueness of literary expression' by 'reducing good literature to poor Freudianism… the Freudian system, in and of itself, can provide little more than points of critical departure, corresponding to the points of creative departure'. Burns believes 'the prime critical function of psychoanalysis… is to raise critical sensitivity to the highest imaginative power'. Freud 'confers' on both the critic and the creative writer 'new powers of vision; and just as the serious modern writer uses these powers to probe further into the mystery of human experience, so the serious critic, whose first business it is to follow the writer as artist wherever he leads, uses the stimulation afforded by Freud to realize (i.e., recreate) what the artist has created'.[58] That the heightening of sensitivity which psychoanalysis can provide is the only aid it can give a critic is a position with which Read agrees. It is also true that many readers already read literature with an intuitive and naturally heightened sensitivity. They ignore or abandon what Read calls 'apparatus' in 'Surrealism and the Romantic Principle' and approach 'the work of genius with... naked eye[s]'.[59] Read is, himself, one of these readers some of the time.

'Surrealism and the Romantic Principle' was the first work I read by Herbert Read many years ago, and I still think it is among his very best. In strictly literary essays, Read seems to feel constrained to be polite and tolerant, often overly cautious, by his recognition of the weight of traditional literature of the past and by the presence of his friends who are his opposition in the field. In 'Surrealism and the Romantic Principle' he writes with the feeling that he is the first to arrive on this scene, unique in his stance, and free to write without restraint. He is more direct, more assertive (even confrontational) in this essay than in any of his other works except those specifically anarchist ones. I think this essay is the most successful merging of Read's anarchism and his views on literature, painting, and sculpture.

In many of his critical essays Read writes of oppositions: romanticism and classicism, organic form and abstract form, personality and character, are three of them, and they all involve some form of natural intuitive growth of ideas opposed to learned thought. In 'The Nature of Criticism' he sets up the conflict between romanticism and classicism in Jung's character-type terms: romanticism is the introverted type; classicism is the extraverted type. Following Jung, Read sees this 'as the natural expression of a biological opposition in human nature'.[60] Usually, in spite of his own predilection for the romantic side, Read tries to give the two opposites equal treatment if not always equal status, but in 'Surrealism and the Romantic Principle', he strides into assertion without equivocation. He takes up the subject again only reluctantly because he thinks 'that Surrealism has settled it... not, as I formerly hoped, by establishing a synthesis which I was prepared to call "reason" or "humanism" – but by liquidating classicism'. They have done this by showing classicism's 'complete irrelevance, its anaesthetic effect, its contradiction of the creative impulse. Classicism, let it be stated without further preface, represents for us now, and has always represented, the forces of oppression. Classicism is the intellectual counterpart of political tyranny.'[61]

A bit later Read continues this frontal attack, this time against the comments of Herbert Grierson:

> A certain type of society is regarded as a 'synthesis', a natural order or balance of forces, a state of equilibrium; and any deviation from that standard is regarded as abnormal, degenerate or revolutionary. Actually such types of society merely represent the dominance of one particular class – the economic dominance and therefore the cultural dominance of that class... the norms of classical art... are the typical patterns of order, proportion, symmetry, equilibrium, harmony and of all static and inorganic qualities... intellectual concepts which control or

repress the vital instincts on which growth and therefore change depend [are] merely an imposed ideal... There is a principle of life, of creation, of liberation, and that is, the romantic spirit; there is a principle of order, of control and of repression, and that is the classical spirit.[62]

Identifying romanticism with the artist and classicism with society, Read concludes: 'whereas the universal truths of classicism may be merely the temporal prejudices of an epoch, the universal truths of romanticism are coeval with the evolving consciousness of mankind'.[63]

Among the deletions which were made from 'Surrealism and the Romantic Principle' for *The Philosophy of Modern Art* in 1952 is a passage of about 550 words in which Read takes up the accusation that he contradicts himself from essay to essay. He dismisses the charge, relating it to unimportant contradictions in his nature about which he 'is not particularly uneasy' for, in the final analysis:

> it will be seen that my main affiliations have always been romantic, in the sense in which I have interpreted romanticism in this essay. I have always had an instinctive preference for those poets and painters who have exceeded the limits of convention, which are the limits of moral experience; and in the history of criticism my interest quickens from the moment that romanticism begins to acquire a rational and scientific basis in psychology and philosophy; the line of development from Vico to Freud.[64]

Read may be practising a bit of poetic licence here, but in the main his best arguments have been those informed by romanticism as he defines it in this essay. The problems occur when he is too much influenced by Jung or when he is trying to stay in touch with the prevailing modes of literary criticism in order to have some influence on them. When he established his own version of surrealism – superrealism – he could speak directly all the time without compromise or equivocation. In that sense he was a pioneer, an original, and though he had little lasting effect on literary critics of his time and less in our time, he did influence others through his combination of anarchism and criticism; that influence was strongest during the 1950s and 1960s.[65] Even though it is now pretty much forgotten, his work on Wordsworth and Shelley, some of his work on psychoanalysis and criticism, and 'Surrealism and the Romantic Principle' are significant contributions whether the rapidly changing fashions of criticism recognize them or not.

Notes

1   David Thistlewood, *Herbert Read: Formlessness and Form: An Introduction to his Aesthetics* (London: Routledge and Kegan Paul, 1984); Herbert Read, *A One-Man Manifesto and Other Writings for Freedom Press*, edited with an Introductory Essay by David Goodway (London: Freedom Press,

1994); Francis Berry, *Herbert Read* (London: Longmans, Green and Co., 1961); Herbert Read, *Selected Writings: Poetry and Criticism*, with a Foreword by Allen Tate (New York: Horizon Press, 1964). All agree that, as Goodway says it, 'to assess the stature of the man each of his individual achievements has to be added together (and the total is greater than the sum of the parts)' (p. 12). However, Goodway believes Read's anarchism is central, Berry and Tate believe the poetry is, and Thistlewood makes art criticism central. In an unpublished book written in the 1940s (British Library Add. MS. 71,198), Louis Adeane, *To the Crystal City*, believes Read is most important as a poet, least important as an art critic, but it 'is as an educationalist that he comes closest to achieving greatness' (pp. 398–400).

2 *Wordsworth* (London: Faber and Faber, 1949). My page references are to this edition, which is a corrected and slightly revised edition, with a new preface and appendix on 'Wordsworth's Philosophy', of *Wordsworth: The Clark Lectures, 1929–30* (London: Jonathan Cape, 1930).

3 Read, *Wordsworth*, p. 19.

4 Ibid., p. 23.

5 James King, *The Last Modern: A Life of Herbert Read* (London: Weidenfeld and Nicolson, 1990), pp. 90–91.

6 Read, *Wordsworth*, p. 31.

7 Ibid., pp. 32–33.

8 Ibid., p. 49.

9 Ibid., pp. 71–72.

10 Ibid., pp. 125–27.

11 Ibid., p. 127.

12 Ibid., p. 168.

13 Published as 'Wordsworth's Remorse' in *A Coat of Many Colours: Occasional Essays* (London: George Routledge and Sons, 1945), pp. 182–90.

14 Read, *Wordsworth*, pp. 173–74.

15 Ibid., p. 112.

16 See also 'The Adamantine Sickle', *The Contrary Experience: Autobiographies* (London: Faber and Faber, 1963), especially pp. 344–45, and throughout *The Cult of Sincerity* (London: Faber and Faber, 1968).

17 King, *The Last Modern*, pp. 90–91.

18 Read, *The Contrary Experience*, p. 279.

19 King, *The Last Modern*, p. 80.

20 On Schachtel see 'The Problem of Pornography', *To Hell With Culture and Other Essays on Art and Society* (London: Routledge and Kegan Paul, 1963), pp. 152–70, and 'The Cult of Sincerity', *The Cult of Sincerity*, pp. 16–22. I suspect that this idealization of his childhood also led to the streak of prudery he shows in his comments on D. H. Lawrence in the first of these essays and in his treatment of Swift, Sterne, and Charlotte Brontë. It also made him more comfortable with Jung's desexualized concept of libido, rather than with Freud's concept, and with Jung's position that sexuality begins at puberty rather than Freud's discovery of sexuality in the infant. See Edward Glover, *Freud or Jung?* (New York: World Publishing Co., 1956, first printed London: Allen and Unwin, 1950), especially chapter 3, 'Mental Energy', for Jung on sexuality, and pp. 177–78, where Glover discusses Read's Jungianism disguised as Freudianism.

21 King, *The Last Modern*, p. 6. Read provides his idealized version of his early life in *The Contrary Experience*, and King provides the more realistic details.

22 Herbert Read, *Icon and Idea: The Function of Art in the Development of Human Consciousness* (New York: Schocken Books, 1965, reprint of 1955 edition), p. 3. Not, it is important to notice, to revise in response to criticism nor to make the argument more forcefully clear through revision

and expansion but to find support in the work of other writers.

23 Herbert Read, 'Psycho-analysis and the Critic', *Criterion*, vol. 3, no. 10 (January 1925), pp. 214–30; Herbert Read, 'Psycho-analysis and Criticism', *Reason and Romanticism: Essays in Literary Criticism* (New York: Russell and Russell, 1963, reprint of the London 1926 edition), pp. 83–106; Herbert Read, 'The Nature of Criticism', *Collected Essays in Literary Criticism* (London: Faber and Faber, 1938), pp. 124–46. In the *Criterion* version Read used Blake's 'The Defiled Sanctuary' for his example of the 'unprofitable task' of translating the poem into 'crude terms of sexual phantasy', but changed to 'I saw a Chapel all of Gold' in the other two. In the *Criterion* version 'extraverted attitude' is mistakenly attributed to the romantic and 'introverted' to the classic artist (p. 228). The error remains in *Reason and Romanticism* (p. 103), even in the 1963 reprint. It is corrected in 'The Nature of Criticism' (p. 144).

24 'The Nature of Criticism', pp. 124, 125 and 126. David Cohen, 'Herbert Read and Psychoanalysis', in Malcolm Gee (ed.), *Art Criticism since 1900* (Manchester and New York: Manchester University Press, 1993), pp. 164–79, chronicles Read's fascination with psychoanalysis; my own comments owe much to that essay even when I diverge from some of Cohen's conclusions. See also Thistlewood, *Herbert Read: Formlessness and Form*, pp. 64–73.

25 D. H. Lawrence, 'John Galsworthy', in *Phoenix: The Posthumous Papers of D. H. Lawrence*, edited and with an introduction by Edward D. McDonald (London: Heinemann, 1936), p. 539.

26 Cohen, 'Herbert Read and Psychoanalysis', p. 165. I work this out in the case of Freud in 'Herbert Read's Use of Sigmund Freud', see pp. 70–82 below.

27 Herbert Read, *The Forms of Things Unknown: Essays towards an Aesthetic Philosophy* (Cleveland and New York: Meridian Books, 1960), pp. 51–55.

28 See Alex Comfort, *Darwin and the Naked Lady: Discursive Essays on Biology and Art* (London: Routledge and Kegan Paul, 1961), for development of ideas beyond and correcting Read, especially pp. 47, 52, 57 and 60.

29 Read, 'The Cult of Sincerity', pp. 24–25. Read ignores Wordsworth's confused religious sentimentalism about the passage of the 'soul' from 'that imperial palace whence [it] came' through birth which 'is but a sleep and a forgetting' in order to bring forth his own belief in the 'innocence' of childhood.

30 Herbert Read, 'In Defence of Shelley', *In Defence of Shelley and Other Essays* (London: Heinemann, 1936), pp. 3–86, reprinted in a slightly revised form in *The True Voice of Feeling*; Herbert Read, 'The Notion of Organic Form: Coleridge', *The True Voice of Feeling: Studies in English Romantic Poetry* (London: Faber and Faber, 1953), pp. 30–37; Herbert Read, 'The Creative Experience in Poetry', *The Forms of Things Unknown*, pp. 124–32.

31 Read, 'In Defence of Shelley', p. 80.

32 Ibid., pp. 69–70. An exasperated reader of my used copy wrote in the margin next to this passage, 'bosh, prove it'.

33 Ibid., pp. 70–71.

34 Herbert Read, *The Sense of Glory: Essays in Criticism* (Cambridge: Cambridge University Press, 1929). The nine essays are: 'Froissart', 'Malory', 'Descartes', 'Swift', 'Vauvenargues', 'Sterne', 'Hawthorne', 'Bagehot', and 'Henry James'. When Read reprinted these as 'II: Particular Studies' in *Collected Essays in Literary Criticism* in 1938, he added four more: 'Tobias Smollett', 'Charlotte and Emily Brontë', 'Coventry Patmore', and 'Gerard Manley Hopkins'. In *The Contrary Experience*, pp. 190–91 and 348, Read offers an explanation of the title, *The Sense of Glory*: 'Traherne… confirmed me in that sense of glory which from my early youth I have identified with the source of all virtuous and unselfish actions. I have given this title… to a collection of essays which help to define, however obliquely, what I mean by the phrase.'

35 Warren Tallman, 'Swift's Fool: A Comment upon Satire in *Gulliver's Travels*', *Dalhousie Review*,

vol. 40, no. 4 (1960), pp. 470–78; Norman O. Brown, *Life against Death: The Psychoanalytical Meaning of History* (New York: Random House, 1959), pp. 179–201.

36 Read, 'Sterne', *Collected Essays in Literary Criticism*, p. 263.

37 Laurence Sterne, *The Life and Opinions of Tristram Shandy, Gentleman* (New York: The Odyssey Press, 1940), chapters 1–4, pp. 4–9.

38 Arthur Efron, *Don Quixote and the Dulcineated World* (Austin: University of Texas Press, 1971); Wayne Burns, *The Panzaic Principle* (Vancouver: Pendejo Press, n.d., reprinted several places); Wayne Burns, 'The Critical Relevance of Freudianism', *The Western Review*, XX (Summer 1956), pp. 301–14; Philip Rahv, 'Fiction and the Criticism of Fiction', *The Myth and the Powerhouse* (New York: Farrar, Straus and Giroux, 1956, reprinted several times and places including *Kenyon Review*, Spring 1956).

39 Read, *The True Voice of Feeling*, p. 11.

40 Read, *The Forms of Things Unknown*, p. 124.

41 I realize there is much controversy over these matters, but this is not the place to develop it. See Gene W. Ruoff, *Wordsworth and Coleridge: The Making of the Major Lyrics, 1802–1804* (New Brunswick, NJ: Rutgers University Press, 1989) for a summary of it and for his own different conclusions.

42 Read, *The Forms of Things Unknown*, pp. 127 and 128.

43 The distinction is asserted often. See especially Read, 'The Nature of Criticism', pp. 125–26; Read, *Art and Society* (New York: Schocken Books, 1966, first published in 1936 and revised and republished in 1945), p. 87; Read, *The Forms of Things Unknown*, p. 91.

44 Read, *The Forms of Things Unknown*, pp. 129–30.

45 Ibid., p. 131.

46 Ibid., p. 132.

47 Ibid., p. 131.

48 Alex Comfort, *Art and Social Responsibility: Lectures on the Ideology of Romanticism* (London: The Falcon Press, 1946), especially pp. 33 and 57; Herbert Marcuse, *Eros and Civilization: A Philosophical Inquiry into Freud* (New York: Vintage Books, 1962, first published Beacon Press, 1955), especially chapter 9, 'The Aesthetic Dimension'. See also Wayne Burns, *The Vanishing Individual: A Voice from the Dustheap of History or How To Be Happy Without Being Hopeful* (Alpine, California: special issue of *Recovering Literature*, XXI [1995]), especially pp. 177–87 and pp. 195–97. Read's consideration of Marcuse's position seems to cry out for an extended discussion of their differing positions: Herbert Read, 'Rational Society and Irrational Art', *Art and Alienation: The Role of the Artist in Society* (London: Thames and Hudson, 1967), pp. 29–39.

49 Comfort, *Art and Social Responsibility*, p. 57.

50 Sigmund Freud, *The Standard Edition of the Complete Psychological Works of Sigmund Freud*, trans. and ed. James Strachey *et al.*, vol. 9 (London: Hogarth Press, 1959), p. 150.

51 Read, *The Forms of Things Unknown*, p. 92.

52 Read, 'The Nature of Criticism', p. 141.

53 Ibid., p. 143.

54 Read, 'The Personality of the Poet', *Collected Essays in Literary Criticism*, p. 23.

55 Read, 'The Nature of Criticism', pp. 126–27.

56 Ibid., p. 126.

57 Burns, 'The Critical Relevance of Freudianism'. During the 1950s, Wayne Burns was a member of a small but very active group of critics interested in psychoanalysis and literature who met once a year in the USA at the Modern Language Association where they read papers they had written and discussed the uses of psychoanalysis. They also published a newsletter called *Psychoanalysis and Literature* which circulated beyond their group.

58 Burns, 'The Critical Relevance of Freudianism', pp. 302 and 305.

59 Herbert Read, 'Surrealism and the Romantic Principle', in Herbert Read (ed.), *Surrealism* (London: Faber and Faber, 1936), pp. 19–91. This quotation is from p. 49. In this, its first edition, the essay was titled, 'Introduction', but I have given it the title by which it was known thereafter in its several printings. In later versions deletions were made so that in Herbert Read, *The Philosophy of Modern Art: Collected Essays* (London: Faber and Faber, 1952), and Read, *Selected Writings*, with a foreword by Allen Tate, about 550 words were deleted, some of which I quote, and about a dozen were added at the very end. Read himself makes one clarifying correction in *Selected Writings* (pp. 267–68), restoring 'the original reading' of the sentence.

60 Read, 'The Nature of Criticism', p. 144.

61 Read, 'Surrealism and the Romantic Principle', pp. 22–23.

62 Ibid., pp. 25–26.

63 Ibid., pp. 27–28. This statement ties in with the later one quoted above from *The Forms of Things Unknown*. See note 51.

64 Read, 'Surrealism and the Romantic Principle', p. 88.

65 I am thinking in part of my own graduate-school days at the University of Washington (Seattle, Washington) and the widespread reading of Read's work there, not only among those who taught us but also among the students of many different persuasions. But I am also thinking of Read's many invitations to speak and to give lecture series, perhaps especially in the USA but also in Europe, of the anthologies which included his work, of Allen Tate and some of the New Critics who found something in his criticism to use, and of the reissuing of his books.

Herbert Read's Use of Sigmund Freud

JOHN R. DOHENY

ERBERT Read's main interest as a literary critic was poetry. He was himself a practising poet. Even when he did write about novels, he was not very much interested in characters in emotional and social relationships. Rather he was concerned with form, style, language, and those he found supreme in Henry James: 'the indispensable virtues of form'.[1] And for poetry, his life-long focus was a search for, even sometimes an explanation of, the source of poetic inspiration, the nature of poetry, and the social function of poetry.

From about 1950 to the end of his life he saw himself as, and was seen by others to be, a philosopher of art and only secondarily a poet. The artistic symbol, the form, the image, the psychic wholeness of the expression of vitality and beauty, these were his constant subjects in essay after essay. He distinguishes between the symbols of psychoanalysis, which are to be analysed in order to reveal their origins in the psyche leading to understanding and, perhaps, relief from the distress of symptoms, and the symbols and images of poetry, which are meant to suggest feeling and to require sensitive response to that feeling but remain themselves resistant to analysis: to analyse the poetic symbol in order to understand its origins is to destroy it.

For Read 'it is the mode which finally matters', the 'mode' is the art. 'But by the mode we mean more than the externals of beauty; we mean above all the driving energy, the vitality of the forces which well up from the unconscious.'[2] This interest allowed Read to move almost seamlessly into the philosophy of art – of poetry, painting, sculpture, design, and even music. That philosophy is at its most abstract in the essays collected in *The Origins of Form in Art*, especially in 'Originality' and in 'The Origins of Form in the Plastic Arts'.[3]

In the less formal 'The Cult of Sincerity', written in the last year of his life, Read states his position more simply.

> Once we become conscious of a feeling and attempt to make a corresponding form, we are engaged in an activity which... is prepared... to moderate the feeling to fit the form... So long as inner drives, motives, passions involved in a conflict... remain undefined, it is not possible to resolve the conflict. The conflict is... resolved by means of a symbolic form, a unitary structure in which conflicting forces are reconciled. Not all art is tragic, but tragedy is the highest form of art and the paradigm of its reconciliatory function.[4]

The form, then, is the aesthetic quality of art, and its function is 'reconciliatory', a 'civilizing agency' and 'a progressive agency, in that it can modify (direct, concentrate, focus) human sensibility'. The artist creates works 'of art, symbolic structures, myths… with the aim of linking together "the whole complex" of ideas, aspirations and feelings that give meaning to the life of the community'. The work of art is 'an instrument for tilling the human psyche, that it may continue to yield a harvest of vital beauty'.[5] This position is one which Read held all his life and stated in different forms in different works. In all his readings he sought, not always consciously, confirmation of his own definitions by finding them suggested or directly stated by other writers. And it was a characteristic of his mind to take lines or paragraphs from many writers for his own purposes without acknowledging the conflicts between them.

When he used the various claimants to psychoanalysis – Freud, Jung, Adler, Trigant Burrow, Melanie Klein, E. G. Schachtel – to give support to what he called the 'science of criticism',[6] he took what suited his own views without attention to context or completeness; and often, I believe without conscious intention to distort, he simply understood passages and concepts as if they were presenting his own position. This non-deliberate form of distortion is most obvious in Read's use of Sigmund Freud, and I wish to illustrate it with some examples.

Over a period of roughly twenty-five years (1925–1950) Read made use of surprisingly few passages from Freud's work, some of which he used in more than one essay.[7] One of them he uses three times and three of them he uses twice each over that period. In three different works Read uses a passage from the end of 'Lecture XXIII' of Freud's *Introductory Lectures on Psycho-Analysis* where Freud, after pointing out that 'everything I have said here applies only to the formation of symptoms in hysteria', adds a footnote of sorts: 'I should like to direct your attention a little longer to a side of the life of phantasy which deserves the most general interest. For there is a path that leads back from phantasy to reality – the path, that is, of art.'[8] Read quotes only a portion of the passage of slightly more than a page in Freud.

> The artist 'is one who is urged on by instinctive needs which are too clamorous; he longs to attain to honour, power, riches, fame, and the love of woman; but he lacks the means of achieving these gratifications. So, like any other with an unsatisfied longing, he turns away from reality, and transfers all his interest, and all his libido too, on to the creation of his wishes in the life of phantasy'.[9]

From this Read draws the idea that the artist gives his phantasies 'the impersonality and universality of art' which make them 'communicable and desirable' to others. The Joan Riviere translation used by Read doesn't quite say this, and the subtle difference is important to Freud's discussion as well as an indication of the position for which Read is seeking support. The Strachey translation for the *Standard Edition* makes the difference even more clear, although with less flair.

> [The true artist] understands how to work over his day-dreams in such a way as

to make them lose what is too personal about them and repels strangers, and to make it possible for others to share in the enjoyment of them. He understands, too, how to tone them down so that they do not easily betray their origin from proscribed sources. Furthermore, he possesses the mysterious power of shaping some particular material until it has become a faithful image of his phantasy; and he knows, moreover, how to link so large a yield of pleasure to this representation of his unconscious phantasy that, for the time being at least, repressions are outweighed and lifted by it. If he is able to accomplish all this, he makes it possible for other people once more to derive consolation and alleviation from their own sources of pleasure in their unconscious which have become inaccessible to them; he earns their gratitude and admiration and he has thus achieved *through* his phantasy what originally he had achieved only *in* his phantasy – honour, power, and the love of women.[10]

Freud's main argument in this passage (which I shall return to later), and in the other passages which Read uses, is that artists manage to construct their own phantasies in such a way as to allow both themselves and their audience to derive pleasure from the act of protesting against the reality principle by reaffirming their own commitment to their own versions of the pleasure principle. But Read is aiming toward his own conception of 'impersonality' and 'universality' which will fit into his reading of Coleridge's insistence on objectivity and aesthetic distance in art as well as Read's own use of Jung's collective unconscious and archetypes.

Read makes two other comments about the nature of the artist which he associates with the passage he has quoted. First, he quotes an assertion by Alfred Adler which Read believes is consistent with Freud: 'every neurosis can be understood as an attempt to free oneself from a feeling of inferiority in order to gain a feeling of superiority'. On his own, Read locates this conflict generally at the onset of puberty and 'the withdrawal of parental protection, the period of intense conflict between instinctive desires and social control'. Read believes 'the artist is born of this conflict' and that Freud lends support to this view in the passage.[11] If we stretch it a bit, we can see what he means, but Freud is hardly necessary for this common assertion if it means that art is protest against the prevailing conditions of society and that the artist successfully presents his own phantasies in such a way as to allow us, as vicarious participants, to join in the protest and gain some significant insight into the human dilemma in the process. This is certainly consistent with Freud's argument here, but it is probably not quite Read's meaning, as I have already suggested. Freud's assertion that introversion is 'not far removed from neurosis'[12] is passed over unnoticed by Read because he needs Jung's version of the term later in the essay to discuss classicism and romanticism. Freud's discussion of the conflict between the pleasure principle and the reality principle in this lecture complicates the situation beyond Read's assertions and probably beyond his wishes.

72

Read's second comment is drawn directly from the Freud passage, and it is a consistent position which Read often maintained in his discussions of the artist from 1925 on: 'the artist is initially by tendency a neurotic' who, through his art, 'finds his way back to reality'.[13] Freud's intention is not so grand as Read's, since Freud is merely saying that through luck or skill the artist can make his unrealized day-dreams of 'honour, power, and the love of women' come true by means of his fame as an artist. Freud's main emphasis is on admiration and fame since he uses other examples of success for his list in other places. It is also clear from the whole of Freud's discussion here that he never intended to suggest that art eliminated the possibility of hysteria: 'it is well known, indeed, how often artists in particular suffer from a partial inhibition of their efficiency owing to neurosis'.[14] Read is, himself, a bit confusing on this issue because there is a suggestion in his Shelley essay that he may be willing to accept that Shelley wrote great poetry and prose yet remained neurotic.[15] However, in the revision of 'Psycho-analysis and Criticism' for its 1938 republication, Read writes that Freud discovered a similarity between the phantasies of his patients and those which the artist expressed in his work; the difference being that the act of putting them into art, projecting and objectifying them, allowed the artist's mind to remain 'stable': 'Art, therefore, was conceived as a way back from phantasy to reality'.[16]

When Read uses 'stability' and 'reality' he may not mean to imply a 'cure' for neurosis. It is certainly conceivable that Read means to accept that the insight of the self-analysis, which he argues for in the Shelley essay, allowed Shelley to create great poetry whatever the state of his psyche in general, if only because Read does not make any claims for the disappearance of Shelley's neurotic patterns. The issue of Read's position in 1925 is further confused, though, when he expresses a hope that psychoanalysis can provide the 'exact course' of the borderline between 'the real and the neurotic' art.[17]

In 1936 in *Art and Society* Read quotes a longer section of the passage from 'Lecture XXIII' which I have been discussing.[18] In his use of the passage there is a glaring error. He decides that Freud's use of 'neurosis' is the wrong term and he substitutes Freud's 'psychosis' instead, thus making nonsense of the discussion: Read has, in a footnote, reversed the definitions of the two terms. We can easily ignore his error here in order to understand what he is doing with the passage.[19]

Read's concern about Freud's use of 'reality' and his wish to substitute 'normality' into Freud's thought indicates a case of careless reading or careless memory or, what is most likely, an unacknowledged sifting in of Jungian thought. Freud's use of 'reality' is extremely clear not only in this passage but in the whole of the lecture. He simply means concrete, ordinary, even mundane reality. This, combined with the equally clear discussion of the conflict between the pleasure principle and the reality principle (i.e., the impossibility of accepting less than full and immediate satisfaction of needs and pleasures and the life-preserving need to do so) which leads to the retreat into phantasy and thereby at least partially paralysing the individual's efforts to carry out ordinary functions such as walking, for example, is one of Freud's important arguments. The result of the development of the neurosis is not Read's excessively dramatic 'explosion into madness'. He has forgotten that the comments concern hysteria. He has ignored Freud's comment that everyone (hysterical or not) resorts to phantasy often. And he also ignores Freud's repeated assertion that the difference between neurosis and ordinary psychic health has no clear dividing line.

Read is reading through a lens of his own making which leads him to regard Jung's more mystical and vague approach as congenial. Freud does not suggest in the lecture or the passage or, for that matter, anywhere else that the artist so 'projects his phantasies that they become external to his mind' or that the artist makes his phantasy 'material and objective', unless Read means by these remarks that the artist transfers it on to the page or the canvas. But Read does not mean this. His comment that the artist 'possesses the power of universalizing his mental life' is not only a distortion of Freud's quoted comments, it is also a clue which indicates that Read is merging Jung and Freud in order to arrive at his own view about art. The work of art does have something to do, in Freud's view, with the 'origin of the work... in the unconscious of the artist', contrary to Read's assertion that it doesn't, because, as Freud writes in the passage Read has just quoted, the artist 'opens out to others the way back to the comfort and consolation of their own unconscious sources of pleasure'.[20]

Later, in the 1950 Ernest Jones Lecture, Read uses this passage again as one of his two jumping-off places in pursuit of his argument that 'form' and 'symbol' are the art rather than the 'theme' which he believes Freud promotes.[21] This time he uses the passage to indicate that Freud can offer hints but has no way to explain the method by which the artist reaches the emotions of an audience and, therefore, has no means of arriving at aesthetic value. This is only true if we accept Read's definition of aesthetic value along with his idea that Freud is more interested in the psychic process than he is in the artistic result.[22] It is clear that Read's definition of aesthetic value and Freud's evaluative criteria are different.

Though Read doesn't acknowledge it, Freud does suggest some criteria for the evaluation of art in the very passages from which Read quotes, and to reach them is sometimes a crucial point for Freud. I quote from the *Standard Edition*:

> ... our actual enjoyment of an imaginative work proceeds from a liberation of tensions in our minds. [The writer enables us] thenceforward to enjoy our own day-dreams without self-reproach or shame.

> [The artist makes use of] special gifts to mould his phantasies into truths of a new kind, which are valued by men as precious reflections of reality... But he can only achieve this because other men feel the same dissatisfaction as he does with the renunciation demanded by reality, and because that dissatisfaction, which results

from the replacement of the pleasure principle by the reality principle, is itself a part of reality.

> [The artist] possesses the mysterious power of shaping some particular material until it has become a faithful image of his phantasy; and he knows, moreover, how to link so large a yield of pleasure to this representation of his unconscious phantasy that, for the time being at least, repressions are outweighed and lifted by it. If he is able to accomplish all this, he makes it possible for other people once more to derive consolation and alleviation from their own sources of pleasure in their unconscious which have become inaccessible to them.[23]

As I said earlier, these are all passages which Read quotes without taking up their intention, nor does he take notice of Freud's insistence that phantasy has its root in 'either ambitious wishes, which serve to elevate the subject's personality; or they are erotic ones'.[24] They are, according to Freud, not fixed, not universal; in other words, they are not part of a 'collective ego'. Therefore, Read's plan, consciously or unconsciously, is to ignore the context and much of the content of Freud's thought in his 'expropriation'. To have read and understood Freud accurately would have threatened, perhaps even destroyed, Read's idealistic criticism. In order to follow that idealism from its early stages, I return to the 1925 essay and its revisions for its 1938 publication.[25]

There are several interesting and revealing revisions to the 1925 essay which appear when Read republished it in 1938 as 'The Nature of Criticism': deletions and additions, some of which eliminate comments which Read thought better of or which seemed merely distractions from his main argument. On page 222 of 'Psycho-analysis and the Critic', for example, just after the footnote sign referring to E. Rignano, Read deleted 'and this theory is, I think, entirely satisfactory as an explanation of poetic inspiration. It will not, perhaps, satisfy the poets themselves, who all, like Blake, imagine that they take down from the dictation of angels. But we are none of us very exact in the description of our own emotional states.' This deletion satisfies both the above objections, but it also satisfies another, I think, which is that it is too personal, as is another deletion from the following paragraph where in the first sentence he deleted the following parenthetical comment: 'and it is based both on my reading of psychology and on the analysis of my own putative experiences'.[26] This latter comment would have been too closely allied to the later discussion where the 'outburst of poetic impulse' is associated with 'the awakening of the adolescent sexual instincts, the time of the withdrawal of parental protection, the period of intense conflict between instinctive desires and social control'[27] from which Read believes the artist is born: that is, at the very period when he was himself incarcerated in the school for boys after the traumatic loss of his father and the family income and expectations, the very period, also, when he began the process of idealizing and closing off from experience and influence his own childhood.[28]

In a less direct way, I believe that Read's need to desexualize the earlier periods and to remove them from full actual experience by intellectually developing a theory about the poetic impulse rising spontaneously from a desexualized 'seething cauldron', which Read borrows from Freud's definition of the Id and defines through Jung's 'Collective Unconscious', manifesting itself in 'sudden promptings of words, sounds, or images from which the artist constructs his work of art', gets its earliest expression in these revisions. Read was always happier with what Jung had to offer than he was with Freud's concepts. The desexualized libido, the idea of a collective unconscious, sometimes a collective ego, suited Read's theory, and when he read Freud's definition of the Id through the use of 'images' – 'a chaos, a cauldron of seething excitement'[29] – ignoring the rest of Freud's definition, he grasped the 'seething cauldron' as an icon for his own use as a descriptive term for his own idea of the untapped and natural source of poetic inspiration.

Between the paragraph discussing 'the state of ecstacy', which ends 'And the full creative process is but a summation of many of these primary creative moments', and the next one beginning 'If this be a correct description of the process of poetic creation',[30] Read added about 2,000 words. In these added pages, he offers a brief history of 'inspiration' through its religious and secular stages to reach the view that:

> It was only with the romantic revival that the concept was once more reinstated, and began to be seriously investigated... One might almost say that the historical distinction between classicism and romanticism is determined by this concept. The classicist... refuse[s] to see in the highest works of art anything but the exercise of judgement, sensibility, and skill. The romanticist cannot be satisfied with such a normal standard; for him art is essentially irrational... whilst hitherto romanticism has had to rely on subjective convictions, and has thus earned a certain disrepute in philosophy and the science of art, it can now claim a scientific basis in the findings of psycho-analysis.[31]

It is also in these added pages that Read extends his use of psychoanalysis further and continues his translation of Freud into his own more Jungian terms. He refers to the essay on 'Creative Writers and Day-dreaming' in order to add the Jungian translation of Freud's 'phylogenesis' into a 'collective ego': 'the technique of the artist is in some way a means of breaking down the barriers between individual egos, uniting them all in some form of collective ego'.[32] And from the newly translated *New Introductory Lectures* (1933), he draws on Freud's discussion of the Id, the Ego and the Superego in order to solidify his own notion of the source of inspiration and its development into poetry, another version of the process he found in Wordsworth's 1800 and 1802 prefaces to the *Lyrical Ballads*.[33]

> The work of art, therefore has its correspondences with each region of the mind. It derives its energy, its irrationality and its mysterious power from the id, which

is to be regarded as the source of what we have called 'inspiration'. It is given formal synthesis and unity by the ego; and finally it may be assimilated to those ideologies or spiritual aspirations which are the peculiar creation of the super-ego. The old metaphor underlying the word 'inspiration' is to this extent confirmed: that out of the darkness of that region of the mind we call the id, come these sudden promptings of words, sounds, or images from which the artist constructs his work of art.[34]

Of course, by 1938, none of this has anything to do with Freud except for the appropriated terms and almost everything to do with Jung. Freud gives no hint of 'words, sounds, or images' as part of the content of the Id. Strachey translates a crucial sentence, 'We approach the id with analogies' rather than 'images' which Riviere uses, and Freud describes it as 'a chaos, a cauldron full of seething excitations' because it is 'the dark, *inaccessible* part of our personality… filled with energy reaching it from the instincts… it has no organization… [it strives] to bring about the satisfaction of the instinctual needs subject to the observance of the pleasure principle'.[35] His summary comes a few paragraphs later:

> The id of course knows no judgements of value: no good and evil, no morality. The economic or… the quantitative factor, which is intimately linked to the pleasure principle, dominates all its processes. Instinctual cathexes seeking discharge – that, in our view, is all there is in the id. It even seems that the energy of these instinctual impulses is in a state different from that in the other regions of the mind, far more mobile and capable of discharge.[36]

In the 1925/1938 essay are the ideas, or the beginnings of ideas, which Read held for the rest of his life in one form or another. He supports them, even sometimes modifies them in minor ways, with references to a growing collection of works by other authors where he finds something which will bolster his own position, but he never changes them in any important ways. He believes that the artist manages somehow to reach some

> archetypal form, some instinctive association of words, images, or sounds, which constitute a basis of the work of art… deeper intuitions of the mind [than 'ideas, and all the rational superstructure of the mind'], which are neither rational nor economic, but which nevertheless exercise a changeless and eternal influence on successive generations… these are accessible only to the mystic and the artist, and only the artist can give them material representation, though naturally the mystic may be, and often is, one kind of artist – a poet.[37]

Read's definition of the function of criticism in this essay is not very clear: 'Criticism is a process of cystallization, of the discovery and elaboration of general concepts'.[38] It is not a call for 'interpretation' which was on the verge of becoming the usual view; it is more nearly a vague statement of modern 'critical theory', and I believe that 'crystallization' is the cardinal fault of both. In a later work Read writes a more clear summary of his position. He sees art as an essential part of the human evolutionary process of 'expanding consciousness... Without the creative arts there would have been no advance in myth or ritual, in language or meaning, in morality or metaphysics.'[39] Therefore, I think we must assume that, for Read, the function of criticism is to call attention to and to elaborate on that evolutionary process. In a footnote Read adds: 'To interpret art as a "manifestation of man's cognitive capability" may be another way of expressing the same idea: but what makes the capability?'. He claims to have developed his own answer in *Icon and Idea: The Function of Art in the Development of Human Consciousness* where he argues that both in history and in individual development the human condition begins with thinking in pictures which develop into ideas.[40]

Idealistic and sometimes vague it is, but I think that here we have the whole of Read's theory of the sources of art, both literary and representational, and his idea of its value to the individual and to society. It is not consistent with Freud's psychoanalysis and not always consistent with Jung's or consistent with any of the other psychological or philosophical writers whom he musters for his support. He borrows terminology from them more than he borrows ideas. When his own concepts are not consistent with theirs, something in his own nature leads him to understand their positions as if they are consistent with his own. The examples of this are many; I have illustrated it here with Freud.

Read's Achilles heel is his wish for some discovery of eternal truth or even sameness in humans hidden in the deep recesses of the unconscious which only art can bring forth into at least semi-consciousness or intuitive awareness: 'Art... is precisely the search for the infinite and the eternal'.[41] This wish is countered by his stubborn suspicion of 'monolithic systems, all logical categories, all pretences to truth and inevitability'.[42]

As a critic he wavers between these two poles, the latter being most evident in the 1930s and in his anarchism generally, and the former most evident as he grew older. Caught between these two poles his only recourse is to celebrate 'form', the means of expressing 'vital beauty', which is, in his view, the continuing progressive development of the indirect expression of the eternal truth or sameness. I don't think that Read ever worked out this conflict in himself. Instead, he presents it as a fatalism which is also active rather than passive:

> I... combine anarchism with order, a philosophy of strife with pacifism, an orderly life with romanticism and revolt in art and literature... This principle of flux, the Keatsian notion of 'negative capability', justifies everything I have done (or not done) in my life... My understanding of the history of culture has convinced me that the ideal society is a point on a receding horizon. We move steadily towards it but can never reach it.[43]

In psychoanalytical interests the conflict left him trapped between Jung, whose wish was to create monolithic, even airtight, systems, and Freud, whose explorations of the human condition continually broke down potential monolithic systems into ordinary human complexity, the results of which were never noble enough for Read.

Herbert Read's need to see the criticism of literature and the other arts as a science seems to me to be a means of separating himself intellectually from the prevailing criticism of his day in order to identity his work as new and important. He did do that even though T. S. Eliot, I. A. Richards and others became the main progenitors of the 'New Criticism', which held the day for so long and is even now reappearing in new forms.

I believe that a wider and deeper exploration of his life and work than has so far been accomplished needs to be done in order to reach an understanding of Herbert Read's rightfully important position in recent intellectual history. One of the issues which needs exploration and expansion can be raised with a question. Given Read's wide-ranging reading in psychoanalysis, why was he never interested in the work of Wilhelm Reich? Reich's fundamental argument that the human 'organism is capable of *self-regulation*' ought to have appealed to Read's anarchism, as it appealed to other anarchists in the 1940s, notably his associates of the Freedom Press Group.[44] The most obvious part of that exploration would have to consider Read's attitudes about human sexuality which is one of Reich's main subjects, but I believe that there is much more to it than that. We would also need to know why Read never noticed Reich's *The Mass Psychology of Fascism*, for example, and why he was attracted by Martin Buber, Kierkegaard, Jung, Simone Weil, and the many other religious writers he finds so useful but cannot wholly join in their belief, turning instead to Chinese classics in a search for harmony.[45]

Appendix

Read quoted other works by Freud during his life, but during this period the following seem to be the ones which formed the basis for his use of Freud. 1.) 'Lecture XXIII, The Paths to the Formation of Symptoms, *Introductory Lectures on Psycho-analysis*', *The Standard Edition of the Complete Psychological Works of Sigmund Freud*, trans. and ed. James Strachey *et al.*, vol. 16 (London: Hogarth Press, 1963), pp. 376–77. Read used this passage three times: all three versions of 'The Nature of Criticism' (*Collected Essays in Literary Criticism*, p. 140); *Art and Society*, pp. 85–86; and *The Forms of Things Unknown: Essays towards an Aesthetic Philosophy* (Cleveland and New York: Meridian Books, 1960), p. 83. 2.) Freud, 'Creative Writers and Daydreaming', *The Standard Edition*, 1959, vol. 9, pp. 149 and 153. Read used the first passage once in *Art and Society*, pp. 87–88, and the second one twice, in 'The Nature of Criticism' (*Collected Essays in Literary Criticism*, p. 135), and in *Art and Society*, p. 88. 3.) Freud, 'Lecture XXXI, The Dissection of the Psychical Personality, *New*

Introductory Lectures on Psycho-analysis', *The Standard Edition*, vol. 22, 1964, pp. 73–74. Read used this passage twice, once in 'The Nature of Criticism' (*Collected Essays in Literary Criticism*, p. 136), and once in *Art and Society*, p. 89. 4.) Freud, 'Formulations on the Two Principles of Mental Functioning', *The Standard Edition*, vol. 12, 1958, p. 224. Though Read used this passage only once (in *The Forms of Things Unknown*, pp. 82–83), I include it here because it is an early (1911), one-paragraph summary of ideas Freud developed further over time, notably in 1.) above and because it contains the idea which was a core element in Read's borrowing from Freud during the period I am considering. It was part of a work translated only in 1925. As was typical with Read in his use of Freud, he ignores its context, especially its association with repression and sexuality: see pp. 222–23, 225 of Freud for evidence of this. 5.) During this period Read also used and seriously distorted the following: Freud, 'Group Psychology and the Analysis of the Ego', *The Standard Edition*, vol. 18, 1955, pp. 107–08 and 136–37. Read quotes the second passage in *Art and Society*, p. 88, and the first in *The Forms of Things Unknown*, p. 87. His commentary ignores Freud's demonstration of the regressive nature of mass behaviour and thought: a further indication that Read was leaning more heavily on Jung's assertions of a group unconscious than on Freud's ideas about mass behaviour.

Notes

1 Edward Dahlberg and Herbert Read, 'On Henry James: 2', *Truth Is More Sacred: A Critical Exchange on Modern Literature* (New York: Horizon Press, 1961), p. 137.

2 Herbert Read, 'Art and the Unconscious', *Art and Society* (New York: Schocken Books, 1966, first published in 1936 and revised and republished in 1945), p. 95.

3 Herbert Read, *The Origins of Form in Modern Art* (New York: Horizon Press, 1965).

4 Herbert Read, 'The Cult of Sincerity', *The Cult of Sincerity* (London: Faber and Faber, 1968), p. 18.

5 Ibid., pp. 19–20.

6 Herbert Read, 'The Nature of Criticism', *Collected Essays in Literary Criticism* (London: Faber and Faber, 1938), p. 125. See also my 'Herbert Read as Literary Critic' above, pp. 54, 67n.23, for the publishing history of this essay beginning as 'Psycho-analysis and the Critic', *Criterion*, vol. 3, no. 10 (January 1925), pp. 214–30; revised and reprinted as 'Psycho-analysis and Criticism' in *Reason and Romanticism: Essays in Literary Criticism* (London: Faber and Gwyer, 1926), pp. 83–106; then extensively revised and renamed 'The Nature of Criticism' for this 1938 collection.

7 I say 1950 instead of 1960, when *The Forms of Things Unknown: Essays towards an Aesthetic Philosophy* (Cleveland and New York: Meridian Books, 1960) was published, because that book's chapter 5, on psychoanalysis, is the Ernest Jones Lecture which Read delivered in 1950. See Appendix, pp. 79–80.

8 Freud, 'Lecture XXIII, The Paths to the Formation of Symptoms, *Introductory Lectures on Psychoanalysis*', *The Standard Edition of the Complete Psychological Works of Sigmund Freud*, trans. and ed. James Strachey *et al.*, vol. 16 (London: Hogarth Press, 1963), p. 376.

9 Read, 'Psycho-analysis and the Critic', p. 224. Read uses the translation by Joan Riviere published in 1922.

10 Freud, 'Lecture XXIII, The Paths to the Formation of Symptoms', p. 376.

11 Read, 'Psycho-analysis and the Critic', pp. 223–24.

12 Freud, 'Lecture XXIII, The Paths to the Formation of Symptoms', p. 376. See also p. 374 for a comment on Jung's use of the term.

13 Read, 'Psycho-analysis and the Critic', p. 225. Read repeats the same phrase almost word for word in *The Forms of Things Unknown*, pp. 81–82, where he attributes the idea to both Rank and Freud.

14 Freud, 'Lecture XXIII, The Paths to the Formation of Symptoms', p. 376.

15 Herbert Read, 'In Defence of Shelley', *In Defence of Shelley and Other Essays* (London: Heinemann, 1936), pp. 3–86. See especially pp. 59–60.

16 Read, 'The Nature of Criticism', p. 135.

17 Read, 'Psycho-analysis and the Critic', p. 225.

18 Read, *Art and Society*, pp. 85–86.

19 In *The Forms of Things Unknown* and in the revisions for the 1938 'The Nature of Criticism' Read reverts to the correct term, 'neurosis'. In the Shelley essay of 1936, he uses 'psychosis' where it seems appropriate: 'In general I have preferred to use the term "psychosis" rather than "neurosis", following the distinction made by Freud' ('In Defence of Shelley', p. 36). However, later in the essay, he reduces Shelley's condition to 'neurosis': 'From the pathological point of view, Shelley was a neurotic, in conflict with the social imposition of normality… from a more general and human point of view, Shelley was a genius whose neurotic reaction, for all its distortion, represents an organic urge towards "a completer oneness of life"' (ibid., p. 59).

20 Read, *Art and Society*, pp. 86–87. Read quotes from the Riviere translation.

21 Herbert Read, 'Psycho-analysis and the Problem of Aesthetic Value', *The Forms of Things Unknown*, p. 83.

22 Read, 'Psycho-analysis and the Critic', p. 215. Read discusses this issue at length in chapter 5 of *The Forms of Things Unknown*.

23 In the order in which they appear here: Freud, 'Creative Writers and Day-dreaming', vol. 9, p. 153; 'Formulations on the Two Principles of Mental Functioning', vol. 12, p. 224; 'The Paths to the Formation of Symptoms', vol. 16, p. 376. See Appendix pp. 79–80, for full documentation.

24 Freud, 'Creative Writers and Day-dreaming', vol. 9, p. 147.

25 See note 6 for the three versions of the essay.

26 Read, 'Psycho-analysis and the Critic', p. 222.

27 Ibid., p. 224.

28 Herbert Read, 'The Innocent Eye', *The Contrary Experience: Autobiographies* (London: Faber and Faber, 1963), pp. 15–55.

29 Read, 'The Nature of Criticism', pp. 136–37.

30 Read, 'Psycho-analysis and the Critic', p. 222.

31 Read, 'The Nature of Criticism', p. 134.

32 Ibid., p. 135.

33 Herbert Read, *Wordsworth* (London: Faber and Faber, 1949), p. 112.

34 Read, 'The Nature of Criticism', p. 137.

35 My italics. Freud, 'The Dissection of the Psychical Personality', vol. 22, p. 73. Read's quotations are from the Joan Riviere translation.

36 Ibid., p. 74.

37 Read, 'The Nature of Criticism', p. 138.

38 Read, 'Psycho-analysis and the Critic', p. 228.

39 Read, *The Forms of Things Unknown*, p. 92.

40 Herbert Read, *Icon and Idea: The Function of Art in the Development of Human Consciousness* (New

York: Schocken Books, 1965, first published 1955), pp. 1, 2, 53, for example; and see the final paragraph of the book, p. 140, for one of Read's ringing statements praising art.

41 Read, 'The Cult of Sincerity', p. 29.

42 Read, 'What is There Left to Say?', *The Cult of Sincerity*, p. 55.

43 Ibid., pp. 55–56.

44 Wilhelm Reich, *The Sexual Revolution: Toward a Self-Governing Character Structure*, trans. Theodore P. Wolfe (London: Vision Press, 1951), p. 7; George Woodcock, *Anarchism: A History of Libertarian Ideas and Movements* (Harmondsworth: Penguin Books, 2nd edn 1986), p. 383. In a discussion of the widening of anarchist perspectives during the 1940s, Woodcock writes: 'the teachings of Erich Fromm… and Wilhelm Reich… were notably appealing to the anarchist intellectuals of the time'. For example, Marie Louise Berneri lectured 'on Reich's work and the sexuality of children' (*Marie Louise Berneri, 1918–1949: A Tribute*, [London: Marie Louise Berneri Memorial Committee, 1949], p. 20). See also her 'Sexuality and Freedom', *Now*, no. 5 (n.d. [internal evidence indicates a date no earlier than late 1944 and probably early 1945]), pp. 54–60, which is an anarchist consideration of Reich's discussion of sexuality and society, primarily as it appears in *The Function of the Orgasm* (New York: Orgone Institute Press, 1942). Read also published in this issue of *Now* and must have read the essay. I thank the editor, David Goodway, for help with these references and much other good advice.

45 Read, 'The Cult of Sincerity', pp. 34–37. Though this reference is to an essay which Read wrote near the end of his life, the issues were lifelong.

Herbert Read as Autobiographer

PETER ABBS

But Spain was not where he designed to stay; for though the Spanish language had become natural to him, so that he habitually used it in thought and speech, his real nationality was English, and the ruling desire in all his present conduct was to return to his native land and particularly to the scenes of his childhood.

The Green Child, I

I

HERBERT Read's writing is, often, deeply autobiographical. He was not a detached thinker, not a scholar, not an academic. His writing was a continuous expression of his own distinctive personality and its existential concerns. While his life was active and varied – he was, of course, a seminal figure in the life of English culture for the best part of fifty years – his own sense of value and meaning always returned, in one form or another, to his visionary childhood on a remote farm in Yorkshire. At a philosophical level this commitment to his early experience entailed a consistent belief in the importance of direct perceptual experience and an unselfconscious attention to things, to objects, to the immediate world before the eye; while at a more intimate level it determined the trajectory of his own life. He moved from innocence to experience to a kind of innocence regained; from the innocence of a country childhood to the alienation (at the age of ten, after the death of his father) of an orphanage school, to the trauma of the First World War, to the business of establishing himself in the world as an intellectual, to the inevitable return in 1949 to the Vale of Pickering, to the landscape, walks and buildings of his childhood memory. In brief, one can discern a strong personal mythology at work in Herbert Read's critical writing as also in his imaginative work, his poetry and his novel *The Green Child*, a circular narrative journey driven by the power of opposites, of contraries. The mythology of Innocence and Experience and the image of the mandala journey mark a great deal of Read's prolific work and make it inherently autobiographical. At one level, of course, one can separate the work out into neat and distinct genres; the novel, the poems, the autobiography, the biography (on Wordsworth), the literary-critical essays, the studies of visual artists, the political work, the educational work and so on. But at a deeper level the pattern of generic differentiation breaks asunder to disclose a consistent autobiographical rhythm, a constellation of personal values (resting on temperament and childhood experience) and an indivisible narrative journey leading, at the end, to a profound sense of isolation from the dominant culture and an intense attachment to the flora and fauna, the buildings and paths, the streams and rivers of his local world, of his earlier childhood Paradise.

There is nothing original in this interpretation and any assiduous biographer would be quick to notice it. Moreover, Herbert Read in his own writing explicitly referred to the deep personal rhythm of his writing. Not only did he affirm the insight of Coleridge which proclaimed an inevitable correlation between existence and style, he also described the autobiographical nature of his critical work. In the closing section of *The Contrary Experience* he wrote:

> But the mere acquisition of knowledge has never been my aim – otherwise I could so easily have become an academic scholar or an archaeologist. I am only inter-ested in the facts that feed an interest which is total, directed to the universe and to life as an existing whole; and it is my intuition of the nature of that wholeness, my desire to hold it within my mind as a coherent conception, which drives me on to the discovery of facts and their reconciliation in a philosophy of life.[1]

This may seem centred more on the other than the self and more abstract than personal, but Read continues as follows:

> In a sense I am a solipsist: that is to say, I believe that the world I discover, as well as the philosophical interpretation I give to it, is contained within myself, and inevitably conditioned by my temperament. Nietzsche's command: Become what thou art, seems to me to be an improvement even on the Delphic oracle.[2]

He then concludes, perhaps not entirely aware of the philosophical slippage:

> Thus, so long as I remain true to that command, I find myself continually returning to certain fundamental beliefs or attitudes which have their unity or reconcilia-tion in my personality.[3]

Under the power of such axioms writing becomes a dynamic activity of intellectual self-disclosure. Thus we find Herbert Read's critical essays essaying into his own personality, consciously and unconsciously, and we find his autobiography often working at a very abstract and philosophical level. The genres with their classifica-tory points of order, difference and decorum dissolve and writing itself becomes a precise instrument for self-affirmation and self-amplification. *Become what thou art.*

Such a position is deeply problematic, of course. If insight is a matter of tempera-ment, how can we generalize from it? And if we do, are we not always in danger of imposing a personal answer on to a larger collective dilemma? The mythical elements of Herbert Read's thinking may not illuminate that of others, just as the mandala narrative may not be the narrative of other lives and journeys. Sincerity is impor-tant, we might say, but what about truth? In autobiography one expects and respects a personal truth, but in critical writing on art, society and education one expects a larger circumference. This is a question that I will return to at the end of the chapter. Here I want only to register two points; Herbert Read's work has a powerful autobiographical current running through it and the philosophy espoused cannot be dissociated from the life of the man and the extraordinary magnetic power of his childhood experience. There is a single psychological *Gestalt* at work, a consistent constellation as specific and distinctive as a finger print. Any full study of Read's autobiographical writing would have to come to terms with this fact.

But the very questioning of the usual generic distinctions makes us look again at Herbert Read as autobiographer, to redraw the map of his writing. What can we list as obvious works in explicit autobiography? Clearly much of the essential material is gathered together in *The Contrary Experience*. This volume was first published in 1963 and is made up of four parts: 'The Innocent Eye' (first published in 1933), 'A War Diary' (extracts from letters written between 1914 and 1918 and presented in the form of a diary), 'The Falcon and the Dove' based on the second part of *Annals of Innocence and Experience* (first published in 1940), and 'A Dearth of Wild Flowers' (largely written around 1960–62). The book is not a continuous narrative, nor does it have a single mode of narration. It is discontinuous, fragmentary, perspectival – yet the first section and the last section are both essentially concerned to elaborate and recreate the original landscape of childhood vision. But *The Contrary Experience* is not the only autobiography. There is also the volume *The Cult of Sincerity* (published in 1968) which for the most part reads very much like conventional apologia (defending the intellectual development of his own ideas) and, at times, like memoir; the essay on his friend T. S. Eliot is actually subtitled 'A Memoir' while the essays 'The Early Influence of Bertrand Russell' and 'Richard Aldington' could also have carried the same generic tag. Some of the poems, too, are clearly a direct form of autobiography: in particular, some of the early poems in *Eclogues* (1919) and such poems as 'Sonnet' (1955) and 'The Visionary Hermit' (1965). Also of central significance is the verse-drama *Moon's Farm* (1955), where the second voice represents Read himself and where the dramatic location is the actual site of a vanished farm several miles from Muscoates, Read's childhood farm. All of these works need to be considered in any study of Read's explicit autobiographies.

II

Of all the varied experiments in autobiography *The Innocent Eye* is the most distinctive and stylistically the most accomplished. The work is, to some extent, prefigured in a number of poems first published in *Eclogues* in 1919. Some of these poems have simple titles based on places ('Woodlands', 'Pasturelands', 'The Pond', 'The Orchard', 'On the Heath') and clearly their content derives from vivid memories of his Yorkshire childhood. The poem entitled 'Childhood' evokes, in a few precise images, the geography which will be more fully amplified and articulated in the later prose autobiography:

> The old elm trees flock round the tiled farmstead; their silver-bellied leaves dance in the wind. Beneath their shade, in the corner of the Green, is a pond. In Winter it is full of water, green with weeds: in Spring a lily will open there.[4]

The writing is sparse and precise. The aim is simple: to throw the object minimally described on the screen of the reader's imagination. While the writing is the antithesis of rhetoric, it is not naïve. Feeling is held back while the language is chiselled into laconic form. In those early autobiographical poems the verse is generally free of formal metre but it is firmly cadenced. One of the poems reads:

> To the fresh wet fields
> And the white
> froth of flowers
>
> Came the wild errant
> swallows with a scream.[5]

A moment of perception is starkly caught in a sentence whose ending is as definitive as the blow of a sharp axe.

The movement informing those early poems was, of course, imagism, and Herbert Read, who always loved manifestos and sudden new schools of thought, was a passionate advocate of its programme. In Part Three of *The Contrary Experience* Read outlines the principles on which the movement was based. The following points are particularly significant:

> to employ always the *exact* word... To create new rhythms... a new cadence means a new idea... To present an image... poetry should render particulars exactly and not deal in vague generalities... To produce poetry that is hard and clear, never blurred nor indefinite... concentration is of the very essence...[6]

These axioms were to shape many of the poems written before and after the First World War: the poems of Ezra Pound, H.D., T. E. Hulme, T. S. Eliot and others. But what has not been commonly noticed is that they were to exert a profound influence on the writing of *The Innocent Eye* which could well be described as an imagist prose-poem, where all particulars are presented exactly and where there are no vague generalities. If *Eclogues* is a young man's fashionable experiment in poetic composition then *The Innocent Eye* is the consummate realization of that experiment and the best 'poem' that Herbert Read ever wrote.

The Innocent Eye is a short work, made up of thirteen brief sections, twelve of which are based around key physical locations or objects: the vale, the farm, the green, the orchard, the foldgarth, the stockyard, the cow pasture, the abbey, the church, the mill, the attic and the musical box. Only the uneven and unlucky chapter

13 has a different title and an entirely different resonance. It is simply called 'Death'. This chapter describes the death of Herbert Read's father in 1903 and with it the sudden traumatic close, at the age of ten, of the child's visionary universe. The loss is described, for the most part, indirectly through physical detail in a highly concentrated poetic writing – for, strangely, there is little direct subjectivity in Read's autobiographical work. The outer landscape bears the inner meaning:

> Then we all drove to Kirkdale, slowly over the frozen flint roads, and there a grave was ready dug at the east end of the Church, by the side of Mariana's. The dark cirque of fir-trees rose in the background, sighing in the frosty wind. The bell in the grey tower clanged its toneless note. The horses were not unyoked. Six friends of my father carried his coffin into the ancient church, and then to the grave. The earth fell with a hollow sound on to the lowered coffin. My mother sobbed against my uncle's shoulder. The last amen was murmured in that immemorial stillness, and when we had taken a last look at the forlorn coffin, we drove back swiftly over the frozen flint roads, horse-hooves beating clearly in the metallic air.[7]

A few weeks after the burial the animals were auctioned and nearly every item of the farm sold off. A few months later Herbert Read and his elder brother were sent off to an orphanage. The world of innocence was over; the age of experience – of alienation, of anxiety, of loss – had begun.

It is the aim of *The Innocent Eye* not to explore that excruciating loss but to affirm the child's prior vision. As vision is timeless so Read does not offer a chronological narrative. It is true that the first chapter involves his birth and early memories and that the last chapter involves his father's death when he is ten, but in the chapters between there is a kind of poetic simultaneity – events happen around places and it is those places which provide the nodal points for the eclectic recall of memory. The actual writing has an extraordinary clarity and sharpness of line yet the method is largely that of free association. The child is not a developing character so much as an eternal eye who sees into the essence of things. Here, for example, is the description of milking in the cow-sheds:

> Morning and night, and most often by lanthorn light (perhaps it is only the winter scene which is impressed on my memory) the cows were milked in a glow and atmosphere which is for me the glow and atmosphere of the Nativity. The patient beasts stood in their stalls, exuding the soft slightly sickly smell of cow breath; a girl or a man sat on a three-legged stool, cheek against a glossy flank, and the warm needle stream of milk hissed into the gleaming pails. At first it sang against the hollow tin drum of the base, but as the pail filled it murmured with a frothy surr-surr.[8]

And here is the description of the threshing-machine in action:

The engine stood before us, merry with smoke and steam; the big fly-wheel winked in the sunlight; the bright balls of the revolving 'governor' (Jabez had taught me the technical names) twinkled in a minor radiance. Jabez was in the cabin stoking the glowing furnace. The big leather belt swung rhythmically between the fly-wheel and the threshing-machine. Two men on the top of a stack threw down the sheaves; two others cut them open and guided them into the monster's belly; the master groaned and gobbled, and out of its yammering mouth came the distracted straw; elsewhere emerged the prickly chaff and below, into sacks that reached the ground, trickled the precious corn. A cloud of dust and chaff swirled round everything.[9]

The language is that of observation so heightened it seems to convert perception into vision. It is as if through the visionary act of seeing the object bears witness to itself. In such autobiographical writing the usual 'I' of the first personal singular becomes subordinate to the eye which unselfconsciously records its exterior world with a quiet sustained ecstasy.

This absence of the reflexive 'I' means that in this volume there is virtually no exploration of relationships. Although the traumatic experience of the father's death is recorded, there is no sense of the boy's relationship to him, indeed no struggle to reconstruct his life or experience; the same is true of the mother (who remains indistinct throughout); and the same is true of the two brothers who, in the first chapter, at least, share the same large bed. There are brief descriptions of family relations but the only figures with any power are those who, larger than life, break in dramatically to alter the slow ritual of rural life: Jabez ('with a little twinkling face and a fuzzy black beard'[10]) with his threshing-machine and Fiddler Dick ('a natty little man, with a hot swarthy complexion and waxed moustaches'[11]) with his fiddle. Without doubt there was a powerful reticence in Herbert Read's character which would have prevented the direct re-creation of turbulent feeling, but it is most likely that his childhood was remembered largely as he described it; as a continuous unfolding of engaged vision and objective perception.

Yet the autobiography is not confined to the re-creation of childhood perception; it is also deeply philosophical. In Herbert Read there were always contraries at work seeking resolution and the contraries in *The Innocent Eye* could be described as *vision* and *speculation*. I have pointed to the vision and its poetic quality; it is now time to glance at the philosophy and its formal elegance. The reflection in the work is in intimate and subordinate relationship to the vivid stream of memory and its poetic re-creation. Elsewhere in Read's writing the ideas seem to float rather unhappily between the rigours of philosophical analysis and poetic enactment – here, for once, the balance is right: the thought attends vision, reflects briefly on it and then returns to it. For once, the division which haunted Read – the seeming irreconcilable struggle between passion and intellect – is transcended and an artistic relationship established between the two forces with experience (as remembered) at the centre.

The philosophical reflections which close the first and last chapters are exemplary. They enact in poetic language the experience of memory and then reflect, with impressive conciseness, on its human significance. They offer brilliant amalgams of poetic re-creation and intellectual reflexivity. This is the final paragraph of the work:

> To-day I found a withered stem of honesty, and shelled the pods between my thumb and finger; silver pennies, which grew between the fragrant currant-bushes. Their glistening surfaces, seeded, the very faint rustle they make in the wind – these sensations come direct to me from a moment thirty years ago. As they expand in my mind, they carry everything in their widening circle – the low crisp box-hedge which would be at my feet, the pear-trees on the wall behind me, the potato-flowers on the patch beyond the bushes, the ivy-clad privy at the end of the path, the cow pasture, the fairy rings – everything shimmers for a second on the expanding rim of my memory. The farthest tremor of this pertur-bation is lost only at the finest edge where sensation passes beyond the confines of experience; for memory is a flower which only opens fully in the kingdom of Heaven, where the eye is eternally innocent.[12]

This formulates with elegance a certain theory and practice of autobiography. The author of autobiography finds those instants of time where the present is illuminated by the past; in the experiences a certain unity is attained which has within it the sensa-tion of eternity. Autobiography as a means to Paradise. Yet there is something else as well; there is a search back in time to find the sources of one's own identity. The philosophy is brilliantly outlined at the end of the first chapter:

> If only I can recover the sense and uncertainty of those innocent years, years in which we seemed not so much to live as to be lived by forces outside us, by the wind and trees and moving clouds and all the mobile engines of our expanding world – then I am convinced I shall possess a key to much that has happened to me in this other world of conscious living. The echoes of my life which I find in my early childhood are too many to be dismissed as vain coincidences; but it is perhaps my conscious life which is the echo, the only real experiences in life being those lived with a virgin sensibility – so that we only hear a tone once, only see a colour once, see, hear, touch, taste and smell everything but once, the first time. All life is an echo of our first sensations, and we build up our consciousness, our whole mental life, by variations and combinations of these elementary sensations. But it is more complicated than that, for the senses apprehend not only colours and tones and shapes, but also patterns and atmospheres, and our first discovery of these determines the larger patterns and subtler atmospheres of all our subse-quent existence.[13]

Autobiography thus becomes the task of tracing one's later commitments and experiences back to their origin in their first characteristic expressions and in their original intensity. Herbert Read's eye for painting and sculpture clearly had its origin in the visionary eye of the child; his love of books, triggered by learning to read at the age of seven, is seen as insatiable and innate; his concern to make art and literature is seen as deriving from the pleasure experienced in creating small bullets from melted-down lead and from watching the blacksmith at work. ('But fire was real, and so was the skill with which we shaped hard metals to our design and desire'[14]). To know itself, to find itself, to own itself the mind is drawn back to analyse its earliest encounters and memories. The innocent years are seen as the key to all that follows.

In *The Innocent Eye* poet and philosopher are beautifully integrated; re-creation and generalization lock powerfully together to create a unified work of autobiography. Elsewhere the attempt is much less successful. In *Moon's Farm*, for example, the writing verges on the vapid. In this free-verse drama the First Voice represents the Spirit of Place (the North York Moors close to where Read was born), the Third Voice represents Time and the Second Voice the author's questing self.

> First Voice   ... I have always
>   lived in this dale.
>
> Second Voice   Then perhaps you can help me. I too
>   used to live in this dale
>   but farther down.
>   I left fifty years ago
>   as a boy of ten
>   I went far away
>   into another country.
>   Today, for the first time
>   I have come back.
>   I find everything changed.[15]

It is, without question, a work of explicit autobiography in which the author through the dramatic device of voices (representing Time and Place) is able to interrogate his own experience. How to keep integrity? How to relate to the past? How to secure continuity? Where to live? How to die? The work discloses, once again, the circular pattern of life's journey from birth to death and asserts at the end some of Herbert Read's most cherished values:

> First Voice   Yes: men should hold on to tangible things.
>   Stay with me in these hills and glens
>   where the birds cry lovingly to their young
>   and the waters are never silent.

Third Voice	Die to the day and its trivialities Die to the sense of time.
First Voice	Or to the sense of place to the place of generation and birth.
Third Voice	Live with the sun by day and with the stars by night.
First Voice	Live with your eyes and ears and the exercise of your subtle fingers.
Third Voice	Live in the moment of attention.
First Voice	Live in the presence of things.[16]

Yet, for all this, *Moon's Farm* remains an embarrassing artistic failure. The abstractions lack concrete embodiment and float in a verse so free it seems entirely formless. The protective restraints of imagism with its demand for precision and cadence had been cast aside but no other principles of effective organization had taken their place. The writing *does* show the influence of T. S. Eliot's *Four Quartets* but the influence is hugely destructive, creating lines of an irredeemable deadness where philosophy (of a kind) merely uses words as the functional elements of intellectual description. The verse-drama is a disaster but it does enable us to identify one of the major weaknesses of Herbert Read – a tendency to write in a thin cerebral manner – as also to isolate in contrast the few, very few, autobiographical poems which work as *poetry* – 'Sonnet' and 'The Solitary Hermit', for example. It also enables us to see the actual poetic achievement of *The Innocent Eye*.

If the first brilliant part of *The Contrary Experience* re-creates the child's vision, the second and third parts are largely about its loss in the alienation of adolescence, in the trauma of the First World War and in the development of intellectual life. The reader who is curious about the specific fate of the ten-year-old boy has to turn to 'The Falcon and the Dove' to discover what happened to him. There in the opening chapter entitled 'A Callow Nestling' the story is continued:

One day in the year 1904, a bewildered and fatherless boy, I was quietly withdrawn from this world and taken a devious train journey across the country. I still retain some memory of the nightmarish impression made by the cavernous stations where we changed trains; and I remember our cab rattling along the roughly cobbled streets of the town which was our destination. We climbed up steep hills, past dark satanic mills, and emerged eventually on a high bare moor, at the other side of which rose the largest building I had ever seen. Built of local stone in a style that must, I now realise, have been copied from some monument of the French Renaissance, blackened by the smoke which drifted across the moor from the surrounding factories, this was the orphanage school in which I was to spend the next five years of my life, in an isolation no less absolute than that of my infancy.[17]

And yet just as the narrative begins, the author intervenes and informs his reader: 'I do not intend to write much about this period of my life because I do not think it is of general interest'. The visionary world of innocence is to be re-created but not, it seems, the divided and often anguished world of experience. Why is this? The reason given by Read is, of course, defensive and insufficient. Again and again, in his writing Herbert Read evades self-exposure and vulnerability. In his final apologia *The Cult of Sincerity* he writes:

> I have never written about the real horror of fighting, which is not death nor the fear of mutilation, discomfort or filth, but a psychopathic state of hallucination in which the world becomes unreal and you no longer *know* whether your experience is valid – in other words, whether you are any longer sane.[18]

This is a characteristic confession; extreme turbulent states of feeling are to be avoided. Later in the same essay, considering a certain cynical habit of mind among modern artists, he writes: 'I was born with an innocence that is abashed by such cynicism, and for this reason alone I must retire into silence, or into the sacrificial busy-ness of committees'.[19] *Retiring into silence* – but that is a peculiar trait for an autobiographer! It is, however, a trait that Herbert Read saw as an indelible part of his own character. In fact, his most honest self-portrait is given to us obliquely and half-consciously in his biography of Wordsworth. In portraying Wordsworth he betrays himself:

> Yorkshire men are imaginative, like all northmen, but a matter-of-factness, a strong sense of objectivity, a faculty for vivid visualisation, keep them from being profoundly mystical. The same qualities make them wary in their actions, and canny in their reckonings. But their most extraordinary characteristic – a characteristic with which in the process of time they have leavened almost the entire English race – is their capacity for masking their emotions. It is not a question of suppression, nor of atrophy; the normal feelings of the human being are present in more than their normal force, but banked up against this impenetrable reserve. No doubt, as a protective device, this iron mask has had historical advantages. And in the domestic sphere it ensures a business-like despatch of those affairs, such as births, deaths and marriages, which tend to choke up the existence of a more expansive people.
>
> In all this, Wordsworth was a true northerner. Indeed, it is almost impossible to understand his life and character unless we remember his racial capacity for masking the strength of his feelings. Wordsworth, as his sister Dorothy once said, was a man violent in affection. But it was necessary to affirm that fact. Outwardly

he was cold, even hard. Inwardly he was all fire. But true to his type, he was not going to give himself away – not even in his poetry, not even in the most inspired moments of his creative activity. Passion, of course, does blaze from many a poem of Wordsworth's; but not the direct passion of profane love, not even the direct passion of sacred love, but passion transmuted into impersonal things – rocks, and stones, and trees.[20]

'That', writes George Woodcock, quoting this passage in his study *Herbert Read: The Stream and the Source*, 'is Read almost to the life.'[21] The paradox seen in Wordsworth the poet is also the paradox that marks Read the autobiographer. We will be given impersonal things: rocks, and stones, and trees – and orchards, and greens, and mills. We will be given a map of intellectual ideas and abstract conceptions; but the extreme moments of human experience, such as birth, death and marriage, will be despatched quietly in a business-like manner. It is interesting that in *The Innocent Eye* Read refers to the 'overweening objectivity' of his 'childish mind'[22] – for it is precisely this overweening objectivity that inhibits the painful subjectivity of the adult mind. Read is not going to give himself away; that is the conscious intention. Yet there *are* moments in his writing when his own predicament and division are presented to the reader but, then, not exactly in the places where the reader would expect.

The most dramatic example of this kind of writing is in the essay 'Apology for E.S.' in *The Cult of Sincerity*. In this short memoir Herbert Read describes his encounter with Eugene Strickland, a born administrator he meets in the Civil Service after the First World War. Herbert Read writes of this ambitious man, who discards his gift as a poet because the age has no place for poetry and selects the life of politics for his career: 'I did not at first succeed in penetrating the reserve of this strange man... I even once or twice introduced him to the young poets... but his attitude to them was one of icy disdain'.[23] He then reveals that Strickland was drawn to the author: 'there must have been something in my personality which attracted him, and which in due course led to the confession which has prompted this short memoir'. What follows is a long letter sent by Strickland to Read. It is introspective and explores the repression of feeling and the final denial of poetic reverie:

> According to the circumstances that then began to determine my development, I became a poet because words were the first tools that were put into my hands to express the desperate need I had to find signs or symbols for my inmost feelings... The daily usage I made of speech was at first a sufficient art, and it was only when I went to school and was taught that speech had uses other than the communication of feeling that I became aware of some sundering of my very self. From that moment I spoke two languages – the inner language that expressed my feelings and the outer language that I addressed to other people to satisfy their

expectations. I answered the questions that tested my knowledge of the world, and discovered, as all children do, that in order to please my parents and teachers, I had to acquire a knowledge of external facts – of numbers, measurements, grammar and history. The language of my feelings I might still use for intimate occasions, to convey to those I loved my affections and desires; but it so happened that my family life came to a sudden end in my tenth year and I was then suddenly thrown into an alien world where there was no use for a language of feeling. My sensitive antennae recoiled into my innermost being, and for eight years I remained a dumb and frightened animal.[24]

The aim of the last half of the 'Apology for E.S.' is to put a convincing case against this intelligent and calculated denial of the poetic life. That is the intention of the memoir. But reading the letter from Eugene Strickland we sense an uncanny resemblance to Herbert Read's life. He, too, had been preoccupied with the nature of feeling and reverie; he, too, had wondered whether to enter politics or the life of poetry; he, too, at the age of ten had been thrown out of his childhood world and its security.

Who, then, is this twin-brother? The status of E.S. becomes clear as soon as we know that Strickland was Read's mother's surname and the E.S. were her initials (Eliza Strickland). He had also used this name once before as a pseudonym when submitting an article in 1920 to the *Athenaeum*. The fictional letter reveals the kind of character and decision that his mother would like to have seen; it also discloses that one of the reasons for his ambition was the image of his father: 'The thought of my own father's brief and obscure life was perhaps always present to my consciousness'.[25] Through the mask of the *other* Herbert Read is able to tell us more about his adult identity than he can in his explicit autobiographies. Through the personae of Eugene Strickland, Wordsworth and Shelley he is able to disclose more fully his own inner conflicts than through the vulnerable first-person singular of confessional autobiography.

The implications of this iron mask and impenetrable reserve for the explicit autobiographies are not too difficult to define. It means that we will find virtually no analysis or re-creation of states of feeling, of the dialectics of human relationship, of actual moments of crisis, division, ambivalence, ambiguity, extremity. It means that where strong emotional states are at work they will be transferred to other objects (to rocks and stones and trees) and that this will require the reader to make a similar transposition but in reverse, from the object back to the author's consciousness. It will require, at times, a psychoanalytical disposition in the reader: the art of reading at a tangent, of detecting masks, of sensing displacement, of re-locating the meaning of metaphors in the concealed life of the author. But even so, much will not be available for knowledge or scrutiny. It means also that the explicit concerns of *The Contrary Experience*, once the innocence of childhood has been poetically re-created, will be mostly confined to the general life of ideas or, at the end of the book, with the objects and places, established in the first section, but now without the earlier visionary intensity.

At first sight, an exception to the above remarks would seem to be the autobiographical writing relating to Read's experience as an officer in the First World War. There are three chapters in *The Contrary Experience* re-creating this experience: 'The Impact of War', 'The Raid', 'In Retreat'. Also the whole of Part Two is called 'A War Diary 1915–18'. The former pieces are carefully constructed narratives and, while clearly deriving from Read's experience, have the shape and impact of stories. Lieutenant P—, in 'The Raid', strikes one as an alter ego allowing the author to explore his own negative feelings, his anxiety and potential cowardice, rather than an actual person encountered in the trenches. They are vivid accounts of the drama and absurdity of the First World War. The 'War Diary' is different and requires some deconstruction. The 'War Diary' was not composed as a diary but as a series of letters written to Evelyn Roff, the woman who was to become, rather tragically, his first wife. The so-called diary is made up of extracts from seventy-six letters written between 28 January 1915 and 14 November 1918. According to his biographer, James King:

> Read instructed his typist (his daughter Sophie) to remove all salutations, closings and endearments, and later he blue-pencilled many passages in the typescript before it was sent to the printer. Then, he burned the letters. (None of Evelyn's letters to him have survived.) Earlier, he or Evelyn destroyed the letters in which he frankly discussed the sexual aspects of their courtship.[26]

In the opening remarks, setting the diary in context, Herbert Read gives a most devious explanation of its genesis and its context. He explains that the author was at a provincial university in 1915, where he met:

> … an unexpected supporter in a young student of biology, a woman of approximately his own age. It was with this almost casual acquaintance that he began to exchange letters as a relief to the otherwise intolerable loneliness of his new surroundings. As there was at first no possibility of pursuing the friendship 'face to face' the letters were given the impersonal form of a diary, and it is as such that they are presented in the following pages.[27]

If not false, this account is very economical with the truth. The diary came out of love letters to the woman he married and later deserted and who became progressively deranged as a result of the experience. This is 'a business-like despatch', if ever there was one, and an all but dishonest masking of emotion, the topping and tailing of all endearment.

What remains of the so-called 'War Diary' shows for the most part a young man's intellectual fascination with all things intellectual. It is brittle with the thin play of ideas and intellectual movements, and at the end, in the closing entries, it reveals a shrewd man adept at what today we call 'networking':

> Met Ezra at 11.30... I broached the future and found him rather sympathetic.[28]

> I am meeting Osbert Sitwell on Thursday to discuss the future.[29]

> Ezra had advised me to go and see Miss Weaver (Editor of the *Egoist*) re project 4.[30]

As a record it has a certain psychological and historical value, but little significance beyond that.

What follows in *The Contrary Experience* is closer to the 'War Diary' than to *The Innocent Eye*. The writing could best be described as intellectual apologia of a rather gentle kind. The dominant tone is modest and calm. The chapters are rather prolix: occasionally eloquent, occasionally bland, but almost never as good as the authors they discuss – Kierkegaard, Bergson, D. H. Lawrence, Jung, Freud, etc. We are taken through a gallery of pictures – I am thinking here of *The Cult of Sincerity* as much as *The Contrary Experience* – with a genial guide, apt to digress. There is, though, another tone of voice which destroys the gentle pattern and increasingly breaks in as we move towards the last writing. This tone is one of utter despondency, of terrible despair, of an irredeemable sense of futility. As so often in Herbert Read, this is most fully projected on to another figure:

> I despair when I think of John Ruskin, for he was a man endowed with sense and sensibility, energy and leisure, who throughout a long lifetime fought with eloquence and passionate clarity for the values I have fought for, and in the end was utterly defeated. The younger generations no longer read him and their elders no longer teach them to read him. His numerous works are the cheapest remnants in the boxes reserved for books that nobody will even steal. Yet what Ruskin has to say, about civilization and culture, about art and literature, about politics and economics, is still relevant to the problems of our own time. The evils and wrongs he denounced have continued to flourish since he died more than sixty years ago, a sad and demented old man.[31]

That Read felt his own work was to follow the same course as his intellectual mentor is almost certain. At the end of his life he despaired of a civilization he no longer wanted to be part of:

> It is difficult for the modern poet to have any confidence in the future of poetry. It is the first art to perish in the depersonalised desert of a cybernetic civilization; music and painting will soon follow, and art in general will cease to be a meaningful dialogue between man and man.[32]

> All modern developments – weed-killers, motor-cars, tractors, mechanization, tourism, the radio, the cinema, urbanization (words as ugly as the things

they signify) – have combined to destroy the countryside that was evident to my innocent eye.[33]

Here, then, we finally encounter one further paradox. The modernist art-critic who believed in a dialectic of historical advance, who was quick to promote new ideas and relate them to the urgency of their historical moment, confessing (and not able to identify the inner contradiction) that all modern developments had been aesthetically ugly and had destroyed all that was most pleasing to the eye of innocence. The acclaimed champion of the new becomes the solitary despairing hermit! At the heart of *The Contrary Experience* lurks an unresolved and unsublimated contradiction.

III

How, then, are we to evaluate Herbert Read's contribution to autobiography? At a stylistic level we discover a plurality of forms. Herbert Read makes use of letters and diaries; he writes memoir and apologia; he writes clear autobiographical poems as well as employing verse-drama; he writes straight impersonal autobiography and he also uses fiction (inventing characters such as Lieutenant P– and Eugene Strickland). An astonishing range of experimentation, yet the work also confronts us with a number of paradoxes and problems which make any quick judgements impossible.

The greatest paradox lies in the guarded reticence of the man. Here is an author who writes autobiographically for so much of the time and who also writes various works of explicit autobiography, yet who is, by disposition, extremely guarded and deeply reserved: a man with 'an iron mask'. His contribution to the great tradition of subjective autobiography established by St Augustine and running through Rousseau into the nineteenth century is virtually nil. There is no astute or sustained analysis of inner states of personal feeling. Yet, at the same time, *The Innocent Eye* is a remarkable re-creation of childhood experience or, more accurately, childhood experience mediated through the transforming power of memory and poetic language. It is a unique prose-poem of memory as vision. It will survive as such. If Herbert Read had possessed the same gift for exploring states of inner division and self-consciousness, if he had been able to put against the open eye of innocence the infected weeping eye of experience, then he would have written a broader masterpiece. This, as we have seen, Herbert Read was unable to do.

What else does his work offer? Some limited but moving accounts of the First World War, a few poems of moderate achievement and many essays of intellectual self-justification and examination which are nearly always lucid but, in the final analysis, too eclectic, too general, too diffuse to be of lasting significance. They offer an historical and personal record but they rarely disclose a philosophical mind equal to those who are examined.

There is a further problem which, at the beginning of the chapter, I promised to return to. Informing Herbert Read's work is a major myth concerning Innocence and Experience. Again and again, not unlike Rousseau, he compares himself to an Innocent lost in a confusing world of Experience. The state of Innocence, the category of ultimate self-validation, is seen to have its origin in childhood; thus a dynamic is set up of *going back*, of *returning*, of *final re-union*. In this myth (which Herbert Read lived out with a certain consistency) civilization becomes inherently ambiguous because while it 'educates' it also corrupts, destroys, falsifies, divides. In *The Cult of Sincerity* Herbert Read, affirming the absorbing power and beauty of the senses in childhood, goes on to claim: 'These are the sensations and feelings that are gradually blunted by education, staled by custom, rejected in favour of social conformity'.[34] As we have seen, the childhood experience of unity in his own life was broken by the death of his father and by compulsory attendance at a repressive orphanage. In other words, the verbal abstractions of Herbert Read carry an invisible autobiographical trauma which, in turn, carries an archetypal schema: Innocence/Experience, Vision/Corruption, Unity/Alienation. But questions have to be asked. How true is this schema? Does it apply to most people's lives? Could it even constitute some kind of defence against a more plural and ambivalent reality? In Herbert Read's case, for example, does it show an impossible idealization of experience before his father's death psychologically necessary for him to survive the trauma and the terrible loss?

The latter question cannot be resolved easily, but the former questions can – for many people simply do not possess visionary memories from their childhood which subsequently form the centre of their lives. For these individuals, history is an inescapable dimension of personal existence and culture (and even schooling) an essential and 'natural' means of self-development. These people do not look backwards for the resolution of their lives, but forward. Any meaning they might claim for their existence would reside in that arc of time which moves always from the instant now into an open future. For them, 'a return to innocence' is not a meaningful imperative. For them, the act of becoming has more significance, the adventure forwards into the undisclosed.

The myth of Innocence and Experience so crucial to Herbert Read's autobiography is, also, crucial to much of his theoretical writing, particularly to his theory of aesthetic education – where there is a marked tendency to see the child's creativity as original and pristine and the influences of culture and history as corrupting and alienating. The Innocent Visionary Child has to be kept out of that terrible orphanage for as long as possible! A hidden autobiography, driven by mythical absolutes, runs through the writing. As readers we need the skills to excavate the concealed, personal and mythical elements. We may want to respect those elements but, at the same time, we must analyse the ways in which they distort the general argument for, in the last analysis, good autobiography is not, necessarily, good philosophy and a myth of any kind is dangerous when it is made literal or when it remains unconscious.

98

Herbert Read's autobiographies, both the explicit and implicit, call for new acts of critical interpretation. In this chapter I hope I have shown some of the possibilities and some of the problems, both in the critical reading of autobiography and in the evaluation of Herbert Read's uneven contribution to the genre.

Notes

1 Herbert Read, *The Contrary Experience: Autobiographies* (London: Secker and Warburg, 1973), p. 344.
2 Ibid.
3 Ibid.
4 Herbert Read, *Collected Poems* (London: Sinclair-Stevenson, n.d.) p. 18.
5 Ibid., p. 16.
6 Read, *The Contrary Experience*, p. 175.
7 Ibid., pp. 53–54.
8 Ibid., p. 27.
9 Ibid., p. 31.
10 Ibid., p. 30.
11 Ibid., p. 50.
12 Ibid., p. 54.
13 Ibid., pp. 16–17.
14 Ibid., p. 24.
15 Read, *Collected Poems*, p. 191.
16 Ibid., pp. 223–24.
17 Read, *The Contrary Experience*, pp. 149–50.
18 Herbert Read, *The Cult of Sincerity* (London: Faber and Faber, 1968), p. 54.
19 Ibid., p. 57.
20 Herbert Read, *Wordsworth* (London: Faber and Faber, 2nd edn, 1949), pp. 37–38.
21 George Woodcock, *Herbert Read: The Stream and the Source* (London: Faber and Faber, 1972), p. 152.
22 Read, *The Contrary Experience*, p. 37.
23 Read, *The Cult of Sincerity*, pp. 60–61.
24 Ibid., p. 62.
25 Ibid., p. 64.
26 James King, *The Last Modern: A Life of Herbert Read* (London: Weidenfeld and Nicolson, 1990), p. 44.
27 Read, *The Contrary Experience*, pp. 60–61.
28 Ibid., p. 140.
29 Ibid., p. 141.
30 Ibid., p. 142.
31 Read, *The Cult of Sincerity*, p. 56.
32 Ibid., p. 74.
33 Read, *The Contrary Experience*, p. 342.
34 Read, *The Cult of Sincerity*, p. 17.

Herbert Read as Novelist: *The Green Child*

BOB BARKER

IN *Homage to Catalonia* (1938), Orwell referred to 'the deep, deep sleep of England, from which I sometimes fear we shall never wake until we are jerked out of it by the roar of bombs'.[1] Yet ironically, he himself had lived from October 1934 to August 1935 in Hampstead, where 'England' had been in one sense anything but 'asleep'. Here was Read's 'nest of gentle artists',[2] that concentration of internationally significant talent including Henry Moore, Paul Nash, Ben Nicholson, Barbara Hepworth, and indeed Read himself, who called the period 'the happiest of my life'.[3] Amongst the varied works which the 'nest' produced, his only completed novel casts interesting sidelights both on those other 'gentle artists', and on much of his own writing. *The Green Child* is also a significant work in its own right, remarkable for its cool yet vivid style; the latter is scarcely surprising, given Read's talent

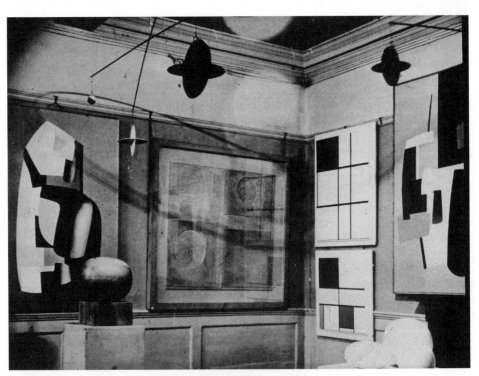

The Abstract and the Concrete Exhibition, February 1936, Oxford

The summer house at 3, The Mall Studios where Read wrote most of *The Green Child*.
(photo Simon Shorvon)

as a poet and his incisive *English Prose Style*, written a few years earlier.[4]

He composed the novel relatively quickly (with most of the text complete after six to eight weeks),[5] and there may be a trace of his growing interest in unconscious composition in that the first sixteen pages of the manuscript (written out separately on a different type of paper) seem to record a dream or reverie.[6] This memorable opening, which has a touch of Gothic fantasy about it, leads to two other fantastic realms, one political and one aesthetic. A look at the manuscript, and comparison with the sources, however – especially with the two which Read never publicly acknowledged (Jowett's 1892 *Phaedo* and John and William Robertson's *Letters on Paraguay* [1838–39]) – suggest a style of composition that could hardly have been unconscious. Nineteenth-century sources should not surprise us, and modernist though he may have been, Read during this period was neither an anarchist nor a surrealist. He was dallying (like Eliot and Pound) with the politics of Social Credit and (like the others in the Unit One group) with constructivist aesthetics. Both of these philosophies are detectable in the novel.

In the first paragraph President 'Olivero', ex-ruler of some South American state, is returning, after a faked assassination, to the England where he was born. His motive for this return is 'to escape from the sense of time, to live in the eternity of what he was accustomed to call *the divine essence of things*',[7] which highly Platonic imagery aptly foreshadows the novel's conclusion. It is also significant that Part One begins as it (and the novel's other two parts) ends, with Olivero's apparent death; which in each case signifies his translation to a profounder level of existence.

When he arrives at the village he had left thirty years before, everything already seems tinged with timelessness, and the local stream is quietly flowing backwards. Olivero follows it in the moonlight, retracing paths familiar from childhood:

> Nothing occurred to interrupt his progress – the stream flowed on before him; he could both see and hear the direction of the water. It went laughing over the stones in its bed, mocking him, luring him onwards.[8]

The participles here – laughing, mocking, luring – recall those tales about fairies leading travellers away to a land where time almost stands still. The original twelfth-century story of the Green Children which Read used, both here and in *English Prose Style*,[9] is indeed part of this fairy tradition; typically, he had found it in a nineteenth-century source, Keightley's *The Fairy Mythology* (1833). The stream leads Olivero to a mill, where he sees a decidedly Gothic tableau through the window: a frail woman, bound to a chair and being forced by the miller to drink from a bowl of blood. Olivero starts to climb through the window, but it drops down and traps him temporarily with his legs 'waving wildly inside the room',[10] before he can emerge, like Alice, into the fantastic world beyond the glass.

The surreal tone may have been intentional, since it recalls an event which André Breton recounted in his *Manifeste du Surréalisme – Poisson Soluble* (Paris, 1924); as he was going to sleep one evening, he distinctly 'heard' the phrase: 'There's a man cut in two by the window'. Read himself mentioned this in his *Concise History of Modern Painting* (1959)[11] to illustrate the origins of surrealism. Olivero's return is also a reworking, in reverse, of part of Read's poem 'Huskisson Sacred and Profane', published in 1919. The protagonist, rather than returning to England after disappearing in South America, here sets out for South America after disappearing in England, although his escape too leads somehow back to childhood. The fourth and final section of the poem (not subsequently republished) closely prefigured Olivero's journey:

> At the age of forty-seven
> Having settled an annuity on his wife Emily,
> Huskisson disappeared one August evening.
> The newspapers talked of him for less than nine days,
> And the detectives were anything but active at that time of the year.
> Emily, after a spasmodic grief lasting fourteen days,
> Found consolation in the works of Boehme.

Huskisson, down in the docks,
Booked a passage in the *Queen of the Incas*.
En voyage
He grew a beard like Walt Whitman's
And became
Companion of low men and lascars.
He disembarked at Rio...[12]

Read himself attempted a mid-life return to his Yorkshire origins in 1949, when he moved to Stonegrave. One of his favourite excursions then was to walk up Hodge Beck, the original of Olivero's stream, to the mill at Bransdale, which he called 'my spiritual hermitage, the "bright jewel" to which I often retire in moods of despair'.[13] In his verse drama *Moon's Farm*, broadcast on the Third Programme in January 1951, the autobiographical 'Second Voice' ('Self' in the manuscript)[14] returns, after a life of action, to find peace and, in the end, death, in such a childhood environment:

As boys we used to come here
    to gather wild daffodils.
At Moon's Farm the pump was in the kitchen
    a well of clean crystal water.
And there was an old clock
    standing opposite the kitchen door.
It had a robin
    or perhaps a wren
painted on its white face
    but the fingers never moved.
It was always 12.25 at Moon's Farm.
12.25 is God's time.[15]

The timelessness of this spot is also conveyed in the prose piece 'The Mill At The World's End' (1963): 'the windows are all broken and the loosened tiles slither one by one into the beck. Time and life stand still.'[16] The title alludes to William Morris's *The Well at the World's End* (1896), and 'Time and life stand still' is an ironic reference to the inscription placed on the Bransdale sundial by a nineteenth-century ancestor of Read's: 'Time and life move swiftly'. In 'The Visionary Hermit' (1965), he referred to both of them again:

An ancestor of mine lived here
    a century and a half ago
carved his name on the lintel
    and a verse from the Greek bible

built a sundial on a grassy mound

incised:
    'Time and life move swiftly
     Quod hora est vide'

Now the doors are rotted
    the glass in the windows broken
the road obliterated: only the black-faced sheep
    visit this place

the silence substantial
    the millwheel unmoving
the granaries empty
    the wide moors
      an oasis enfolding

a mill at the world's end[17]

After he stopped using the loose sheets of these opening sixteen pages of manuscript, Read employed one section of the exercise-book paper on which the bulk of the novel is written for the title:

INLAND FAR

by

HERBERT READ

This original title clearly alludes to Wordsworth's Immortality Ode and the 'bright landscape'[18] of childhood that casts its spell over later life. A second page of this section bears the phrase 'Part 1' and this epigraph, just as follows:

Reminiscence

~~Self~~

~~La~~ ~~The power of reflection~~ is
R   the condition of all productivity

S. KIERKEGAARD

Once more Read, far from being forever 'progressive' was again placing his novel in a nineteenth-century context; in 1940 he classed Kierkegaard very much with Wordsworth, as 'essentially a poet, a child of the Romantic Movement'.[19]

At the point where the initial sixteen pages of manuscript end, neither the man nor the woman at the mill has been identified, but almost immediately the manuscript text recommences on the exercise-book paper used from here onwards (as if Read had started writing again after a gap and with some new ideas); Olivero exclaims: 'It is the Green Child' and recalls what he had heard of her first arrival, which created a 'sensation, not only in the village, but throughout the whole world of newspapers, the very day he left home thirty years ago'.[20]

Having recognized the girl, whose appearance in the world was 'obscurely connected with his departure, and connected too with the inevitability of his return',[21] he now remembers the miller too, and explains that, thirty years before, as 'Oliver' the village schoolteacher, he had resigned in despair after he saw the boy Kneeshaw commit an act of vandalism, deliberately over-winding a prized clockwork engine.[22] It is in a sense to this unfinished business that Olivero has now returned.

The Green Child herself is a symbolic sibling or *alter ego* to both Olivero and Kneeshaw; she represents a state prior to all sentiment and is not only vegetarian, but herself curiously vegetal. Her preferred diet (trout, watercress) is appropriate to a water-nymph, as are her coloration and her few interests:

> Only the sound of rippling water interested her and she would play for whole days in the pebbly bed of the stream [*manuscript:*... making waterfalls][23]

and the final paragraph of Part One refers to 'her green naiad figure'.[24]

At this point in the manuscript, on the next left-hand page, are pencilled notes outlining the rest of Part One:

> the parlour again
> g g sleeping – O's love revealed
> return
> man to man
> a crescendo of hate
>   sudden attack
>   race around the house – in the yard – ?the mill
>   the sluice and mill wheel
>   at grips – moonlight
>   the end of K
> back to the g g
> waiting for dawn
> the early sunlight
> the walk in the alders
>   K's body drifting past
> Olivero's story[25]

This suggests that Read had not planned the plot of Part One much before he reached this point, and even these notes seem provisional, as in the evident uncertainty over whether the fight should continue into the mill, in that the 'alders' became willows and that Kneeshaw's drowned body is not 'drifting past', but floating among 'withered sedge'[26] in a backwater.

From the moment Olivero struggles through the window out of the moonlit night he has been in a world whose patterns are increasingly those of the unconscious mind, in which fragments of memory are reassorted or transformed. Significantly, in *The Innocent Eye* (1933), Read recalled that at school:

> my own imagination was most strongly fired by Rider Haggard, and never have I known such absorption and excitement as gripped me when I first read *King Solomon's Mines* and *Montezuma's Daughter*.[27]

Both of these romances influenced the novel. For example in *Montezuma's Daughter* the hero, after many years of adventures (imprisoned in Cadiz, ruler for twenty years of an independent state in South America), returns in the moonlight to his native village in England, where firmly, but with a Spanish courtliness, he saves his former sweetheart from marriage to his unsavoury brother. Olivero and Kneeshaw are quasi-brothers, sharing the same surrogate mother, obsessed with the same quasi-sister, and each eventually meeting his fate in a pool in the same stream.

Kneeshaw is distinguished from Olivero, however, by adjectives including 'instinctive',[28] 'dumb', 'blind',[29] 'unread', 'inarticulate',[30] 'primitive',[31] 'simple',[32] 'animal'[33] and especially 'sullen';[34] he also 'breathes like a doomed bull'[35] and it is no accident that it is animal blood that he is trying to force between the Green Child's lips when Olivero returns. Like the ignorant eleven-year-old boy he had been thirty years earlier, Kneeshaw still lacks the command of language which Olivero has now gained. In *Annals of Innocence and Experience* (1940), Read wrote as follows of this 'pre-adolescent' phase:

> From the age of ten or eleven to the age of fifteen or sixteen is the least genial period in the life of a boy. He has lost the innocent eye of childhood and has not yet become an experiencing nature. It is a callow and confused phase... the vague emotions which are aroused by our environment, by strange experiences, by the unknown – for these we have no ready words. We cannot impart our moods, even to our most intimate friends. Children of this intermediate age suffer like animals, dumbly and vaguely.[36]

'Kneeshaw' is a name that also appears in 'Kneeshaw Goes to War', a poem which Read wrote while still on active service in 1918. It describes the catharsis endured by one inexperienced infantryman (from the name, a Yorkshireman) in Flanders. This early 'Kneeshaw' combines characteristics of all the three personae of the novel. He begins almost as plant-like as the Green Child, becoming anaemic for lack of sunshine:

> Ernest Kneeshaw grew
> In the forest of his dreams
> Like a woodland flower whose anaemic petals
> Need the sun.[37]

However, like the novel-Kneeshaw, he displays an extreme of Yorkshire phlegm, being 'Like a cold steel mirror – emotionless'. Eventually his mind (like Olivero's) is broadened by action and experience, and he achieves inner peace in the contemplation of beauty:

> *I stand on this hill and accept*
> *The flowers at my feet and the deep*
> *Beauty of the still tarn...*[38]

The interdependence of the three in the novel is evident from the neat choreography whereby 'Oliver' leaves the village when Kneeshaw first threatens the innocence of which the Green Child is the 'objective correlative' and they return together to her original world once Kneeshaw is overcome. In the terminology which Read employed in *Form in Modern Poetry* (1932), the green innocence of the 'personality' was nearly always repressed beneath the chrysalis of the inarticulate 'character' in the contemporary world.[39] However, some few individuals might (like Olivero, or many of the painters and poets whom Read admired) recover the 'innocent eye' through creative reflection and reminiscence.

Furthermore, like Kneeshaw, the Green Child reappears in Read's poetry, as he himself acknowledged in 'Daphne' (1961),[40] which also refers to the nymph's 'green tresses'.[41] His very first volume of verse, *Songs of Chaos*, had contained a long sub-Keatsian work, 'The Song of the Lark', in which the poet is beguiled by supernatural music, a magic stream and a mute fairy into 'deep caverns' where music echoes.[42] 'Tourists in a Sacred Place' (written about ten years before the novel) invoked another musical proto-Green Child, 'Cecily' (St Cecilia?), with 'naiad face' to 'rebuild the strong defences of age and innocence' of (perhaps) Rievaulx, invaded by tourists:

> Your tresses are wet from the rushing river
> a green weed clings like a vein on your breast.[43]

Olivero is able to redeem the Green Child because, since leaving England, he has mastered a series of new languages and new philosophies. Imprisonment in Cadiz results from his initial political and linguistic ignorance, but his fellow prisoners teach him both their liberal politics, and also to express himself 'clearly and fluently' in Spanish.[44] His journey from Buenos Aires to Roncador, like his return to the mill, has a dream-like intensity, as he travels 'inland far' along the banks of the river and towards his upland utopia. Soon after arriving, he composes a new provisional constitution, in a passage that perhaps reflects the manner in which Read wrote the novel itself (i.e., quickly, but with careful revision and reference to suitable authorities):

it was only after several cups of yerba tea, and frequent recourse to Rousseau and

Volney, that my phrases began to take form once again. Then I wrote swiftly and clearly, and was able to spend the second day in reviewing and correcting the periods of our proclamation.[45]

A passage, describing the assassination of the ruling Dictator, is one of those in the novel which was 'reviewed and corrected' quite closely, and in which the style rises above its usual unadorned clarity to the intensity of a prose-poem, especially in the manuscript version, which differs significantly from the published text. At first, during the *corrida*, time seems to 'drag on interminably',[46] but after the last bull is killed there is a growing sense of expectancy. Both versions develop a staccato rhythm, but in the manuscript a sudden lack of verbs creates an almost impressionist immediacy (or could we say that Read has again adopted another Victorian style – of Carlylean condensation?):

> Intent. Now through the frame. The ring swinging idly behind. On unswervingly, swift, swift; an indrawn cry, a confused rising of men. The body of the rider very low, one with the horse and its far-flung hooves. The flash of sunlight on the lance. The horse upreared, high against the palisading. Then the downward lunge. The action of St. George. Then all confusion, aimless and astonished cries. People running across the ring from all sides.[47]

It may seem ironic that Olivero overthrows this dictator, only to become one himself. However, in 1934–35, Read did express a belief in some social regimentation, at least of economic activity, e.g., in the essay first published as 'The Intellectual and Liberty':

> From certain points of view, therefore, I can welcome the notion of the totalitarian state, whether in its Fascist or Communist form. I am not afraid of the totalitarian state as an economic fact, an economic machine to facilitate the complex business of living in a community.[48]

(He later muted these remarks, and finally removed them altogether, in versions of the essay republished, as 'Essential Communism', in 1935 and 1938.)[49]

Olivero's second opponent in Roncador, the river-pirate Vargas, is shot in the throat and dies speechless, whereas Olivero is by now eloquent in several languages, including Guarani. Vargas's death, trapped in a hut among the bullocks' skulls, has something of the ignominious clumsiness of Kneeshaw's. Olivero, however, leaves both Vargas's camp, and eventually Roncador itself, in moonlit river journeys (recalling his journey upstream to the mill):

> The funeral pyre still burned with a lurid light in the darkness behind us; before us the stars hung above Roncador. In spite of our victory we were silent; only the creaking of our saddles, and the jingle of our equipment, rose above the soft thunder of hooves.[50]

108

When Read began the novel he seems to have intended to make Olivero in South America simply a 'man of action', who only later returned to art and contemplation; but in the published text President Olivero becomes in some respects 'an artist seeking a mode of expression'.[51] However, having created a rustic Utopia, he deliberately refuses to spoil the simple innocence of its citizens (as he had earlier refused to spoil that of his school pupils) by complicating matters. Convinced that he himself must leave or else stagnate, he decides that he must depart 'in a cloud of glory'[52] (undoubtedly another deliberate echo of Wordsworth).

Olivero's Napoleonic rise to sole authority very accurately reflects the more sinister career of the historical Dictator Francia in nineteenth-century Paraguay, chronicled in the novel's main source. Benedict Read has identified two volumes of that work[53] (which, however, in 1952 his father apparently could not 'come across'[54] when Louis Adeane was researching *The Green Child*) in the library at Stonegrave. They are from the first (1838–39) edition of John and William Robertson's *Letters on Paraguay* (Volume 2 is now wrapped in the inside-out dust-jacket of a copy of Read's *Collected Poems 1913–25*). At the back of this volume, where an appendix gives the census figures for the chief towns of the Jesuit *Misiones*, one line of figures was marked in pencil; these are for Candelaria, and prove to be identical with those which Read gave to his city of 'Roncador' (754 families, 3,064 souls, 4,632 tame cattle, 1,780 oxen, 1,510 horses, 3,791 mares, 501 mules, 198 asses, 4,648 sheep and a few goats).[55] Read seems not to have begun using the *Letters* until after he had written a substantial amount of Part One, but in Part Two there are dozens of very clear borrowings from this source; the name Roncador itself, for example, can be found on a map inside the front cover of Volume 1. Generally the details borrowed were such names and aspects of local history, geography and culture, but Read rigorously omitted all the Robertsons' hostile comments on the regimes of both the Jesuits and of Francia. He usually pruned the descriptive passages, typically to just over four-fifths of their original length, but did not much alter the style, which fits remarkably well with his own. For example, in this description of the pampas:

> I saw thistles higher than the horse, with the rider on his back; here and there a few clumps of the Algarroba tree; long grass; innumerable herds of cattle, wild and tame; deer and ostriches bounded over the plain; bearded biscachas (a sort of rabbit) coming out at evening by groups from their thousand burrows which intersect the country; now the whirring partridge flying from under my horse's feet, and anon the little mailed armadillo making haste to get out of the way.[56]

Read's version, but slightly more energetic, is:

> The grasses and plants that grew by the side of the road were of gigantic size – the thistles in particular rearing their crowns and jagged branches like fantastic

trees above our heads. Great herds of cattle moved like migrations over the plain; deer and ostriches bounded from our path, and smaller animals, the bearded biscachas and the mailed armadillo, met our onset with sudden surprise; whilst every few hundred yards a covey of partridges would rise whirring from under our feet.[57]

There was also a third volume to the *Letters*. To have used this (entitled *Francia's Reign of Terror* in an American edition) as a source for Olivero's peaceful utopia required quite a transformation, but Read certainly did so, though there seems now not to be a copy at Stonegrave. In this volume William Robertson wrote concerning the Catholic priesthood:

> Francia hated them for the influence which they exercised over the people, and for the open profligacy of their lives. The simple minded and superstitious Paraguayans reverenced a *pai* (or father), as the immediate representative of God; they blindly and implicitly followed the instructions given to them, and did whatever was required at their hands. Many of the licentious brotherhood took advantage of this superstitious confidence placed in them by the people.[58]

This clearly inspired a cognate passage in *The Green Child*. For another example, 'a lieutenant by the name of Iturbide', who had boasted of being a favourite of the Dictator, is publicly stripped of his uniform and drummed out of his regiment; he must be the origin of Read's Iturbide, who suffers the same fate at the hands of the Dictator of Roncador.[59]

Part Three of *The Green Child* was prefaced in the manuscript by the following extract from the *Phaedo*: 'Wherefore, if ye desire of me a tale, hearken to the Tale of the things that be beyond upon the Earth under the Heaven'. The translation, despite its antique style, is that of J. A. Stewart's *The Myths of Plato* (1905).[60] Part Three as published omits this and begins with the water curving around Olivero and the Green Child; it makes 'a perfect spheroid'.[61] (This geometric precision is symptomatic of the ideals of both Plato and of the 'nest of gentle artists'.) They emerge into her universe and she soon remembers her original name, 'Siloën' (the other inhabitants are decidedly abstract, and none is ever named), her native tongue and her original *mores*.

Social life here begins in groups of about fifty, but individuals (at least, men) then join progressively smaller groups and eventually may become solitary hermits. In Part Two, the reverse had happened: Olivero became part of progressively larger social groups: the tailor's shop (two), the family in Poland (three), the ship's crew, the prison (100), and finally the nation of Roncador (14,000 families). Olivero and Siloën join one group of fifty, and a life of unsentimental carnality. He soon picks up both the language and the manners of her world; the former turns out to be 'simple' with no 'irregular inflexions' and 'devoid of abstract concepts';[62] the only sample

110

of it given is the four words which Siloën utters: '*Si Siloën, Si Siloën*'[63] ('I am Siloën') which have an appropriate symmetry, both in the repetition of the phrase, and in the syllable 'Si' within the phrase. The idea of a language 'devoid of abstract concepts', however, is not easy to understand, and Read would have been hard pushed to expand it much beyond this level of self-ostentive definition; the later discussions between Olivero and the sages on the nature of Time and Order would surely have been impossible.

He tires before her of innocent sensuality, and passes on to the next life-stage, that of manual work, within which there is a gradual development through increasing levels of craftsmanship. He starts, almost as if to recapitulate the development of terrestrial cultures, with simple food-gathering, and progresses to spinning and weaving, of which Read gives a fairly detailed description, reminiscent of his careful analysis of textile manufacture in *Art and Industry* (1934).[64] After 'works of irrigation, sanitation, stone-polishing and the like', we then hear rather more about the 'manufacture of gongs and crystals' and more still about 'the highest type of workman... engaged on the polishing of crystals'.[65] This begins with a paragraph on the green people's crystallography, which in the manuscript was even longer and more technical.

After an apprenticeship studying natural crystals, Olivero moves on to the creation of pure but non-natural forms, relying now upon insight as well as intellect. At first the novice practises on opaque materials and later upon the more highly valued rock-crystal (one thinks of some of Naum Gabo's translucent geometrical constructions, or Ben Nicholson's white reliefs): 'though there was no actual control of the supply of this precious rock, it would have been regarded as a kind of blasphemy to employ the material for an imperfect work'.[66] The ultimate criterion of a craftsman's success is to have five finished stones accepted by a sage.

Next, Olivero joins a group of five peripatetic philosophers. He attempts to vindicate a belief in Newtonian Absolute Time, but is unable to make any headway against their conviction that 'Time is change',[67] and not therefore absolute or infinite (ironically, a view which philosophers of our own generation might endorse). For them, the true Parmenidean reality is Order, 'motionless and unchangeable, everywhere similar to itself'.[68] His inability to convince them recalls the fate of the man who has left the cave in Plato's *Republic*.[69] In *The Education Of Free Men* (1944) Read described the *Republic* as: 'the creation of a poet, but its beauty is objective, calculated, classical: it is like a crystal of ice'.[70] (Ironically, such opinions have sometimes also been expressed about *The Green Child*.)

Later, Olivero rather more successfully contributes to a discussion of aesthetics. The Green People recognize both an absolute, natural beauty and an artificial order which may diverge from it, and associate the former with the mind and the latter with the senses. He eventually convinces them of the reverse view: that it is the mind which appreciates the artificial forms; and leads them, in stealthy Socratic fashion, to a comprehensive synthesis in which the craftsmen who make artificial crystals employ their senses to appreciate human 'order', while hermits employ the mind in appreciating the higher, natural order.[71]

Olivero himself now embarks on the life of such a hermit. He walks twice round the uppermost terrace and listens to 'perhaps sixty'[72] directional chimes, most of them composed of seven notes. He selects that which most appeals to him and follows it, again like the conventional enchanted traveller led away by fairy music. Eventually he comes to a suitable cell, which is vividly described with a combination of precise geometrical and organic vocabulary:

> the walls arched upward, shallowly concave until they reached the high apex, which was round and deep, glistening and bluish, like the freshly exposed socket of a bone. To gaze upwards was like gazing into the iris of an immense illuminated eye.[73]

This could be a hermit's cave designed by Henry Moore; and the fusion of organic and inorganic foreshadows Olivero's impending integration into the matrix of the material world. He chooses to contemplate a crystal 'varying between pale gold and steely blue' which consists of 'seven planes without symmetry, but with axes meeting at a single point'. It echoes 'the melody of the music outside his grotto', so he is now contemplating similar forms through both sight and sound, 'lost in the ecstasy of objective proportions, crystals and bells'.[74] 'Ecstasy' had been a key word in Read's vocabulary in the 1920s, signifying then fusion of intellect and emotion, though on the one occasion when it occurs in his poetry of the 1930s ('Hulk', 1932), it celebrated, as here, 'the white ecstasy of intellect' alone.[75]

Olivero's life of aesthetic asceticism now reaches its logical conclusion. Two paragraphs convey his meditation upon finally extinguishing his organic existence. The first expresses his growing conviction that perfect harmony can only be obtained when the body is no longer troubled by the soul. For this, Read turned to the *Phaedo*, in which the Platonic Socrates argues that a true philosopher welcomes death. It may be significant that the particular passage can be found early in Bridges's *The Spirit of Man*[76] which Read took with him to the front in May 1917 (with the *Republic* and *Don Quixote*).[77] However, the specific translation is not Bridges's, but that of the third (1892) edition of Jowett,[78] whose quasi-Biblical style is retained in Read's text, where it may evoke Olivero's adoption of a transcendental mode of thought. The variety of styles in *The Green Child* is indeed impressive, including this grandiloquent archaism, the cool scientific description of geometric forms, the impressionism of the Dictator's assassination, and the novel's usual remarkably lucid flow. Their unexpected conjunctions are reminiscent (or perhaps, in the context of Read's development, premonitory) of surrealism, but also typical of his poetry, rich in pastiche and quotation from earlier writers.

The passage obviously derived from Jowett consists of about 400 words, from

'When Olivero considered all these things…' to '… which is no other than the law of truth'.[79] Read's adherence to the original here is very close, taking over verbatim several phrases of considerable length, such as 'it fills us full of loves, and lusts, and fears, and fancies of all kinds'; but he again trimmed his source to just over four-fifths of the original length, as with *Letters on Paraguay*. There is apparently one outstanding difference, though. Socrates's argument, that his spirit will be better off when separated from the body, is reversed, since Olivero argues that it is his body which will be better off when released from the spirit. Nevertheless, the difference in the end is not great, because where Socrates talks of the 'soul' he means the rational or intellectual soul, and the material impediments that he attributes to the 'body', Olivero ascribes to the inconstant, immaterial soul. Plato himself elsewhere would have ascribed them to the 'vegetative' or 'appetitive' soul. The 'law of truth' which Olivero believes can only be attained by the body is very close to that knowledge of the ultimate (usually geometrical) truth which Plato says can only be attained by 'the soul'. They both seek purity and harmony, and they both deplore its corruption by carnal desires. Whether one assigns the latter to the 'body' or the 'mind' eventually makes little difference.

The tale which Socrates tells about the afterlife near the end of the *Phaedo* suggests that our own world is one among many others (connected by underground rivers) that are all really just hollows in the 'true earth', which , like Siloën's world, is rich in gems and crystals, a world of harmony without decay or disease. Such imagery also occurs in Read's inter-war poems, e.g., in 'The Seven Sleepers', 'The Lament of St Denis' and 'Beata l' Alma' (from Michelangelo's line *'Beata l' alma, ove non corre tempo'*).[80]

Read's contemporary critical writings also paralleled the philosophy of the underground world, even in its more surprising facets. For example, the essay that he contributed to the *Listener*'s series 'What I Like in Art' (published in October 1934, during the exact period he was writing the novel) contrasts two elements in a work of art: the 'universal' and the 'temporal' or sentimental. Like the Green People, he prefers the former:

> In the universal are all those elements of form, colour, material, and their inter-relations, which appeal directly to the senses, or sensibility…[81]

Such was his commitment to the 'universal' that he here attempted a strictly geometrical, even algebraic, analysis of Seurat's *Bathers* with the same cool precision as the underground campanology and crystallography:

> In each compartment made by the diagonals an equation is set up, which holds good for both sets of compartments. The dominant colours are blue and yellow, with red as a constant multiple.
>
> The equation might be symbolized as:

$$Y+r^1 + b^2 = B +r^1+ y^2$$

but I do not guarantee the mathematical rectitude of such a symbol... what is important is that everything is meant, everything is mathematical... there is no slopping-over of irrelevant emotion. The temporal elements are conscious and intellectual, and that is my own personal preference in the plastic arts.[82]

(One could be excused for thinking he was discussing a painting by Mondrian, rather than one of people bathing in the Seine.)

Georges Seurat, *Bathers at Asnières* 1884. Oil (identified) on canvas 201 × 300 cm (© National Gallery, London)

However, that Read did not commit himself irrevocably to this constructivist analysis, and perhaps that he felt he had rather let it carry him away, may be inferred from the fact that he never republished this essay, and also from its rather disarming conclusion, where he admitted that the approach was characteristic of his generation, rather than 'universal':

There are special reasons why intellectual values appeal to my generation. They are a part of our zeitgeist – that impalpable spirit of the times which is created by the air we breathe, the manner of our lives, our work and pleasure, our hopes and fears – all the spiritual and material factors of our mode of being.[83]

There seems some confusion in the essay over whether the 'universal' elements such

114

as form and colour appeal to the intellect or to the senses, but significantly the same dilemma was a central question to the Green People, which they first answer in favour of the senses, until Olivero suggests first the contrary view, and finally a synthesis whereby Art (Order) appeals to the senses of craftsmen and to the intellect of sages (and critics?).

In 'What is Revolutionary Art?', another essay roughly contemporary with the novel, Read was again concerned with the distinction between the 'universal' and the 'temporal' in art, claiming that dialectical materialism could interpret only the latter, whereas 'pure form' has its own 'relatively permanent' criteria, which he compared to crystallography:

> The recognition of such universal formal qualities in art is consistently materialistic. It no more contradicts the materialistic interpretation of history than does a recognition of the relative permanency of the human form or of the forms of crystals in geology.[84]

In *Annals of Innocence and Experience* (1940) Read sketched the philosophical foundations which had supported this mathematical aesthetic, referring to the Golden Section, Pythagoras, D'Arcy Thompson and Plato, who had 'found in *number* the clue to both the nature of the universe and the definition of beauty'.[85] This fits well the simpler aspects of the Green People's 'art', though less so their more advanced work with crystals, where the aim is to create a subtly non-natural order. That too, however, accords with Read's own contemporary aesthetic in its fuller development. He had long felt a sympathy for 'organic' as well as 'abstract', pure or mathematical form, and even in *The Meaning of Art* (1931) he had followed a passage on the Golden Section with one emphasizing the importance of sometimes deviating from mathematical regularity:

> It is well known that a perfectly regular metre in verse is so monotonous as to become intolerable. Poets have therefore taken liberties with their measure; feet are reversed within the metre, and the whole rhythm may be counterpointed. The result is incomparably more beautiful. In the same way, in the plastic arts certain geometrical proportions, which are the proportions inherent in the structure of the world, may be the regular measure from which art departs in subtle degrees.[86]

Likewise in *Art and Industry* (1934), although he wrote that

> Nature herself is abstract, essentially mathematical: and our human needs simply acquire the conditions of their greatest freedom when they conform to that discipline 'whose golden surveying rod marks out and measures every quarter and circuit of the New Jerusalem' (Milton)

and also quoted with approval Ruskin's dictum that 'All beautiful lines are drawn under mathematical laws organically transgressed'.[87] In 'The Importance of Living' (1938) he expressed similar ideas, in words some of which might have come straight from Part Three of his novel:

> It is tempting to identify our aesthetic emotions with our awareness of the structural harmony of the universe, but a closer examination of the aesthetic creations of mankind shows that their forms tend to depart in some degree from the mathematical patterns which result from physical laws. The emotion we experience when we perceive the form of a crystal or of the solar system is not the same as the emotion we experience when we read Shakespeare's poetry or listen to Beethoven's music. This latter emotion is rather the thrill we experience from daring to depart from the patterns inherent in the universe. Art is thus an adventure into the unknown, and therefore purely subjective. This has not always been perceived, and a confusion has arisen between the imitation of universal patterns (the 'beauty' of classical art) and the creation of free patterns (which is art properly so-called).[88]

'Art properly so-called' is clearly that which the aesthetics of the Green People attributes to the craftsmen who make artificial crystals, while 'the "beauty" of classical art', imitating universal patterns, provides the more intellectual satisfaction which the hermits derive from an appreciation of Order.

In a review of *Either-Or*, published in 1938,[89] Read called Kierkegaard 'one of the subtlest thinkers who ever lived', and given also that the manuscript of the novel originally began with a quotation from Kierkegaard, it seems quite possible that its culmination points towards Kierkegaard's 'third way' (the transcendental, after the aesthetic and the ethical). This is not inconsistent with the novel's Platonic elements, or Read's own contemporary views on aesthetics. In 1940, he wrote of Kierkegaard's 'aesthetic' standpoint as:

> aesthetics, which Kierkegaard, like Plato, recognised as the world of pure form – 'form seeking and symbolising the austere peace of eternity'... a philosophy of pure form derived, ultimately, from the physical laws of the universe...[90]

The art of pure mathematical form which Read thus idealized is also clearly apparent in the contemporary work of his artistic associates. For example, Barbara Hepworth's *Three Forms* (1935) was her first completely abstract work, and is not only contemporary with, but structurally akin to, *The Green Child*. Even Paul Nash (usually the most representational of the 'gentle artists') was at this period boldly geometrical in *Equivalents for the Megaliths* (1935). Nash wrote of the experience from

Barbara Hepworth, *Three Forms* (carving in Serravezza marble) 1935. Photos courtesy Tate Gallery, London (© Alan Bowness, Hepworth Estate)

Paul Nash, *Equivalents for the Megaliths* 1935. Oil on canvas (© Tate Gallery, London)

which this painting seems to have grown in a style that sounds much like *The Green Child* or Read's 'What I Like in Art' essay:

> Last summer I walked in a field near Avebury where two rough monoliths stood up, six feet high, miraculously patterned with black and orange lichens, remnants of an avenue of stones which led to the Great Circle. A mile away, a green pyramid casts a gigantic shadow. In the hedge, at hand, the white trumpet of a convolvulus turns from its spiral stem, following the sun. In my art I would solve such an equation.[91]

The last two paragraphs of the novel, in which Olivero attains 'final harmony', have a vivid style and dense imagery, so that *The Green Child* ends on a final peak of poetic intensity. There is a parallel here with Read's practice in some of his contemporary poems (e.g., in *Poems 1914–1934* [1935]) in which the last few lines are particularly concentrated, often rhyming or with an alliterative element; the rhymes at the end also often create a link with the opening. Good examples are 'September Fires', exactly contemporary with the novel, or the dream poem 'Love and Death' (*c.*1935–38), whose conclusion is tied tight with alliteration and rhyme, and even has a content similar to the novel's:

>   ... There in my bed
> The lovely girl and the destitute lad
> Are lying enlaced. And I know they are dead.[92]

The novel ends, describing the posthumous union of Olivero and Siloën, as follows:

> The tresses of Siloën's hair, floating in the liquid in which they were immersed, spread like a tracery of stone across Olivero's breast, twined inextricably in the coral intricacy of his beard.[93]

'Tracery' and 'intricacy' rhyme, while there is alliteration in 'spread like a tracery of stone across' and 'beauty' and 'beard'; 'coral' is appropriate to their submerged state. That reference to Olivero's beard perhaps also recalls the first mention of it in the novel's opening paragraph. The enigma of their simultaneous deaths is not explained.

Notes

1   George Orwell, *Homage to Catalonia* (Harmondsworth: Penguin Books, 1962), p. 221.
2   Herbert Read, 'A Nest of Gentle Artists', *Apollo*, vol. 77, no. 7 (September 1962), pp. 536–42. References are to its publication in the catalogue *Art in Britain 1930–40 Centred around Axis, Circle, Unit One* (London: Marlborough Fine Art, 1965), pp. 7–9.
3   Read, 'A Nest of Gentle Artists', p. 7.
4   Herbert Read, *English Prose Style* (London: G. Bell and Sons, 1928).
5   From late (?) summer to the end of November 1934. The manuscript and the text of the first edition end with the date '27 xi 1934'. In a letter to C. G. Jung dated 25 October 1948 (Read Archive, University of Victoria Library, British Columbia, Canada) Read stated that the composition of the novel took 'five or six weeks'. In an interview in July 1961, he said: 'two or three months in the summer of 1935' (*sic*) (Hans Bosshard, 'Mythisches und Utopisches Dasein in Herbert Reads Erzählung "The Green Child"', PhD thesis, Zurich, 1964). In 'A Nest of Gentle Artists' (1962), he wrote that he had composed *The Green Child* 'during that first summer' in his wooden garden cabin behind Number 3, The Mall Studios.
6   Herbert Read, *The Green Child* manuscript (Read family, Stonegrave House).
7   Herbert Read, *The Green Child*. There have been six editions:

First edition, subtitled *A Romance* (London: Heinemann, 1935);
Second, with illustrations by Felix Kelly (London: Grey Walls Press, 1945);
Third, with introduction by Graham Greene (London: Eyre and Spottiswoode, 1947);
Fourth, with introduction by Kenneth Rexroth (New York: New Directions, 1948);
Fifth, with 1947 Graham Greene introduction (Harmondsworth: Penguin Books, 1979); and
Sixth, with 1947 Graham Greene introduction (London: R. Clark, 1989, 1995).

All references are to the Grey Walls Press edition; in this case, p. 6.
8   Read, *The Green Child*, p. 14.
9   Read, *English Prose Style*, pp. 139–40. Read cites his source as 'T. Keightley, *The Fairy Mythology*, p. 281'.
10 Read, *The Green Child*, p. 19.

11 Herbert Read, *A Concise History of Modern Painting*, third edition with preface by Benedict Read (London: Thames and Hudson, 1974), p. 130.

12 Herbert Read, 'Huskisson Sacred and Profane', *Coterie*, December 1919.

13 Herbert Read, *The Contrary Experience: Autobiographies* (London: Secker and Warburg, 1973), pp. 334–35.

14 Read Archive.

15 Herbert Read, *Collected Poems* (London: Faber and Faber, 1966), p. 225.

16 Read, *The Contrary Experience*, p. 335.

17 Read, *Collected Poems*, p. 257.

18 Read, *The Green Child*, p. 5.

19 Read, *The Contrary Experience*, p. 192.

20 Read, *The Green Child*, pp. 15–16.

21 Ibid., p. 16.

22 This perhaps parallels the anecdote which A. S. Neill described in *The Problem Child* (1926) of his neurotic nephew who broke a stolen gold watch because, according to Neill, he had not been told where babies come from, and whose 'wish to find out the truth took a form of symbolic gratification'; he also claimed that the boy was 'unconsciously thinking of the deep cavern in which his life began' (A. S. Neill, *The Problem Child* [London: Herbert Jenkins Ltd, fourth edn, 1935], pp. 10–12).

23 Read, *The Green Child*, p. 25.

24 Ibid., p. 38.

25 Read, *The Green Child* MS. 'g g' presumably stands for 'green girl', a phrase also used to describe her in the text, e.g., on p. 36.

26 Read, *The Green Child*, p. 37.

27 Read, *The Contrary Experience*, p. 152.

28 Read, *The Green Child*, pp. 27, 29.

29 Ibid., p. 29.

30 Ibid., p. 19.

31 Ibid., p. 26.

32 Ibid., pp. 27, 34.

33 Ibid., p. 34.

34 Ibid., pp. 16, 22, 25, 29, 30, 31.

35 Ibid., p. 34.

36 Read, *The Contrary Experience*, p. 150.

37 Read, *Collected Poems*, p. 29.

38 Ibid., p. 33.

39 Herbert Read, *Form in Modern Poetry* (London: Vision Press, 1964 edn), p. 23.

40 Written in Venice in 1961 (see *A Tribute to Herbert Read 1893–1968*, catalogue to exhibition at The Manor House, Ilkley [Bradford: Bradford Art Galleries and Museums, 1975], p. 15).

41 Read, *Collected Poems*, p. 245.

42 Herbert Read, *Songs of Chaos* (London: Elkin Mathews, 1915).

43 Read, *Collected Poems*, p. 90.

44 Read, *The Green Child*, p. 48.

45 Ibid., p. 71.

46 Ibid., p. 77.

47 Read, *The Green Child* MS.

48 Herbert Read, 'The Intellectual and Liberty', *Listener*, 19 September 1934.

49 First published as No. 12, Pamphlets on the New Economics (London: Stanley Nott, July 1935)

(where the passage quoted is modified on p. 21); then, with revisions, in *Poetry and Anarchism* (London: Faber and Faber, 1938), chapter 4.

50 Read, *The Green Child*, p. 103.

51 Ibid., p. 82.

52 Ibid., p. 106.

53 Personal communication to the author, *c.*1980.

54 Louis Adeane's letter to Herbert Read dated 27 February 1952 (Read Archive) which asks 'If you do come across the South American book, however, please let me know'.

55 Read, *The Green Child*, p. 82.

56 John and William Robertson, *Letters on Paraguay* (London: John Murray, 3 vols, 1838–39), vol. 1, p. 194.

57 Read, *The Green Child*, p. 55.

58 Robertson, *Letters on Paraguay*, vol. 3, p. 28.

59 Ibid., vol. 3, p. 297; Read, *The Green Child*, p. 74.

60 J. A. Stewart, *The Myths of Plato: Translation with Introduction and other Observations* (London: Macmillan, 1905), p. 2. Benedict Read confirmed that there was a copy of this work at Stonegrave.

61 Read, *The Green Child*, p. 111.

62 Ibid., p. 121.

63 Ibid., p. 118.

64 Herbert Read, *Art and Industry: The Principles of Industrial Design* (London: Faber and Faber, 1966 edn), pp. 133–37.

65 Read, *The Green Child*, p. 122.

66 Ibid., p. 126.

67 Ibid., p. 124.

68 Ibid., p. 128.

69 Plato, *The Republic* (Harmondsworth: Penguin Books, 1955), p. 281.

70 Herbert Read, *The Education of Free Men* (London: Freedom Press, 1944), p. 8.

71 Read, *The Green Child*, pp. 130–31.

72 Ibid., p. 133.

73 Ibid., p. 134.

74 Ibid., p. 135.

75 Read, *Collected Poems*, p. 128.

76 Robert Bridges, *The Spirit of Man: An Anthology in English and French from the Philosophers and Poets* (London: Longmans, Green and Co., 1916), Book I, No. 16 (unpaginated).

77 Read, *The Contrary Experience*, p. 92.

78 Benjamin Jowett (trans.), *The Dialogues of Plato*, 3rd edn (Oxford: Clarendon Press, 1892), vol. 2, pp. 205–06.

79 Read, *The Green Child*, pp. 136–37.

80 Read, *Collected Poems*, pp. 120, 83, 75.

81 Herbert Read, 'What I Like in Art', *Listener*, 10 October 1934.

82 Ibid.

83 Ibid.

84 Herbert Read, 'What is Revolutionary Art?', in Betty Rea (ed.), *Five on Revolutionary Art* (London: Wishart, 1935).

85 Read, *The Contrary Experience*, pp. 345–46.

86 Herbert Read, *The Meaning of Art* (London: Faber and Faber, 1936 edn), p. 28.

87 Read, *Art and Industry*, pp. 64 and 36.

88 Herbert Read, 'The Importance of Living', in *Poetry and Anarchism* (London: Freedom Press, 1947 edn), p. 78.

89 Herbert Read, review of Søren Kierkegaard, *Either/Or*, in *Spectator*, 1 July 1938.

90 Read, *The Contrary Experience*, pp. 193–94.

91 Herbert Read (ed.), *Unit One: The Modern Movement in English Architecture, Painting, and Sculpture* (London: Cassell, 1934), p. 81.

92 Read, *Collected Poems*, p. 143.

93 Read, *The Green Child*, p. 137.

Herbert Read and Contemporary Art

ANDREW CAUSEY

ERBERT Read was Britain's most energetic supporter of contemporary art for twenty years from the early 1930s, and in the six years from 1933 was part of a group living in Hampstead that included some of the most adventurous artists anywhere at the time. Though Read championed experiment till his death – if with increasing misgiving – it was with those artists and others of the early modern period that his deepest loyalty lay. 'There can be no doubt where revolutionary energy has been most manifest', he wrote in 1948, '... the work of the younger men is still but the prolonged reverberations of the explosions of thirty or forty years ago. The general effect is a diminuendo.'[1] This was not Read's last word, and he continued to promote new art, but in so far as his outlook was formed by contact with artists, it was those he met or got to know of in the 1930s who influenced him most.

Before Read was on close terms with any artists at all, however, he had spent most of the 1920s as a curator at the Victoria and Albert Museum, where the gathering of artefacts from numerous cultures and epochs under one roof stimulated ways of looking that lasted beyond Read's museum career. His search for connections between objects from widely different times and places, and attempts to compose an account of art that would transcend cultural differences, started at the V & A. Read liked to order and categorize, and his museum training and desire to synthesize and find common bases and goals in widely different art, were carried into his writing on friends and contemporaries. As a result, historicism and the way the contemporary can be fitted into patterns of thought evolved to account for the art of the past became issues.

Read was a relative latecomer to writing on contemporary art, aged 35 when he started contributing on art in September 1929 to the *Listener*, the newly founded journal of the BBC. The acknowledged English text on the modern movement at that point was R. H. Wilenski's *The Modern Movement in Art* (1927), which argued that the modern movement represented the reinstatement of the classical or architectural, by which he meant something akin to Bloomsbury's significant form. Wilenski argued that the key developments had occurred in Paris, from which he drew most of his examples. Read's ambition was to shift the discussion from a rather generalized formal account to the will or impulse that underlay the artistic expression of different regions and races. In one of his first articles on twentieth-century art, looking at Picasso and Matisse as acknowledged leaders of the new art, Read

123

Weekly Notes on Art

Picasso

PABLO PICASSO is generally admitted to be the most significant of modern painters, but it is difficult to know what is implied by this blessed word 'significant'. Is a significant painter necessarily a good painter, a man whose sense of beauty is expressed in forms that will endure because they have universal value? Or is a significant painter merely one who appeals to the co-opted jury of snobs which in most ages secures a judgment for any odd and outrageous escape from banality? It is not easy to say, and in the case of Picasso especially, the protean nature of his activity precludes any summary answer. He has, at all costs, avoided a manner. He can be as human and as caustic as Toulouse-Lautrec, as careful as Ingres, as massive as Michelangelo and as sentimental as Greuze; and he can be completely abstract and devoid of any value beyond the bare physical reaction to form. The two paintings illustrated here do not show the extremes, either of abstraction or sentimentality, to which Picasso can go, but they show a wide contrast in the treatment of a similar theme. Yet Picasso himself has declared that he never changes; that we must seek the same principles of design in all his pictures; the same values, the same objectivity.

Picasso was born at Malaga in Spain in 1881. He therefore belongs to a younger generation than Matisse, who was born in 1869. I mention Matisse because some people might regard him as a still more significant painter, and certainly he does not give rise to the same feelings of doubt and unconfessed dismay. The reputation of Matisse is secure, even though the significance is by no means fully recognised. But it carries with it a sense of achievement; it is a tradition, the tradition of Cézanne, carried to its logical conclusion. Picasso, however, is the beginning of a new tradition, and half his fascination is his capacity for arousing our sense of wonder.

Though Paris has absorbed him (he settled there in 1903), it has never assimilated him. He has preserved his native integrity, and this, as Mr. Uhde has pointed out in a recent book (*Picasso et la Tradition Française*, Editions des Quatre Chemins, Paris, 40 frs.), this is more Germanic than French. 'Germanic' is perhaps a strange word to use in this connection, and it will perhaps be interesting to return some time to the suggestion which Mr. Uhde makes of an underlying similarity in the Greek, Spanish and German genius: their common tendency to express a longing for the infinite, for the transcendental. Meanwhile we can agree that in its superficial aspects, at any rate, the manner of Picasso is 'sombre in its colouring, essentially tormented in its inspiration, vertical in its tendency, romantic in its tonality, embodying in its totality the Gothic or Germanic spirit'. Picasso himself would scarcely approve such a generalisation. Like every artist, he is necessarily an individualist: 'I paint what I see', is one of his sayings. But there is no such thing as an individualist; we all express the complex organisations into which we are born as a dependent unit.

Picasso's own reflections on art, originally contributed to a Russian review, have been translated into French and published in the second number of an interesting new magazine called *Formes* (Paris, 18, Rue Godot-de-Mauroy, 25 frs.). Some of his remarks are directed at his critics. For example: 'Art has neither a past nor a future. Art which is powerless to affirm itself in the present will never come to its own. Greek and Egyptian art do not belong to the past: they are more alive to-day than they were yesterday. Change is not evolution. If the artist modifies his means of expression, that does not mean that he has changed his mind'. Again: 'Cubism in no way differs from other schools of painting. The same elements and the same principles rule in all'. And, in further explanation of cubism, there are these maxims: 'Nature and art are two entirely dissimilar phenomena'. 'Cubism is neither the seed nor the germination of a new art: it represents a stage in the development of original pictorial forms. These realised forms

Baigneuse en Vert (Periode Cubiste), by Picasso
Size 36½ x 25½ inches
From the private collection of M. Paul-Guillaume

Les deux Arlequins, by Picasso
Size 30 x 40 inches
From the private collection of Mr. Brandon-Davis

describes Matisse's reputation as secure because 'it is [in] a tradition, the tradition of Cézanne carried to its logical conclusion'.[2] Matisse is within the canon of great art, Read implies, and so, he was to feel, was Derain when he came to write about him two years later.[3] To Derain Read attributed the quality of 'virtue' which he used in an eighteenth-century sense meaning moderate, within the tradition, or canonical. As a literary critic contributing to the *Criterion* in the mid-1920s Read had agreed with Eliot, its editor, that tradition is crucial and that artists only come to maturity as individuals by subsuming themselves within it in such a way as to become the new end link in the long chain of tradition.

Read's article on Picasso, and others as well, show him to have been uncomfortable with any view, such as Clive Bell and Wilenski held in relation to Paris, that there was a dominant tradition or canon. The *Listener* articles are concerned with different national, racial and regional traditions (North European, Jewish, etc.), and Read recognized Paris as a focus for national achievement but also as a melting pot where other traditions come together. More than that, Read was concerned with what was 'not Paris', and it was here that his remarks on Picasso were unusual. Having identified Matisse as within the French canon, he describes Picasso as the beginning of a new tradition. The article's context was a book *Picasso et la tradition française* (1928) by the German Paris-based author and longstanding friend of Picasso, Wilhelm Uhde, who had built up a picture of Picasso, in Read's description, as Romantic, tormented, and Germanic. Read added judiciously that Picasso himself might not agree, but was clearly struck by Uhde's notion of the enduring effect of Picasso's Catalan background in engendering an art of vivid and vital character that long residence in Paris could never subdue.

Read was not overtly critical of Wilenski, but his dissatisfaction with Roger Fry, and in particular Fry's inability to appreciate German and Flemish art, became clear in 1932.[4] From the early 1920s, in literary criticism, Read had shown himself to be dissatisfied with 'significant form'.[5] He felt it was a cul-de-sac, the end-product of a split within eighteenth-century aesthetics between ethics and beauty, which had left the formal development of art in its pursuit of beauty lacking any outside check or standard. Read's starting-point in this respect was closer to Ruskin than Bloomsbury, and underlying the *Listener* articles is a desire to redress the overbalance in British taste for Paris.

Read's way of pursuing this is original within an English context. He had been interested since the mid-1920s in the German aesthetician Wilhelm Worringer, translating into English in 1927 Worringer's *Form in Gothic* and writing an introduction which paid tribute to Worringer's distinction between abstraction and empathy. Abstraction, Worringer said, was characteristic of the art of cultures where

'Picasso': Read's article in the *Listener*, 5 March 1930

the outside world was felt as alien or unfriendly, while empathy implied the objectification in the outside world of people's sense of ease and vitality, and a culture that empathizes thus with its surroundings produces a naturalistic art. It was a distinction considered by Worringer in relation to Egyptian, Byzantine and Gothic art, but it was Read, following the English aesthetician T. E. Hulme, whose papers Read edited for publication as *Speculations* in 1924, who developed it in relation to the twentieth century.

Read was alone in England in 1930 in being interested in modern German art. Following Worringer, Read saw a recurrent theme in German art which was not precisely, in Worringer's distinction, towards abstraction but was certainly opposed to naturalism. The tendency of the artist to retreat into abstraction was countered, as Read saw it, by the pressure of actuality that makes such an escape impossible, and the result is caricature, a way of facing reality without resorting to naturalism. It was actually a theory of expressionism, though Read did not define it as such, and tended to use the word 'expressionism' rather vaguely, to mean little more than the use of paint directly to reflect personal feeling. Through reading Worringer and other German aesthetic theory Read arrived at a definition of North European art (applied not only to Germany but to Scandinavians like Munch and to the art of the Low Countries) which seemed applicable to both historic and contemporary art. It provided the theoretical basis for his understanding of George Grosz and Otto Dix, who were more or less unknown in Britain when Read discussed them in articles in the *Listener* in 1930.[6] Read's interest in art as the reflection of nationality and geographical location led him to see the underlying principles of the art of peoples and places as relatively constant through time, and to that extent his viewpoint was a-historical.

The Meaning of Art, published towards the end of 1931, gathered many of Read's *Listener* articles into a book. The selection did not altogether reflect the vigour with which Read had engaged with contemporary art in his articles, but *The Meaning of Art* was effective in suggesting how North European art, German or Flemish, or the Catalan inheritance of Picasso with which, he thought, it had affinities, could be seen in terms of geography and the accretion of cultural characteristics over history. It was not intended to highlight any period, certainly not the twentieth century. *Art Now*, published two years later, was Read's first fully worked out account of contemporary art, but was underpinned nonetheless by an historical perspective. Read attacked eighteenth-century rationalism and the notion of a classical tradition searching for formal perfection, a canon of beauty. An alternative, vitalist theory emerged: 'Art may flourish in a rank and barbaric manner from an excess of animal vitality; but it withers and dies in the arid excesses of reason'.[7] As opposed to a classical theory of perfection, Read, basing himself on Giambattista Vico's *La Scienza Nuova* of 1725, presents a theory of art, specifically of poetry, as the primitive expression of man while 'he is still living in a direct sensuous relation to his environment, before he has learned to form universals and reflect'.[8] Read was working out a notion of the origins of culture in society which had been implied rather than stated in *The Meaning of Art*.

The order in which Read made certain discoveries, and the problem of living in a country that was slow to acknowledge modern art, led to his arrival, under Vico's influence, at a theory of art as the first collective expression of society before he had sufficient knowledge of late Symbolist and Surrealist painting to make full connections between his new theory and contemporary art. De Chirico, Miró, and Ernst, artists concerned with myths of origin, are all illustrated in *Art Now*, but the commentary on them is brief from lack of space and suggests that Read did not recognize their potential significance for the theoretical argument contained in the book. Read's first essay on Surrealism, published in the *Listener* in 1930[9] but not reprinted in *The Meaning of Art*, related to automatism, making the connection with Freud and, in literature, Joyce. It included discussion of Ernst's collages but did not explore Surrealist painting. Read's 1920s background was in literature and poetry and it was these, together with a growing interest in psychoanalysis, that gave him his entrée to Surrealism. Indeed it is arguable that Surrealism was never well understood in Britain because the literary basis of British culture led much of the commentary on it in the mid-1930s (by Paul Nash, Hugh Sykes Davies and others, as well as Read)[10] to appropriate Surrealism, which was by then a major issue, for British culture by reference to the Gothic novel and Romantic poetry.

Art Now shares the assumption of Wilenski and others at the time that 'abstract' means 'abstracted from' rather than 'non-figurative'. *Art Now* is the last of Read's writings in the 1930s to assume a middle-of-the-road, *École de Paris*, view of contemporary art and contains a very wide range of illustrations. English artists include the former Vorticists Wyndham Lewis and William Roberts, who were not involved in the experimental Unit One which Read was at that very moment helping to organize. When Read wrote *Art Now* he knew nothing of Constructivism, the Dutch De Stijl movement or the innovations opened up by Gropius at the Bauhaus. There was no mention of Mondrian or non-figuration in the 1933 edition of *Art Now* – a gap that Read filled in later editions – because non-figurative art was unknown in England, and its role after 1918 in European countries such as Russia, Germany and Holland in providing a model for a restructuring of society had no parallel in Britain. It was a gap soon to be occupied with the arrival in London as refugees of artists and architects, like Gropius and Moholy-Nagy, Gabo and Mondrian, none of whom is mentioned or has work reproduced in *Art Now*.

Writers in Britain and America, experiencing non-figurative art only after it had declined in significance in Holland or been forcibly uprooted in Russia and Germany, missed the ethical implications it had originally possessed, the ambition of the Constructivists, for example, to re-order the relationship between art and society, or the De Stijl movement to reach beyond the subjective to collective expression.

127

Beyond Realism

MOST people have heard by now of 'Surréalisme', but as the movement is not, so far as I know, represented in England, it might be worth while to define its character. In speaking of Cubism a few weeks ago, I pointed out that the principles of that revolutionary phase of art are essentially classical: it is a formal art which more and more tends in the direction of intellectualism—towards an art of number and proportion and away from the art of emotion or sentiment. Naturally the whole of the modernist movement could not follow in this direction; some people are romantic by nature and others are romantic in spite of themselves. So in opposition to Cubism we had first 'Dada' and then 'Surréalisme'. 'Dada' was only a joke; or rather it was the gesture of men too bored with the tragedy of life to be anything but irreverent. It was born at Zurich in 1916 and died at Paris in 1924. In 1924 'Surréalisme' rose from the ashes—and took visible shape in a manifesto by two poets, André Breton and Louis Aragon. The movement is still thriving, and, indeed, I see no reason why it should not expand, for the romantic spirit on which it feeds is plentiful enough.

In literature the phenomenon is perhaps more familiar to us. I should describe Mr. James Joyce, especially in his latest developments, as a super-realist (if that is how we should translate the word). As the word implies, the main doctrine of the school is that there exists a world more real than the normal world, and this is the world of the unconscious mind. I doubt if 'Surréalisme' would ever have existed in its present form but for Professor Freud. He is the real founder of the school, for just as Freud finds a key to the perplexities of life in the material of dreams, so the 'Surréaliste' finds his best inspiration in the same region. And with reason. In my opinion, you can no more dismiss 'Surréalisme' than you can dismiss Psychoanalysis. But even if you deny the validity of both as theories, the test, so far as the art is concerned, remains the simple one of enjoyment.

My own preferences are classical: that is to say, I derive most pleasure from a work of art, whether literature or painting, in which expression is achieved with some degree of formal precision. But I could never see why, though a classicist, I should be forbidden the enjoyment of romantic art. Granted that both impulses, the romantic and the classic, exist in their own right (and the history of art is a sufficient demonstration of that), then perfection may be achieved in the expression of either, and enjoyment is the perception of any kind of perfection. A perfect representation of the workings of the unconscious, such as Mr. Joyce's *Ulysses*, is, therefore, in my opinion a great work of art. If I have not yet seen a 'Surréaliste' painting which convinces me in the same degree, the fault is probably my own: I have not seen enough. The least I can do is to admit that the *genre* is possible.

The Cubist movement has at its head a Spaniard, Picasso; by a strange coincidence (but why strange?) Intellectually Spain is as wideawake as any country in Europe) the leader of the 'Surréaliste' movement is also a Spaniard—Joan Miro. The earlier work of Chirico is 'Surréaliste' in inspiration; other members of the movement are Paul Klee (a German), Max Ernst (presumably also German), Papazoff (a Bulgarian), the monosyllabic Arp, and, though he may not be officially allied to the school, that extremely interesting Russian painter, Marc Chagall. Though the centre of the school is Paris it will be seen that none of these names is French, and there is indeed something incompatible between this informal literary mode of painting and the French genius. It should also be remembered that in France the theories of Freud have never made any great headway.

Max Ernst has recently published a book which is a good example of super-realism. It is called *La Femme 100 Têtes*, and is published by Editions du Carrefour, 169 Boulevard Saint - Germain, Paris (45 francs). It is a novel in pictures, but very strange pictures. Max Ernst did not draw them himself: they are taken from the illustrated books of adventure, technical treatises and journals of the middle of the last century, but not quite simply. For Mr. Ernst has cut out a figure from one source, an instrument from another, and cleverly introduced them into the groundwork of still another engraving. The results are very surprising; they are, in fact, exactly like Freudian dreams. I reproduce a comparatively simple specimen. It may be a joke, but it is an amusing one, and Mr. Ernst makes it still more amusing by his witty captions. The one which accompanies this page reads: *'Chaque émeute sanglante la fera vivre pleine de grace et de vérité'*.

'Chaque émeute sanglante la fera vivre pleine de grace et de vérité'

In an introduction to the volume, André Breton says that Max Ernst has the most magnificently haunted brain of to-day, and after looking through this book, no-one will be inclined to dispute the claim. But why be haunted? I think Mr. Breton would reply that it is better than being bored. A statue, he says, which is quite devoid of interest in its proper place, becomes an object of wonder if put in a ditch. And so with life in general: it is too dull for anything in its proper place. It is the function of art to upset the apple-cart: to snatch things from the security of their normal existence, and put them where they have never been before, except in dreams.

HERBERT READ

Switzerland (Western and Southern) has now been added to the series of 'Picture Guides' issued by the Medici Society (7s. 6d.). This consists largely of charming views of mountain scenery, lakes and costumes, together with an end-paper map and a descriptive text. The range of the book is from Neuchatel and Geneva to Ticino, and the photographs are most superbly reproduced in photogravure—which makes the book equally valuable to the traveller both in anticipation and in retrospect,

The kind of modernism that Read was ultimately to propose, which saw advanced art as an enclosed activity primarily concerned with its own limits and development, was characteristic of English-speaking countries which had least experience of the socially idealistic phase of modernism after the First World War.

A change of emphasis took place in Read's thinking with the formation of Unit One in the summer of 1933 and his involvement in the group's exhibition and publication in spring 1934. Unit One was the brainchild of Paul Nash, and included painters, Nash himself, Wadsworth, Nicholson and others, the sculptors Moore and Hepworth, and avant-garde architects. It stood for experiment, believed in the effectiveness of group activity, and echoed pre-war Vorticism, though without a leader of the fire or bile of Wyndham Lewis. The *Unit One* book reproduced the first fully non-figurative works of Nicholson, and between his work and Nash's semi-abstractions reaching towards landscape there is already evidence of the divide that was to widen swiftly and make an avant-garde group with a common pursuit untenable. Though shortlived, Unit One was important in bringing Read, who had returned from two years as Professor of Fine Art at Edinburgh University only months before the launch of the group in June 1933, into the centre of the most vigorous debate on avant-garde art since the war, a debate which was important in shifting British modernism towards a sharper emphasis on experiment than existed in Wilenski's writing, or even Read's in *Art Now*.

However, the arrival in England of artists as refugees from Hitler's Germany was at least as important as Unit One in redefining Read's attitude. Gropius arrived in October 1934, and though Britain was in the end to prove a disappointment to him, his relationship had already begun encouragingly with an exhibition of work in May at the Design and Industries Association, where he gave a lecture that was printed in the *Listener*.[11] Read's *Art and Industry*, published later in 1934, pays a generous tribute to Gropius. His return to London from Edinburgh coincided with a debate on the artist in industry following the Gorell report of 1932 on the role of design in the competitiveness of British industry and a thrust, further stimulated by the underemployment of artists in the Depression, towards the involvement of avant-garde art in industrial design.

In *Art and Industry* Read came to terms with non-figurative art, insisting that 'not until we have reduced the work of art to its essentials, stripped it of all the irrelevancies imposed on it by a particular culture of civilisation, can we see any solution of the problem'.[12] This is a bold statement, applied in a context not of industrial design but of art, because it suggests that style is a supplement to something more fundamental, and that arrival at a pure non-figurative art (Mondrian, Nicholson and Hélion are mentioned in the book) is the final state of an evolutionary and reductive

'Beyond Realism': Read's article on Surrealism in the *Listener*, 16 April 1930

A page from Read's *Art and Industry* showing an architectural sense of design exemplified in engineering units: *above* the 'B' amplifier Output Switching Relays at Broadcasting House, London (photo, © BBC), *below* Settlement at Dammerstock, Karlsruhe, Germany. Architects: Gropius, Haesler, Riphahn and Good.
Read comments: *The resemblance between these two illustrations is not merely fortuitous; the same laws of design end in the same effects of harmony.*

process. The kind of abstraction that these artists would bring to industry was based, in Read's view, partly on formal organization, related to the golden section and other proportions that were demonstrably satisfying, and partly on the artist's intuition of form that was beyond analysis.

Read was, as often, concerned with positioning his ideas historically and reiter-ated the distinction between humanistic (Renaissance) and abstract art, rooted in his earlier study of Worringer. More specifically he compared the present moment with two other moments in history, Greece of the fifth century BC and Christian art of the twelfth to thirteenth centuries. 'There is one significant fact about such periods: they are without an aesthetic. What they did, they did as the solution of practical problems, without taste, without academic tradition.'[13] Read was adapting an idea he had worked out in the mid-1920s, when he was writing on medieval stained glass,[14] that cultures pass from early and primitive to late and decadent phases, with the latter dominated by taste and decorativeness (Hellenistic art or Decorated architecture). Read's preference is for the early, which in Gothic he thought of in a way described by Jacques Maritain as the balance of logic and intuition that produces a rational attitude, an immediate solution to a social need using techniques and materials appropriate to the desired solution.[15] The comparison Read is making is functionalist in its correspondence between need and provision, and makes the proposal, common enough then but unacceptable now, that the modern movement was free of style rather than a style in itself. Just as Read's earlier examples of the moment of balance – where the early phase of a cycle comes to maturity but is as yet without hint of decadence – were times when architecture was eminent among the arts, so now it was the example of Gropius that was pivotal in suggesting to Read that the modern movement was both rational and responsive to social need in the way early Gothic had been.

Read's 'What is Revolutionary Art?', a vigorous defence of non-figurative art, appeared a year later in November 1935 in a Marxist publication in which Read was surrounded by defenders of realism. He started by rejecting the Mexican muralist Diego Rivera, who was coming to be seen in Europe as having found an acceptable middle way between a popular Socialist art and an élite modernism. Read's judgement of Rivera as 'competent but essentially second rate'[16] was coloured by the conviction that non-figuration was the only truly revolutionary art. His starting-point was still Gropius, posing against 'the anecdotal and literary art [of Rivera]... the vitality and intellectual strength of the new architecture'.[17] Architecture was the leading art because it was closest to social need, and at a time when techniques and materials were developing rapidly it was an art that made use of what was clearly modern.

Read still, in 1935, saw contemporary art basically as a problem of form, with taste and style as supplements, and he now divided the elements of art between the timeless and abstract on the one hand and, on the other, the different styles – each of only momentary validity – which are imposed by history. Taste and style he describes as the 'mannerism' through which 'the prevailing ideology of a period is expressed',[18] plainly exposing his belief that it was the timeless, formal element that mattered. His argument started once again from the rightness of early Gothic architecture, but now claimed that it was an élite taste at the time it was imposed.

Read was saying in 'What is Revolutionary Art?' that the artist was a special kind of person who could legitimately escape within society into a position of detachment which, in terms of art, was represented by pure form. In another article of the same date he wrote more specifically of the artist within modern society.

> Art is socially functional... but it has always functioned through the intellectual elite of any period. We... the critics and apologists of the modern movement, are increasingly impelled to justify the social relevance of such art. Society today is disunited; there is no accepted mythology on which the artist can rely for a medium of communication. The élite, in this decaying stage of capitalism, feels insecure, is without intellectual confidence, and therefore aimlessly dilettante. We live, it is only too obvious, in an age of transition.
>
> What can an artist do in such an age – an age of transition which is going to outlast his own lifetime? If he refuses to be a mere time-server, he can only withdraw upon himself, creating his own world... In the present spiritual and economic condition of Europe, there is no other choice to make.
>
> The values of this age, in so far as they are social values, are not spiritual values. They are values of wealth, comfort, amusement, excitement, sexual stimulation... There is no spiritual integrity in our life, and no artist of any worth will put his skill and sensibility at the service of any less worthy cause.[19]

Read's position closely parallels the modernism which Clement Greenberg evolved in 1939–40, putting integrity above popularity, and insisting that art must preserve itself and wait for better times.

Read argued in 'What is Revolutionary Art?' that the new Russian art was dogged by its own past, an apparent paradox considering how Read, like Eliot, had put high value on tradition. But Read's argument was that Stalinist art was making a fraudulent appeal to tradition when all it was really doing was reviving a specific bit of the past, nineteenth-century realism. What Read saw happening in Russia he thought was also being imposed in Germany. With Germany, however, Read's position was different, because he had a personal commitment. *Art Now* had been dedicated to Read's German colleague and friend Max Sauerlandt, formerly of the Kunstgewerbemuseum in Hamburg, who had been in the first group of avant-garde museum curators to be dismissed, in March 1933, when the National Socialists assumed power. In *Art Now* Read became perhaps the first writer in Britain to condemn unequivocally National Socialist art policy and his passionate endorsement of avant-garde art over the next few years, and total opposition to regressive tendencies, need to be seen in the context of his affection for Germany and, especially, respect for Sauerlandt.

In October 1935 Read published a damning review of *Art in the USSR*, published in Britain by the *Studio*, but written by official Russian authors.[20] Read tore into the notion that the newly established official Soviet art was a reconnection with tradition as the writers claimed, stressing that it was to the limited achievement of the nineteenth century that the new academicism appealed, and condemning the suggestion that art must have popular appeal. Read never lost the conviction he shared with Eliot that art was difficult and had to be fought for, and that to popularize was to vulgarize. As in his attitude to National Socialist art, he was quick to criticize Soviet Socialist Realism, linking the Soviet Union with Germany, and finding it odd that two countries which, in common with most people, Read saw as opposed politically, should be so alike in their contempt for modern art. He referred to Hitler's and Goering's visit in 1933 to the Schreckenskammer exhibition in Dresden, which ridiculed pre-1933 German modernism and was to be a model for the Degenerate Art exhibition in Munich in 1937.

Read admitted he knew little of the post-revolutionary Russian art of Constructivism, which had barely been heard of in the English-speaking world before Alfred Barr fitted it into his pattern of non-figurative developments in *Cubism and Abstract Art* (1937). Read's lack of knowledge of Constructivism was bound up with the arrival from Paris in 1935 of the Russian Naum Gabo, who had left his native country in 1922, and had appropriated the word Constructivism for his own work and his brother Antoine Pevsner's. The brothers had published in Moscow in 1920 the Realist Manifesto in which they described with clarity the need for sculpture, in line with modern thinking and modern science, to switch from a concept of reality as mass towards reality as force or energy, away from a sculpture of solid volume towards one of open structures.

Writing the catalogue for the Gabo–Pevsner exhibition at the Museum of Modern Art, New York, in 1948, Read credited the brothers' contribution to this key development beyond Cubism, adding that the new Soviet Union could not tolerate such innovation, and Gabo and Pevsner had had to leave. Read was not alone in not understanding that Constructivism was an ideology and set of practices that attempted in the early 1920s to reorder the relationship of art to industry and work, and that the principal theoretical texts relating to Constructivism had actually been published from 1922 onwards after Gabo had left. The contribution of Rodchenko and others to Constructivism was not well understood, even by Alfred Barr who had visited Russia and exhibited examples of their work at the Museum of Modern Art in New York. Far from Gabo being forced to leave Moscow by the Bolsheviks, he had left voluntarily because his concept of Realism, a radical formal development but without the social implications of Constructivism, was out of step with the direction other members of the avant-garde were taking.

Read's first reaction, in 1933, to the art of the dictators was thus to the National Socialists' condemnation of the recent German art that he alone in Britain had championed, as well as being a response to the fate of a friend deprived of a senior museum post. Then in 1935 he was incensed by a British art publisher issuing a craven account of Socialist Realism, and linked this with developments in Germany. Thirdly, having become convinced that non-figurative art was the true revolutionary art, and now a close friend of Gabo – a sculptor of distinction and influence, but not in the original sense a Constructivist – Read misapprehended Gabo's role in the new Russian art. In one sense this was a minor confusion over the meaning of a name, since Read understood quite clearly what Gabo's contribution was. But the misunderstanding of Constructivism, which was possible because of the delayed contact of the Anglo-Saxon world with non-figurative art, led to the word being used to describe formal developments alone, the revolutionary contribution of the early Soviet years to be overlooked, and Gabo's withdrawal from Russia in 1922 to be presented by Read to an élite American audience in 1948, at the start of the Cold War, as an escape. This would not have been possible if he had had a clearer picture of the beginnings of non-figurative art during and after the First World War. As it was, his knowledge, like Nicholson's and Hepworth's, was mediated through Paris and *Abstraction-Création*, a group and publication which took the sting out of the radical, socially reformist ideology of the early non-figurative movements.

In 'What is Revolutionary Art?' Read also looked at Surrealism, which was now in the front of his mind as the British avant-garde fractured during 1935 into Surrealist and abstract groups. Read admired Surrealists like Arp and Miró whose abstractness meant they could not be simply labelled literary or narrative. He had explored for ten years a Classical–Romantic polarity which he could now translate from its literary-poetic origins in his thought to the visual arts, and he could use Classical to mean formal and Romantic broadly to mean poetry added to the formal structure. In 1935 Read was clear that it was through abstraction that the new art would finally come into being, that Surrealism was what he called 'destructive', a part of the necessary fragmentation of the old aesthetic order, and thus had 'only a temporary role in the art of a transitional period', while abstract art had a positive function, keeping 'inviolate, until such time as society will once more be ready to make use of them, the universal qualities of art – those elements which survive all changes and revolution'.[21] Though his commitment at that point was to non-figuration, by the time of the International Surrealist Exhibition in London in 1936, to which his contribution was to edit and introduce a book titled *Surrealism*, his approach was shifting, not least because his mind was focusing increasingly on British rather than continental art.

Early in 1934 the Royal Academy organized an exhibition of British Art and, though it did not extend to the twentieth century, its reverberations were considerable and put a spotlight on British art as a whole. Coinciding with the revolutions in artistic policy in Germany and the Soviet Union, the exhibition stimulated a parallel interest in nationality in Britain. Looked at from a different angle, the issue was the way political deterioration in Europe set in motion the search for national identity in different countries. Read, who had always been interested in nationality, as the *Listener* articles show, would have noticed with interest Paul Nash's references to traditional British monuments and archaeological sites such as Avebury in his writing for the *Unit One* volume which Read edited in 1933. Read at the same time wrote his inaugural article, in December 1933, as editor of the *Burlington Magazine*, on 'English Art',[22] and attempted, as others including Wilenski and Fry also did at the time, a definition of Englishness: for Read it meant precise observation, particularity, earthiness, a tendency to the burlesque and satire, an empirical outlook and mistrust of idealism. He saw British art as personal, even eccentric, but not extreme, allied to nature but not naturalistic. It was a judicious summary, overlapping what he had already written in the *Listener* about German and Flemish art and adding to his conviction that there was an art that could be called North European.

Read's closest artist friend was Henry Moore and the article on English art leads naturally towards an appreciation of Moore, who, it could be argued, started from nature but was not dominated by it, whose interest in the life and energy even of inanimate things could be fitted into the pantheistic strain Read observed in English art and had previously recognized in English poetry. Read was an established authority on English Romantic poetry and the interest that led him to devote his first monograph on a visual artist, in 1934, to Moore, followed naturally from his concern with poetry. Read's appeal to Worringer's precepts of the vital and the abstract reappears, and Moore is cast as exemplar of a middle way which draws on the austerity of pure abstraction and also masters the vital rhythms implicit in the forms of nature.

> Mr Moore... believes that behind the appearance of things there is some kind of spiritual essence, a force or immanent being which is only partially revealed in actual living forms. Those actual forms are, as it were, clumsy expedients determined by the haphazard circumstances of time and place. The end of organic evolution is functional or utilitarian, and spiritually speaking a blind end. It is the business of art, therefore, to strip forms of their casual excrescences, to reveal the forms the spirit would evolve if its aims were disinterested.[23]

Read associates Moore with the pattern of his thought inspired by Worringer by denying, first, that Moore fits into the Renaissance humanist type, because he is not naturalist, but refusing also to allow that Moore can be shoe-horned into a narrowly formal concept. Moore's model, Read says, is that of the Egyptians, Mexicans and Etruscans. It is archaic, which means that it responds to features that show the vitality of the subject, which it exaggerates and distorts until a significant rhythm and shape is arrived at. Plainly, Read's writings on poetry, on English art, and then on Moore, do not accord with his pressing defence of non-figuration in 1935.

Read's introductory essay to *Surrealism* turns the tables on classicism with his declaration that 'wherever the blood of martyrs stains the ground, there you will find a doric column or perhaps a statue of Minerva'.[24] Read had always been concerned with the polarity of romanticism and classicism, as he was with that between the personal and the collective, freedom and order, logic and intuition. In the 1920s he had belonged intellectually with Eliot in the party of order, and his resolution of the romantic–classical conflict had been through reason. He had called Gothic art up to 1350 the Age of Reason and regarded it as the peak of medieval intellectual achievement, the Thomist resolution of faith and rationality and, in art, of naturalism and abstraction.[25]

Read's commentary on Moore in 1934 falls into a similar pattern; Moore is archaic, primitive, belonging, Read might have said, to the early phase in an historical cycle when it had not been overgrown with ornament and excrescence. But there is a respect for nature, also, as point of origin. But in *Surrealism* Read describes 'a principle of life, of creation, of liberation, and that is the romantic spirit'.[26] He no longer treats romanticism and classicism as opposites to be reconciled, but sees romanticism as the seed, classicism the husk, and it is the seed that must at all costs be preserved. Read's recasting of the debate follows from his new conviction that classicism always reflects authority imposed from the outside and not arrived at by reasoning.

The International Surrealist Exhibition was a flamboyant late expression of the movement, corresponding in terms of Surrealism to the position in the Middle Ages of the late Gothic which Read had earlier dismissed as ornamental and decadent. When his introduction to the 1936 book was republished in 1952 with the new title 'Surrealism and the Romantic Principle', Read added a footnote, acknowledging, in effect, the suddenness of his apostasy in the classical–romantic debate, and claiming that the pressure of external events in 1936 might have affected his judgement.[27] No doubt his attitude was bound up with events in Germany and Russia and a passionate contempt for predetermined styles and ideologies. Read's writing on advanced art between 1933 and 1939 was strongly influenced by his resistance to the regressive art of the dictatorships. He was opposed in principle to academic art anywhere, but in England, where it remained relatively mute through the 1930s, it did not concern him as it did in countries where modernism was under positive attack.

With London isolated from Europe by war, and the Hampstead group scattered and not to reconstitute itself, the 1940s were less internationalist and provided fertile ground for the development of the arguments about national identity hinted at in Read's writing on Surrealism. New possibilities for British art emerged with radical developments in the institutional framework of contemporary art represented by the foundation of the Arts Council and the Institute of Contemporary Arts within a few years of each other and the expansion of the British Council's visual art activities. Read had seen in the early demise of Vorticism and through his work with Unit One how little institutional support Britain offered artists. His contribution to the *Unit One* book had been focused on the need for artists to find strength in groups, and his writing in the 1930s was from the vantage point of a polemical participant. Read's experience as curator and organizer fitted him to help administer the new art scene. As he did so, his writing on contemporary art – often on the same artists he had supported in the 1930s – shifted slightly towards historical context and cross-cultural analogies.

Read edited or introduced an impressive series of monographs on the work of his friends, Moore (1944), Nicholson (1948), Nash (1948) and Hepworth (1952), all published commercially by Lund Humphries but conveying the sense from their size and the completeness of their record of artists' work that, in the context of the new institutions for promoting British art, there was beginning to be an official modern British art with Read as its leading authority. Read's introductory essay in the Moore volume is interspersed with illustrations of Cycladic, Etruscan, African, Mexican and other European and non-European sculptures and artefacts, mainly of the kind

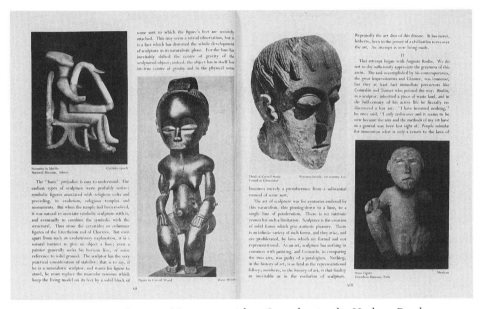

From *Henry Moore: Sculpture and Drawings*, with an Introduction by Herbert Read (London: A. Zwemmer, 1944)

Read had referred to as archaic in the 1934 introduction. The Nicholson volume has Bronze Age metalwork from Britain and Cyprus, a mosaic from Torcello, and Cubist and abstract art by Kandinsky and Picasso, Gris and Mondrian. In neither text are most of the comparative illustrations referred to, though it is plain from the argument why they are there. The Nicholson book starts with an essay on abstraction and revives Worringer's analysis of empathy and abstraction, the tendency to turn to nature or to be 'space shy' depending on the degree of a culture's well-being in relation to the external world:

137

Ben Nicholson is the leading representative in Great Britain of that tendency in art which has been called *abstract*... The tendency to abstraction in art is by no means specifically modern. It has recurred repeatedly throughout the history of art, and was already recognised as an historical phenomenon, and called 'abstract', before the modern movement came into being... Indeed, it is possible that the *theory* of abstract art not only preceded the practice of it in modern times, but actually inspired and influenced its development.[28]

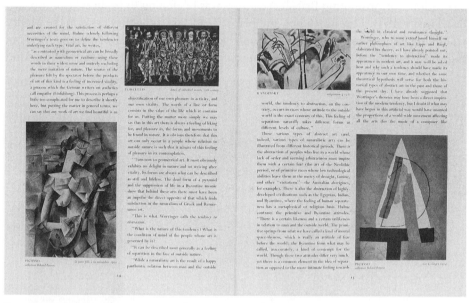

From *Ben Nicholson: Paintings, Reliefs, Drawings*, with an Introduction by Herbert Read (London: Lund Humphries, 1948)

Read had appealed to Worringer's ideas since he edited the writings of T. E. Hulme for publication in 1924, and to that extent there is nothing new, and there is no period in Read's professional life when he considers the contemporary apart from history. It happens again in 1952 in his introduction to the Hepworth volume. Read points to Hepworth's own account of contemporary influences on her work, and adds that 'she might have mentioned more, for by quite consciously situating herself in the historical tradition of sculpture, she allowed her roots to strike deep into the past, as well as to spread widely in the present'.[29] Read adds as influences the Roman copy of Praxiteles's *Aphrodite of Knidos*, African, Mexican, Egyptian and early Italian Renaissance art. The point is not that Hepworth may not have been influenced by all of these at some point, but that none is linked by Read to a specific work or period of Hepworth and none is in fact particularly relevant to the period of writing. This is not a criticism of Read in the sense that, in relation to Hepworth, anything he said

138

was wrong, but there is a certain artificiality in building her up as a 'world sculptor' in this way.

Though historical reflection was always involved in Read's consideration of contemporary art, it was less common in the Hampstead years when he was bound up in the day-to-day lives of artists and was defending the modern against the historically oriented art of the dictators. The debate over the incidence of naturalism and abstraction in history shifted in the 1930s to a book such as *Art and Society* (1936), which was not primarily concerned with present-day art. The new monographs of the 1940s and early 1950s, especially those on Moore and Nicholson, restored the connection between ideas derived from Worringer and contemporary art. They removed the artists some way from their immediate context and located them in world terms. Moore, with his longstanding passion for the British Museum's non-European collections, offered himself for this treatment, and the affinity between Read and Moore related to the way both connected being modern with having a world view of art. With Nicholson, however, Read's strategy worked less well, and the trans-historical view of abstraction that Read proposed is less convincing. Read had thought in the mid-1930s of Nicholson's switch to pure form as the essential way forward for revolutionary art, but had never felt the need, as he did in 1948, to relate Nicholson's abstraction to history. The revolutionary character of abstraction in the face of the art of the dictators had been a sufficient account. Unlike Moore, Nicholson did not favour comparisons of Read's kind, and in any case parallels with the cooler sensibility of post-Giotto Italian art and with Cézanne would have been more appropriate to Nicholson than with Byzantine art which was Read's choice, perhaps because it carried the endorsement of Worringer.

When Read came to write his most comprehensive work on sculpture, *The Art of Sculpture* (1956), which was forming in his mind as lectures at the time he wrote the Hepworth monograph in 1952, he saw Moore, Hepworth and Gabo as climactic figures in modern sculpture and it was to those three that he dedicated the book. The Hepworth monograph itself compares the three, distinguishing their different contributions to modern sculpture, with a view, in part at least, to giving each a particular role in the outcome of historical trends. It is a form of writing backed by a particular purpose, which was to frame the British contribution to art in as positive a way as possible and, like Greenberg's support at the same time of Pollock or David Smith, it aimed to put compatriot artists on the world stage without descending into chauvinism.

Read particularly did this with his close friends of the prewar generation, feeling, as he wrote in the passage from the *Hudson Review* from 1948 quoted at the beginning, that post-war art was a 'diminuendo'.[30] But there was another way in which Read saw pre- and post-war art differently. The first remained for him a world art that to a large extent transcended history and demonstrated with a high degree of refinement the way the artists assimilated the examples of Africa, Mexico and Egypt, integrating the best of history into the present in order, Read infers, to give the present resilience in the face of the debasement of art in Russia and Germany. On the other hand Read saw the younger, post-war artists more in terms of what by 1951 he was to call 'regional norms'.[31] Nationality and geography became more important and, in debates involving the new generation particularly, the notion of a world art receded.

Read's catalogue for the British section of the Exposition Internationale de Peintures Modernes, the inaugural exhibition of UNESCO in Paris in 1946, opened with the comment that a few years earlier the British contribution would not have been distinctive or of interest to anyone outside Britain. It seems a curious remark in view of Moore, especially, already having international prestige in the 1930s. But Read was thinking now not of an international art, such as London had given a home to in the 1930s, but of the international standing of art that could be seen as distinctively British. He looked back to the earlier prestige of Turner, Constable, Blake, Gainsborough and Hogarth, after whom, he thought, British art had lost its nerve, dissipating its talent in anecdote, with artists of promise such as Palmer, Calvert and Danby withering early in the acrid atmosphere of the industrial revolution. Now Britain begins to recover its native tradition, Read says. Before looking at Sutherland, Minton, Craxton, Colquhoun and MacBryde, who were the core of the exhibition, he addressed himself to Paul Nash, valuing Nash's lyrical landscape watercolours with their references back to the eighteenth century above the more experimental Surrealist work, by which Nash, who had died in 1946, would have himself liked to have been remembered.

Read had got to know Nash in 1933 in the context of Unit One, but Nash had been on the edge of the Hampstead avant-garde, and it was only after the International Surrealist Exhibition, which had focused the minds of both on the poetic and the nature of Englishness, that Read first wrote about Nash – an introduction to a collection of colour plates published in 1937. That was followed by a volume in the Penguin Modern Painters series in 1944, a tribute in the memorial volume published in 1948, and a preface to Nash's posthumously published autobiography *Outline* (1949). Long before they met Read had felt an affinity with Nash on seeing his exhibition of war art at the Leicester Galleries in 1918,[32] which, he felt, expressed the same outrage at the destruction imposed by the war on nature as his own writing did. Read had much in common with Nash, particularly in terms of their response to romanticism, but this did not emerge during the 'international' years of the mid-1930s or until the issue of Englishness rose to the top of the cultural agenda towards the end of the decade. There was a marked change not only in Nash's art in the late 1930s, as his concern for the modern lessened, and criticism of his work – not only Read's – made more of his links as a landscape watercolourist with earlier English art.

Read's proposal in the Moore and Nicholson monographs that art has enduring cross-cultural and trans-historical properties emerges clearly in 1948 in his catalogue introduction for the Institute of Contemporary Art's 'Forty Thousand Years of Modern Art: A Comparison of Primitive and Modern'. Read argued that the purpose of bringing together works from prehistory to Picasso's *Demoiselles d'Avignon* was not to point to particular primitive influences, but to highlight.

> the universality of art, and, more particularly, the eternal recurrence of certain phenomena in art which, on their appearance, are labelled 'modern'... like conditions produce like effects, and, more specifically... there are conditions in modern life which have produced effects only to be seen in primitive epochs... these conditions... are archetypal, and buried deep in the unconscious ... a vague sense of insecurity, a cosmic anguish... feelings and intuitions that demand expression in abstract or unnaturalistic forms.

There is a problem with reading an essentially post-Enlightenment concept, the modern, back into history, and to suggest, as Read seems to, a stable identity for it. The 'universality of art' is another concept that is open to criticism: was abstract art the same thing even in the late 1940s as it had been for Hampstead in the 1930s? Certainly the sculpture of Reg Butler, Lynn Chadwick and others, to which Read was to give the title 'geometry of fear' in 1952,[33] had very different priorities from those of Gabo and Hepworth or even Moore. Gabo, in an exchange of letters with Read published during the war, had stated unequivocally that his sculpture made no response to the war because there was nothing particular that he could say through his art that people could not experience and feel for themselves, and that his art should be a reminder of better times.[34] Gabo was speaking the language Read had used of non-figurative art in 1935. Though 'geometry of fear' seems an overstated title, the sculpture it alludes to certainly did, on the other hand, reflect in some way the sense of insecurity and anguish Read refers to. Nowhere more than at this point do Read's two roles, as contemporary critic and historian of world art, coexist so uneasily.

Contemporary British Art (1951) is linked with Read's role in framing an 'official' British art for the Festival of Britain in that year, and is rooted in a concept of nationality derived ultimately from German theory.

> The cultural unity we all desire as the basis of political unity will be artificial and insecure unless it is a focus of the diversity and multiplicity of local and individual forces. Unity is not the spiritual counterpart of uniformity, and each country will contribute most to the unity we all desire by exploiting its own idiosyncrasies, and by remaining true to the traditions which have become part of its character and destiny... We cannot escape our mental climates, because they are in a literal sense the creation of our prevailing winds and the chemistry of our soils.[35]

It is inconceivable, Read suggests, that British art should be *decisively* influenced by

Indian art or French by African, and such effects as that of Africa on Picasso or Mexico on Moore should be seen as like injections of a drug, a temporary stimulus to restore the body to health, and not the basis of habit or fashion. History, in Read's view, showed that the art of a particular region always tends to revert to a regional norm – to a mode of sensibility and style of expression determined by ethnic and geographic factors. If the vitality of art comes from cross-breeding of styles, its strength comes from stability, from roots that grow deep into a native soil.[36] This was an argument belonging to a post-war Britain which had narrowly escaped oblivion and wanted continuity as it faced Americanization on one side and Communism on the other. As an essentially post-war attitude to art, it parallels the *rappel à l'ordre* that followed 1918, with the reappropriation of classicism as the 'real' tradition of French art in opposition to Cubism, and the resurgence of eighteenth-century tastes in England against Vorticism. As a critic in the 1920s, Read had been well aware of the trend, and his connection in 1932 of Derain with the traditional idea of 'virtue' had been a late manifestation of it.

Read wanted two things that were not altogether reconcilable. He wanted to assert Moore's and Nicholson's equality with the greatest of world art, and made comparisons in monographs on them to demonstrate it. But he also wanted to press 'regional norms' and, recalling his mid-1930s defence of non-figurative art, he argued again in 1951 that style is the ephemeral addition to what is fundamental, defined earlier in terms of pure form, and now in terms of nationality. Read's strength was that, unlike other critics ploughing the same furrow, he had, in Worringer's distinction between abstraction and empathy and theory of expressionism as *the* mode of north European art, a theoretical basis for his case. Read was conscious of this, and in *Contemporary British Art* enlarges the context beyond Britain to northern Europe; he refers to the effect of the war in disseminating true German art across the world as artists fled from National Socialism, and he explains his reasons for seeing romanticism as the true British art in terms of a form of expression which he sees as typical of northern Europe as a whole. He repeats his earlier argument founded on Worringer that the typical art of northern Europe alternates between abstraction and expressionism. We may, Read says, be successful for a time if we absorb southern European styles, which are idealistic and naturalistic, but our talent lies in styles that are introspective and personal, and such styles are romantic by nature. The genius of our greatest painters and architects no less than of our greatest poets was always romantic and the trend of contemporary art may be interpreted as a return to our romantic tradition.[37]

Read never entirely reconciled the twin roles of critic and historian, or his excitement at new art as it actually was with what as a historian he felt it ought to be. His difficulties were a measure, first, of the ambition of his project, which was to turn British criticism back from consideration of the end result alone, the form, to the starting-point, the will or impulse in society or individual that gave rise to one kind of expression rather than another. But there was a complicating factor in the discontinuity of the modern movement, which Read had already recognized in *Art Now*, which always presented difficulties to his dialectical frame of mind. 'We have in some way telescoped our past development', he wrote in 1933, 'and... the human spirit, which in the past had expressed itself... diversely at different times, now expresses the same diversity... at one and the same time'.[38] It was not, after all, a matter of Romantic *or* Classic, North *or* South; such was the twentieth century's knowledge and consciousness of history that such opposites now coexisted.

Notes

1   'The Situation of Art in Europe at the End of the Second World War', *The Hudson Review*, New York, vol. 1, no. 1 (1948), reprinted in Herbert Read, *The Philosophy of Modern Art: Collected Essays* (London: Faber and Faber, 1952), p. 57.
2   *The Listener*, 5 March 1930.
3   Ibid., 5 October 1932.
4   'The Painter-Critic', *The Listener*, 7 December 1932.
5   See especially the 'Readers and Writers' column, *New Age*, 1 October 1921.
6   'Modern German Painting', *The Listener*, 29 October 1930, and 'Post-War Art in Germany', ibid., 5 November 1930.
7   *Art Now: An Introduction to the Theory of Modern Painting and Sculpture* (London: Faber and Faber, 1933), p. 30.
8   Ibid., p. 33.
9   'Beyond Realism', *The Listener*, 16 April 1930.
10 See, for example, Paul Nash, 'The Life of the Inanimate Object', *Country Life*, May 1937, and 'Surrealism and the Illustrated Book', *Signature*, March 1937; and Hugh Sykes Davies, 'Surrealism at this Time and Place', in Herbert Read (ed.), *Surrealism* (London: Faber and Faber, 1936).
11 Walter Gropius, 'Rehousing in Big Cities', *The Listener*, 16 May 1934.
12 *Art and Industry: The Principles of Industrial Design* (London: Faber and Faber, 1934), p. 1.
13 Ibid., pp. 2–3.
14 *English Stained Glass* (London and New York: G. P. Putnam's Sons, 1926). See especially 'Introductory' and chapter 2, 'The Age of Reason'.
15 For Read and Maritain see especially 'Art and Scholasticism', *The Listener*, 19 March 1930.
16 'What is Revolutionary Art?', in Betty Rea (ed.), *Five on Revolutionary Art* (London: Wishart, 1935), p. 12.
17 Ibid., p. 13.
18 Ibid.
19 'Jean Hélion', *Axis*, November 1935.
20 'Soviet Realism', *The Listener*, 2 October 1935.
21 'What is Revolutionary Art?', p. 20.
22 *Burlington Magazine*, December 1933, reprinted in *In Defence of Shelley and Other Essays* (London: Heinemann, 1936), and *The Philosophy of Modern Art*, op. cit.
23 *Henry Moore* (London: Zwemmer, 1934), p. 12.
24 Read, *Surrealism*, p. 23.
25 *English Stained Glass*, chapter 2, passim.
26 *Surrealism*, p. 26.

27 *The Philosophy of Modern Art: Collected Essays*, p. 105.
28 *Ben Nicholson: Painting, Drawings, Reliefs*, vol. 1 (London: Lund Humphries, 1948), p. 13.
29 *Barbara Hepworth: Carvings and Drawings* (London: Lund Humphries, 1952), p. ix.
30 See above, note 1.
31 In *Contemporary British Art* (Harmondsworth: Penguin Books, 1951), p. 39.
32 See *Paul Nash*, no. 1 in the series 'Contemporary British Painters', ed. D. A. Ross and A. C. Hannay (London: Soho Press, 1937), unpaginated.
33 In the catalogue of the British Pavilion at the 1952 Venice Biennale.
34 See 'An exchange of Letters between Naum Gabo and Herbert Read', *Horizon*, July 1944.
35 *Contemporary British Art*, pp. 38–39.
36 Ibid.
37 Ibid.
38 *Art Now*, p. 60.

Herbert Read and Design

ROBIN KINROSS

Preamble

THIS essay needs some explanation. Written from outside the academy, by a typographer and publisher, it starts and ends in the realm of personal anecdote. But perhaps this informality is no more than a true reflection of the pragmatic and worldly nature of the activity of designing.

In 1980, on the day I first met Norman Potter, the author of the first book I published, we had an argument about Herbert Read. Norman Potter is English, and of that generation just too young to have fought in Spain, but old enough to have resisted call-up in the Second World War. As he once wrote in a letter to me, by 1949 he had seen the inside of four English prisons in various episodes of youthful dissent, including refusal of an identity card. Potter is a lifelong anarchist, a designer and maker, a workshop person in love with tools, especially certain big heavy cutting machines. One might describe him as a modernist cabinet-maker; and as a poet. Our argument went like this.

RK: But Read was so woolly and vague in his writing. Yes, he was generous, but too generous.

NP: Read was exceptional in Britain, then and now. He bridged the cultures, between the visual and the literary. Britain's literary culture has been so stifling. Those literary people had no clue about design. Bloomsbury visual culture was a matter of pattern-making and ornament: Omega Workshop amateurism. Ornament went along with their essentially literary cast of mind; it is like narrative. Read was different: he understood abstraction, and he was European-minded. So he got quite vigorously involved in design. His book *Art and Industry* had a kind of talismanic quality for us: the book itself was a modern object, like the buildings designed by Wells Coates or the furniture by Aalto, which we regarded as icons. The tweedy later editions of the book showed how the English literary culture smothered what Read was trying to do.

RK: But in fact the first edition of *Art and Industry* isn't such a perfect book. The design, credited to Herbert Bayer, is muddled. And the argument of the book, too, is so diffused and evasive.

NP: No. The book had real spirit and presence. And I remember Read at that public meeting in defence of the Freedom Group in 1945: obviously a shy man, but with real courage, speaking up for anarchism.

And so the argument was carried on, intermittently, over the years. One piece of evidence turned up when I found Norman Potter's old copy of *Poetry and Anarchism* in a second-hand bookshop. I bought it and gave it back to him. He re-read the book and remarked on how powerful and intoxicating it had been for him, on his first encounter with it. Then I wrote an essay about the book *Art and Industry*.[1] I was interested in trying to trace the history of the writing and production of that work, in as much detail as I could find. My essay was also intended as one of a set of pieces which would diagnose the ills of British culture through case histories.

In what follows here I take the argument of that essay a little further: beyond the book *Art and Industry*, and beyond Read, to include some things that happened outside the terms of his discussion. In doing so, I make criticisms of what seem to me the limitations of Herbert Read's activity in, and his ideas about, the field of design. These criticisms are not meant as a point-scoring attack, but rather as an attempt to tackle something larger than Read. In that spirit they are a compliment to Read, as an enabler, for opening things up.

A theory of design in 1934

Art and Industry: The Principles of Industrial Design was published first in 1934. The book was issued in four further editions, finally going out of print in the 1970s. *Art and Industry* is a discussion of the aesthetics of manufactured products. It addresses a 'problem', as Read himself put it (or a 'problematic' as we might put it now, more pretentiously). The problem is this: what might be the new aesthetic standards for the new methods of production that were by then widespread in the industrializing western world? So the book extends and applies the aesthetics that Read was then working out in relation to sculpture and painting, into this hybrid field of industrial design. It also represents an extension of his already existing interest in applied art: he had worked for almost ten years, until 1931, in the Department of Ceramics at the Victoria and Albert Museum.

A crude summary of Read's position on design, in 1934, might run as follows. He was worrying about form, and especially about abstract form: by then he had taken up his role as principal critic and explainer-to-the-British of modern, especially abstract art. He was also concerned to think about the social dimension of art: a dimension that would take on a greater presence for him as those years in the 1930s, of social and political crisis, wore on. Design appeared to Read, rather suddenly I think, as the field where these two interests – abstraction and the social place of things – could come together.

146

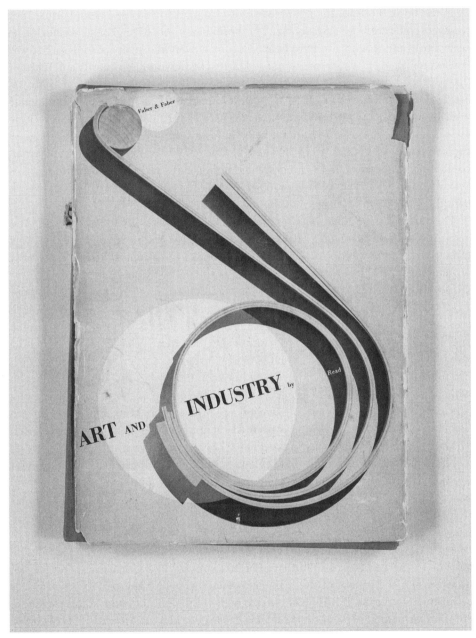

Front of the book jacket of the first edition of *Art and Industry*, 1934, designed by Herbert Bayer. The image is a plywood model, designed by Alvar Aalto.

In the book of 1934, the conjunction of form and society is, I would argue, not resolved coherently or sufficiently. The book bears too strongly the weight of its early aim – and it seems to have been conceived even five years or so before it was finally published. It was to be, to quote David Thistlewood, 'primarily a defence of the abstract artist... whose researches into pure form were crucial to both the aesthetic and commercial well-being of the community'.[2] In Read's correspondence with his publisher, as the book was being prepared, its title was – even as late as June 1934 – 'Art at Work'. The shift towards 'industry' was given considerable help by the events of 1933 and 1934 in Central Europe. This was the moment when continental modernism in architecture and design came to Britain. Bauhaus masters – Walter Gropius, Marcel Breuer, László Moholy-Nagy – came to live and work here then; although, as it proved, their stays were only temporary.

Gropius and the Bauhaus became the exemplifications of Read's argument. And in getting another *Bauhäusler,* Herbert Bayer, to design the book, and Moholy-Nagy to help obtain photographs, the hope was to make the Bauhaus ideas a materially present part of the argument. In the design of the first edition of the book, a determined effort was made to break with the traditions of English literary publishing. Text is set two columns to a page, and pictures are integrated as much as possible into the text. There are reminders of Bauhaus typography as it first flourished in the mid-1920s. For example, notes to text are signalled by an 'elemental' form (a dot) rather than by conventional reference marks (asterisk, dagger, etc.) or numerals. But the final product was a compromise between the wishes of a designer in Berlin with imperfect command of English and hazy in his technical instructions, and a printer (Cambridge University Press) and a publisher (Faber and Faber) in England – neither of them used to being instructed by a designer, let alone a modernist one. The correspondence surviving in the archive of Faber and Faber makes all this clear.

Nevertheless, as some of its first reviewers registered, *Art and Industry* did present a strikingly different appearance as an artefact, and this supported and was indeed part of its argument. The photographs were the most powerful element here. In his 'Explanations & acknowledgements' to the book, Read brought the qualities of these images into his larger argument about the need to accept and use the possibilities of design: 'What is known as commercial photography is in this country immeasurably inferior to the commercial photography in a country like Germany – and for the usual reason: the refusal of the manufacturer to recognise and pay for the services of a competent artist. If it is objected that some of the photographs I have used here are too artistic, and present their subjects in a too striking or dramatic light, I would claim that I have been careful to exclude any photographs which in any way distorted or misrepresented their subjects; and that otherwise I do not see why a product of industrial manufacture should not be given the same chance as a work of fine art.'[3]

The pages from *Art and Industry* reproduced here show the book's use of pictures at its most argumentative. Vernier depth gauges are juxtaposed with a Dornier sea-

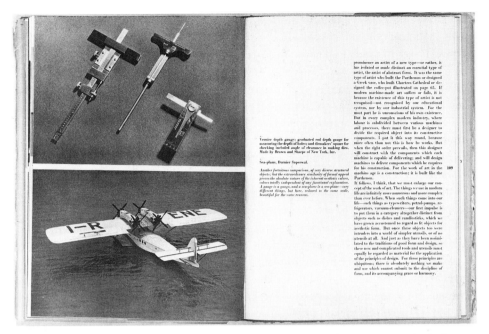

Spread from *Art and Industry*, 1934 (page size 253 × 192mm), showing its method of comparing merely technical objects with the products of modern design. The design of the book itself uses a central horizontal axis, around which headings, captions and page numbers are oriented.

plane. The caption suggests that these things are 'beautiful for the same reasons', and 'the extraordinary similarity of formal appeal proves the absolute nature of the inherent aesthetic values' (p. 108). Elsewhere a switching relay in use at the BBC's new Broadcasting House is juxtaposed, and compared for harmony, with an aerial view of the new housing estate at Dammerstock, designed by Walter Gropius and others (see above, p. 130). Such pages provide easy bait for anti-modernist critics who have seen the new architecture as merely mechanized and inhuman.

If, over the span of his life, Read engaged in a dialectic of classic and romantic, of the rational and the felt (or of form and formlessness, in David Thistlewood's analysis), then these pages show most clearly that just then, in 1934, he was inclined to pursue a modernist technological rationalism. Now, after a succession of revisionist accounts, we may view the modern movement in architecture and design – with the Bauhaus as its most vocal and perhaps typical institution – as a fragile and contradictory coalition, already falling apart in the European crisis of the 1930s. But in 1934, the Bauhaus seemed to represent a better, more complete integration of art and industry than anything that was then possible in Britain. A tubular steel chair designed by Marcel Breuer was, it was implied by Read, both 'artistic' and

149

'industrial', in ways not achieved elsewhere, and certainly not in Britain.

My criticism of Read's book would be that this key element in it, of the argument for design, is too much implanted as a late addition. The weight of the book falls too strongly on pure aesthetics. There is very little discussion of industry or of politics. German design is sometimes held out as a model; but Read offers no real explanations as to why in this field Germany is different from Britain. The book relies far too heavily on photographs of objects-as-sculpture. There are no plans or diagrams to indicate how these things are constructed, or how they operate. For a striking contrast, in these and in other respects, one might look at Siegfried Giedion's *Mechanization Takes Command* (1948).

One can see Read's book as an important step in the habilitation of continental modernism in Britain. *Art and Industry* became one of the gospels of design in Britain: thus the evidence of its longevity in print. Nikolaus Pevsner's *Pioneers of Modern Design* should be mentioned here, as a work of comparable significance for the culture of British design. It was published in its first form in 1936, and has stayed in print ever since. In this book, too, Gropius is a key, emblematic figure. Pevsner was of course German: but someone who managed to integrate remarkably thoroughly into British life, and whose work turned into a seamless synthesis of German and English traits.

After 1934: theory and practice

After the publication of *Art and Industry*, there was a hiatus in Read's involvement in design. Other things occupied him, and, in tune with the public mood of the middle and later 1930s, he became politically more explicit in his writings. If he had since his youth been politically conscious, he now 'came out' politically – as an anarchist. But if one goes to Read, looking for an anarchist or left-wing theory of design, this disjunction or time-lag is something to remember.[4] His ideas about design were put down in print a few years before he began to develop the explicit anarchism for which we may think of him now. He never had the occasion or the will to write an anarchist text on design, although one can find hints and passages in later texts which do at least raise some of the difficult considerations that this idea entails.

One can trace Read's modifications to his ideas about design in essays and statements that he published in the 1940s. The separation of 'form' from 'society' and from 'function', which is clear in *Art and Industry*, begins to dissolve, at least in theory. The second edition of the book was published in 1944, and the work was now returned to a standard 'literary' format. (This may have been for reasons of war economy – the first edition had been quite a lavish production – and for reasons of inertia: to revise the work, but maintain the structure of its original layout, would have required some ingenuity. Herbert Bayer was by then in the USA.) The text was little changed, but Read did insert these words at a crucial point: 'But in the end, we shall find that the fundamental factor in all these problems is a philosophy of life.

150

The problem of good and bad art, of a right and wrong system of education, of a just and unjust social structure, is one and the same problem.'[5] A lecture to the Design and Industries Association (DIA) of 1943 raised the awkward questions of the possibilities for design in existing political systems, looked forward to a 'Plastic Age' of material abundance, and proposed a 'duplex civilization'; 'objective rationality' in industrial, public products; and a coexisting private realm of handicrafts.[6] In an essay of 1945, Read began to raise the political dimension that I think is missing from *Art and Industry*. He discussed design in the different contexts of two prevailing and opposing systems of communist totalitarianism and monopoly capitalism. He marginally prefers capitalism, but states his preference for something else: a pattern of life 'based on co-operation and mutual aid'.[7]

It was just in these years – the early 1940s – that Read was entering the practical world of design. This happened through Design Research Unit (DRU). This was an idea for a design practice that could provide 'new designs' in the reconstruction that would come after the war. Each of the three words of the name of this outfit – design, research, unit – was loaded with the promise of something modern, rational, scientific.

Design Research Unit was formulated in 1942, by Marcus Brumwell and Herbert Read. Brumwell worked in advertising, and was one of the enlightened left-leaning patrons of modernism in Britain then. One finds him now in the footnotes of British cultural history, as a patron of artists – among them Ben Nicholson, Naum Gabo, Piet Mondrian.[8]

DRU started operations in London in 1943. At the start, while the other partners were engaged in war work, Read was in sole charge of DRU's office. A year or two later he became less centrally involved: attending directors' meetings, and perhaps also weekly meetings where current work was criticized. One of their early projects suggests that, at its outset, DRU was a rather literal attempt to implement the ideas of *Art and Industry*: the abstract artist finding a social role. This was the design of a car body, which the artist Naum Gabo carried out for Jowett Cars. There was perhaps some altruism here on the part of Read and Brumwell – it would have been a way of getting some money to Gabo – but certainly the project came to nothing, beyond sketches and models.[9]

The story of DRU is really the story of what one has to call – in shorthand – the British design establishment.[10] At the end of the war, DRU's two leading partners, Misha Black and Milner Gray, returned from their work with the Ministry of Information where they had been in the exhibition design section. DRU then became the central practice in the formative years of professional design in Britain: from 1945 into the 1950s. As a designer from that period once put it, DRU was a kind of finishing-school.[11] In other words: in the absence then of any plausible or adequate design education in the colleges, this was where you went after an art-school education, to become a designer. Certainly, looking at the records of those times, design

Clay model for a Jowett car, made by Naum Gabo in collaboration with Bernard Leach, 1943 (photo Studio St Ives)

in Britain – the kind of conscious design that got officially backed and which was discussed in magazines – seems like a not a very large family of people, working together, employing each other, occasionally writing about each other.[12]

DRU overlapped with and complemented the government's Council of Industrial Design (established in 1944), which was later called the Design Council. The Royal College of Art, where Misha Black would become Professor of Industrial Design, was another central player. A succession of public exhibitions provided focuses for the development of design: 'Design for the Home' (1945), 'Britain Can Make It' (1946), 'Design at Work' (1948), culminating in the Festival of Britain in 1951. DRU was heavily involved in this last event. With completion of work for the Festival its office numbered around forty people.

This was then the culture into which Read's discussion of design, and to some extent Read himself, was now absorbed. To make another phrase or term, one could call it 'establishment modernism'. And here I think that Read's *Art and Industry,* with its deficient social analysis and its estranged aesthetics, worked bad effects. The book could be taken without trouble into the curriculum of this design establishment. In the slogan of the time, 'form' may have followed 'function': but in the absence of fruitful interplay between the two, both had to live in reduced circumstances.[13]

This absorption after 1945 of what had been potentially radical in the 1930s, is the same mechanism whereby Moore, Nicholson and Hepworth were turned into heroes of British culture – or, to be more precise, into heroes of the British Council. What in the early to mid-1930s had been experimental and definitely a minority pursuit was now transmuted into something bigger and safer. One simple index of this development would indeed be the physical size of the works of these artists: from small things, constrained by material shortage, towards larger, sometimes monumental pieces.[14]

One can understand this development well enough, as part of the long-established pattern of life in Britain or (more exactly) England: of co-option and incorporation. It is the pattern by which extremity and clarity, which characterized modernism in continental Europe, was diffused and blurred here. It is the difference between Bertolt Brecht and J. B. Priestley, between Piet Mondrian and Ivon Hitchens, between Marina Tsvetaeva and Virginia Woolf, between Marlene Dietrich and Vera Lynn… As has been remarked often enough: the explanation is that there they had revolution, invasion, fighting in the streets, occupation, and here we did not. There the state was overthrown, and in Britain we are still bound by political arrangements made in the seventeenth century.

It might be interesting, though it is difficult, and perhaps mistaken, to compare Read's endeavours with those of some of his near contemporaries in other countries: people who were writers about art and culture, but also to some extent 'men of affairs'. For example, Clement Greenberg or perhaps Lewis Mumford in the USA, or figures such as Franz Roh in Germany, or Karel Teige in Czechoslovakia. There is not much to compare between them. But even the attempt to make such a comparison reminds one – if one had ever forgotten it – of how English Read was. Compare Read with a Scottish generalist like Hugh MacDiarmid – sharp, angry, uncomfortable – and the point becomes clearer. There is something about England that softens. Read did not avoid this, and he cannot have wanted to.

I do have a sense of Herbert Read as someone whose hopes were defeated by his circumstances: and partly this was just the terrible load of freelance writing, meetings, openings and so on, that he had to take on. There is the evidence of that very telling all-purpose reply postcard which he had printed:

> Herbert Read begs to thank you for your letter, but has to inform you that he has retired from all unsolicited correspondence, from lecturing, attending meetings and conferences, joining committees, writing prefaces and introductions, visiting studios and opening exhibitions, reading unsolicited manuscripts and books, offering his opinion on drawings and paintings submitted to him through the post, and generally from all those activities which render his present existence fragmentary and futile.[15]

This one-sentence lament was written in the 1940s. But it seems not to have helped.

153

Reading about Herbert Read's life, the impression one has is that the burden of having to do these things carried on. But the greater question is this. How did it happen that his social radicalism, which was certainly public on occasions, proved no impediment to – to use this shorthand again – his British Council commitments?

Other design

There are people and events in British design that belong to the 'problem' addressed by Read, but which have so far been largely passed by in the annals of design history. There was a stream running alongside, but outwith the design establishment. It was dissatisfied: dissenting, socialist, anarchist.

One would think first of architecture: and remark or concede that it is perhaps easier to be radical in architecture – if the architect finds a good commissioner – than it is for a designer of products. But perhaps this has to be put in the past tense: with the proviso that it refers to Read's lifetime. The point is that architects then were not dealing with market forces so directly as they do now in Britain. By its nature, architecture deals with space – more or less public – where social meaning becomes very clear. People gather and move around together in buildings. With products, by contrast, exchange value comes much more to the fore.

There was a succession of students at the Architectural Association (AA) School of Architecture, in London, just before and just after the Second World War, who went on to do work that was radical and also 'modern' in a stronger sense than that of the design establishment. One can see the first seeds of this work in their magazines *Focus* (1938–39) and more especially *Plan* (1943–51). In one of the very few historical discussions of these students, Andrew Saint described their spirit.

> Intellectually, politically and pragmatically, the post-war students were more sophisticated than before. Lethaby, Morris, Geddes, Mumford, even D'Arcy Thompson the biologist on growth and form – all these authors were devoured. A few students were drawn to Marxism, some others to a constructive type of anarchism, many more to simple socialism which endorsed the ideals of reconstruction. The pages of *Plan*, the student magazine which succeeded *Focus*, are imbued not with rebelliousness but with a sense of jobs to be done and problems to be solved. A symposium on the various methods of group-working, fully reported in 1948, exemplifies the intense practicality of outlook.[16]

Typically these students went on to work in local authority architectural departments, the schools built in Hertfordshire and also Nottinghamshire being the most notable achievements.

In this post-war work, use and function lead, and formal interest is not treated separately. Yet it is there, subtly and consciously, as it hardly is in the establishment design promoted by the Council of Industrial Design. I am thinking, say, of the

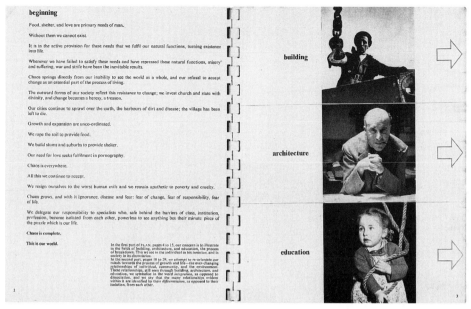

Spread from *Plan*, no. 6, 1949 (page size 204 × 162mm). This programmatic issue put forward a social vision of architecture, in a poetic, documentary spirit.

Routemaster bus, designed by Douglas Scott, and championed by the *Plan* students in a remarkably thorough analysis – as against, say, furniture designed by Gordon Russell (Chairman of the Council of Industrial Design) or packaging designed by Milner Gray at DRU.[17] And while Read's *Art and Industry* had become a fixture on the booklists of establishment modernism, I think it was missing from the books read by these AA students. I can imagine that Read's anarchist writings were important for some of those architects and designers: but not his writing that was explicitly about design.[18] Equally, Read in those years does not seem to have taken much or any interest in the work of these people who were, I think, trying harder to implement his ideals than the designers with whom he had become associated at and around DRU.

In the course of a retrospective essay, Norman Potter touched on this moment in post-war English culture, when he too was coming of age as a designer and maker.

> … there seemed a limited number of 'alternatives in principle'. One was to go into public housing or service building such as hospitals and schools. The Hertfordshire school building programme emerged as one option, and had much about it to interest students and young architects (for instance, using lightweight hollow core sheet materials such as Holoplast, perhaps more an exercise in polemic than practicality). Another approach was to arrive at a selective view of

155

Above: Cover of *Plan*, no. 7, 1950, using an abstract image but with some human reference. This issue aimed 'to continue our argument in a more detailed way, taking up again some of the threads of enquiry which we left incomplete in our last number'.

Right: Card for Norman Potter's workshop at Corsham in Wiltshire, designed and printed by Anthony Froshaug, 1951 (105 × 148mm). The stick furniture idea was typical of the spirit of the venture: as-if-for-mass-production, indifferent to the craft's totems, but striving for good manufacture and the well-resolved detail.

156

acceptable design; that is, of those opportunities that a self-conscious lefty was prepared to entertain, or to specialize in. This embodied the notion of the 'sticking point', and carried an implied rejection of the unacceptable. Yet another possibility was to ally oneself with a do-it-yourself anti-professional working stance – architecture without architects, or with architects as enablers, advisors and technical consultants. John Turner and Pat Crooke finally took this position and went off to Peru. There they began a life-time involvement with Third World problems, and with owner-controlled housing in theory and practice. The English proliferation of self-help groups of many kinds in the housing field was in part an outcome, in part an accompaniment, to this thinking.[19]

In the 1950s Potter established and was the leading figure in a joinery workshop at Corsham in Wiltshire. It was an anarchist venture: doing jobs for people in the community; like a garage, they hoped. This workshop also made furniture in small batches, for sale. The work was modern in spirit and form. Powered machinery was used, and some of their materials (plywood, plastics, industrial bolts) contradicted the craft expectations of the time. Potter had some idea of inviting Pierre Boulez to the workshop opening. In other words it was very different from – consciously antagonistic to – the English Arts and Crafts tradition.

Another venture of that time was the workshop that the typographer Anthony Froshaug ran in the far west of Cornwall, from 1949 to 1952.[20] Like Potter's work-

Norman Potter

Stick furniture

Cabinet-makers Shop   Corsham   Wiltshire

In production 1952 at the new workshop : scaffolding system of minimal storage and stick furniture ; its strictly utilitarian character being patent in its simple assembly & jointing

Designed to be inexpensive and freely adaptable to individual requirements , the basic framework of hardwood section is free-standing , stable , and accessible all sides ; unit assembled and fully demountable without special tools

For direct connection to the scaffolding are certain accessories conforming to the structural module : pre-cut sheet materials providing shelving & cupboards ; bed frame at seating height to take all standard mattresses ; desk and/or table etc

Reference W N details and list prices per ft run/super

Froshaug printer . PZ

Kitchen designed by Norman Potter, *c*. 1960. The structure, which stood in the large living room of a nineteenth-century house in London, was made in Potter's Corsham workshop. Following a thorough consultative report, a design emerged that was 'all detail', with no backs and nothing hidden.

shop, it is suggestive beyond its results. This was a one-man affair, limited to what one person could produce with his hands and feet. I suppose that Froshaug might have used a powered press if he could have afforded it, and if his minimal-rent cottage had had electricity; he was more interested in setting type than in printing from it. (Another printer in England, Desmond Jeffery, who followed Froshaug's path rather consciously later in the 1950s, did use a powered Heidelberg press.) The simple point to make here is that the designer Froshaug was more or less driven to make this experiment of being his own producer, because this was the only way he could function without his work going wrong in production. He wanted to experiment, and that was not possible, fully, in the English printing trade of that time. So he had to use almost pre-industrial methods to make modern work. At that time Froshaug and Potter – they were close friends – turned to Lewis Mumford, especially *Technics and Civilization,* for a theoretical justification of what they were doing.[21]

These two workshops were lonely ventures. There are no comparable instances of modern designers working in that way at that time in Britain. Modern design was then being worked out in the metropolis, by firms like DRU. From the viewpoint of the Gropius-inspired modernism that was becoming orthodox then, country workshops were a heresy: design was for industry; and it happened by command, separated off from industrial production. Someone from the circle to which Potter and Froshaug belonged once remarked to me that they were not understood by critics and commentators: 'even Herbert Read, who should have understood what they were doing, didn't seem to...'.[22] I have a sense that by this time, the early 1950s onwards, Read himself was simply not available to these dissenting designers and architects. And yet, it was they – more than the orthodox modernists – who were attempting something of real spirit: something in the spirit of *Poetry and Anarchism.*

Coda

It feels right to close these remarks here, without any neat resolution, because that is how the theme of 'Herbert Read and design' developed. After the initial statement in *Art and Industry* there were some modifications of the theory, a brief practical engagement, then a dying away. *Art and Industry* ran on into its further editions. But it was as if on automatic pilot: rehearsing, hardly reconsidered, the thesis of 1934.

One could perhaps extend this discussion to 1968, the year of Read's death, and the time of the political turbulence that had some effects on design, particularly design education. Norman Potter's book *What is a Designer* was published first in 1969 and was partly shaped by the experiences of the rebellions at the schools of art at Hornsey, Guildford and elsewhere. Potter was a committed supporter of the student movement. Herbert Read had written an introduction for a first (pre-1968) draft of Potter's book; but this was not used. Not content to be a simple text-book, *What is a Designer* has an intention of imagining things differently: a proposition as

Reprinted here as a conspectus are specimens of jobbing
printing selected from the first two years' work of this press

Equipment is deliberately minimal and simple in mechanical
design; rather than behaviourist engines, it tends towards
workshop tools & machine-tools enjoying maximal degrees
of freedom, within which one individual may solve new
problems in configuration

Postulates of hand composition and hand & foot presswork
have bound output to 180 jobs each year – ranging from
visiting cards to 24-page catalogues, and printed for various
individuals & organisations – standards of typesetting are
therefore high, those of machining reasonable; resultant
prices are a mean between country and London rates

Reproduced in Swiss & English periodicals, work has also
been chosen for the printing section of the South Bank
Exhibition; the press is included in the 1951 Stock List

Though interested in general jobbing, the predilection is
for bookwork and other jobs whose required solution is in
terms of variation & counterpoint on a theme; orders for
work and/or requests for type sheets and other mailings are
welcomed from addressees, their friends & acquaintances

Better Books Limited
Design & Industries Association
St.George's Gallery Limited
Church Street Bookshop
Herbert Rieser Photography
William Campion
Clive Latimer MSIA
Gerik Schjelderup Esq
Triangle Film Productions Limited
Ian Gibson-Smith Photography
Editions Poetry London Limited
Norman Potter Constructions
Children & Youth Aliyah
Mill House (Penzance) Limited
New Europe Medical Foundation
Beltane School Limited

La Terrasse Coffee Garden
Toy Trumpet Workshops
Roger Wood Photography
Norwegian State Railways
Penwith Coiled Baskets
T H Verran & Son
Barbara Hepworth
Penwith Society of Arts in Cornwall
Taylor's Foreign Press
Jesse Collins FSIA
Michael Wickham Photography
London Opera Club
St.George's Gallery (Books)
Design & Research Centre
Gaberbocchus Press Limited
Whitehill Marsh Jackson & Co
Picture Post
Rupert Qualters Esq
Institute of Contemporary Arts
Delbanco Meyer & Company Limited

Lea Jaray
F H K Henrion FSIA
Festival of Britain
Joseph Rykwert Esq
Religious Drama Society
&c

Front of a four-page 'conspectus' of work by Anthony Froshaug, 1951 (281 × 215mm).
The statement encapsulates the philosophy of his workshop venture. On the right the list
of customers (printed red) grouped by years: 1949, 1950, 1951.

much as a question. I worked with Norman Potter, as an editor and publisher, on a second edition of *What is a Designer*. It appeared in 1980, just at the start of the years of radical conservatism in Britain, and of post-modernism in architecture and design. Eventually Potter and I made a third edition, in the time of the last government led by Margaret Thatcher, when 'designer' had become a well-deserved term of abuse. Norman Potter recently said to me that if we ever made a further edition, it would have to be called 'What *was* a designer'. Like Herbert Read, we had our tries.[23]

Notes

1 Robin Kinross, 'Herbert Read's *Art and Industry*: A History', *Journal of Design History*, vol. 1, no. 1 (September 1988), pp. 35–50.

2 David Thistlewood, *Herbert Read: Formlessness and Form: An Introduction to His Aesthetics* (London: Routledge and Kegan Paul, 1984), p. 108.

3 Herbert Read, *Art and Industry: The Principles of Industrial Design* (London: Faber and Faber, 1934), p. 1.

4 These inconsistencies were noticed at the time (1945) by George Orwell in his sharp review of Read's *A Coat of Many Colours*: George Orwell, *Collected Essays, Journalism and Letters* (Harmondsworth: Penguin Books, 1970), vol. 4, pp. 69–73.

5 Herbert Read, *Art and Industry: The Principles of Industrial Design* (London: Faber and Faber, 2nd edn, 1944), p. 170.

6 'The Future of Art in an Industrial Civilization', in Herbert Read, *The Grass Roots of Art* (London: Lindsay Drummond, 1947), pp. 57–73.

7 'The Present System of Design and Its Relation to the Industrial System', *Architects' Year Book*, vol. 1 (1945), pp. 86–91.

8 One could refer here to the family relations that have connected the patrons and 'movers' of British modernism. Thus Su Brumwell, Marcus Brumwell's adopted daughter, married, first, the architect Richard Rogers (latterly, Chairman of the Trustees of the Tate Gallery), and, second, the architect John Miller. Among the jobs of John Miller's practice have been the remodelling of the Whitechapel Art Gallery, the Royal College of Art, and the Institute of Contemporary Arts (ICA): the arts centre that Read had imagined first in the 1930s. Such interconnections and their role in British life deserve an essay of their own. For a passing description, see Bryan Appleyard's striking *Richard Rogers: A Biography* (London: Faber and Faber, 1986).

9 For some brief description of this project, see James King, *The Last Modern: A Life of Herbert Read* (London: Weidenfeld and Nicolson, 1990), pp. 215–16.

10 John and Avril Blake, *The Practical Idealists: Twenty-Five Years of Designing for Industry* (London: Lund Humphries, 1969) is a brief company history of DRU, with wider pretensions; but still the best source of information on the firm.

11 This was the late Jock Kinneir's phrase, in conversation with me in 1993. His career followed a characteristic path for a designer of his generation (born 1917): art school, army service, DRU, freelance practice and part-time teaching.

12 See, for example, the anthology of essays, introduced and edited by Herbert Read, *The Practice of Design* (London: Lund Humphries, 1946). Of thirteen contributors, seven worked for DRU, and one was married to a DRU associate.

13 Tim Benton provides evidence for and expands on this point of view in 'The Myth of Function', in Paul Greenhalgh (ed.), *Modernism in Design* (London: Reaktion Books, 1990), pp. 41–52.

14 Evidence for the suggestions in this paragraph can be found in the film *England's Henry Moore*, made for ICA TV by the writer Anthony Barnett and director Hugh Brody, and shown first in 1988 on Channel 4.

15 This text is partially quoted by King, *The Last Modern*, p. 242. It is given in full by Vernon Richards in his contribution to 'Remembering Herbert Read', *Anarchy*, no. 91, September 1968, p. 286.

16 Andrew Saint, *Towards a Social Architecture: The Role of School Building in Post-War England* (London: Yale University Press, 1987), p. 31.

17 See *Plan*, no. 5 (1949).

18 Thus the books cited in a synoptic issue of *Plan* (no. 6 [1949], p.33), include (only) Read's *The Education of Free Men*, along with writings by Geddes, Mumford, Giedion, Kropotkin, Marx, Martin Buber, Wilhelm Reich.

19 Norman Potter, *Models & Constructs: Margin Notes to a Design Culture* (London: Hyphen Press, 1990), pp. 81–82. This book contains plentiful illustration and documentation of Potter's work.

20 I have discussed Froshaug's work in a number of short articles, of which the best illustrated is 'Technics and Ethics', *Octavo*, no. 1 (1986), pp. 4–9.

21 *Technics and Civilization* was first published in 1934, like *Art and Industry*, one of whose epigraphs comes from Mumford's book.

22 This was the artist Susan Einzig. Around 1945, the Artists International Association – dissenting and often Communist-influenced – was one focus of activity for people in this circle. Thus, for the AIA exhibition 'Sculpture in the Home' of 1945, Potter designed the installation, Froshaug the catalogue, while Einzig was named as 'secretary' of the AIA in its *Bulletin*. Here they would not have met Read, who in the 1930s had been hostile to the realist art that the AIA tended to foster. See King, *The Last Modern*, pp. 158–60.

23 The publishing history of the three editions of *What is a Designer* is: London: Studio Vista, 1969; Reading: Hyphen Press, 1980; London: Hyphen Press, 1989.

Herbert Read: Word and Object:

In response to Robin Kinross

NORMAN POTTER

I HAVE a designer's eye-view to train upon the matters of common concern in this book, but I had better begin by sketching in my own small part in the Read story.

Actually I hardly knew Herbert Read in a personal way, although always holding him in warm regard. He once asked me to tea at the Reform Club, and I remember him seated mischievously at the extreme edge of a very large club armchair, making it quite clear that there was a perceived incongruity that he was very willing to share. This was a nice way of putting me at my ease. Many years earlier, in 1945, I had sat near him at the protest meeting for the editors of *War Commentary*, three of whom were imprisoned. He was trembling with nerves, and although I was very young then, I thought I understood how difficult it was for him to speak publicly in the way demanded by such occasions (that is, with more regard for an intended effect than for truths, options, or loyalties of any complex or balanced kind). He could anyway be expected to be a naturally diffident man in such contexts. However, he got up, climbed the platform, and said his piece. Afterwards, I thought there could be a couple of lessons worth taking to heart. First, that the worlds of poetry and of social rhetoric were sharply to be distinguished (a difficult lesson for a very young man), and second, that an intellectual should be held to be first and foremost a man or woman of honour and high calling, who kept faith with principle, spelled out a position, and defended it openly in the public realm. From then on Marie Louise Berneri and Simone Weil were the heroines, George Orwell and Herbert Read the heroes, that I looked up to as models of an active personal integrity. These four still burn brightly among other stars in my firmament; upon occasion, reliably to steer by.

My youthful respect for intellectuals (as such) faded somewhat. Of the two really brilliant men I came to know intimately, one went mad and the other committed suicide: for me an inoculation, perhaps, against any excess of involvement with late-comers such as Foucault and Derrida. However, I was able to keep indirectly in touch with Herbert Read through my friend George Woodcock and my brother (writing under the name Louis Adeane),[1] both of whom wrote books about him. George, fluent and unhesitating, got in first, and in my opinion did an excellent job with *Herbert Read: The Stream and the Source* – doing equally well for Orwell and Aldous Huxley in the course of his own copiously fruitful writings. Sadly, my brother shared a family weakness for getting it right at damaging cost to getting it written. His unpublished manuscript is now in the British Library for any who might be interested. Read evidently thought well of the project, and seems to have been specially intrigued by Louis's analysis of *The Green Child,* as is attested by the lengthy correspondence in the Read Archive.

When Herbert Read died, the resolve grew upon me to take over and continue his work as a bridge-builder between the deeply divided literary and visual disciplines in English cultural life, deriving in part from long isolation, or insulation, from actively creative influences abroad. Hitherto this has been an unmentioned and privately contractual matter between myself and the departed spirit of Herbert Read. It seems right to give it passing mention in the context of the present book. Although possessing only a small fraction of Read's vast learning in so many fields, I felt that I had certain advantages, notably as a well-informed field worker in design practice and education, and as a practised manual worker. I also wrote poetry, had the anarchist connection, and had done research into diagnostic method and 'words and things' at the Royal College of Art. The related series of books begun by *What is a Designer* and furthered by *Models & Constructs* has been, therefore, a Read-inspired project. Volume three, linking in architecture with other areas of design, is currently frustrated by the recession.

The more intimately ambitious verse-drama *Icarus,*[2] which carries forward these bridging concerns, attempts altogether more complex and intricate connections, as befits its theme; not least those between the private and public functions of language. The audience takes away a full copy of the script and the performance notes. The design of the 'hall' (an enclosure), the set, a related slide programme, drum score, and lighting score, reinforce the script (which is primary) isomorphically: it is not a multi-media production as such. The 'place and occasion' – to use the words of Aldo van Eyck – and in particular, the physical space of the enclosure during its short life, then hosts and formally introduces unknown and therefore open-ended happenings related to the theme: the possibilities for young people attempting to change their world. There is therefore a built-in metaphor of social action emerging, briefly, into an experience of its practical outcome. *Models & Constructs* has the script.

The Bristol Construction School (1963) owed much to Herbert Read's adventurous spirit. Initially the school was revolutionary in spirit and programme by the English standards of the time, though not so unfamiliar to anyone properly acquainted with the work of the Bauhaus *and* that of the Hochschule für Gestaltung at Ulm. Still, it is decidedly unusual for design schools to employ a full-time professional philosopher and an English literature specialist; to dismiss by redefining the ridiculous categories of 'two' and 'three' dimensional design; to attempt, as we did, to heal the disastrous split between 'design' and modern architecture; to have a fully argued and documented academic position (as unfamiliar in England as a written constitution); to have students urged to co-operate rather more than compete – they had done that; and to find it normal that books like Pound's *ABC of Reading*[3] would be on a first-year reading list for designers. Of course it couldn't work, but we had a go. The early loss of Richard Hollis[4] was a serious one. The school fought off opposition from every quarter, and was finally deprived by the establishment of the recognitions and the students it needed (conspiracy theory is unnecessary to this statement); seeing me off into the 1968 student movement after five years of intense and exhausting involvement.

It had certainly been a design project of major difficulty – it was all of that – but a prolonged deviation, I later thought, from my own proper concerns at the bench, machine, board, and typewriter; just as Read came to feel that the incessant pressure of his public duties had taken him away from himself. This question of duty and its reward – not the most fashionable of topics if identified in those terms – is one, or rather two, questions that need looking at, and I shall comment on Read's seeming entrapment or personal fulfilment in the exercise of duty. For the moment, and merely to conclude these remarks about the Read-like aspects of my own work, I will simply say that *What is a Designer* was, indeed, a work of social duty, while *Models & Constructs*, which is about making, designing, and the artefacts that result, is a work of love.

The loss of vertical dimension – a theme of *Icarus* – and concurrently a loss of the vital distinction between the concreteness of first-order work and the lesser orders of its history, criticism, and theory, has been a contentious matter in the second half of this century, but the distinction was deeply understood by Read. His holding to it, tenaciously and – as it were – with his teeth as much as his thought, against all inducement from his own widespread cultural life, was and is a decisive affirmation. A very widely read man – perhaps exceptionally so – one could not say he was bookish. He knew a good thing when he saw it, and what he saw, he was able to respond to with all his faculties, and certainly with heart, mind, and spirit. It is a point missed by Robin Kinross and perhaps reduces his estimate of *Art and Industry*. Robin might look more for the image, sign, info., and the virtual, and might take more kindly than I do to what has become, or threatens to become, of the cultural studies syndrome. To look and not to *see* – not to grasp intently with the spirit, to enter relation with, to be moved and affected by – is a condition less uncommon than often realized. As a disengagement from source, it seems confirmed rather than liberated by theoretical work upon cultural relativism and 'the parameters of discourse'. The philosophical training necessary to elucidate such work (on its own terms) is rarely forthcoming either. Those of us who struggled years ago, ahead of our time, to introduce connective cultural studies, analytical thinking, and problem-solving disciplines, as a follow-up to fine-art-guided foundation studies, saw these as no more than essential elements in the build of a design education. Hoisted on our own petard, we have sometimes seen them become a substitute. It might be said, therefore, that a dose of Read, like an old-fashioned chemist's remedy, could restore colour to paling cheeks and generally do a power of good in such quarters.

Artists and designers out in the world and at work – with whom Read closely identified – will usually seek and find nourishment almost anywhere but in criticism bearing on their own subject: typically, they learn from growth and mistakes in their own work, and of course from the work of others. If the artist and the artefact (to use no more than a convenient shorthand) were Read's home base, and art and design students one significant focus of address, the principal targets were the public at large and (in the case of product design) the design conscience of industry and the retail market.

Here the situation was picking up a little, as evidence from *The Flat Book* (1939) rather thinly suggests. So far as this gain was observable, Read's own contribution should not be underestimated, as witnessed by the tribute from the architects J. L. Martin and Sadie Speight (to be quoted further on). Far more lively and promising things were happening on the continent, as Read was only too impatiently aware; against which the full weight of temporal defeat was yet, in 1933, gathering its destructive momentum. Since then – one can hardly speak of cultural continuities in those terrible years – there has been the more mundane realization that product design would suffer from mal-definition in being assigned a pivotal role in the discussion of design. Read was still hopeful at this time, if intuitively cautious, as I think the tone of *Art and Industry* probably indicates. Good work in domestic product design was scarce then as it is scarce now, and would be found in a coldness and a blankness of public regard, with Read later putting his faith in education through art. A poem by Louis Adeane is nearly contemporaneous with *Education through Art*:

The Night Loves Us

This is our love, these wheels and chains,
Walls, windows, vistas, fettered edge of foam.
Our blood blew red and melted; these remains
Are love cooled down to solid shapes of home.

Yet outside place, beyond our brittle light
Spread fields incredible, the planes of love;
Invisibly they flood towards our sight,
Our little city stands within a wave.

And growing greenly in subversive park
Their secret fountains flourishing impel
The child to feel love falling from the dark,
The wishing girl to dream beside a well.

So leaping flowers in the burning town
May light the marble gardens of our thought

> And running visions melt our coldness down
> To fire the insurgent freedom of the heart.

If designers may nod in approval at Read's pursuit of what we may call 'real presences'[5] in the world, as distinct from their shadows (philosophically suggestive as these may be), and speculations concerning them, it is plain that he earned his bread very largely as a one-man-band public educator, at a rather different level from his more occasional investigative criticism, his work as a philosopher and historian of art, his autobiographical work, and of course his poetry. (It is hard to compass Read's output without starting to make lists.)

That he preferred so free-range and insecure a way of life to skulking about in the corridors of academe – an obvious alternative – may have kept his findings fresh for him, and an edge on his perceptions. Read could also indulge his inconsistencies the more happily, bringing them to the point of outright contradiction, or dialectical opposition, where the tension invoked – the crack and jump of a healthy spark across polar opposites – could be a source of energy to him, keeping him free, on the move, open (he was the most open-hearted and open-handed of men) and as happy with approximation as anarchists usually are. Not one for epistemological niceties, he certainly knew enough to know the limits of his own knowledge, and beyond that: the unknowable. For that reason, and in that largeness of spirit, he might judge that a position he took up was adequately defensible, on its own terms, but there was no useful and final sense in which it could be said to be right, as distinct from preferred. His sometimes disconcerting critical method of oversteer and understeer – frequently writing rather roughly, with broad sweeps, and making his points within the sweeps (a bit like the workshop 'offering up' or 'trying for size') – which may be worrying to the tidy-minded, is capable, I believe, of a sympathetic interpretation. Not so, of course, the soft spots that every writer needs a shrewd editor to uncover – dote in otherwise healthy timber – such as Read's habit of sinking back rather too often into the cushioning of terms (unexamined) such as 'sensibility'.

It is possible to take these thoughts further and see Read as a pamphleteer in the grand manner – excepting always his work at the extremes (the most personal and the least), and his work as a poet. Such a view would accommodate the range and restlessness with which his talent for exposition was exercised, the variable quality of percipience entailed, and the sometimes hit-or-miss character of the polemic that so engaged him.

It is on record that Read himself was in doubt, by the late 1950s, of his own identity and status in 'criticism' as such, fearing even that a sensuous response to aesthetic values had surrendered to intellectualism. Self-assessment of this kind, often anecdotal in origin, or prompted by circumstances of the time, should never be given undue weight. Read's 'coat of many colours' may have kept the weather out and the prospect economically cheerful, but it could be taken off and hung up somewhere

(I have already suggested) when more vital matters were encountered at first hand, as is more directly testified in his earlier experiences with Moore, Hepworth and Nicholson.

My own interpretation goes further. It is supported only by a sense of closeness to him, by intuitive sympathy (empathy might be a better word) and by a less than scholarly acquaintance with his working life, its background, and its extraordinary range of productive outcomes. In fact – now – I keep only two Read books on my shelf: *Poetry and Anarchism*, and *Art and Industry*. Both I value highly. I suspect that students went off with others in long-forgotten exchanges of enthusiasm. The impression I have of Read, and shall develop further in discussing *Art and Industry*, is that he was a man committed quite involuntarily to salvation through works, on the one hand, and to a related and pertinacious sense of public duty, on the other. He was doing what he had to do. It is hard *not* to believe this, I think, when putting together what we know of his character with the enduring effect of his experience of the First World War and its demands upon him (then and subsequently); the social and cultural aftermath of this unequalled sacrifice of young life; the claustrophobic and ominous unfolding of the 1930s; the collapse of anarchist hopes in Spain; a further world war to be confronted and lived through; Auschwitz; the Bomb. It was no accidental quirk of character that made Read so endlessly generous, patient, and helpful, to young people; and always ready to succour and encourage even the least promising shoots of new growth. Much of the value implicit in Read's life situation, and the way in which he rode to it, lay in what he may not clearly have seen himself, yet was exemplified in the totality of his striving – even in those aspects of his life that he came to think were diversionary or wasted effort.

The reason it is hard to compare Read's accomplishments with those of his contemporaries is the very measure to which he fulfilled his potential and his unique-ness; and in the latter respect I think of something from Martin Buber's *The Way of Man*.

> It is the duty of every person… to know and consider that he is unique in the world in his particular character and that there has never been anyone like him in the world, for if there had been someone like him, there would have been no need for him to be in the world. Every single man… is called upon to fulfil his particularity… [His] foremost task is the actualization of his unique, unprece-dented and never-recurring potentialities, and not the repetition of something that another, and be it even the greatest, has already achieved.[6]

(I recall – from memory – that, possibly in reviewing *Between Man and Man,* Read said of Buber, 'merely to read him is an education'.) It is in this perspective, I believe, that Read's life and attainment should be viewed, and it is from this angle of discern-ment that much of his activity can be valued – including the blind alleys and false starts, and quite beyond a literary tally of the books he produced.

In the critical field things have moved along, as we all know. With Leavis Read was still sharing common ground – approximately – and, uncharacteristically, it seems that Leavis treated him with something approaching a distant respect. Whether this was mediated by relations with Eliot (shared if unequal) I do not know. Much further down the line, and to cut a long, barren, and pettifogging story mercifully short, it is unsurprising to find no mention of Read in Terry Eagleton's congenial book *The Function of Criticism: From the 'Spectator' to Post-Structuralism* (1984). Eagleton is a Marxist, decidedly high church (Read is chapel) and often sharp and good fun (Read is neither). It might be hoped of the Warton Professor of English at Oxford that he will simplify and render more accessible his own use of the English language (dare one suggest George Orwell's *Animal Farm* as a model?), but he states with simple conviction: 'The single most important critic of post-war Britain has been Raymond Williams'. Well, family loyalties have their place. Each to his own?

Fortunately I am not called upon to tread lightly across the quicksands of post-Saussurean literary theory, or surely I would be engulfed and never write another poem, even. Turning abruptly to design matters, in the more familiar sense as to what these are, Read's contribution cannot be ranked with Giedion's indispensable *Space, Time, and Architecture* and its sequel *Mechanization Takes Command* (1941 and 1947 respectively), or with vigorous earlier testament from original sources such as Le Corbusier. Two considerations arise here, both of them interesting.

The first is something I hope for Read but cannot substantiate. If it is fair, there is no reason to do any rank-ordering anyway. Leavis would have no one near him, work-wise, without denunciation, but I feel sure that the very dispersal of Read's explorations, and the mosaic of responses that steadily accrued, would have inclined him quite otherwise, since, here, he was more of a cultural anthropologist than a collector of specimens. He speaks of 'creating meaningful relationships between the various spheres of knowledge', and of 'the courage and even the foolhardiness' that must be brought to the task. He was not especially well suited to such a programme, except by the pressures of internalized compulsion and the need to earn his living, because – I shall argue – he was not naturally gifted as a generalist or as a synthesizer, although at first sight he might seem to be both. Whether or not this was so, his anarchism and his attachment to the modern movement would join in giving him a relational and collaborative approach to creative work: he would not have seen his findings and doings and makings as discrete entities, self-contained, definitive, and competing with their neighbours for the world's exclusive attention. Rather, he might see a book like *Art and Industry* as a contingent affirmation, to some extent provisional and open-ended in character, taking account of relational work already in the field: in a word, as a contribution.[7]

It is only in using this fine old socialist word, with its faintly Quaker-like overtones and rich implication of common endeavour (and much else) that a sense of what is lost to us becomes suddenly overwhelming; and the need of restitution, of fresh beginnings, the more urgent. The word is still there; it hasn't shrunk to a fraction of its size like 'great', or 'disinterested'. A natural casualty of social norms collapsing into money worship and the life of self-advantage, the word has simply fallen into disuse. It is still there, like faith; summoning us.

I am suggesting, therefore, that Read should never be approached with his social beliefs out of mind, and that then – excepting as ever the most personal work – we do well to take account of the immediate neighbours; i.e., related books published between 1934, when *Art and Industry* appeared, and 1939, when the Second World War was declared. The two essential accomplices – acknowledged as such – are Mumford's *Technics and Civilization,* and Moholy-Nagy's *The New Vision.* To these might be added two books by Gropius, who was certainly Read's man, *The New Architecture and the Bauhaus*[8] and the mandatory *Bauhaus* (heavily illustrated) which came from the Museum of Modern Art in 1938. Pevsner's *Pioneers of the Modern Movement* was usefully complementary to Read. The charismatic and canonic *Flat Book* came last (1939). This was a catalogue of design-conscious products and interiors, with a brief but good commentary by Martin and Speight. The authors note 'a special debt to Herbert Read at whose suggestion this book was undertaken and to whose outstanding book on the general principles of design, *Art and Industry,* they have made constant reference'. This tribute is worth noting, because Martin and Speight were first-rate designers. So was F. R. S. Yorke, whose excellent home-grown *The Modern House* appeared in 1934. This book, and other specifically architectural references, are unmentioned by Read (seemingly as irrelevant to his subject).

This, then, is a small collection of books published, or readily available, in England between 1934 and 1939, the reading or even the scanning of which – collectively – would tell and show the reader what modern design is all about; and would still do so today. Read's contribution would be a strongly welcome one in this company, but certainly he gains from it. That Read knew what he was about is clear from one thing. He went straight for the key insight in Mumford's *Technics* and used it as an epigraph for *Art and Industry*:

> Our capacity to go beyond the machine rests upon our power to assimilate the machine. Until we have absorbed the lessons of objectivity, impersonality, neutrality, the lessons of the mechanical realm, we cannot go further in our development toward the more richly organic, the more profoundly human.

In my workshop days I certainly knew this by heart; in fact, it might have been carved into the doorpost, with Marcel Breuer's comradely 'Where Do We Stand?' (1934) never far from mind either (this may now be read in Benton and Sharp's *Form and Function* [1975]). The two together will fire a modernist workshop quite adequately since, in the search for zero and the poetic principle, answers are sought in the conditions of the job itself (and who needs pictures). This was (approximately) how we saw it. Read remarks, but of organic poetry, not organic design:

> It is the form imposed on poetry by the laws of its own origination, without consideration for the given forms of traditional poetry. It is the most original and most vital principle of poetic creation; and the distinction of modern poetry is to have recovered this principle.[9]

Could we have enlisted Read in our anti-style campaign? It would have been rather too late, I fear; by then, the 1950s and 1960s, he was back on the fine art wagon, and *Art and Industry* far behind him. The workshop slogan, 'meaning not look', might have had a wan reception. It was good starting rhetoric, no more, and if designers have to start somewhere, better that way round than the opposite, which has become more fashionable. The reason was clear enough in the 1980s.

I suppose it is possible, as Robin Kinross half suggests, that the sheer dullness of Read's establishment experiences may have put him off design altogether. It is also the case that heavy and repeated doses of committee work will set any creative-minded person back on their heels, if not actually putting them to sleep: the collaborative stance loses its freshness of appeal, and the artist's garret comes up for re-estimation. The mentioned introduction that Read wrote for some of my own writings[10] certainly wouldn't do, but I do not wish to dwell upon it. I did not realize he was so seriously unwell: it was very good of him (and of course, wholly typical) to respond at all. I cannot follow Robin's connected remarks about Nicholson, Hepworth, and Moore, because I cannot affirm too strongly that this is wonderful work; at its best moving me to tears as it has more than once in the Hepworth museum. Nicholson's painting has been a source of pure joy in my own life – the more so, if anything, as I grow older. The only equivalent I can think of (though such comparisons are unsatisfactory) is with Glenn Gould's playing of Bach; perhaps the French suites, and some of the partitas.

Arriving (at last) at the second 'interesting consideration' mentioned much earlier, there may be another reason for a certain falling-away of Read's design commitment. There is an evident lack or weakness of orientation that is actually rather mysterious. I refer to a lack of any really excited interest in modern archi-tecture. If it had been there, he couldn't have kept it so well under wraps in his writings and particularly those on design. It was in architecture, and chiefly from designers who happened to be architects,[11] that almost everything was going on – from fiercely argued theory, to educational programmes, to building and planning, to furniture, interior and exhibition design, to industrial product design, to graphics – in all these fields extraordinary things were happening in the way of a spatially-hosted experience of modernity; visibly at the Bauhaus, yes, sharply apparent from the Pavillon de l'Esprit Nouveau (1925) onward, but far more widespread than that as in the triangular relations between Germany, Holland, and Russia after the revo-lution. Few could have had more understanding of post-cubist space in painting than

Herbert Read, but there is little or no sense of parallel involvement outside the picture frame on his part, suggesting (to put it probably too extremely) a degree of object-fixation at the cost of spatial anaesthesia. Does this go too far?

If it is seen more as a personal bias, a tendency of approach (the point I am making is conjectural), then certain consequences might still be entailed. There was never too much going on in the industrial design field: as Robin Kinross properly comments, Read was weak on economics in *Art and Industry*, but this was normal to modernist pronouncements. The Gropius 'type-form' – a standardized form for a product – was deemed apparently invulnerable to the ordinary operations of market capitalism, which could replace a carefully evolved 'solution' overnight to stimulate fresh demand. Nizzoli's Olivetti 22[12] typewriter is as sound and satisfactory as at the day of its birth in 1950, but as with most (not all) industrial products worth having, it was taken – as designers sometimes say – by the Devil, with really quite a good run for its money (which, in a faster-moving throwaway society, is now more unusual). As to replacement for the Olivetti 22, the fall from grace was precipitous. Disgusted-Tunbridge-Wells complains often enough that modern buildings are durable. Graphic design is not seen by Read as industrially product-worthy for inclusion in *Art and Industry*; though, very greatly to his credit, the book itself is treated as one such object. The ephemeral aspects of graphics (i.e., outside book design) become actually instrumental to the conduct of what we now call a market-led economy, and modern work there has been relatively invulnerable – indeed, has proliferated.

I can now address comment more directly to the book *Art and Industry,* and – in the usual spirit of our exchanges – to disagreements with Robin Kinross. Read comes on strong about design education – stronger, I think, than Robin Kinross gives credit for. In the introduction to *Art and Industry* and again near the end of the book, in 'Art Education in the Industrial Age', he discusses design teaching in art schools at length, gaining little satisfaction from it. Speaking of 'a paradox', he remarks that it is in the industries where 'the artist as such never enters... we find the best formal designs'. This after an attack on the 'abominations' produced by artists using surfaces in industrial design contexts as though they were canvas for painting on. He goes as far as saying: 'what we need more than anything is the total suppression of the professional art schools and colleges'.[13] Not a meliorist statement, surely, RK, and hardly sporting behaviour for one so allegedly English? No wonder Read's popularity has receded in the schools, where strapped-for-cash painters and sculptors are often quite confident that they can teach design perfectly well, preferably to their weaker students. However, it must be admitted that Read is less than specific about design education as such (apart from doffing his hat to the Bauhaus). Far from thinking through a constructively coherent position, he merely says, in effect, 'scrap the lot, involve the factories, and start again'. He may be right, but God or an anarchist revolution are left unmentioned as the moving agents in such a programme. This is

172

oversteer: in the context of his analysis, it may keep readers awake to the seriousness of the situation as he then saw it.

For my purposes though, in checking-out Read's spatial credentials, he markedly
fails to pick up, even to notice, the English split between design and architectural
education, and thus, of course, to speculate upon its damaging effect – to both
parties. His perceptions short-circuit back to the art schools, which he still obscurely
feels to be the 'fountain-head'; a view later under powerful attack at Ulm, but properly in question at any time. The design and architecture issue (which, once
appreciated, rapidly becomes a design *in* architecture issue) is left regrettably undis-
turbed, though there is a rather conventional mention in *Art and Industry* – very far
short of the tearaway radicalism in Le Corbusier's early writings.[14]

It is true that relatively little advanced architecture had been established in
England, compared with the ferment on the continent, at the actual time of writing,
but this should have been no deterrent to Read's critical involvement abroad.
Definitive work had been done in the brief and frostbitten springtime of the century,
chiefly between 1923 and 1932. His references to the phenomenon, from which all
else followed, are muted and rather conventional, though I suppose that, in the main,
he was addressing a readership a good deal more 'English' than he ever was. Apart
from the industrialized thinking in Bucky Fuller's Dymaxion House, unmentioned,
assured and substantial and formative work was in being from Le Corbusier and
others. Breuer, who more unaccountably escapes notice, had a remarkable wealth
of pre-1934 product design to show to his credit.[15] If Read was strong on pots, as
undoubtedly he was, he was weak here, both in presenting the evidence and
discussing it. His intuitive sympathies are not in doubt, but all he can do is to point
rather helplessly toward the Bauhaus.

At this point, as one who took the path, both toward the Bauhaus and of making,
I had better declare my own hand with respect to *Art and Industry*. At a sixty-year
remove, it is actually surprising that such a book might still claim our attention except
in its own historical context. In ways I have already discussed, there are shortcomings, objections, that might seem to undermine the book's legitimacy and certainly
its relevance today. 'Not a bit of it' has to be my own response. Turning over the
salt-stained pages of my own copy, which survived falling in the sea, I am amazed at
how good a book it was and still is; how heartening, how properly informing, how
pleasing to the eye, how inviting to explore further. I hasten to say, and to say firmly,
that I refer to the Bayer edition only. I do not know if the later ones fully retained
the illustrations even, because I wouldn't have one of these in the house, any more
than I would now be typing on an Olivetti *32* (and I don't suppose Robin Kinross
would either). These things matter. Principle is involved: moreover, the whole
nature of the book, its plea, belongs with its physical substance – a rare thing indeed
in English publishing. Bayer's work is not exactly 'muddled', I would say, so much
as imperfectly realized. The art cover, which is well executed, is probably the worst

bit. This doesn't matter: the whole approach communicates a principled quality of intention, and that is what matters.

The pictures are brilliant, super, remains my reaction, just as when I first had the book it felt like unwrapping a Christmas stocking – what would be next! This must have been some time in the late 1940s, I think; maybe earlier – my restored copy of *Poetry and Anarchism* (thanks be to Robin) is dated 1941 on the flyleaf. There are 130 illustrations, of which 46 are pre-twentieth century. He puts in, so to say, a part in the bass line of his musical argument, apparently no more than reticently supportive to the leading melody, but which, before you notice it, is fully integrated into the subtle process of authentication that he is concerned to make good. If Read was alive now, I reckon he might want to improve on a couple of dozen of these images, perhaps more. There are a few of truly transfixing dullness; mostly furniture and interiors. A further alternative would have been to add a supplement. I cannot follow Robin Kinross on the wretched outcome that in fact ensued. The expensive cloth-and-board cover might have been allowed to go for a burton, leaving the rest of the book as a paperback facsimile. There would be very little loss of object-integrity down that route. The cover was not without interest, but expensive to do and chancing its arm a bit in the art department. There could have been a wartime-type explanation, a photograph of it, and an apology. Why are publishers so chary of direct communication with the people who buy and read their books? The stimulus of a proper job might also have jolted Read into losing or replacing just a few obviously duff illustrations.

For such regrets the word has to be 'academic'. The question now has to be the standing of the book as it first appeared, and its continuing relevance. Surely the first question can be answered in short order (consider the visually barren publishing scene of the time). Both in content and presentation, the book was a small publishing miracle. As in seeking out the very few good modern buildings – say, around London – such happenings were come upon with the thirst of a desert traveller alighting upon an oasis. It should be remembered that continental work and energies were abandoned, inaccessible, destroyed, or dispersed, for a considerable time before and after the actual war years. No matter about defects and omissions: it was good work, and work of the spirit.

Now is a very different situation. Unless *Art and Industry* has the good fortune to be re-issued and re-edited (as, for instance, was very well done for Kropotkin's *Fields, Factories and Workshops* by Colin Ward) it has little more than a conceptual life and the threat of historical status – although it might be said that most out-of-print books turn out to be available if you want them enough. So vestigial a contemporary presence is to my mind decidedly unjust, and in a curious way, the book presents – or could present with a supplement – to entirely fresh advantage. One reason I have already suggested. The book has its minders (Mumford, Giedion, Moholy-Nagy, and Gropius), substantial men and none of them, one would hope, too deeply into retirement. It even has its antidote, the peripatetic Victor Papanek with an inventive student following for his *Design for the Real World* (1972), which does have diagrams, eschews aestheticism, and goes for the jugular in attacking the western world's priorities. Pictorial records of modernity, and/or the search for it, are now plentiful. Then there is Norman Potter, rooting for Read on all fronts...

So, the book no longer has to stand as lonely testimony, nor need more be asked of Read than he had to offer. He was never a generalist. He moved from one area of specificity to another. He was a particularist, and this would seem to follow from the acuity of his sense-responses, their vividness, and an almost child-like faith in the authentic reality of their sources: the truth-claim, the artefact, the solid object, and their demands upon his full attentiveness. The local immediacy of his perceptions is familiar enough to the anarchist temperament, but they are not of the classifying and system-building order of detachment available to the natural generalist. Read was happy enough in seeking to order and relate his experiences, without losing *touch* with them, and as I have said, he could relish contradiction in himself, but it is not for his synthesizing power that we go to him. Others can take care of that. Oddly, therefore, *Art and Industry* now stands before us in a purified form of Read's own contribution: he is aided by his aides, and minded by his minders, but on his own ground he has not been bettered since. In the last analysis, perhaps it is because Read was a poet, and pure in heart, and not trivial, and was socially aware, that this book still has a distinction of mind and eye largely denied to the subsequent history of design in Britain.

The designer Tom Quinn recently put it more directly, in conversation: 'The thing I like about Read', he said, 'is that he puts something on the table. "Look at this", he says. "It's good." I liked that about him. He stood his ground.'

As for me, I don't really need Herbert Read's books. My whole life has been blessed by the spirit of this man, and I hope I have said so. Not that there is enough to show for it, as yet; but that is another's story.

Notes

1 Born 1921 as Donald Louis Sargent Potter; died 1979. Early poems (the book *The Night Loves Us*) and some acute critical writing in various journals. Reviewed Read's and Alex Comfort's poems in Woodcock's magazine *Now*.

2 Written and first performed in 1975. Revised version 1989.

3 The prolific American poet Denise Levertov once told me that this was the only book of criticism that had helped her writing. Pound's abrasive irascibility certainly acts as a goad.

4 Richard Hollis is a graphic designer, author of *Graphic Design: A Concise History* (1994).

5 I am aware that these words are also the title of a book by George Steiner (1989). I am using them rather differently, but not, I think, in a spirit contrary to his. Steiner usually finds good reason for putting first things first; in keeping with which, the opening sentence of his *Tolstoy or Dostoevsky* is: 'Literary criticism should arise out of a debt of love'. Yes!

6 Martin Buber, *The Way of Man: According to the Teachings of Hasidism* (London: Routledge and Kegan

Paul, 1950), p.17.

7 I first heard the word in this use by the veteran anarchist Matt Kavanagh; many years later, in use by John Turner and Pat Crooke of the *Plan* architectural student group. As an aside of possible interest, aged seventeen I had the privilege of a brief imprisonment with Matt. Shaking hands with him upon release, I couldn't forget that he had (among many distinctions) shaken hands with William Morris. What an inspiration to a seventeen-year-old! It may be this that caused me to say in *What is a Designer* 'the history of consciousness is a chain of hands...'

8 This book has Gropius on the 'type-form' and industrial design.

9 Herbert Read, *Collected Essays in Literary Criticism* (London: Faber and Faber, 2nd edn, 1951), p.20.

10 An earlier and slighter version of *What is a Designer*.

11 I mean the creative minority at home and abroad in this otherwise rather conservative and timidly-minded profession.

12 Has survived well and is occasionally to be found second-hand now that word-processors are widespread in their use. A delightful classic of product design. Poets should use no other.

13 Herbert Read, *Art and Industry: The Principles of Industrial Design* (London: Faber and Faber, 1934), p.131.

14 Le Corbusier's early writings are not confined to architecture. The celebrated *Towards a New Architecture* (first English translation, 1927) sweeps all before it and includes a future for industrial design. Strong medicine. Too strong for Read's milder prescription for the English public? He left it on the shelf.

15 There is a very good book by Christopher Wilk, *Marcel Breuer: Furniture and Interiors* (London: Architectural Press, 1981).

The Politics of Herbert Read

DAVID GOODWAY

IT was the Spanish Revolution of 1936 and ensuing Civil War that caused Herbert Read in 1937 to declare for anarchism – at first extremely mutedly in the *Left Review* survey, *Authors Take Sides on the Spanish War*, and then forthrightly in 'The Necessity of Anarchism', a three-part article in the *Adelphi*.[1] This latter was included the following year in the substantial statement, *Poetry and Anarchism:*

> To declare for a doctrine so remote as anarchism at this stage of history will be regarded by some critics as a sign of intellectual bankruptcy; by others as a sort of treason, a desertion of the democratic front at the most acute moment of its crisis; by still others as merely poetic nonsense. For myself it is not only a return to Proudhon, Tolstoy, and Kropotkin, who were the predilections of my youth, but a mature realization of their essential rightness...
>
> I am thus open to a charge of having wavered in my allegiance to the truth. In extenuation I can only plead that if from time to time I have temporized with other measures of political action... it is because I have believed that such measures were part way to the final goal, and the only immediately practical measures. From 1917 onwards and for as long as I could preserve the illusion, communism as established in Russia seemed to promise the social liberty of my ideals. So long as Lenin and Stalin promised a definitive 'withering away of the State' I was prepared to stifle my doubts and prolong my faith. But when five, ten, fifteen, and then twenty years passed, with the liberty of the individual receding at every stage, a break became inevitable. It was only delayed so long because no other country in the world offered a fairer prospect of social justice. It comes now because it is possible to transfer our hopes to Spain, where anarchism, so long oppressed and obscured, has at last emerged as a predominant force in constructive socialism.[2]

In later writings Read was very precise about the 'predilections of his youth'. In 'My Anarchism', a review article of 1968, the year of his death, he said:

> my own anarchist convictions... have now lasted for more than fifty years – I date my conversion to the reading of a pamphlet by Edward Carpenter with the title *Non-Governmental Society*, which took place in 1911 or 1912, and immediately opened up to me a whole new range of thought – not only the works of professed anarchists such as Kropotkin, Bakunin and Proudhon, but also those of Nietzsche,

177

Ibsen, and Tolstoy which directly or indirectly supported the anarchist philo-sophy, and those of Marx and Shaw which directly attacked it.[3]

In *Annals of Innocence and Experience* (1940) he had also named Marx and Bakunin, and went on:

> ... I was much influenced by Kropotkin's *Fields, Factories and Workshops*, and by his pamphlets on *Anarchist Morality* and *Anarchist Communism* (published by the Freedom Press in 1912 and 1913). A pamphlet by Edward Carpenter on *Non-Governmental Society* (1911) was even more decisive...[4]

To these writers must be added also Max Stirner and Georges Sorel.

Another question that demands an answer is why Read's political convictions of the pre-1914 years, formed around the time he was a student at the University of Leeds, were not manifested until a quarter of a century later. He accounts for this partly in the passage already quoted from *Poetry and Anarchism* (by confessing to the hold over him of the Bolshevik Revolution); makes clear his support of Guild Socialism during the First World War and his occasional advocacy of it in the *New Age* and the *Guildsman;* and also says:

> ... when, after the war, I entered the Civil Service, I found myself under a much stricter censorship, and though I never 'dropped' politics, I ceased to write about them. When in 1931 I left the Civil Service and was once more at liberty to take part in the public discussion of political issues, some people assumed that I had 'just discovered Marx', that the turn of political events had forced me from the seclusion of an ivory tower, that I had adopted anarchism as a logical counter-point to my views on art. Actually there was an unfailing continuity in my political interests and political opinions. I would not like to claim that they show an unfailing consistency, but the general principles which I found congenial thirty years ago are still the basic principles of such political philosophy as I now accept.[5]

Read was well advised not to claim a political consistency throughout these years, since in the early 1930s he had some distinctly authoritarian sympathies: 'From certain points of view... I can welcome the notion of the totalitarian state, whether in its Fascist or Communist form'.[6] Nor is *The Green Child* (1935) in any way liber-tarian. I have always found the comparison A. L. Morton draws between Read's Utopia of the Green People and the final part, 'As Far as Thought Can Reach', of *Back to Methuselah* (1921) most insightful, for Read's inclinations are here identical to those of Bernard Shaw, the bloodless, Fabian admirer of the inter-war dictators, in contrast to those of the libertarian communist, William Morris, in *News from Nowhere*.[7]

What is also missing is any mention – by Read himself or by his biographers – of his adherence to Social Credit. This was a common enthusiasm in the 1920s and

1930s amongst members of Read's milieu. It was his mentor, A. R. Orage, who in the *New Age* had 'discovered' and edited Major C. H. Douglas and led a section of Guild Socialism in support of Social Credit. Other followers, temporary or for life, of Douglas included Ezra Pound, Edwin Muir and Hugh MacDiarmid. The scale of Read's involvement remains to be documented; but it is readily apparent that *Essential Communism*, a pamphlet of 1935, a 'drastic revision' of which was incorporated in *Poetry and Anarchism*, was a Douglasite tract – and it was indeed reprinted in *The Social Credit Pamphleteer* (1935).[8]

Read continues in *Annals of Innocence and Experience*:

> In calling these principles Anarchism I have forfeited any claim to be taken seriously as a politician, and have cut myself off from the main current of socialist activity in England. But I have often found sympathy and agreement in unexpected places, and there are many intellectuals who are fundamentally anarchist in their political outlook, but who do not dare to invite ridicule by confessing it.[9]

There is considerable irony in the ultra-modern trend-setter in the visual arts electing for so permanently unfashionable a political creed as anarchism. Read has been accused, especially by bitter figurative painters, whose work he caused to be shunned, of jumping ceaselessly on to the bandwagon of the latest artistic novelty, of imposing upon practising artists a procrustean schema of aesthetic evolution culminating in the abstract. As his thoroughgoing enemy, Wyndham Lewis, put it in 1939:

> Mr Herbert Read has an unenviable knack of providing, at a week's notice, almost any movement, or sub-movement, in the visual arts, with a neatly-cut party-suit – with which it can appear, appropriately caparisoned, at the cocktail-party thrown by the capitalist who has made its birth possible, in celebration of the happy event.[10]

In politics, however, for thirty years, Read was resolutely (and, with the exception of his knighthood, consistently) against the tide by professing his anarchist convictions.

The Russian-American anarchist, Emma Goldman, spent the years of the Spanish Revolution and Civil War largely in London, acting as representative for the CNT-FAI and running a propaganda office for them. So after Read had announced his anarchism in 1937 he was contacted by Goldman and recruited as a sponsor for the English Section of the SIA (Solidaridad Internacional Antifascista).[11] For several months they worked together fairly closely. Goldman later told Read that he and the novelist Ethel Mannin were the only 'two real comrades and friends' she had made during her entire three-year stay in London.[12] Read donated small sums of money; reviewed anarchist books for the *Criterion*; acted on behalf of anarchist authors with the two publishers, Heinemann and Routledge, for which he worked;

spoke on anarchist platforms; and published articles and poetry in *Spain and the World* (the paper launched in 1936 by the twenty-year-old Vernon Richards).

This set the pattern for the fifteen years of Read's association with the Freedom Press Group. *Spain and the World* became *Revolt!*, which was revived as *War Commentary*, which in turn became, in 1945, a resurrected *Freedom*. Read published in all these titles,[13] and in addition he wrote or edited for Freedom Press (which also reprinted *Poetry and Anarchism*) six books and pamphlets: *The Philosophy of Anarchism* (1940), *Kropotkin: Selections from his Writings* (1942), *The Education of Free Men* (1944), *Freedom: Is It a Crime?* (1945), *Existentialism, Marxism and Anarchism* (1949) and *Art and the Evolution of Man* (1951).

Anarchists have always revered the written word but, traditionally, they have esteemed public speaking almost as much; and so Read was pressed to participate in this area also. But, as Vernon Richards remembered in his affectionate obituary of Read:

> he not only reluctantly agreed to speak at meetings but,… having agreed to he wrote out his speech and delivered it with all the revolutionary fervour he could summon up for the occasion. Which meant that more often than not some of the public were so disappointed by his delivery that they failed to take into account the important things he had to say![14]

All this came to a dramatic end with Read's acceptance of a knighthood in the New Year's Honours for 1953. It is significant for two reasons that this was awarded 'for services to literature', not to art. The State was unable to stomach his promotion of contemporary art; and Read, who always thought of himself as primarily a poet and that his literary achievement had been unfairly overshadowed by his other activities, felt it was at last properly recognized. Anarchists, not unnaturally, found his conduct insupportable – in any case they found themselves the laughing-stock of their revolutionary rivals on the left for what was perceived as the opportunism or, at best, ingenuousness of their most prominent advocate – and he was ostracized by *Freedom*.

Yet as far as Read himself was concerned he remained an anarchist, even if an anarchist knight. His gravestone at St Gregory's Minister, Kirkdale, bears the inscription: 'KNIGHT, POET, ANARCHIST'. Benedict, Read's youngest son, commented in 1974:

> Read attempted to justify his decision to accept, but it is clear that there was more behind it than he cared to state publicly; perhaps the heart had its reasons. In any case it did not in any way lessen the strength of his [political] views.[15]

Read's biographer, James King, has now disclosed how eager Ludo Read was to become Lady Read: 'Ludo had no doubt that Herbert had to accept the Palace's invitation'. T. S. Eliot had in 1948 been appointed to the Order of Merit, but Ludo asked 'what's the use of being Mrs OM?'. The couple were partially estranged because of a passionate friendship which Read had formed with Ruth Francken, a woman painter thirty years his junior, in Venice earlier in 1952. The relationship was platonic, but he had wanted it otherwise and been so foolhardy as to tell Ludo so. Thus King concludes: 'Finally, Read succumbed to Ludo's considerable powers of persuasion'.[16]

All the same, I still find it very relevant that Read was a countryman, coming from a Conservative farming family – his first politics (from the age of fifteen) was a romantic, Disraelian Toryism.[17] In 1949 he had returned to Yorkshire: to live in Stonegrave, only two or three miles from his birthplace and childhood home at Muscoates. He had explained in *Poetry and Anarchism*:

> In spite of my intellectual pretensions, I am by birth and tradition a peasant. I remain essentially a peasant. I despise the whole industrial epoch – not only the plutocracy which it has raised to power, but also the industrial proletariat which it has drained from the land and proliferated in hovels of indifferent brick. The only class in the community for which I feel any real sympathy is the agricultural class, including the genuine remnants of a landed aristocracy. This perhaps explains my early attraction to Bakunin, Kropotkin, and Tolstoy, who were also of the land, aristocrats and peasants.[18]

It needs to be said that Read's second marriage had some very negative consequences for him. Ludo certainly provided him with psychological and emotional sustenance – their partnership and his second family were extremely happy. But the acceptance of the knighthood demolished whatever reputation Read had had on the left and, in addition, made many writers and painters (who do indeed often have much of the anarchist in them), especially avant-garde artists, down to the present day, scornful of someone so entirely compromised by absorption into the establishment. Further, Ludo was responsible for a lifestyle at odds with her husband's published principles. Read the atheist assented to his daughter being sent to a (very bad) convent and his sons to the nearby Catholic public school, Ampleforth, when naturally he would have preferred them to have gone to a school like A. S. Neill's Summerhill.[19]

Read's anarchist political theory was unremarkable. He was an anarcho-syndicalist – at the outset at least – with respect to means. 'The ethical anarchism of Bakunin has been completed by the economic syndicalism of Sorel… wherever anarchism is a considerable political force, as in Spain, it is combined with syndicalism. Anarcho-syndicalism is a clumsy mouthful, but it describes the present-day type of anarchist doctrine.'[20] In terms of ends, Read seems always to have been an anarchist communist. Kropotkin is the anarchist theorist most frequently (and approvingly) mentioned by him.

In 1942 Read concluded:

... all the practical aspect of Kropotkin's work is astonishingly apt for the present day. Though written more than fifty years ago, a work like *Fields, Factories and Workshops* only needs to have its statistics brought up-to-date; its deductions and proposals remain as valid as on the day when they were written.[21]

Colin Ward has now done just this for Kropotkin in his edition of *Fields, Factories and Workshops Tomorrow* (1974; 2nd edn, 1985). On a visit to China in 1959 Read wrote:

All these communes are virtually self-supporting – the only things they need to get from outside are heavy machinery like tractors & perhaps coal & minerals like cobalt. It is the complete decentralization of industry advocated by Kropotkin in *Fields, Factories and Workshops*...[22]

George Woodcock recalls how:

On his return from his first visit to the United States after World War II... he came to see me and talked mostly about supermarkets, which he had seen for the first time, and which interested him because people took what they wanted from the shelves; it seemed to him that, if only the cash desks at the entrances could be removed, the supermarket would be the perfect model for free anarchist communist distribution as envisaged by Kropotkin in *The Conquest of Bread*.[23]

These three comments demonstrate one of Read's most attractive qualities: keeping abreast of modern developments and assessing the continuing relevance of anarchist analysis – and, if necessary, pointing out how it needed to be updated. From the mid-1940s he often anticipated the 'new anarchism' of Alex Comfort and Paul Goodman, Colin Ward and Murray Bookchin – an anarchism informed by such disciplines as psychology, sociology, biology and ecology. His impressive lecture of 1947 to the London Anarchists, 'Anarchism: Past and Future', is particularly noteworthy in this respect.[24]

It remains the case, though, that the broad outlines of Read's anarchism are unexceptional:

I have said little about the actual organization of an anarchist community, partly because I have nothing to add to what has been said by Kropotkin and by contemporary syndicalists like Dubrueil;[25] partly because it is always a mistake to build a priori constitutions. The main thing is to establish your principles – the principles of equity, of individual freedom, of workers' control. The community then aims at the establishment of these principles from the starting-point of local needs and local conditions. That they must be established by revolutionary methods is perhaps inevitable.[26]

As Read himself observes:

I realize that there is nothing original in [my] outline of an anarchist community: it has all the elements of essential communism as imagined by Marx and Engels; it has much in common with Guild Socialism and Christian Socialism. It does not matter very much what we call our ultimate ideal. I call it anarchism because that word emphasizes, as no other, the central doctrine – the abolition of the State and the creation of a co-operative commonwealth.[27]

On the other hand, Murray Bookchin, the most innovative anarchist theorist since Kropotkin, has revealed that:

Kropotkin had no influence on my turns from Marxism to anarchism – nor, for that matter, did Bakunin or Proudhon. It was Herbert Read's *The Philosophy of Anarchism* that I found most useful for rooting the views I slowly developed over the fifties and well into the sixties in a libertarian pedigree…[28]

Read breaks with the classic anarchist political thinkers in just one way, but it is of decisive importance. This is his rejection of force. 'Anarchism', he says, 'naturally implies pacifism.'[29] Writing in 1938, he explained:

There is no problem to which, during the last twenty years, I have given more thought than this problem of war and peace; it has been an obsession with my generation. There is no problem which leads so inevitably to anarchism. Peace is anarchy. Government is force; force is repression, and repression leads to reaction, or to a psychosis of power which in its turn involves the individual in destruction and the nations in war. War will exist as long as the State exists. Only a non-governmental society can offer those economic, ethical and psychological conditions under which the emergence of a peaceful mentality is possible.[30]

He explicates further, in 1953:

Revolt, it will be said, implies violence; but this is an outmoded, an incompetent conception of revolt. The most effective form of revolt in this violent world we live in is non-violence. Gandhi temporarily inspired his followers to practise such a form of revolt, but we are still far from a full awareness of its potentialities.[31]

Read became a member, one of the 'names', of the Committee of 100, the most important anarchist – or near-anarchist – political organization of modern Britain; but he resigned, after only a year, in 1961 in protest against the mass action at the Wethersfield air-base, regarding the intention as aggressive:

Such a policy is not passive. It is an organized threat to authority that provokes the threat of counter-forces to preserve public order or protect public property. In their immediate effect such demonstrations are directed against the police and military forces and not against the real enemy, which is the people in their massive ignorance and stupidity.[32]

Read's anarchism was not peripheral to his other, varied activities. Rather it was – knighthood and all – at the core of how he viewed the world in general. When he came to collect the essays he had written 'specifically on the subject of Anarchism' he very rightly insisted:

> There is no categorical separation... between what I have written on this subject and what I have written on social problems generally (*The Politics of the Unpolitical*) or on the social aspects of art (*Art and Society* and *The Grass Roots of Art*) or on the social aspects of education (*Education through Art* and *Education for Peace*). The same philosophy reappears in my literary criticism and in my poetry.[33]

In his aesthetics Read attempted to assimilate classicism to romanticism. As he explained in 1937:

> From 1918 I have been a close friend of T. S. Eliot, and to some extent his influence is responsible for my early attempt to reconcile reason and romanticism – not entirely, because the contradiction exists in my own personality.

Other major influences on Read in this respect were Orage and T. E. Hulme, whose *Speculations* he edited for posthumous publication.[34]

> Wisdom, as I have insisted ever since I became intellectually conscious, is the needle which comes to rest between reason and romanticism (a word which comprises instinct, intuition, imagination, and fantasy).[35]

So it is when Read deliberately situates his politics within his overall philosophy that what he has to say is at its most unusual and, I think, impressive. Let me, in Read's own style, quote two lengthy extracts in illustration:

> When we follow reason... in the medieval sense, we listen to the voice of God; we discover God's order, which is the Kingdom of Heaven. Otherwise there are only the subjective prejudices of individuals, and these prejudices inflated to the dimensions of nationalism, mysticism, megalomania, and fascism. A realistic rationalism rises above all these diseases of the spirit and establishes a universal order of thought, which is a necessary order of thought because it is the order of the real world; and because it is necessary and real, it is not man-imposed, but natural; and each man finding this order finds his freedom.
>
> Modern anarchism is a reaffirmation of this natural freedom, of this direct communion with universal truth. Anarchism rejects the man-made systems of government, which are instruments of individual and class tyranny; it seeks to recover the system of nature, of man living in accordance with the universal truth of reality. It denies the rule of kings and castes, of churches and parliaments, to affirm the rule of reason, which is the rule of God.
>
> The rule of reason – to live according to natural laws – this is also the release

of the imagination. We have two possibilities: to discover truth, and to create beauty. We make a profound mistake if we confuse these two activities, attempting to discover beauty and to create truth. If we attempt to create truth, we can only do so by imposing on our fellow-men an arbitrary and idealistic system which has no relation to reality; and if we attempt to discover beauty we look for it where it cannot be found – in reason, in logic, in experience. Truth is in reality, in the visible and tangible world of sensation; but beauty is in unreality, in the subtle and unconscious world of the imagination... We must surrender our minds to universal truth, but our imagination is free to dream; is as free as the dream; is the dream.

I balance anarchism with surrealism, reason with romanticism, the understanding with the imagination, function with freedom.[36]

This Heraclitean principle of flux, of chance, of fortuity issues out of the tragedy of war, and is basic to my anarchism and romanticism... That I can combine anarchism with order, a philosophy of strife with pacifism, an orderly life with romanticism and revolt in art and literature – all this is inevitably scandalous to the conventional philosopher. This principle of flux, the Keatsian notion of 'negative capability', justifies everything I have done (or not done) in my life, everything I have written, every attack and defence. I hate all monolithic systems, all logical categories, all pretences to truth and inevitability. The sun is new every day.

A fatalistic philosophy should imply more resignation than I have shown. But fatalism does not imply inactivity; on the contrary, since we are counters in a child's game, we are condemned to action. It is in changing, as Heraclitus said, that things find repose. I have called my politics 'the politics of the unpolitical', but I have striven for change, even for revolution. My understanding of the history of culture has convinced me that the ideal society is a point on a receding horizon. We move steadily towards it but can never reach it. Nevertheless we must engage with passion in the immediate strife – such is the nature of things and if defeat is inevitable (as it is) we are not excused. The only excusable indifference is that of Zeus, the divine indifference.[37]

As this second passage in particular suggests, Read was, as Henry Moore considered, 'fundamentally... a romantic', he himself admitting to his 'native romanticism',[38] and I would contend that the politics of romanticism is most naturally and properly anarchism. So Read could write:

It is true that we come into the world trailing clouds of glory; a Heaven which is universal and impersonal lies about us in our infancy, and though the shades of the social prison-house begin to close on the growing boy, he is still, in Wordsworth's exact phrase, 'Nature's Priest'.[39]

At root Read adhered to the values of romanticism: sincerity, simplicity, organicism, spontaneity, emotion, individualism. And it is when, drawing upon the well-spring of locality, he is writing as a Yorkshire romantic (even if balancing this with classicism) rather than as an internationalist revolutionary that his political voice is most distinctive.

The point at which Read's anarchist thought is most grievously lacking is in his failure to extend his professional concern with the visual arts into a generalized theory of human emancipation. George Orwell, reviewing a collection of his essays, astutely chose 'to concentrate mainly on one point – the clash between Read's political beliefs and his aesthetic theory'.[40] In the title essay of *The Politics of the Unpolitical* Read names the six modern 'philosophers and prophets… whose message is still insistent, and directly applicable to our present condition – Ruskin and Kropotkin, Morris and Tolstoy, Gandhi and Eric Gill'.[41] Although Read is sincere in his admiration of Morris as a 'great artist and great socialist', he is withering in his dismissal of Morris's rejection of the machine:

> I am no yearning medievalist, and have always denounced the sentimental reaction of Morris and his disciples. I have embraced industrialism, tried to give it its true aesthetic principles, all because I want to be through with it, want to get to the other side of it, into a world of electric power and mechanical plenty when man can once more return to the land, not as a peasant but as a lord.[42]

Read is, of course, fully aware of the way in which the names and ideas of Ruskin, Morris and Gill are interlinked,[43] but neither Ruskin nor Gill receive the stick which he gives in his writings to Morris. Ruskin he reveres as a great and visionary writer and as a master of English prose. His high opinion of Gill, a personal friend, is indicated by his surprising inclusion among 'the Six' and influenced by Gill's having come to terms with mechanization and mass production (as actually Read considered Morris would also have done).[44]

Read is predominantly concerned with the role – indeed with the unshackling – of the designer in modern industry rather than, as Morris was, with the liberation of the worker. But in one important and provocative lecture, 'The Future of Art in an Industrial Civilization' (later retitled 'Towards a Duplex Civilization'), he speculates on the future not only of industrial design and the industrial designer but also of 'industrial man in general'.[45] He envisages a future in which the

> defects in the existing economic system have been removed, and… there are no further obstacles to the full and free application of design to the products of the industrial system. Production is for use rather than profit, everything is made fit for the purpose it is to serve, and everyone has the necessary means to acquire the essentials of a decent life at the highest level of prevailing taste… virtually the

industrial designer's paradise will have come into being, and we shall have not only a machine age but also, what we have so far lacked, a machine art.

The standards for machine art are 'economy, precision, fitness for purpose – all qualities of classical beauty'. 'It is', says Read, 'a very possible, and even a very probable Utopia.' Yet such a Utopia would be liable to suffer fundamental social and, especially, aesthetic problems.

> We shall have factories full of clean automatic machines moulding and stamping, punching and polishing innumerable objects which are compact in form, harmonious in shape, delectable in colour. Gone are the jointed and fragile objects which to-day we ingeniously construct from wood and metal; almost everything will be made from one basic plastic material, and beds and bath-tubs, plates and dishes, radio cabinets and motor-cars, will spill out of the factories in an unending stream of glossy jujubes. I am perhaps exaggerating: if we get tired of glossiness, we can have our surfaces matt. Nothing will be impossible. The technologist and the designer between them will be able to satisfy every whim and fancy. From a technical point of view, it will all be fearfully easy, and we may well ask ourselves: where is the restraint to come from? What is to prevent this search for quality and variety degenerating into an avalanche of vulgarity?[46]

Technological advances will have largely eliminated the human element from production and so, in addition to the problem of leisure, there will be the problem of 'the atrophy of sensation': so few people will be required 'to use their hands in creative contact with a material' that they will be 'quite unable to check a general atrophy of sensibility…'[47]

Read's solution to these interrelated problems, 'if we are to go forward to the logical conclusion of the machine age', is to 'create a movement in a parallel direction, and not in opposition'. It will be necessary to establish a 'double-decker' or 'duplex civilization', in which there will be a division between a public machine art, abstract and geometrical, and a private naturalistic or humanistic art.[48] He gives the example of ancient Egypt, where a religious art, mainly of public buildings and sculptured monuments, and which was geometric, rational, objective, abstract, co-existed for centuries with a domestic art, largely of paintings, small carvings and various kinds of decorated vessels, and which was naturalistic, lyrical, even sentimental. Obviously contemporary society already exemplifies to a significant extent a double-decker civilization. What, in addition, Read prescribes is to

> let every individual serve an apprenticeship in handicrafts… creative arts of every kind should be made the basis of our educational system. If, between the ages of five and fifteen, we could give all our children a training of the senses through the constructive shaping of materials… then we need not fear the fate of those

children in a wholly-mechanized world. They would carry within their minds, within their bodies, the natural antidote to objective rationality, a spontaneous overflow of creative energies into their hours of leisure.

The result would be a private art standing over against the public art of the factories. But that – in our painting and sculpture, our poetry and dancing, our artist-potters and artist-weavers – we already have. That is to say, we have a tiny minority of people calling themselves artists. I am recommending that everyone should be an artist.[49]

Here, belatedly, in a lecture given in 1943 and first published in 1947, we have Read standing more-or-less foursquare alongside his great predecessors – Ruskin, Morris, Gill – and stressing the fundamental, liberatory importance of the arts and crafts in any free society. It must be noted, though, that the argument is not unproblematical for, as the reviewer of *The Grass Roots of Art* in *Freedom* observed, it is:

not one that would be acceptable to anarchists; indeed, the argument as it stands seems to be in sharp contradiction to the general thesis of the book... the anarchist would argue that the syndicate and the commune, operating a decentralized industry, would exert a direct influence upon design as well as distribution and exemplify the kind of communal creativity Read has in mind. This particular essay in speculation is a brilliant one, but the steps by which Read mounts to its launching would seem to the anarchist reader to be conspicuously shaky.[50]

Read's views continued to develop to such an extent that by 1961, as the designer Misha Black, who as a young man had been fired by *Art and Industry*, recalled, 'he had completely changed his attitude' and believed that 'one must accept that most things which are made by industry have no real aesthetic value at all and one must look for aesthetic satisfaction in other things... and he was getting very close in fact to... a kind of William Morris attitude'.[51]

Read's undeniably original, although not unproblematic, contribution to anarchism was as an educational theorist. When the British Council was established in 1940, it was decided to 'project' British art overseas during wartime not by sending valuable works by professional artists but to substitute collections of drawings by British children. Read was given the task of selecting the works and visited schools throughout the country. In the year before his death he was to recall it as 'an experience that may be said to have redirected the course of my life'.[52] He was appointed to a Leon Fellowship at the University of London for the two years 1940–42, and the result was the imposing *Education through Art*, published in 1943. As Read was to stress:

It is not often realized how deeply anarchist in its orientation... *Education through*

Art is and was intended to be. It is of course humiliating to have to confess that its success (and it is by far the most influential book I have written) has been in spite of this fact. I must conclude that I did not make my intention clear enough...[53]

He himself admitted: 'It is a general complaint that my book, *Education through Art*, is a difficult one – too difficult for the people it might most benefit.'[54] Freedom Press brought out *The Education of Free Men* in 1944, the year of the Butler Act, as 'a shorter statement of the theory of education' put forward in *Education through Art*, announcing:

> We are glad to publish this pamphlet by Herbert Read because... it covers new ground by relating the problem of education to that of liberty. This is particularly important at a time when many people think that the question of education can be solved by State legislation.

Back in 1940 what had so moved Read was the gestural and emotional content of the children's art. In particular, it was a working-class girl of five from a Cambridgeshire village who gave him 'something in the nature of an apocalyptic experience' with the drawing she described as 'a snake going round the world in a boat'. Not only had the child drawn a mandala, 'a magic circle divided into segments', 'one of the oldest symbols in the world', but she had found a verbal equivalent, for 'the snake surrounding the world is one of the most ancient of primordial images'. Read was a convinced Freudian and had been one of the first in Britain to apply psychoanalytical concepts to literary and art criticism. What he had previously known largely from reading Jung and regarded as merely an interesting hypothesis 'suddenly became an observed phenomenon, a proof', as he recognized the girl's drawing as 'a symbol that was archetypal and universal'. (He now transferred his allegiance to Jung and was to become both publisher and editor-in-chief of the collected works of Jung in English.) In total Read recognized in the children's drawings a range of imagery that suggested that young children were naturally in harmony with deeply-embedded cultural and social experiences. As he put it:

> The more I considered my material the more convinced I became of the basic significance of the child's creative activities for the development of consciousness and for the necessary fusion of sensibility and intellect.[55]

What are the implications for anarchism of all this? Read begins *Education through Art* by stating:

> The purpose of education can... only be to develop, at the same time as the uniqueness, the social consciousness or reciprocity of the individual. As a result of the infinite permutations of heredity, the individual will inevitably be unique,

and this uniqueness, because it is something not possessed by anyone else, will be of value to the community... But uniqueness has no practical value in isolation. One of the most certain lessons of modern psychology and of recent historical experiences, is that education must be a process, not only of individuation, but also of integration, which is the reconciliation of individual uniqueness with social unity... the individual will be 'good' in the degree that his individuality is realized within the organic wholeness of the community.

Here we have the egoism of Max Stirner assimilated in the anarchist communism of Kropotkin. (Read mentions Stirner in *The Education of Free Men*; writes approvingly of him elsewhere, recounting how he bought his copy of the first British edition of Stirner's great book, *The Ego and His Own*, in 1915; and goes so far as to conclude that 'Jung sometimes seems to echo Stirner's very words'.)[56]

As we have already seen, in his discussion of a duplex civilization, Read advocates that 'creative arts of every kind should be made the basis of our educational system'. On the one hand, 'a child's drawings, produced as a result of spontaneous activity, are direct evidence of the child's physiological and psychological disposition' and 'once the psychological tendency or trend of a child is known, its own individuality can be developed by the discipline of art, till it has its own form and beauty...'; on the other hand: 'We know that a child absorbed in drawing or any other creative activity is a happy child. We know just as a matter of everyday experience that self-expression is self-improvement.' As a result: 'We do not claim an hour or a day of the child's time: we claim the whole child'.[57]

For Read the choice between authoritarianism and a free, libertarian society therefore lies in the schoolroom:

> The first charge on the educator... is to bring the uniqueness of the individual into focus, to the end that a more vital interplay of forces takes place within each organic grouping of individuals – within the family, within the school, within society itself. The possibilities are at first evenly weighed between hatred, leading to crime, unhappiness and social antagonism, and love, which ensures mutual aid, individual happiness and social peace.[58]

Only a few years later Alex Comfort was to conclude that the task of modern revolutionaries is to abandon political intrigue and insurrectionary fantasy and instead become practitioners – or at least propagandists – of 'child psychiatry, social psychology and political psychology'.[59] Similarly, and rather more practically, Read is in effect calling on anarchists to bring about the social revolution by becoming schoolteachers, trained in the pedagogy of his freedom in education:

> ... a choice must be made which inevitably dictates the form which our society will take. In one direction we can institute objective codes of conduct and

morality to which our children are introduced before the age of understanding and to which they are compelled to conform by a system of rewards and punishments. That way conducts us to an authoritarian society, governed by laws and sanctioned by military power. It is the kind of society in which most of the world now lives, ridden by neuroses, full of envy and avarice, ravaged by war and disease.

In the other direction we can avoid all coercive codes of morality, all formal conceptions of 'right' and 'wrong'. For a morality of obedience we can substitute a morality of attachment or reciprocity... Believing that the spontaneous life developed by children among themselves gives rise to a discipline infinitely nearer to that inner accord or harmony which is the mark of the virtuous man, we can aim at making our teachers the friends rather than the masters of their pupils; as teachers they will not lay down ready-made rules, but will encourage their children to carry out their own co-operative activities, and thus spontaneously to elaborate their own rules. Discipline will not be imposed, but discovered – discovered as the right, economical and harmonious way of action. We can avoid the competitive evils of the examination system, which merely serves to re-enforce the egocentrism inherent in the child: we can eliminate all ideas of rewards and punishments, substituting a sense of the collective good of the community, to which reparation for shortcomings and selfishness will be obviously due and freely given.[60]

Education is a common preoccupation of anarchists, both theoretically and practically. Amongst the principal anarchist thinkers Godwin, Stirner and Tolstoy have all shared Read's concern, but only he went so far as to identify the school as the primary arena for anarchist action. What he originated was, in his words, 'a revolutionary policy', which would 'bring about a revolution in the structure of our society'.[61] Read's vision is an inspiring one and not, I consider, unrealistic – nor dependent on the ultimate validity of Jungian theory or on his own abstract schematizations. There is, however, one major difficulty with it. All societies regard their educational systems as of vital importance to social well-being, none more so than contemporary societies. The kind of intervention and social change that Read advocates would be far from uncontested – as is witnessed by the educational reforms of Thatcherite and Blairite Britain, which to a significant degree have been directed at reversing the pedagogy and curriculum, especially in the primary school, which had been developed over the decades after 1944 and which the ideas of Read and the Society for Education through Art (of which he was President) had done much to influence. So we are necessarily returned to the struggle for social power, which is required in order to implement such far-reaching educational innovation.

As a prolific writer on anarchism and related matters, and as a large fish in the small pool of international anarchism between 1937 and 1968, Read's reputation as a political and social thinker was considerable in libertarian circles. His anarchist writings deserve to be read and studied – particularly for the ideas on education, but also for the many perceptive and sometimes profound things to be found scattered throughout them.

Notes

1   *Adelphi*, September–November 1937. Cf. the letter from Read to V. F. Calverton, 20 February 1937, in Eric Homberger (ed.), 'A Transatlantic Correspondence', *Times Literary Supplement*, 22 May 1981.

2   Herbert Read, *Poetry and Anarchism* (London: Faber and Faber, 1938), pp. 13–14. All quotations are, where possible, from first or early editions of Read's works since he always extensively revised the texts of later editions, but not, as he himself emphasized, 'to give an air of caution to the impetuous voice of youth' (Herbert Read, *Anarchy and Order: Essays in Politics* [London: Faber and Faber, 1954], p. 9).

3   Reprinted in Herbert Read, *The Cult of Sincerity* (London: Faber and Faber, 1968), p. 76.

4   Herbert Read, *Annals of Innocence and Experience* (London: Faber and Faber, 2nd edn, 1946), pp. 127–28.

5   Ibid., pp. 129–30, 133–34. And indeed on 14 December 1934 he was telling Calverton that he was 'too good an anarchist' to become 'a complete Marxist' (Homberger, 'A Transatlantic Correspondence').

6   This is from the *Listener* article of September 1934 quoted by Bob Barker, 'Herbert Read as Novelist: *The Green Child*', p.108 above.

7   A. L. Morton, *The English Utopia* (London: Lawrence and Wishart, 1952), pp. 208–09.

8   Both were published by Stanley Nott Ltd of London, *Essential Communism* in the 'Pamphlets on the New Economics' series. John L. Finlay, *Social Credit: The English Origins* (Montreal and London: McGill-Queen's University Press, 1972), says that it was not until *Essential Communism* that Read made public his acceptance of Social Credit (p. 253) – and considers there is a natural affinity between it and anarchism. (For Eliot and Social Credit, see David Bradshaw, 'T. S. Eliot and the Major: Sources of Literary Anti-Semitism in the 1930s', *Times Literary Supplement*, 5 July 1996.)

9   Read, *Annals of Innocence and Experience*, p. 134.

10 Quoted by Jeffrey Meyers, *The Enemy: A Biography of Wyndham Lewis* (London and Henley: Routledge and Kegan Paul, 1980), p. 310.

11 International Institute of Social History, Amsterdam: Goldman Archive, XXVIII B, carbon of letter from Goldman to Read, 19 January 1938; letter from Read to Goldman, 20 January 1938. For an account of the activities of the English Section of the SIA see my forthcoming edition of the correspondence between Goldman and John Cowper Powys.

12 Letter from Goldman to Read, 5 June 1939, quoted by Alice Wexler, *Emma Goldman in Exile: From the Russian Revolution to the Spanish Civil War* (Boston: Beacon Press, 1989), p. 214.

13 His contributions are reprinted in Herbert Read, *A One-Man Manifesto and Other Writings for Freedom Press*, ed. David Goodway (London: Freedom Press, 1994).

14 V.R., '"A Man Born Free"', *Freedom*, 22 June 1968 (reprinted in *Anarchy*, no. 91 [September 1968], pp. 284–86).

15 *A Tribute to Herbert Read, 1893–1968* (Bradford Art Galleries and Museums: catalogue of exhibition at The Manor House, Ilkley, 1975), p. 15.

16 James King, *The Last Modern: A Life of Herbert Read* (London: Weidenfeld and Nicolson, 1990), pp. 263–66. As Ludo admitted to Vernon Richards, when contact was fleetingly restored after Read's

death: 'It was I who said it was the new Queen's first list and it would be a shame to refuse…' (I am indebted to Vernon Richards for a copy of this letter of 21 June 1968.)

17 Read, *Annals of Innocence and Experience*, pp. 124–26.

18 Read, *Poetry and Anarchism*, p. 16.

19 'A Childhood: Piers Paul Read', *The Times Magazine*, 9 September 1995. See also the obituary of Lady Read (by Piers Paul Read), *The Times*, 15 March 1996. I am indebted to Tom and Celia Read for some information (as well as their hospitality at Stonegrave), but they are not responsible for my interpretation.

20 Read, *Poetry and Anarchism*, pp. 71, 82.

21 Herbert Read (ed.), *Kropotkin: Selections from his Writings* (London: Freedom Press, 1942), p.15.

22 Herbert Read, 'Letters from China, 1959', in *A Tribute to Herbert Read*, p. 47.

23 George Woodcock, *Herbert Read: The Stream and the Source* (London: Faber and Faber, 1972), p. 234.

24 *Freedom*, 17 May 1947 (reprinted in Read, *A One-Man Manifesto*, pp. 117–25).

25 The 'remarkable' book, *A Chacun sa chance* (Paris, 1935), by this little-known writer, Hyacinthe Dubreuil, also deeply impressed Aldous Huxley in his contemporary libertarian treatise, *Ends and Means: An Enquiry into the Nature of Ideals and into the Methods Employed For their Realization* (London: Chatto and Windus, 1937), pp. 74–77, 83–85, 172.

26 *The Philosophy of Anarchism* (1940), reprinted in Read, *Anarchy and Order*, p. 51.

27 Read, *Poetry and Anarchism*, p. 87. I illustrate the extremely conventional nature of Read's political anarchism in greater detail in the original, longer version of this chapter: my introduction to Read, *A One-Man Manifesto*, pp. 7–11.

28 Murray Bookchin, 'Deep Ecology, Anarchosyndicalism, and the Future of Anarchist Thought', in Murray Bookchin *et al.*, *Deep Ecology and Anarchism: A Polemic* (London: Freedom Press, 1993), p. 53.

29 Read, *Poetry and Anarchism*, p. 87.

30 Ibid., pp. 119–20.

31 'Introduction: Revolution and Reason', to Read, *Anarchy and Order*, p. 26.

32 'A note on policy submitted to the Meeting of the Committee of 100 to be held on December 17 1961', printed in *A Tribute to Herbert Read*, pp. 51–52. See also King, pp. 300–01; 'Remembering Herbert Read', *Anarchy*, no. 91 (September 1968), pp. 287–88.

33 Read, *Anarchy and Order*, p. 9. The omission of the art criticism from this list is very noticeable.

34 University of Victoria, Victoria, BC: Read Archive, carbon of letter from Read to Hans W. Häusermann, 6 August 1937. For Read's shifting approach to the romanticism–classicism dichotomy, see David Thistlewood, *Herbert Read: Formlessness and Form: An Introduction to His Aesthetics* (London: Routledge and Kegan Paul, 1984), esp. pp. 7–9, 38–49, 168–73; H. W. Häusermann, 'The Development of Herbert Read', in Henry Treece (ed.), *Herbert Read: An Introduction to His Work by Various Hands* (London: Faber and Faber, 1944), esp. pp. 53–55, 69–71, 79–80; also G. Wilson Knight, 'Herbert Read and Byron', in Robin Skelton (ed.), *Herbert Read: A Memorial Symposium* (London: Methuen, 1970), p. 130.

35 'Chains of Freedom' (1946–52), printed in Read, *Anarchy and Order*, p. 171.

36 Read, *Poetry and Anarchism*, pp. 96–97.

37 'What is There Left to Say?' (1962), reprinted in Read, *The Cult of Sincerity*, pp. 55–56.

38 Henry Moore, 'Remembering Herbert Read', *Anarchy*, no. 91 (September 1968), p. 287; Herbert Read, 'Lone Wolf' (obituary of Wyndham Lewis), *New Statesman*, 16 March 1957. Cf. also Allen Tate, 'Foreword' to Herbert Read, *Selected Writings: Poetry and Criticism* (London: Faber and Faber, 1963).

39 Herbert Read, *The Education of Free Men* (London: Freedom Press, 1944), p. 18. For Read as a

romantic, see Herbert Read (ed.), 'Introduction', *Surrealism* (London: Faber and Faber, 1936), pp. 21–28, 87–91 (this essay was reprinted as 'Surrealism and the Romantic Principle' in Herbert Read, *The Philosophy of Modern Art: Collected Essays* [London: Faber and Faber, 1952]); Herbert Read, *The Tenth Muse: Essays in Criticism* (London: Routledge and Kegan Paul, 1957), p. 4; E. H. Ramsden, 'Herbert Read's Philosophy of Art', in Treece, *Herbert Read*, p. 45; Woodcock, *Herbert Read*, pp. 139–56.

40 George Orwell, review of *A Coat of Many Colours*, *Poetry Quarterly*, vol. 7, no. 4 (Winter 1945), reprinted in *The Collected Essays, Journalism and Letters of George Orwell* (Harmondsworth: Penguin Books, 4 vols, 1970), vol. 4, p. 69.

41 Herbert Read, *The Politics of the Unpolitical* (London: George Routledge, 1943), p. 2.

42 Ibid., p. 44; Read, *Poetry and Anarchism*, pp. 16–17. For Read on Morris, see also Geo. Ed. Roebuck (ed.), *Some Appreciations of William Morris: 24 March 1934* (Walthamstow: Walthamstow Antiquarian Society, 1934), pp. 28–29; Herbert Read, *Art and Industry: The Principles of Industrial Design* (London: Faber and Faber, 1934), pp. 27–33; and 'William Morris', in Herbert Read, *A Coat of Many Colours: Occasional Essays* (London: George Routledge, 1945), pp. 76–79.

43 See, for example, Herbert Read, *The Grass Roots of Art: Lectures on the Social Aspects of Art in an Industrial Age* (London: Faber and Faber, new edn, 1955), pp. 37, 49.

44 For Read on Ruskin, see 'The Message of Ruskin', in Read, *A Coat of Many Colours*, pp. 231–37, and Read, *The Cult of Sincerity*, pp. 56–57. For Read on Gill, see 'Eric Gill', in Read, *A Coat of Many Colours*, pp. 5–16. When he reissued *The Politics of the Unpolitical* as *To Hell with Culture: and Other Essays on Art and Society* (London: Routledge and Kegan Paul, 1963), Read dedicated it to Gill's memory. Robin Kinross, 'Herbert Read's *Art and Industry*: A History', *Journal of Design History*, vol. 1, no. 1 (1988), pp. 37–38, 44–45, provides a helpful discussion of the dialectical relationship between Gill and Read.

45 Herbert Read, *The Grass Roots of Art* (London: Lindsay Drummond, 1947), p. 58.

46 Ibid., pp. 63–65.

47 Ibid., p.68.

48 Ibid., pp. 68–69. The distinction between these two kinds of art is introduced in Read, *Art and Industry*, pp. 11–13.

49 Read, *The Grass Roots of Art* (1947 edn), pp. 71–72. Cf. Read's initial conclusions on art and education in *Art and Industry*, Part IV.

50 *Freedom*, 1 May 1948. The reviewer was Louis Adeane, author of *To the Crystal City*, a book on Read's writings that has, regrettably, remained unpublished, although now deposited at the British Library as Add MS. 71, 198 (see George Woodcock, *Letter to the Past: An Autobiography* [Don Mills, Ontario: Fitzhenry and Whiteside, 1982], pp. 299–300; Read Archive, letters from Adeane to Read, 1949–52).

51 BBC Radio 3 programme, *Recollections of Herbert Read*, 4 December 1977. This oneness with Morris is also expressed in Herbert Read, *Design and Tradition: The Design Oration (1961) of the Society of Industrial Artists* (Hemingford Grey: The Vine Press, 1962); and in an interview published in 1959 he named Morris with Carpenter, Kropotkin and Stirner as his four major anarchist influences ('Intervista con Herbert Read', *Volontà*, vol. 12 [1959], p. 13).

52 'The Truth of a Few Simple Ideas' (1967), in Read, *The Cult of Sincerity*, pp. 43–45.

53 'My Anarchism', in Read, *The Cult of Sincerity*, p. 90.

54 Herbert Read, 'Education through Art', in Stefan Schimanski and Henry Treece (eds), *Transformation Two* (London: Lindsay Drummond, 1944), p. 63.

55 Read, *The Cult of Sincerity*, pp. 44–45; Herbert Read, *Education through Art* (London: Faber and Faber, 2nd edn 1945), p. 187n ('Snake round the World in a Boat' is reproduced as Plate 1b, facing p. 96). David Thistlewood, 'Herbert Read: Education through Art', *Resurgence*, no. 154

(September/October 1992), gives a useful summary of this and Read's educational ideas in general. See also Thistlewood, *Herbert Read*, pp. 111–14; Michael P. Smith, *The Libertarians and Education* (London: Allen and Unwin, 1983), pp. 118–22. In addition to *The Education of Free Men*, Read provides a clear and compact account of his views in 'The Aesthetic Method of Education', in Read, *The Grass Roots of Art* (1954 edn).

56 Read, *Education through Art*, p. 5; Read, *The Education of Free Men*, p. 17. For Read on Stirner see Read, *A One-Man Manifesto*, pp. 32, 38–39, 106–11; Read, *The Cult of Sincerity*, pp. 84–92; Herbert Read, *The Forms of Things Unknown: Essays towards an Aesthetic Philosophy* (London: Faber and Faber, 1960), pp. 173–76, 205.

57 Read, *The Education of Free Men*, pp. 15–16, 32.

58 Ibid., p. 18.

59 See David Goodway (ed.), *Against Power and Death: The Anarchist Articles and Pamphlets of Alex Comfort* (London: Freedom Press, 1994), pp. 18–20.

60 Read, *The Education of Free Men*, p. 25.

61 Herbert Read, *Education through Art – A Revolutionary Policy* (London: Society for Education through Art, 1955), p. 1. George Woodcock has been an eloquent expositor of this new anarchist strategy, which he compares to anarcho-syndicalism: see especially Woodcock, *Herbert Read*, chapter 8; but also George Woodcock, *Anarchism: A History of Libertarian Ideas and Movements* (Harmondsworth: Penguin Books, 2nd edn, 1986), p. 383, and George Woodcock (ed.), *The Anarchist Reader* (Glasgow: Fontana, 1977), pp. 48–49.

Herbert Read: Art, Education, and the Means of Redemption

MALCOLM ROSS

It is not often realised how deeply anarchistic in its orientation... *Education through Art* is and was intended to be. It is of course humiliating to have to confess that its success (and it is by far the most influential book I have written) has been in spite of this fact. I must conclude that I did not make my intention clear enough...

Herbert Read, *The Cult of Sincerity*[1]

ERBERT Read published *Education through Art* in 1943. For the next forty years there would have been few teachers of the arts unfamiliar at least with the book's title, even if, like me, they were less confident about its precise contents. Teachers of the visual arts in particular would have been aware of his great article of faith: that every child was a special kind of artist. Many would have been members of an organization of art teachers, the Society for Education through Art, committed to the promotion of his ideas, not just nationally but internationally. Nowadays his 'most influential' book has been out of print for over thirty years and your only chance of finding a copy is to have a slice of luck in a second-hand bookshop. References to his writings in new books on arts education are few, and when they do appear it is usually either for historical reasons or as a focus of criticism. For we seem to have moved beyond his orbit, despite the fact that some writers maintain[2] that the influence of Herbert Read is to be found in the National Curriculum for Art. If this were true, it would be because much of his writing on art education, as we shall see, left considerable scope for a positivistic interpretation. On the other hand, I believe he would have found the oppressively bureaucratic and centralist character of the National Curriculum anathema to his personal instincts, and for someone who wrote a book entitled *To Hell with Culture*, the focus upon consumerism and the pillars of the high European canon must surely have been unacceptable.

But trying to second guess what Herbert Read would have thought of this or that occurrence, had he lived to see it, is neither a safe nor a particularly productive activity. For example it is difficult to be sure what he would have made of the decision of the executive of his Society to set aside in 1984 its long resistance to amalgamation with the art teachers' trade union (the National Society for Art Education) and to accept shared identity as the newly named National Society for Education in Art and Design (NSEAD). The impulse that had kept the two organizations in a state of mutual rivalry for so long probably represented, for Read at least, a fundamental difference in principle between them – one that called for two separate organizations through which their distinctive positions could be expressed.

The organization with which Read was to become identified was first established as the Art Teachers' Guild in 1900. From the outset, the Guild had been principally an association of women teachers committed to the importance of expression, creativity and imagination in early childhood education. The Guild set itself the task of promoting and popularizing the radical ideas of such pioneers of progressive art education as Ebenezer Cooke and Franz Cizek. In 1946, after several years of cooperation and negotiation, the Guild amalgamated with the New Society of Art Teachers – founded in 1938 by Alexander Barclay-Russell – and formally adopted the title Society for Education in Art (SEA). Herbert Read's association with the Guild began in 1940 when he became Chairman of its joint Advisory Panel of External Consultants, charged to develop policy and to lobby government in the lead up to the Butler Education Act of 1944. The change of title to the Society for Education through Art occurred in 1953 and followed upon the sponsoring by UNESCO in 1951 of an International Society for Education through Art. Read, who had been made President of the SEA in 1947, remained in office until his death in 1968. This tradition in art education had always been distinctly separate from that of the slightly older, male-oriented, art-college-dominated Society of Art Masters, founded in 1888 (and renamed as the National Society of Art Masters in 1909 and the National Society of Art Education in 1944). The Art Masters espoused a very different set of priorities from the Art Teachers, focusing instead upon laying a sound foundation in schools for professional standards of craftsmanship in post-school art and design courses. [3]

I am in no position to pronounce upon the genesis of Read's personal philosophy, any more than I am on the calibre or character either of his political or of his personal life. I know him through his published writings, and of those only the most obvious. By any standard, his range of interests and the scale of his activities as a writer and cultural entrepreneur are prodigious. That he should have thought of *Education through Art* as both an anarchist tract and his most influential book is surely extremely important for an understanding of its content and purpose – even if, as he himself suggests, few of his readers have been fully aware of his underlying intentions. Read was driven by quite specific, political ideals. He remonstrated against every manifestation of repression – and in particular such repression as was visited upon the individual citizen in the name of good government. Having fought in the First World War and watched the rise of fascism and of the European dictatorships in the 1930s, Read, the 'philosophical anarchist', turned to education as the instrument through which an alternative to the seemingly endless cycle of violence might be established. He made the connections between psychology and art and psychology and education, and set out to provide a theory of education through art, based upon the latest

197

discoveries in psychology. However, as we shall see, he expresses his hopes of transforming the human personality in rather unfortunate terms: he suggests that the
behaviourists might have the answer to the perversion of the human mind which had
in his lifetime twice brought the world to a state of indescribable horror. If the mind
could be the seat of the aggressive impulse it could surely be trained towards the
opposite inclination. The connection between art and emotion was pivotal to Read's
project. Read's plan, for what was essentially to be a 'moral' education through the
transformation of the human personality, was a controlled programme of benign
indoctrination.

Read launched his anarchist assault upon education with the publication of
Education through Art. From then on, and for the remainder of his life, Read's commitment to and enthusiasm for what he called his 'mission' was absolute. In 1950 he
produced *Education for Peace*. This volume included four papers 'originally delivered
in 1947 or 1948 as lectures in various parts of the world – Sweden, Greece,
Czechoslovakia, Belgium, the United States of America and England'. The final essay
in the collection, *The Education of Free Men*, had been first published by the (anarchist)
Freedom Press in 1944 as a separate pamphlet. As Read himself says in his note of
introduction, 'For a more complete statement of the theory of education which lies
at the basis of them all, the reader is referred to the author's previous book, *Education
through Art*'.[4] His *The Redemption of the Robot* of 1966 includes five of these essays,
omits two and adds a further three. Read makes no reference to the previous publication of any of the material and I have been unable to discover for certain whether
or not the three 'new' essays had themselves appeared in print prior to the collection.[5] Read's practice seems to have been to recycle his work as he felt inclined,
sometimes making revisions, at other times merely allowing a paper to stand more
or less as originally published. Clearly he felt that he had said best what he wanted
to say about education in *Education through Art* and in the writings of the years immediately following upon its publication.

In a paper delivered to the American Committee on Art Education at its Sixth
Annual Conference in 1948, published subsequently as a pamphlet by the Museum
of Modern Art under the title *Culture and Education in World Order* (and incorporated
in both *Education for Peace* and *The Redemption of the Robot*), Read makes clear his
understanding of the connection between art, education and a new world order.
Having drawn a picture of Europe on its cultural knees, Read proceeds to chide
UNESCO for going about its business of renewal in a predictably antiquated and, to
his mind, inappropriate manner. He sees UNESCO in the hands of the old cultural
and educational establishment wedded to lecturing and committee work.
Furthermore, UNESCO, he claims, seems to wish to perpetuate the split between
education of the intellect and education of the emotions, a tradition dating back to
the Renaissance. Read proposes, on the authority of Plato and supported by arguments taken from Rousseau and rooted in the modern educational practices of

Pestalozzi and Herbart, that the basis of the new education needed to build a civilized culture should indeed be a moral education. A moral education, for Read, meant the education of the emotions – and this is where the arts came in. He made the simple equation: 'Aesthetic education develops ethical virtue'.[6] Upon this premise Read was to raise his entire pedagogical project. By way of illustrating how his 'moral revolution' was to be achieved, Read cites the work of the Russian psychologist, Ivan Petrovich Pavlov, and draws this conclusion:

> Human children can be conditioned even more easily than dogs, because of their range of sensibility and intelligence, with infinitely subtler results.[7]

Read's declared aim was 'the total reorientation of the human personality'.[8]

It is perhaps surprising that such talk did not set alarm bells ringing for his audience; perhaps it did for some of them. However, the general thrust of his message and the powerful drive of his speech seem to have carried the day – on that particular day in America in 1948 and upon many subsequent days. Here he is in full flow:

> The rebirth of a tragic sense of life; the re-emergence of transcendental forces so long frustrated by lawless expansion of competitive instincts, by crude materialism or by the elimination of human sympathy from the processes of thought; the restoration to life of significant play and ritual; a moral healthiness which is affirmative, and not an inhibition of all vitality; a sense of personal freedom and a consequent responsibility for the endowment of one's own fate with values; all these changes are involved as groundwork for a new civilisation. But it is unlikely that these deep, subtle and intimate changes can be brought about by secretariats and committees, by international conferences and polyglot organisations. They will be born in solitude, in meditation; in the family circle and in the nursery school; in the field and the factory: in the face of specific problems and by conscious discipline; in creative community and in communal creations; in drama and in the building of new cities; in dance and in song; in moments of mutual understanding and love. For all these moments and occasions, all we need to ask is peace in our time and the end to the exploitation of man by man.[9]

This rhetoric of Read's struck a chord with a great many teachers in the years following the Second World War. If the anarchist message was not picked up, the drive towards an education that stressed the cultural development of the individual child, that sought to relate pedagogical practice to the child's inherent disposition and so to value individuality and particularity, that stressed the creative and expressive potential of each individual – these principles found immediate favour and were easily assimilated into the whole progressive thrust of education over the following twenty years or so. Comprehensive education was introduced to eradicate the waste inherent in a system geared to the perpetuation of class and academic divisions. Primary schools became open spaces for the generation of integrated, fluid learning

experiences driven by the twin principles of 'child-centredness' and 'readiness' –
banished were the old notions of whole-class, teacher-led instruction and learning
by rote. In such an environment it was natural for the arts to flourish and primary
schools in Britain became world models for what such an education through the arts
might be. With the passage of time and the realization that new working circumstances would make different demands upon young people seeking employment, the
school leaving age was raised to sixteen (1969), and a massive programme of
curriculum development put in place geared to the empowerment of students and
the retraining of teachers to more interactive roles in the classroom. Such was the
world of the 1960s and early 1970s. It was a world marked by professional optimism: teachers were to have regular periods of leave for professional development;
schools were reorganizing to accommodate new technologies and new pedagogical
practices: students were becoming active participants in their education rather than
merely passive recipients. Where the arts were concerned expansion was the
keynote; the visual arts were broadening out to include industrial and environmental
design; a revolution in music education was under way stressing creative music-
making as well as musical appreciation; educational drama had arrived and was the
fastest growing subject in the curriculum.

By the mid-1970s the tide was on the turn. The coming changes were signalled
by James Callaghan in his famous Ruskin College speech of 1977. A series of international economic crises followed by social and industrial unrest at home
precipitated a sudden loss of confidence in the dreams of the preceding decade. The
professions as a whole came in for criticism and were soon under direct attack by
the Thatcher administration – all the old certainties were called into question and,
more particularly, called to account.[10] The teacher unions took on the government
in a prolonged and bitter dispute in the mid-1980s and lost – never to recover either
their professional clout or their moral authority. The years of institutionally-based
research and professionally-led, locally-authorized experimentation in education
were halted and, in England and Wales, though not in Scotland, legislation was
invoked by Government as the best way of bringing about 'managed change'. A
wholly new ethos was sweeping the Western world with capitalism triumphant and
international socialism suddenly vulnerable and then, unthinkably, collapsing altogether.

In the world of arts education the change of climate was seen as extremely threatening and a group of experts was assembled in 1978 by the Gulbenkian Foundation
under its Director, the late Peter Brinson, to make the case for the arts. The Report
which resulted from their deliberations, published in 1982, provided a common
rallying ground for the arts in the increasingly difficult circumstances of the 1980s.
But, with its pragmatic, multi-functional approach to the role of the arts in education, in itself it already represented something of a drift away from the
all-encompassing, single-minded vision identified with Read.[11] The Schools

200

Curriculum Development Council's Arts in Schools Project, directed by Ken Robinson, which followed upon that Report, sought to strengthen the position of the arts by creating the first truly national professional network for *all* the arts in education. Schools, local education authorities and teachers of the arts interacted through local centres to promote the cause of the arts.[12] Although publications conceived as providing a theoretical under-pinning for the arts in education abounded at this time, the scope for the institution-based, empirical research typical of the 1970s had become distinctly restricted and the best policy was seen to be the promotion of a broad, practical programme stressing the links between the different arts whilst respecting their particular strengths and traditions – known in the business as 'good practice'. The formulations of the Assessment of Performance Unit[13] took a similar line, treating the 'aesthetic' as a single area of learning manifesting a common pedagogical structure but respecting subject differences – very much in line with the published thinking of Her Majesty's Inspectors at the time.[14]

However, once the principles of the new assessment-led National Curriculum had become clear, those responsible for the Arts in Schools Project opted for accommodation rather than resistance, arguing that the establishing of Attainment Targets and Levels of Performance would present no insuperable problem for arts teachers. In decreeing a subject-based curriculum for the arts, naming only Art and Music as Foundation Subjects and placing Drama and Dance under the auspices of English and Physical Education respectively, the Government dismantled the basic tenet of the Gulbenkian initiative. From then on it was up to the individual arts subjects to fight their own corners as best they could.

Predictably the longer-established subjects managed the crisis better than the more recent arrivals. Visual Art probably had the easiest run-in, with the National Society for Education in Art and Design providing a strong and effective lead to the Working Party. The musicians has more of a struggle due principally to their determination to hold on to the recent changes made to conventional teaching methods, changes the Government at first found difficult to accept. But some strenuous lobbying by prominent professional musicians won the day and the principles of participation and composition were allowed through. For Drama and Dance, life was very much more difficult and both now appear to be in some danger of losing out as arts subjects in their own right. In so far as the notion of an arts collective was central to Read's philosophy it is difficult to see the National Curriculum as anything other than a direct negation of that principle. There is no encouragement given within the legislation to an integrated or collaborative arts curriculum in schools, and although the notion of the child as art maker is retained, the role of art in the development of personality through creative self-expression receives little more than token endorsement.[15]

Read's incursion into education had begun with a commission to create an exhibition of children's art in the early years of the Second World War. His longstanding association with the Modern movement in art well qualified him for such a task. From the beginning of the twentieth century, children's art had been the focus of attention for a number of influential artists. Not only children's art, of course, but the unsophisticated, 'natural' work of so-called primitive and unschooled artists (e.g., Henri Rousseau), of cultures remote from the influence of Western society (Gauguin), and of madmen, criminals and other 'outsiders'. Klee, Kandinsky, Marc, the Dadaists, all explored the naïve power of children's art, brought to public attention through the work, for example, of Franz Cizek (1865–1960), who founded a Jugend-Kunstschule in Vienna in 1897, and of Corrado Ricci in his book *L'Arte dei bambini* (Genoa, 1887). The first exhibition in New York of children's art took place in 1912.

Read's extension of such professional interest in naïve manifestations of artistic expression and creativity to art education, for all the support it received at the level of principle among perhaps two generations of teachers, has always been open to attack from particular factions within the arts. There are, for example, those who argue that, since creativity cannot be taught, a practical pedagogy could not be raised to support it.[16] Read offered nothing practical himself, always insisting that this was beyond his scope since he was not a teacher. His emphasis upon psychology and the allusions to programmes of personality control left his thesis vulnerable to criticism both as indoctrination on the one hand and therapy on the other.

Then there are the criticisms deriving from those whom his contemporary, the English philosopher R. G. Collingwood (*The Principles of Art*, 1938), described as the 'pseudo-arts' people: those whose account of arts in society derives from an instrumentalist philosophy, committed to what he, Collingwood, called the 'craft' theory of art. This opposition comes in various forms. Academics argue for the formal teaching of traditional modes and practices and the authority of the canon; technical-rationalists favour the master-apprentice model of learning in the arts – with expression and creativity reserved for the singularly talented. There is also the art-as-moral-regeneration interest that condemns the romanticism and hedonism of the progressives and wishes to see the arts recover their former role as repositories of ultimate cultural and moral values. Read actually said he preferred the notion of 'morale' to that of morality in connection with the 'spiritual' orientation of the arts.[17]

It was perhaps especially unfortunate that Read's anarchist agenda translated into a pedagogic practice which seemed to advocate total non-intervention on the part of the teacher. Since creativity could not be taught and expression, was by definition, a private, not to say mysterious business, what was there for responsible teachers to do but to avoid corrupting the child's spontaneity and integrity by confining themselves to acting as a 'learning resource'?

It was to counter the damage to arts education being done by the 'hands-off' principle that my colleague Robert Witkin and I worked out a pedagogy of teacher intervention as a consequence of the research we undertook for the Schools Council in the early 1970s.[18] That research was itself the direct outcome of an earlier study[19] which showed the arts subjects in secondary schools failing to achieve what was widely held to be their full educational potential. This sense of the 'potential' of the arts in a general education certainly owed much to the influence of Read, together with the (by now widely appreciated) work of such radical arts educators as Franz Cizek, H. Caldwell Cook, Croce, Dalcroze, Susan Isaacs, Margaret Macmillan, Maria Montessori, Marion Richardson, Rudolf Steiner, R. R. Tomlinson, Wilhelm Viola. It was an article of faith with all these people that the arts were for every child, neither simply for the gifted, nor, to turn the matter about-face, for those who could do little or nothing else. This arts-for-all principle has to be understood as running directly counter to traditional secondary school practice. In Art to some degree, and in Music more particularly, the notion had always been that practical making as distinct from appreciation (i.e., looking at pictures and listening to music) was reserved for those with obvious vocational or academic potential in the subject, the exception being the programmes of instruction in basic drawing techniques which were seen to be necessary to training in a wide range of modern occupations. Such technical instruction in both Art and Music was in the hands of 'master craftsmen' in both subjects, and this was the tradition on to which, somewhat uneasily, the new philosophy was to be grafted. When Drama burst upon the educational scene in the 1940s and 1950s there was no such traditional baggage to be dealt with, and Drama instantly became the 'participatory' art par excellence – a designation it has never surrendered and for which most Drama teachers still struggle despite the new, unfavourable circumstances in which they find themselves.

Read's influence was very clear to Witkin and myself as we worked through the research data collected from teachers and pupils in the early 1970s. Top of the expressed priorities of the arts teachers we worked with, and locked into the consciousness of the pupils (the project explored the full range of the expressive arts taught in secondary schools at the time) were the notions of the pupil's personal development and self-expression. The more purely technical and academic matters were seen as subsidiary to these two fundamental organizing principles. Furthermore, the notion that such a participatory education through art was the natural right of every child was simply too obvious to need mentioning. In assessing the problems teachers seemed to be having in realizing the full educational poten- tial of the arts we focused upon the concept of expression itself and attempted, on one hand to clarify it and to relate it to the (at the time) dominant Piagetian theory of cognitive development, and on the other hand to propose an interventive prac- tice through which the teachers might become participants in the pupil's creative project rather than mere material providers and judges-in-waiting. We also raised questions about the criteria of assessment used by teachers in judging children's creative work – an issue explored in subsequent research.[20] Our approach was to respect what arts teachers were telling us about their work – and what they told us was that they were wedded to a philosophy they identified with Herbert Read – and to try to help them become more effective in delivering the outcomes they sought.

I believe we failed to make any significant impact upon pedagogical practices that polarized art teaching on the one hand as craft instruction and on the other as moral support. The reasons are probably many and various, and this is not the place for a searching analysis. The published outcomes of the research did not make easy reading and the research sponsors at the time had provided neither for a programme of dissemination nor for a strategy of development. We were left simply to cast our bread upon the waters. The project's proposal for teacher participation was itself only sketched in principle and, though rooted in a certain understanding of what artists actually do when they make art, it was subject to no programme either of experimentation or evaluation. Attempts to implement the proposals were patchy and uncoordinated and generally languished as new pressures and perceived remedies began to bear upon teachers. For many years the work was highly regarded but it nonetheless remained largely ineffectual. Where it was misunderstood it proved abortive; where it was understood it was found too threatening to established interests. Eventually criticism emerged consonant with the change in climate to which I have already referred.[21]

The priorities of the different arts subjects became more particularized and, with this progressive differentiation around subject-specific objectives, such broad-based notions as personal development and self-expression increasingly lost currency. (I am presently carrying out research which aims to discover how far this process has progressed.[22]) The Visual Arts, through NSEAD, are now largely restored to the tradition identified with the old Society of Art Masters. Music has placed most of its curriculum eggs in the 'composition' basket in its determination to enhance its profile as a creative subject and thereby, perhaps, its poor standing with students. Whether an appropriate pedagogy has been forthcoming remains an unanswered question – I personally doubt that it has. Drama has become the most written about of all the arts and has been the subject that has split into the greatest number of competing factions. Perhaps the outright winner at this time is the widely valued practice of using Drama as a medium of learning across the curriculum. Whilst this idea is to be found in Read it does not constitute his principal thesis – and seems at some distance from the practice of, for example, Caldwell Cook, from whose writing and teaching Read took so much of his inspiration. Dancers meanwhile tend to see their survival as depending almost entirely upon establishing curricular legitimacy – i.e., a distinctive pedagogical identity – in schools, one devoted to the celebration of specifically high-art, professional, dance values. In accounting for the failure of the 'expressive' project in arts education I would cite these developments within the individual arts subjects – developments identified in each case with the strongest faction actually at work within the particular discipline at the time of the educational 'reforms' of the late 1980s. Having said that, it would not be correct to suggest that schools on the whole have entirely rejected the principle of integrating the arts. My present research will show that the different arts can work productively together to fulfil the subject-based requirements of the National Curriculum. However, although such arrangements may be possible and do indeed exist and flourish, I doubt that they will become the norm in the foreseeable future.

Returning to Read and moving to a critical assessment of his principal writings on arts education, I shall begin by quoting from perhaps the most influential American writer on arts education in recent years, Elliot Eisner. In 1972 he wrote of *Education through Art* in the following terms:

> One cannot help being impressed with the range of scholarship that permeates Read's writing. He freely draws upon ancient humanistic resources as well as modern scientific research to support the ideas he advances. Yet from this wealth of material emerges an unclear eclecticism that leaves the reader in a persistent state of wonder regarding the meaning Read intends... Aside from the laudable goals Read embraces for education and the important position he assigns to art in achieving these goals, he offers little direction to those who would interpret children's drawing with the intention of facilitating the child's growth in this area of human activity. In short, Read's statements on art, children, and education are stimulating and scholarly but in their present form are outside the realm of empirical validation.[23]

I have to say that I cannot quarrel with this assessment. Reading the book today, its faults are more glaring than its virtues – even when you are simply looking for clarity of argument, irrespective of any interest in 'empirical validation'. Eisner went on to lead American art education towards what became known as the 'discipline-based' (i.e., subject-centred) curriculum, which is not a million miles from that which now prevails over here. And as for Read's statements on art, children and education, what Eisner described as 'their present form' was never to be either revised or further elaborated – only retitled and reissued – a publishing strategy which seemed to have had an irresistible attraction for him.

By way of substantiating my own criticism, I want to look briefly at the way Read uses and wishes us to understand the word 'art' in the context of education, and then to try to put together what might count as the essence of his conception of an 'education through art', for exactly what he means, as Eisner has pointed out, is neither clear nor – I believe – consistent. There is a sense in which the more you read the less you know. If we turn first to some of the early writing, for example his *The Meaning of Art* published in 1931, we find a clear and balanced exposition. He begins by insisting that, although his focus – for the purpose of the book – would be principally upon the visual and the plastic arts, he should be taken as speaking for the arts in general. This is also the position he adopts with the later *Education through Art*. The primary condition of art in general, he says, is that it should give pleasure. Music, he says, most perfectly corresponds with this criterion as only the musician is absolutely free to concentrate on this concern of the artist to create 'pleasing forms'. This propensity to take pleasure in certain formal patterns or arrangements in perception Read designates 'the sense of beauty'. These aspects of art Read ascribes to the domain of the aesthetic. He concedes however that art and the aesthetic are not interchangeable terms since art also embraces a further consideration: the notion of 'expression'. For Read, expression seems initially to mean the communication of a pre-existing emotion or feeling. Having defined expression in this way he characteristically finds fault with the word 'expression' itself, indicating that, in adopting the word, he feels he might not have expressed precisely what he meant. He pursues the matter however, and struggles to give 'expression' a more formative, a more creative, connotation. Artists create through expressive acts which are themselves informed by feeling rather than intellect. Read says that artists work intuitively.

> Form, though it can be analysed into intellectual terms like measure, balance, rhythm and harmony, is really intuitive in origin; it is not in the actual practice of artists an intellectual product. It is rather emotion directed and defined, and when we describe art as 'the will to form' we are not imagining an exclusively intellectual activity, but rather an exclusively instinctive one.[24]

Life is nothing like so simple nor straightforward for the reader of the opening pages of *Education through Art*. The basic elements of this earlier definition of art are still there but they are now forced to bear the yoke of a new agenda: an anarchist equation of art with education. Read aims to demonstrate the truth of his claim that the purpose of the new education should be 'the creation of artists'.[25] He begins by presenting a thoroughly confusing schema for differentiating the particular arts within the general description of 'forms of expression'.[26] The term 'design' must be understood according to Read to subsume visual and plastic expression and is to be thought of as 'corresponding' to sensation; music and dance become an education in eurhythmics and 'correspond' to intuition; poetry and drama are forms of verbal expression, 'corresponding' to feeling; what he calls constructive education is also a form of 'expression' much as music and poetry are, and 'corresponds' with thought. One thinks of Collingwood's clarity in his account, for example, of feelings as 'sensation carrying an emotional charge'[27] with absolute relief after being put through Read's theoretical convolutions. Perhaps someone will tell me why Read makes no mention of Collingwood at all. Despite his promise that all will become clear in the discussion to follow, Read seems bent on dragging his reader ever deeper into a maze of theoretical typologies and positivistic schema.

He proceeds to demonstrate how he intends to read art for education and education for art. Art 'is present in everything we make to please the senses'.[28] What pleases the senses? The answer is 'good form' – something done as well as possible, for example, a body kept 'in good trim'. Our model for 'good form'? Why nature itself – the world of nature which everywhere exhibits the principle of good form where that means flourishing as nature intended.[29] The Platonic notion of the moral ideal lying behind or beneath reality underwrites this theory of the aesthetic as the pursuit of perfection. Read points out that the creative quest for good form is not confined to the traditional practices of the artist but informs the work equally of the creative scientist, mathematician and engineer. At this point the approach he has opted for ceases to work as an account of the role of art in education and becomes a way of broadening the concept of art to cover every aspect of learning as the terms 'aesthetic' and 'art' are more or less elided. The pursuit of the beautiful, the pursuit of the 'artist' in the soul of every worker, the intuition of the good that inspires our feelings for and corresponds with the principle of order inhering in nature, these impulses, along with the archetypal imagery which expresses them, are common to us all, Read argues: they cross cultural boundaries and are known equally in developed as in undeveloped communities. Here are the grounds then for establishing a universal and at the same time a moral education through art: i.e., education as the pursuit of good form. This, on my reading, is the gist of Read's case as expressed in *Education through Art*.

Read's idea of art, in order to become the unifying principle in a reformed system of education, has been trimmed radically and now means the concern for good form and commitment to the aesthetic-ethical equation. Every school subject shares with art the pleasure of making things, informed by the pursuit of excellence. Education through art is to be an ethical, a moral programme, and, as such an education for peace. That is what arts education is about: that should be the common ground upon which all teachers of all subjects should meet and begin the process of refashioning the personalities of children.[30] Read's formulation has this supreme overarching goal in mind: the need to change the world through a radical revision of traditional education upon anarchistic principles.

Here is his vision of the 'integrated' secondary school curriculum, spelt out in organizational terms:

> Let us for the moment envisage the actual organisation of a secondary school based on our integral pattern. Under the headmaster there would be four senior masters, or masters of method, in charge of the four main activities – drama, design, music, craft. Under these four masters of method would be a number of assistant-masters, for whom the old-fashioned name of preceptor might be revived, for their function would be to take their place at the head of a class or group of pupils, and initiate them into particular aspects of the group activities. Under the master of design would come a preceptor of drawing; under the craft master, preceptors in mathematics and science; under the music master, preceptors in eurhythmics and dancing; and under the master of drama, preceptors in history, literature and elocution.[31]

Expression, as against the cultivating of a feeling for good form, does make something of a comeback, but never recovers its original force in his earlier writing as the
symbolic projection and refinement of feeling. Two things follow from this: the
distinctiveness of art is sacrificed to a general moralizing aesthetic; the notion of
artistic imagination being affective rather than rational loses focus, as does the project
for a working theory of expression as language – despite the attention lavished in
sections of the book upon psychological research into imagery. Read seems ready to
diminish any claim to the uniqueness of the arts within the curriculum still further
when he declares art to be a universal teaching method, a medium – as we have seen
above – through which all subjects might be taught. We are now adrift from any
theoretical account of the 'proper' function of art as expressive language (I have
Collingwood's *The Principles of Art*, chapter 12, in mind here). Read's own intuitive
artistic understandings would appear to have been sacrificed in this ambitious project
to his political obsession. What is galling is to find Read tracing the absolute essentials of art as an education in feeling, rather than of the emotions, in the section
entitled 'The Purpose of Expression', and then not making this central to an account
of education through art. There is no redress when, towards the end of the book,
he aligns the feeling for form with the acquisition of moral insight – preferring, as
he says, his notion of a moral education through art to 'those systems of religious
instruction which nowadays... make such an insistent clamour for re-establish-
ment'.[32] Eventually one simply becomes exhausted trying to keep up with him.

Read insists upon the connection between 'good form' as aesthetic judgement
and as moral achievement. This is the principal burden of chapter 8 of *Education
through Art*, but is perhaps nowhere more emphatically made than in the closing paragraph of 'The Moral Significance of Aesthetic Education' (see *Education for Peace* and
The Redemption of the Robot). First of all he concedes that for his equation to work, he
'is willing to admit that art... must itself be modified'.[33] An apparently trifling
consideration. There follows an explanation:

> It is too often a wayward, partial, even perverse expression of universal harmony.
> It is too often but an expression of personal phantasies, of egoistic and aggressive
> impulses. It is prostituted to purposes which destroy the aesthetic nature. Our
> whole conception of art will have to be enlarged and purified.[34]

Art may well be said to *invite* a moral response, but this is not to claim that the one
induces the other.

I have earlier drawn attention to Read's prescription for washing out children's
brains with art: I sense in the above prescription for the 'purification' of art an equally
obnoxious aspiration. Read's enforced coupling of art with virtue through an education for peace, laudable though the ends might be, suggests the cost in terms of means
might be prohibitive. I sense Read's whole grandiose plan beginning to break open
at this point – a point where it seems to reveal an alarmingly totalitarian cast of mind.

A kinder interpretation would attribute the flaws in Read's proposals to what Eisner referred to as his 'unclear eclecticism'. For his part, as we shall see, Read preferred to speak of 'mental ecstasy'.

> The perfection of art must arise from its practice – from the discipline of tools and materials, of form and function. For that reason we must give priority in our education to all forms of aesthetic activity, for in the course of making beautiful things, there will take place a crystallisation of the emotions into patterns which are moulds of virtue. Such patterns are in effect social patterns, the patterns assumed by human relationships, and their harmony is part of the universal harmony, made manifest in life no less than in art.[35]

Education through Art is a pot-pourri of theoretical speculations and propaganda, a bewildering muddle of pseudo-science, sympathetic magic and mystical transcendentalism which fails both as a rationale for teaching the arts and as a prescription for bringing in the millennium. Buber is stalled beside Skinner; Köhler with Eysenck. And yet, at the time, the challenge of the vision somehow transcended the confusion of the vehicle. I believe, and am glad, that it does so still:

> Every man is a special kind of artist, and in his originating activity, his play or work (and in a natural society, we have held, there should be no distinction between the psychology of work and of play), he is doing more than express himself: he is manifesting the form which our common life should take, in its unfolding.[36]

I have suggested that Read's initial success was due in large measure to his being in tune with the spirit of the times. In particular, despite the complaints made against *Education through Art* in the paragraphs above, he proved to be a powerful advocate for the intuitive experiments of a number of practitioners in the field of arts education at a time when the need for radical changes in education as a whole claimed widespread support. He was not alone of course in this endeavour.[37] Although his anarchistic intentions were peculiar to him, he must share the credit for reform with others who were practising teachers. The changes where arts education was concerned were to be informed by the spirit of modernism, of which, of course, Read was already a leading authority and promoter. Having Herbert Read preaching a new arts education was to have a most potent ally at that time. With the benefit of hindsight we might want to say that Read's thesis, based upon his readings of a group of psychologist mentors, laid rather too much emphasis upon the make-up of the child and too little upon the making of art. In this regard we should remind ourselves perhaps of Collingwood's enigmatic dictum: 'The arts are about making things, but not material things'.[38] In following arts teachers wedded to Read's philosophy Witkin and I perhaps made the same error of emphasis – despite our attempt to redress the balance through our proposed pedagogy of 'subject-reflexive action'. In stressing the 'inner' experience of the child we insufficiently stressed the full import of the dialogue with the medium and, in particular, the importance for that dialogue of understanding the tradition which nurtures it. Here, as I have come to understand more recently, we would have been wiser to have attended – had we been able to do so at the time – to the writings in cultural hermeneutics and phenomenology by such as H-G. Gadamer[39] and M. Merleau-Ponty.[40] Thereby we might have avoided being pigeon-holed as therapists manqués. The creative-expressivist cause became unnecessarily and unhelpfully entangled in a political struggle between the integrators and the subject-separatists in arts education. Read, as we have seen, customarily used the collective noun. Whether the arts would have fared any better in the curriculum struggle by making common cause is a political judgement: only time will tell.

Had we – and by now I am including, I hope not unreasonably, the stories of all of us concerned for a creative and expressive reading of arts education – managed to provide a better-balanced rationale in making our case, then the writing itself might have been more accessible. I have claimed that Read's writing on the arts in education is far from felicitous – I have in mind not only his *Education through Art* but also *Education for Peace* and *The Redemption of the Robot*.[41] My students tell me that much of the writing on arts education with which they have to deal – including my own – suffers from the same failing. There have been exceptions – most notably perhaps the long-ago writings of Marion Richardson. This absence of the poetic spirit in the bulk of academic writing on arts education is paralleled by a failure to stress what Gadamer calls the 'festive' aspect of the arts in classroom and studio practice. We of the expressivist persuasion have perhaps been rather too preoccupied with understanding how feeling works 'on the inside' at the expense of understanding the social processes of the expression of feeling in rite and ritual. If Read's vision of what he called, in the passage quoted earlier from *Culture and Education in World Order*, 'moments of mutual understanding and love' were to be actually realized within the arts curriculum, we might indeed have an arts education to celebrate. I would argue that our arts lessons will never succeed in enlisting the full participation of students until we are prepared to give full play to the principle of festival in the life of the school. We should also of course pay proper attention to Gadamer's two other principles of the beautiful: play and symbol. I shall not elaborate upon them here. Together with the idea of festival they constitute the basis for a fully participatory experience of the arts for students in schools, with teachers actively and formatively involved at every step along the way. The only question then remaining would be the extent to which schooling as such – and schooling as currently understood – could accommodate such a radical proposal. Arts educators need to play fast and loose, whereas the current management insists upon slow and tight.

Had Read drawn more explicitly upon his own artist friends and acquaintances to formulate an account of artistic practice in schools, he might have been served

210

better than by the psychologists. There is a memorable passage in his *The Meaning of Art*, in which he describes with wonderful insight what is special in the way Henry Moore makes sculpture.

> If you are translating form in one material into form in another material, you must create that form from the inside outwards. Most sculpture – even, for example, ancient Egyptian sculpture – creates mass by a synthesis of two-dimensional aspects. We cannot see all round a cubic mass; the sculptor therefore tends to walk round his mass of stone and endeavours to make it satisfactory from every point of view. He can thus go a long way towards success, but he cannot be so successful as the sculptor whose act of creation is, as it were, a four-dimensional process growing out of a conception which inheres in the mass itself. Form is then an intuition of surface made by the sculptor imaginatively situated at the centre of gravity of the block before him. Under the guidance of this intuition, the stone is slowly educated from an arbitrary into an ideal state of existence. And that, after all, should be the primary aim of every artistic activity.[42]

I don't think there is a passage in *Education through Art* to touch this as an account of education *as* art. And we are light years away from the notion of education as moral conditioning. It is for such an account of art and of education that I want to remember Read – together with his advocacy of Buber; his endorsement of his friend Eric Gill's plea on behalf of 'the poetry of things'; his admiration of the work of Marion Richardson; his intuition concerning Suttie's sense of the expressive act as 'an overture demanding response from others'; his championing of the idea that every child is a special kind of artist. If you are prepared to be 'picky', Read still has a lot to offer. It is said that Socrates was a sculptor, and his dialogical relationship with his students comes closest to my sense of an artistic pedagogy, the final purpose of which has to be the revelation of the child – through art.

We shall subvert the language of 'performance indicators' and 'quality assurance' with poetry rather than rhetoric. So Heaney[43] these days rather than Read. The kind of writing Read himself most favoured – for example the earlier quotation from his American address – can still stir us, but we have learnt to be wary of such stirrings. We have only slowly acquired the vigilance beloved of Read's great contemporary, George Orwell. When Read was preaching his anarchist's gospel of world peace there was still scope for the Great Idea; now, I hope, we are less credulous, perhaps humbler too. Those Churchillian periods of Read's have all the troubling ambiguity of Charlie Chaplin's valedictory oration at the end of *The Great Dictator*. However, Herbert Read the poet – and it was as a poet, rather than as an art critic or educator, that the anarchist was finally knighted – would surely have understood, despite the temptation to exploit the opportunities for 'education' available to dictators everywhere, the dangers inherent in anyone's claiming a monopoly of the means of redemption. Nevertheless, we should probably do best to remember Read for what he himself called his 'zest'. Can arts education ever have had a more zestful, a more tenacious advocate, even if behind that advocacy lay concealed a suspect revolutionary agenda? These lines are from his poem, 'The Analysis of Love':[44]

> Nature has perpetual tears
> In drooping boughs
> And everywhere inanimate death
> Is immemorial.
>
> But I have naught that will express
> The grief I feel
> When men and moods combine to show
> The end of this –
>
> This mental ecstasy all spent
> In disuniting death;
> And the years that spread
> Oblivion on our zest.

The threat to an education through art in our own day is the National Curriculum. The robots *are* coming: a new breed of teachers programmed to deliver art as a business plan, to package culture as a commodity – in short, to consign the children's zest to oblivion. Were we able, at this eleventh hour, to reinvest in the essential elements of his vision – his instinct for play, for creativity, for ritual and romance in education and in art – Herbert Read's witness might yet prove redemptive.

Notes

1   *The Cult of Sincerity*, quoted in *Herbert Read: A One-Man Manifesto and Other Writings for Freedom Press*, ed. David Goodway (London: Freedom Press, 1994), p.90. I am grateful to David Goodway for bringing his collection of Read's writing for Freedom Press to my notice. I found his own Introduction especially helpful and instructive.
2   See David Thistlewood, 'Editorial: Education through Art', *Journal of Art and Design Education*, vol. 12, no. 2 (1993), p.134.
3   I am most grateful to David Thistlewood for helping me uncover this material. His detailed research into the formation of NSEAD is published as 'The Formation of NSEAD: A Dialectical Advance for British Art and Design Education', *Journal of Art and Design Education*, vol. 8, no. 2 (1989), pp. 135–36.
4   Herbert Read, *Education for Peace* (London: Routledge and Kegan Paul, 1950), p. vii.
5   Herbert Read, *The Redemption of the Robot: My Encounter with Education through Art* (New York: Trident Press, 1966).
6   Herbert Read, *Culture and Education in World Order* (New York: Museum of Modern Art, 1948), p. 7.
7   Ibid.
8   Ibid., p. 9.

9 Ibid., p. 15.

10 See Donald A. Schon, *The Reflective Practitioner: How Professionals Think in Action* (London: Maurice Temple Smith Ltd, 1983).

11 Ken Robinson (ed.) *The Arts in Schools: Principles, Practice and Provision*, (London: Calouste Gulbenkian Foundation, 1982).

12 *The Arts 5–16: A Curriculum Framework* was published by the National Curriculum Council in 1990.

13 The Assessment of Performance Unit published its paper *Aesthetic Development* in 1983 (London: HMSO).

14 Department of Education and Science, *A View of the Curriculum* (London: HMSO, 1980). The authors argued that the school curriculum be ordered not subject by subject but in terms of 'areas of experience'. One of the areas was the 'aesthetic', understood as including all the arts subjects.

15 I have criticized the 'logic' of the 1995 revisions by Sir Ron Dearing to the original curriculum orders for Art and Music in a paper published recently: Malcolm Ross, 'National Curriculum Art and Music', *Journal of Art and Design Education*, vol. 14, no. 3 (October 1995), pp. 271–76.

16 For example, Andrew Brighton writing in *Aspects*, vol. 18, Spring 1982.

17 Read, *Culture and Education in World Order*, p. 6.

18 Arts and the Adolescent (1968–1972) was a research project based at the University of Exeter and funded by the Schools Council. Its principal publications were Robert W. Witkin, *The Intelligence of Feeling* (London: Heinemann Educational Books, 1974), and Malcolm Ross, *The Creative Arts* (London: Heinemann Educational Books, 1978).

19 Schools Council Enquiry One, *The Young School Leaver* (London: HMSO, 1968).

20 Malcolm Ross, Hilary Radnor, Sally Mitchell and Cathy Bierton, *Assessing Achievement in the Arts* (Buckingham: The Open University Press, 1993).

21 David Best, *Feeling and Reason in the Arts* (London: George Allen and Unwin, 1985).

22 State of the Arts in Schools (1996–97), a research project based at the University of Exeter, sponsored jointly by the Calouste Gulbenkian and Paul Hamlyn Foundations.

23 Elliot Eisner, *Educating Artistic Vision* (New York: Macmillan Publishing Co. Inc., 1972), pp. 92–93.

24 Herbert Read, *The Meaning of Art* (London: Faber and Faber, 1931), p. 25.

25 Herbert Read, *Education through Art* (London: Faber and Faber, 1943), p. 11.

26 Ibid., pp. 8–9.

27 R. G. Collingwood, *The Principles of Art* (London: Oxford University Press, 1938), p. 162.

28 Read, *Education through Art*, p. 15.

29 Ibid., p. 31.

30 Ibid., p. 212.

31 Ibid., pp.241–42.

32 Ibid., pp. 163–66 and 298.

33 Read, *Education for Peace*, p. 71.

34 Ibid.

35 Ibid., p. 72.

36 Read, *Education through Art*, p. 302.

37 Natalie Cole, *Art in the Classroom* (1940); Victor D'Amico, *Creative Teaching in Art* (1942); Victor Lowenfeld, *Creative and Mental Growth* (1947); Marion Richardson, *Art and the Child* (1948); Marjourie Hourd, *The Education of the Poetic Spirit* (1949).

38 Collingwood, *The Principles of Art*, p. 108.

39 H-G. Gadamer, *Truth and Method* (London: Sheed and Ward, 1975).

40 Maurice Merleau-Ponty, *The Prose of the World* (Evanston: Northwestern University Press, 1973).

41 Read's comments on the children's artwork contained in *Education through Art* are often merely

clinical:

> These two drawings illustrate, at infant and adolescent stages, a type of unreflective and naïve expression which is characteristic of many children, and which persists into adult life. It is essentially the mode of expression of the extroverted feeling type, a superficial decorative style, which can develop into a talent for pretty embroidery, etc., but is not capable of the qualities necessary for art of any deeper significance. (p.178).

42 Read, *The Meaning of Art*, p. 217.
43 Seamus Heaney, *The Redress of Poetry* (London: Oxford University Press, 1995).
44 'The Analysis of Love', in Michael Roberts (ed.), *The Faber Book of Modern Verse* (London: Faber and Faber, 1936), p. 183.

Herbert Read's Organic Aesthetic: [I] 1918–1950

DAVID THISTLEWOOD

THERE is a corpus of twentieth-century art scholarship – distinct yet not easily defined – which may be termed a 'Readian aesthetic'. It is a great deal easier to summarize what it is *not* than to summarize what it is, and this is partly due to its complexity and its eclecticism. It is not an aesthetic of style – for example, as compared to the standard interpretation of early modernism published by Alfred Barr at the Museum of Modern Art, New York, in 1936.[1] Neither is it an updated conventional aesthetic like that of another of Read's eminent contemporaries, Kenneth Clark at the National Gallery, London.[2] In order to appreciate Read's theorizing about the contemporary art of his direct experience we must observe it over its fifty-year unfolding. The way in which it developed by distinct stages, with periodic consolidation, revision and change and no obviously predetermined goal, provides one reason for describing Read's aesthetic as 'organic'. This chapter is an attempt to chart such evolution while also noting other ways in which the term 'organic' is appropriate to his work: his identification – in the creativity of contemporary artists – of a type of plastic development equivalent to his own theoretical development; his corresponding respect for other theories of organicism that would inform his own; and his recognition of a specifically English, avant-garde creativity emanating from the 'soil' of its native culture.

Read's north European – or more properly his English – perspective provides a convenient point of entry into this manifold subject. His criticism throughout his working life, from his first publications during the First World War until his death in 1968, today offers insights into how the achievements of European (later, American) avant-gardes were perceived and appreciated contemporaneously from an English standpoint. For Read this perspective was cultural rather than racial, reflecting traditions of accommodating French, Saxon and Nordic influences, and of uniquely synthesizing these in aesthetic values rooted in the *genii loci* of their adoptive home. Read's 'home', and the spiritual location of his aesthetic, was northern England, a territory bearing evidence, in its field patterns, routeways and buildings, of Roman occupation, Nordic and Germanic settlement, medieval Christianity, and resistance to Norman incursion. The 'mental map' of Read's critical theory is constituted of analogous features – respect for classical idealism, especially as present in German scholarship; acceptance of romantic adaptations; receptivity towards a northern European expressionism; religiosity of purpose; a qualified and highly suspicious appreciation of the School of Paris. Read's work was a constant filtering of received concepts through such predispositions: he 'lived' in a rural northern mental inscape, more vivid for his being condemned to live and work in the south. Well before he was thirty it must have been apparent to him that his hopes of returning to North Yorkshire would be fulfilled only in retirement. Thus he possessed a conception of rural life, rooted in infant memories and nurtured by distant intention, which was highly idealized. Idealized, it was aestheticized and adapted to socio-cultural constructs.

He was an early devotee of Ruskin and Morris, graduating quickly to philosophical anarchism as typified in the writings of Kropotkin. As early as 1912 he began to read the *New Age*, among the leading journals of socialist politics and aesthetics of its day, becoming a regular contributor to this paper throughout a period in which it was a vehicle for promoting socialist alternatives to Fabianism – Read's ruralist instincts naturally opposing Fabian materialism. The *New Age* offered a continuum of modern art and politics, and Read's devotion to the paper coincided with his membership of the Leeds Arts Club, a forum for an exactly similar philosophical interrelationship.

His initial interest in the *New Age* was in its libertarian socialist politics, to which a *plastic* aesthetic was initially peripheral. But in this periodical Read found Thomas Ernest Hulme's defence of abstraction in contemporary British art[3] sustained by theories of 'empathetic identification' Hulme had adapted from the German philosophers Riegl and Worringer. Empathetic identification with fugitive values was here presented as a characteristic of the north – the perceptual residue of generations of coping with climatic instability – in contradistinction to a 'rational identification with the concrete' associated with the more stable climates of southern Europe. There was evidence of this theory beyond Hulme's articles. Michael Sadler, patron of the Arts Club and an enthusiastic collector of modern paintings, provided access to works by Paul Klee and, especially, Wassily Kandinsky which manifested varying degrees of fugacity.

The Arts Club addressed the *problematic* basis of such imagery, for example in practical experiments correlating a fugitive symbolism and the characteristic sounds and structures of contemporary music. The prime objective of a Hulmean scheme was to win concrete symbolism that would be hard, smart and durable from the welter of transient percepts originating in everyday experience. Hence vorticism was welcomed in Leeds debates. Wyndham Lewis addressed the membership in person, Filippo Marinetti in spirit. By 1914 Read was himself practising an art of pure abstraction that he called 'futurist'. This was his grounding in aesthetics, and unless this is appreciated it is easy to regard him as a museologist whose gifts for interpreting 'difficult' modern philosophy swept him into the realm of the avant-garde.

For his early reputation was founded on two things, the first of which was his having sacrificed a fast-track career at the Treasury in order to transfer within the

Civil Service to the Department of Ceramics at the Victoria and Albert Museum. Here he rapidly became an expert in German historical manuscripts, publishing important studies that enabled a proper evaluation of English adaptations of German processes of manufacture. The second plank of his early reputation followed his editing the literary remains of T. E. Hulme, killed in action in the Great War.[4] Hulme had been an erratic theorist, and Read genuinely added value to his work by reductive selection. The result was an unprecedented (in English) explanation of creative origination, which may be drastically summarized as follows. The artist delves into the unconscious stream of experience and 'surfaces' having grasped some vague notion of significant form. The essential irregularity of this form is gradually polished away, resulting in an abstract percept that symbolizes both its *origins* in irrationality and its *destination* in rational contemplation. It is thus both timeless and of immediate signification, offering analogous relationship with religiosity. Modern abstraction is thus the highest order within a system of human constructs (aesthetics) that is akin to morality.

Read published a faithful representation of Hulme's theory, and persuaded himself, throughout the 1920s, to believe in its exclusive validity. It was presentable as a modernist derivative of accepted scholarship. The art of the south is classical, refined, conventional; that of the north is romantic, spontaneous, original. Normal scholarly practice assimilates the 'original' to the 'conventional'. Each is indispensable: the north originates; the south consolidates the primary culture. Read's ability to present the otherwise chaotic body of Hulme's writings in a sequence that made sense to an informed readership gained him an immediate reputation as an analytical thinker. This interfused with his self-perception as an individual torn from a rightful future as a productive member of the agricultural community. His position was summarized in his critical appreciation of Julien Benda's book *La Trahison des clercs*[5] in which a series of propositions were found to be so strikingly familiar that they came as self-revelations.

All real human existence is the existence of an individual or of a group unified by common interest, and is competitive and necessarily aggressive. The '*clerc*' or disinterested person of learning is one who protests against a morality of aggression by proclaiming ideal values revealed in contemplation of matters abstract, universal and infinite. Civilized humanity is made possible by the coexistence and synthesis of aggressive expediency and disinterested philosophy. A world observing only a code of practical necessity would be barbarous: one which practised only a code of ideals would cease to exist. Civilized existence *mediates* between immediacy and idealism.

Read naturally identified with the dislocated individual who, while leading an ostensibly unproductive life, had the special purpose of divining abstract principles for the benefit of the wider community in an age of idealism following and counteracting a period of great international aggression. At this time in his life, like his friend T. S. Eliot, he considered the goals of aesthetic contemplation to be formal

217

precision, harmony and elegant proportion – principles which, he firmly believed, when evident in literature, art and conduct, offered the world the prospect of an international medium of understanding.

In the 1920s Read's growing reputation as a museologist with an unusual background (war hero; contributor to modern literary criticism; frequent traveller to Germany) made him interesting to the fledgling BBC. He became the Corporation's regular art correspondent to *The Listener* and thus a 'media personality'. His first major book on art, the synoptic *The Meaning of Art* (1931),[6] was an anthology of his weekly *Listener* writings. It was substantially a conventional history, but it also confirmed Read's determination to be taken seriously as a critic of the avant-garde by culminating in appreciations of Paul Klee and Henry Moore. In this regard it was a threshold event for Read; in its final passages he switched from summarizing accepted scholarship to interpreting an emergent creativity, offering a first indication of what would become his major preoccupation. The Hulmean distinction between conventional and original creativity now served to distinguish between two forms of *critical* activity, convincing Read that in his desire to recognize significant enterprise in the work of contemporary artists he should be alive to matters *resistant* to conventionalization (thus turning the role of historian–critic into something much more demanding and productive than mere descriptive reportage).

Klee's work, for example, could be assimilated to established art history only with great difficulty. To Read he seemed to be evoking an 'alternative' *nature*, a world of imagery materializing from the shallow unconscious, an emergent formlessness given shape only in the moment when 'the pencil moves and the line dreams'.[7] Moore, on the other hand, appeared motivated by intimate understanding of his *natural materials* – stone, wood, clay – and the forms they *inevitably* had to assume in order to accommodate interpretations of the artist's subject matter. Rather than depicting them, he would *translate* his reclining figures into a language of stone. This necessitated an act of manifold empathy which, once recognized in the work of Moore, remained central to Read's critique for the rest of his life. In order to be a *paragon* modernist the artist had to empathize with subject-matter (whether phenomenal or noumenal), with the nature of materials (respecting their legitimate form), and with organic nature (permitting creative concepts to evolve naturally rather than constraining them with a false aesthetic). Moore's creativity was thus perceived as

> a four-dimensional process growing out of a conception which inheres in the mass itself. Form is then an intuition of surface made by the sculptor imaginatively situated at the centre of gravity of the block before him. Under the guidance of this intuition, the stone is slowly educated from an arbitrary into an ideal state of existence... the primary aim of every artistic activity.[8]

This highly speculative discourse on modernism in *The Meaning of Art* was in effect a postscript. Over the next two years – while he was Professor of Fine Art at Edinburgh University – Read widened the scope of his modernist critique substantially beyond his initial constituencies of interest, certain of the Bauhaus artists[9] and the Yorkshire exile Moore. The result was the tangibly didactic *Art Now*,[10] intended not merely to map modernism but to reveal avant-garde aesthetic 'intentions' in all their plurality. As an academic with research commitment to contemporary art (which did not endear him to his university colleagues) he saw it as his responsibility to model *intentionality* in whatever form it became apparent, which at this time meant attending equally to constructivism and surrealism. He therefore celebrated formal precision, harmony and elegant proportion, and he also provided a defence of the irrational and the imprecise. At a time when modernism was split along such ideological lines this gave rise to accusations that he was hedging his bets.[11]

But he made this into a dialectic virtue, seeking opposing tendencies – within the community of artists and within individual creativity alike – that could be counterposed in explanation. Thus in *Art Now* two tendencies (symbolism and expressionism) were explored in detail but set aside as not specifically modernist, while two more (abstract formalism and subjective idealism) were proposed as belonging uniquely to the avant-garde. There was an attempt to demonstrate their interrelatedness but this led to the rather lame identification of a 'common element' residing in the artists' skill, in each tendency, of transposing 'mental images into linear signs' – their abilities to express personality.[12]

It is clear that here in his early critiques of modernism Read employed a distinct methodology: he would identify intentionality and fractionalize it in order to appreciate its fullest extent. Klee's painting could be fractionalized into constructive and organic strategies. So too could Moore's sculpture: in Read's first dedicated critique of Moore he identified a comparable, though unequal, divergence:

> In one direction the artist tends to create a work whose whole aesthetic significance resides in formal relations and in qualities of texture; in the other direction the artist combines these relations and qualities with a reflection or representation of qualities typical of living things or, at least, qualities due to natural processes. The first type of artist is a purist, and makes no kind of compromise with any world outside the ideal world of subjective creation; he merely gives outer and solid form to conceptions that are as abstract as any conceived by the mathematician... The second kind of artist does not wish to limit his function in this way. He feels that if he can link his formal conceptions with the vital rhythms everywhere present in natural forms, that then he will give them a force altogether more dynamic than the force of abstract conceptions. Henry Moore, though he does not exclude exercises in the abstract mode, and, indeed, finds such exercises a considerable aid to his development, belongs essentially to this second type.[13]

Read's conception of what a modern artist *did* was substantially shaped by this frac-tionalization of Moore's creativity. Read's prototype paradigm featured precisely this periodic alternation: outwardly addressing nature (creating natural equivalents); inwardly addressing self-ordered preferences (exploring abstract relationships in a spirit of play or nervous replenishment). This model had applications beyond the individual artist: it explained the modernist *project*. All contributors to modernism were negotiating this axis, and their individual differences were explicable in terms of that part of the route they travelled most often.

It was in exactly these terms that Read announced the existence of an English modernism in 1934 on behalf of the group of artists and architects named Unit One.[14] Their divergences confirmed his 'shuttle' explanation, and also required its exten-sion to incorporate a more complete introspection as a result of Ben Nicholson's revelation of an almost exclusively metaphysical creativity accommodating a minimum of reference to nature.[15] While typifying the Hulmean principle of the destination of the creative impulse in a form sustaining rational contemplation, Nicholson's work invited speculation as to its *origins* in irrationality. Read's appre-ciation of the geometric abstraction of a typical Nicholson white relief of the early 1930s as the ultimate result of a creative process originating in the fugitive did not in fact challenge the predominant western aesthetic tradition of assimilating 'origi-nality' to the 'refined'. However, his defence of Klee, Moore – and, only a short while later, surrealism – signalled genuinely revolutionary intent in the reversal of this academic principle. What now distinguished Read from other theorists of contemporary art was his interest in the originating principle underlying the formal purity of, for example, a Nicholson relief, rather than its form as *aesthetic*. As Read began to operate this critical principle, he came to suggest that irrational forms might have comparable validity to the refined as *outcomes* of creative activity. He called these alternatives to the refined 'organic', and he thus offered his detractors a first oppor-tunity to declare him an inconsistent theorist.

Within three years Unit One had ceased to operate as a cohort, having become vastly enlarged by the gravitation of European emigrant modernists. Within this greater community the parochial references to an organic creativity, and the mental map which served it, tended to be outshone by the heroic imported causes of constructivism and surrealism. They were evangelical and began to claim the loyalty of individuals,[16] each in fact attracting Read's support. As they were mutually antag-onistic, the sense of beneficial interaction between the different poles of creativity was in danger of being lost. Read was determined to preserve this principle while at the same time explaining to his constituency its sudden saturation with the European avant-garde. The shaping of a paradigmatic critique, which may be seen developing in his work throughout the 1930s, is therefore complicated with political contextu-alization.

He knew well the victimization of artists and intellectuals that was taking place in fascist Germany – a project of his to bring a truly representative exhibition of modern German art to London had been made impossible by much of its proposed content having been declared 'degenerate'.[17] In addition he was made aware, by Russian artists and designers now in London after having earlier sought refuge in Germany, that soviet communism had also stamped on the avant-garde. His conclusion was that contemporary art had to become active rather than contemplative, partisan rather than disinterested, and subliminal rather than super-evident. In other words, artists and theorists had to adopt a militancy of a sort that was at this time most apparent in the work of those irrationalists who had been loosely grouped within dada and surrealism. So while celebrating that Britain was a haven for both constructivism and surrealism, Read momentarily abandoned critical neutrality and called himself a surrealist.[18] It was in this climate, in 1936, that Read published his paradigm partly in order to defend his own position, and in his urgency he published it prematurely and incomplete.[19]

Superrealism   Realism   Abstraction

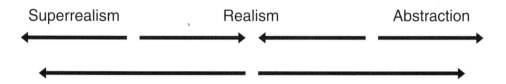

Herbert Read's Paradigm (first version). A characteristic of the English avant-garde is its tendency to range between superrealism and realism; realism and abstraction; and in certain cases superrealism and abstraction.

It was also slightly confusing in its unconventional terminology. In order to avoid giving prominence to *movements* Read emphasized *intentionality* to the extent of replacing 'constructivism' and 'surrealism' with 'abstraction' and 'superrealism' – terms signifying problematics rather than group interests. In 1936 he was confident to maintain the equal prominence of abstract and superrealist intentionality. The former was evident in the work of such painters as Mondrian, Hélion, Nicholson and Moholy-Nagy and sculptors including Brancusi, Gabo and Hepworth, and was essentially formalist. The latter was less essentially formalist and represented by such painters as Ernst, Dalí, Miró and Tanguy and a sculptor, Arp. 'The first tendency', Read had written a year earlier, 'is plastic, objective and ostensibly non-political. The second group is literary (even in paint), subjective and actively Communist'.[20] Consistent with his politicized critique, Read suggested that superrealism had an immediate, dynamic purpose in attacking and breaking down bourgeois values – it was the art of a transitional period. The revolutionary task of abstraction, however, was passive yet constructive: its role was to remain 'inviolate, until such time as

221

society will once more be ready to make use of them, the universal qualities of art – those elements which survive all changes and revolutions',[21] when it would be instrumental in building a new, classless society.

These brief quotations demonstrate Read's preoccupation with avant-garde creativity as an agent of beneficial change and as resistant to malignant socio-political forces. As his model gradually featured more centrally the work of the British avant-garde, it became heavily loaded with implications that the Cultural International had moved from Paris to London, requiring only the presence of Picasso, perhaps, for its completeness. The model contained abstraction (having largely undergone a process of revolution) and superrealism (now occupying a revolutionary phase). They were tending to diverge, but certain artists, responsible for the profoundest creative achievements, were holding the centre:

> Though at their extremes – a Mondrian against a Dalí – these two movements have nothing in common, yet the space between them is occupied by an unbroken series, in the middle of which we find artists like Picasso and Henry Moore whom we cannot assign confidently to either school. Significantly, these intermediate artists are among those most evidently in possession of a fertile and powerful genius...[22]

Read felt compelled to represent the extremes of his theory to opposing audiences. In the first of such efforts – a contribution to the *International Survey of Constructive Art* of 1937 in which he pressed the claims of superrealism – he suggested that abstraction and superrealism were different aspects of a single enterprise. This involved superimposing a model of the creative mentality on that of the broad front of plastic creativity. Just as superrealism could be said to engage a latent imagery *below* the level of the conscious mind, abstraction could be said to address imagery *beyond* the range of conscious attention.[23]

In an article in the *London Bulletin*, organ of the English Surrealist Group, Read elaborated the abstractionist position and in so doing revived his pre-paradigm pre-occupation with the organic. Abstraction took an interest in:

> certain proportions and rhythms which are inherent in the structure of the universe, and which govern growth, including the growth of the human body. Attuned to these rhythms and proportions, the abstract artist can create micro-cosms which reflect the macrocosm... [through] access to the archetypal forms which underlie all the casual variations presented by the natural world.[24]

Read made a further observation which was in effect a statement of philosophical intent:

> Just as surrealism makes use of, or rather proceeds on the assumption of, the knowledge embodied in psycho-analysis, so abstract art makes use of, or proceeds

on the basis of, the abstract concepts of physics and dynamics, geometry and mathematics.[25]

A *latent* revolutionary abstraction acknowledging the physical sciences; an *immediately* revolutionary superrealism informed by psychoanalysis; abstraction and superrealism themselves dialectically opposed: from the late 1930s onwards Read used these co-ordinates to defend the various types of intentionality of the avant-garde.

In the 1940s Read, convinced that the world of avant-garde practice was now centred on England, wrote a number of highly focused studies of Hampstead modernists, and in his efforts to locate precisely the intentionality of individual artists within his paradigm (first version) Read encountered a problem that at first worried him. He realized that Moore, Nicholson, Hepworth and Nash could not be positioned precisely within the broad creative front (as, for example, Mondrian and Dalí had been) for they all periodically tended to shift their ground. Nicholson seemed to combine the geometrical and (for want of a better word) the impressionistic; while Hepworth's work ranged from uncompromising abstraction to an intense and dramatic realism. In a letter to Read she had written: 'Working realistically replenishes one's *love* for life, humanity and the earth. Working abstractly seems to release one's personality and sharpen the perceptions…',[26] and Read had thus grasped the idea of a mutually-nourishing alternation. Hepworth drew Read an explanatory diagram[27] which profoundly informed his writings in the late 1940s (later anthologized in *The Philosophy of Modern Art* [1952]). It is an axial arrangement with at one side realism, symbols of the known, figures, hands, eyes, trees, and so forth, and at the other side abstraction, symbols of the unknown, including erotic, prenatal and primitive forms, dream images and childhood imagery. She said her point of address might be at either extremity, but that during the development of a work there might well be autonomous transition. An initially abstract process might materialize recognizable traces – eye-like hollows or similar presentative features – and drawing from observation might liberate formal ideas for abstract carving. Hepworth's account of such abstract working in which she felt 'in the grip of an emotion… pursuing the unknown form to hold it', together with her relational diagram of creative impulses, provided Read with evidence for linking abstraction and superrealism in productive relationship, and helped complete his great intellectual achievement of accommodating the diverse manifestations of the avant-gardes of his day within a unitary system of relationships.

Within this system Nicholson and Hepworth would now respect the outer world of perceptions, now engage the inner world of structured abstraction; and Paul Nash too, it became clear to Read, would cover this ground while also occasionally giving expression to the irrational or superreal.

In certain cases [Read wrote] it seems possible for an individual to alternate between the extremes represented by this polarity – to tend in one psychological phase towards an affirmation of the world which results in a naturalistic style, and in another psychological phase towards a rejection of that world, which results in an abstract style of art.[28]

And by an extension of this argument to accommodate Nash, Read indicated the possibility of encountering a periodic, complete traversion between the polarities abstraction and superrealism.

The work of Henry Moore also exhibited such complete traversion. In 1936 he

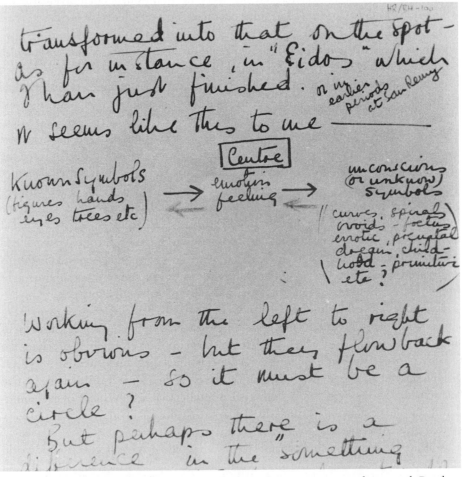

Barbara Hepworth, diagram of creative sensibility, 1947, in correspondence with Read (courtesy Read Archive, University of Victoria Library, British Columbia, Canada, © Alan Bowness, Hepworth Estate)

had exhibited with the surrealists and in 1937 he had featured prominently among the Circle group of constructivists; but his intentionality seemed to Read too complex to be characterized as that of a roving sensibility (as Nash's had been). Apart from his, usually brief, excursions to the extremities of the front, Moore had made objects which seemed to be admixtures or interpenetrations of the abstract and the superreal – that is, he seemed to occupy the centre. But in the 1940s Read's theoretical front now consisted of abstraction-*naturalism*-superrealism and this obviously would not accommodate Moore's work as a central feature unless it could be argued that it was not merely an interpenetration but a *synthetic resolution* of the two polarities, and as such belonged to an advanced condition of art. If this were sustainable, Read's paradigm (first version) would be vindicated as the prior stage within a Marxian dialectic. Read looked to whether this might be supported in his knowledge of Moore's development.

He knew that Moore respected the power of the natural organism to stimulate ideas about sculptural form. In 1934 Moore had said that principles of form discoverable in certain organisms and natural objects would suggest particular material exploitation. The forms found in pebbles would inform stone-carving and those perceptible in weathered timber would inform wood-carving. The structures of tree growth and branching would suggest passages of formal variation for the wood-carver, while the structural strength and tenseness of form discoverable in bones might provide insights for the carver in stone.[29] In pursuit of these interests Moore had filled notebooks with drawings, and constructed numerous maquettes, of forms deriving from studies of bones, stones, shells and weathered wood, and a great many of his finished works overtly manifested organic properties.

Moore had thus placed emphasis on working with the *materiality* of timber and stone. A proper respect for their aesthetic evocations would 'force [the sculptor] away from pure representation and towards abstraction', and the result – far from constituting an 'escape from life' – would afford deeper penetrations into reality than the imitative.[30] This had corresponded to the significance Read had found in Nicholson's art at the time of Unit One. But then Moore had 'returned' to naturalism in his *Shelter* drawings and *Coal Working* studies undertaken for the War Art Commission in the Second World War, though this was a form of naturalistic representation heavily impregnated with abstraction and superrealism. His latest work could be characterized differently: whereas in the *Shelter* drawings abstraction and superrealism served the greater purpose of representation, more recently, Read noted:

> ... a given form is broken down, allowed to suggest associative forms and phantasies. If the first process may be called *crystallization*, this might be called *improvisation*. It is another aspect of the opposition between constructivism and superrealism which [Moore] is always seeking to synthetize.[31]

The work of Moore demonstrated that it was possible to envisage 'an inclusive ambivalent attitude, a taking-into-oneself of the complete dialectical process...',[32] while the work of Hepworth, Nicholson and Nash demonstrated the necessary *preconditions* of such resolution. Their various types of apprehension, fuelling their artistic intentionality, could be:

> arranged along a polar axis, with transcendental metaphysics at one end and an intense self-awareness of physical vitality at the other end. It is along the same axis that we can place abstraction and [super]realism in art. But... choice is not imposed on the individual artist. The axis exists *within* the individual artist if only he [or she] can become aware of it.[33]

These last quotations suggest both the originality of the model that occupied Read's attention during the 1940s and the inherent feature that postponed its authoritative publication. The model contained polarities of modernism fundamentally attracted yet fundamentally opposed. Hepworth, Nicholson and Nash had precipitated the resolution of these opposites in acts of creative *integration*, while Moore had directly achieved their *synthesis* in a condition of art Read now termed 'organic vitalism', the *ultimate* condition of achievement within the second version of his paradigm:

> ... obviously the whole scope of art is altered if you make it, instead of the more or less sensuous symbolization of intellectual ideals, the direct expression of an organic vitalism. No doubt intellectual elements will enter into the choice and elaboration of the [forms of this expression just as sensuous elements enter into the] images which the intellect selects to represent its ideals...[34]

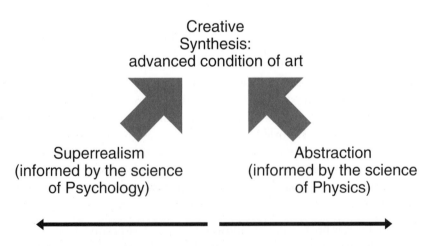

Creative
Synthesis:
advanced condition of art

Superrealism
(informed by the science
of Psychology)

Abstraction
(informed by the science
of Physics)

Herbert Read's Paradigm (second version). A characteristic of the work of a very few artists (principally Henry Moore) is the tendency to engage with both extremes of the modernist front and to synthesis them in the creation of 'new realities'.

226

Other artists drawn to the London International could be afforded roles within this notional system. For example, Gabo seemed to have brought from Russia the fruits of accomplished revolution in abstraction, but as a result of a long correspondence (and ironically after Gabo had left Britain to reside in the USA) Read was persuaded of the fundamentally organic nature of his constructions.[35] Gabo was attempting to create *equivalents* and in this sense merited comparability to Moore. The work of another refugee in London, Mondrian, however, though apparently similar to Gabo's in conception, had been anchored at the abstraction extremity and – because it was positively *locatable* – had memorialized the previous revolution (enshrined in the first version of Read's paradigm). A prerequisite of avant-garde authenticity for Read now was an artist's *resistance to exclusive association with idioms or movements*. His or her responsibility was to be alive to the various fractions of a broad front of creativity linking the most extreme variants of abstraction and super-realism, while consistently avoiding prolonged settlement on any one of them. It was a case of perfecting a roving sensibility – as exemplified either by those artists who practised idiomatic variation (as modelled in the first version of Read's paradigm) or, more profoundly, by those such as Moore and probably Gabo, who practised idiomatic *synthesis* (the highest order of achievement within the second version). An advancement of art – and therefore of culture and eventually human percipience in general – was the product of artists respecting the reciprocal tensions while asserting their right to create realities independent of fractions that had already become conventions.

> Somewhere in this psychic shuttle… freedom intervenes – the freedom to create a new reality. Only on that assumption can we explain any form of evolutionary development in human consciousness, any kind of spiritual growth. A novelty-creating freedom exists by virtue of the intensity generated by aesthetic awareness; an evolutionary advance emerges from the act of expression.[36]

By the mid-century, then, Read had refined a model of contemporary creativity by means of which he could locate all variations of intentionality associated with avant-gardes which had bearing on the notion of an English Cultural International. It is not clear why he did not publish this explicitly,[37] but one reason is surely that his interests were more in finding validation for avant-garde creativity in socio-cultural principles than in taxonomic constructs. While he had been working on his relational model he had also been developing a theory of the fundamental socio-cultural importance of art,[38] something he had found relatively straightforward when confined to discussion of pure form. In 1939 he had written that art becomes more *ethical* with increasing abstract purity because the ultimate goal of abstraction is truth, and that modern art was for this reason unpopular in that it revealed insights into a morality too exacting to be generally acceptable.[39] But it was a half-hearted argument, for he knew that it was only partially applicable to an array of intentionality which also embraced surrealism. In seeking a universal principle applicable to all art in his purview, he asked: 'Where, if not in a moral code shall we find a criterion of art?'

> The answer is, of course, *in nature*. There, absolute and universal, is a touchstone for all human artefacts. And we must understand by nature, not any vague pantheistic spirit, but the measurements and physical behaviour of matter in any process of growth and transformation. The seed that becomes a flowering plant, the metal that crystallizes as it cools and contracts, all such processes exhibit laws which are modes of material behaviour. There is no growth which is not accompanied by its characteristic form, and I think we are so constituted – so much in sympathy with natural processes – that we always find such forms beautiful.[40]

The artist in particular is one gifted with conscious or automatic – but in either case a most sensitive – percipience towards natural form: and all great art, even the most nihilistic example of twentieth-century creativity, in some way transmits a sense of scale, proportion, symmetry and balance.[41] Regarded in this light, the accumulated results of half a century of experiment, including both constituencies of abstraction and superrealism, may be seen to be cohesive. A philosophy of morphology would therefore justify Read in his beliefs that individual artists should reconcile extremes of their creative personalities, and that fractions of the avant-garde should endeavour to cross-represent their principles. This was of course central to the model of modern art Read was constructing: a vital culture will result from the synthesis of such extremes. Morality, then, is not a criterion of creativity but a product:

> morality is essentially mutuality, the sharing of a common ideal. And the process by which we are induced to share a common ideal is… the creation of an empathetic relationship with our fellow citizens by means of common rituals, by means of the imitation of the same patterns – by meeting, as it were, in the common form or quality of the universally valid work of art.[42]

Such arguments constituted Read's major wartime theme. When induced to express them more strongly he would say that art was too often a partial, even perverse, expression of harmonics, and too often an aggressive utterance of personal fantasy. The whole conception of art would have to be revised, and this meant nothing less than achieving a synthesis of pure form and personal feeling such as was being effected by artists he knew well.[43] At mid-century, as he approached his sixtieth year, Read clearly believed he had perfected a critique which did justice to English achievements of the 1930s, had value for post-war western culture in general, and could offer popular purchase on the otherwise obscure activities of the avant-garde. Art, he said, would have no history but for the individual artist's efforts to invent new, significant forms in response to unique, originating intentionality. The paragon modernist artist is positioned at the very growth point of human awareness, winning new forms from numinous and fugitive experience and offering them to the public culture. Culture is a dialectic moving forward, annexing and occupying new experience, an organic event unfolding.

> The point I am trying to make [he wrote], the whole point of my hypothesis, is that the work of art is not an analogy – it is the essential act of transformation; not merely the *pattern* of mental evolution, but the vital process itself.[44]

Notes

1   Barr was inaugural Director of the Museum of Modern Art (founded in 1929) and his sponsors were its patrons, who had quite specific collecting interests in post-impressionism. His responsibility was to devise a mission for the museum which would both validate the taste represented in its founding collections (in which works by Cézanne and van Gogh were preponderant) and establish principles of canonic modernism on which the institution's research commitment could be founded. He constructed pedigrees of descent from cubism and surrealism, locating other discernible movements and idioms in inferior relationship to these principal initiatives. See Alfred H. Barr Jr, *Cubism and Abstract Art* (New York: Museum of Modern Art, 1936)[New York: Arno Press, 1966, 1974], Diagram (frontispiece) and pp. 19ff. See also Alfred H. Barr Jr, *Fantastic Art, Dada, Surrealism* (New York: Museum of Modern Art, 1936), pp. 9–13.

2   In so far as Clark was interested in contemporary art he regarded it as little different in essence from the rest of post-Renaissance culture in that it emanated from a centre (where it was relatively stable and conventionalized) and gradually spread geographically and chronologically, diluting as it did so. This was fundamentally different from Read's initial premise, inherited from T. E. Hulme, that the art of the periphery had its own distinct characteristics which opposed those of the centre. See notes 3 and 4, below.

3   Thomas Ernest Hulme, 'Modern Art I', *New Age*, vol. 14, no. 11 (15 January 1914), p. 341; Thomas Ernest Hulme, 'Modern Art II', *New Age*, vol. 14, no. 21 (26 March 1914), pp. 661–62.

4   Herbert Read (ed.), *Speculations* by T.E. Hulme (London: Kegan Paul, Trench, Trubner & Co., 1924).

5   Julien Benda, *La Trahison des clercs*, trans. Richard Aldington, *The Betrayal of the Intellectuals* (London: Routledge, 1928). See Read's review in *Criterion*, vol. 8, no. 21 (December 1928), pp. 270–76.

6   Herbert Read, *The Meaning of Art* (London: Faber and Faber, 1931).

7   Ibid., pp. 145–48.

8   Ibid., pp. 148–53.

9   While at the Victoria and Albert Museum Read had travelled frequently to Germany and certainly visited the Bauhaus in Dessau. When Professor of Fine Art, in an open 'Proposal for a Scottish Philanthropist', undated [1932], he had sought funds to establish a Bauhaus in Edinburgh (37/55, Read Archive, University of Victoria, British Columbia). His contacts with such as Walter Gropius, Wassily Kandinsky and László Moholy-Nagy and his knowledge of the approaching crisis in Dessau would certainly have led to their being, at the very least, consulted on its formation.

10 Herbert Read, *Art Now: An Introduction to the Theory of Modern Painting and Sculpture* (London: Faber and Faber, 1933).

11 Worse, this brought into question Read's 'modernity' because other celebrated modernists, of whatever idiomatic preference, were investing heavily in the concept of *exclusive validity*. Read

must already have been aware of Barr's intention to map modernism as a succession of move-ments each fitting, and absolutely representing, their times of origin. Barr had consulted Wyndham Lewis who was prominent among Read's circle of friends, and on Lewis's advice Barr had made a 'grand tour' of European avant-garde artists following an ordering suggested by the proposal that all the great aesthetic advances of the previous twenty-five years had descended from cubism. Read is certain to have been aware of this through friendship with Lewis and also because of Barr's subsequent, systematic research in every part of the European arena in which Read was active. In contrast, Read's preference for modelling modernism according to a range of differing artistic *intentionality* was, and remained, a unique feature of his work. Though they seem not to have met at this time, Read and Barr must constantly have encountered traces of one another as they explored the same territory. On Barr's 'grand tour' see Irving Sandler and Amy Newman (eds), *Defining Modern Art: Selected Writings of Alfred H. Barr Jr* (New York: Harry N. Abrams Inc., 1986), p. 103. See also Russell Lynes, *Good Old Modern: An Intimate Portrait of the Museum of Modern Art* (New York: Atheneum, 1973), p. 27.

12 Herbert Read, *Art Now*, p. 144. In subsequent editions 'linear signs' was changed to 'plastic forms'.

13 Herbert Read, *Henry Moore, Sculptor: An Appreciation* (London: Zwemmer, 1934), pp. 10–11.

14 Herbert Read (ed.), *Unit One: The Modern Movement in English Architecture, Painting and Sculpture* (London: Cassell and Co. 1934). The group comprised (sculptors) Barbara Hepworth and Henry Moore; (painters) John Armstrong, John Bigge, Edward Burra, Tristram Hillier, Paul Nash, Ben Nicholson and Edward Wadsworth; (architects) Wells Coates and Colin Lucas.

15 Herbert Read, *Unit One*, 'Introduction', esp. pp. 14–16.

16 Herbert Read, 'British Art 1930–1940', in catalogue of the exhibition *Art in Britain 1930–40 Centred around Axis, Circle, Unit One* (London: Marlborough Fine Art, 1965), pp. 5–6.

17 Instead, Read took a leading role in bringing the Third Reich exhibition of *'Degenerate' German Art* to the New Burlington Gallery, London, 1938, and accepted this opportunity to publish a defence against 'degeneracy': Herbert Read, 'Introduction', in Peter Thoene, *Modern German Art* (Harmondsworth: Penguin Books, 1938), pp. 7–11.

18 Herbert Read, 'Why I am a Surrealist', *New English Weekly*, no. 10 (March 1937), pp. 413–14. For an extensive account of Read's involvement with surrealism, see Paul C. Ray, *The Surrealist Movement in England* (Ithaca, NY, and London: Cornell University Press, 1971), pp. 108–32.

19 Read and Barr both issued their paradigms in 1936 – Read's in a postscript to the second edition of *Art Now* (1936); Barr's in Alfred H. Barr Jr, *Cubism and Abstract Art*, on the occasion of the exhi-bition of the same title. It is tempting to detect competition: each would have been aware of the other's project in outline through their common network of artists, dealers, picture agencies and other sources of information. Read would have known the priority Barr afforded cubism and (since both Read and Barr had simultaneously completed major studies of surrealism and also shared sources in this specific arena) he would have been aware of the dependency on cubism that Barr attributed even to surrealism. See Herbert Read (ed.), *Surrealism* (London: Faber and Faber, 1936); Barr, *Fantastic Art, Dada, Surrealism*. But competition with Barr was less urgent than the need to express solidarity with the Europeans. The fact that Read called himself a surrealist in order to accomplish this weakened the reception of his ideas. In comparison, Barr's control over exhibition interpretation at the Museum of Modern Art enabled him to rehearse his model in all the Museum's publications, conventionalizing the proposal that modernist authenticity descended from cubism.

20 Herbert Read, 'What is Revolutionary Art?', in Betty Rea (ed.), *Five on Revolutionary Art* (London: Wishart, 1935), p. 19.

21 Ibid., pp. 20–21.

22 Herbert Read, *Art Now* (London: Faber and Faber, 2nd rev.ed.1936), p. 146.

23 Herbert Read, 'The Faculty of Abstraction', in J. L. Martin, Ben Nicholson and N. Gabo (eds) *Circle: International Survey of Constructive Art* (London: Faber and Faber, 1937), p. 64.

24 Herbert Read, 'An Art of Pure Form', *London Bulletin*, no. 14 (1939), pp. 6–9. This was a republication of a passage in Herbert Read, *Art and Society* (London: Heinemann, 1937), pp. 259–60.

25 Herbert Read, 'The Faculty of Abstraction', p. 66.

26 Letter from Barbara Hepworth to Herbert Read dated 15 May 1944: 48/61, Read Archive. See also references to this correspondence in Herbert Read, 'Barbara Hepworth: A New Phase', *Listener*, vol. 39 (1948), p. 592; and Herbert Read, 'Realism and Abstraction in Modern Art', republished as chapter 5 of Herbert Read, *The Philosophy of Modern Art: Collected Essays* (London: Faber and Faber, 1952), pp. 88–104 (p. 98).

27 Letter from Barbara Hepworth to Herbert Read dated 6 March 1948: 48/61, Read Archive.

28 Herbert Read, 'Ben Nicholson' (1948), republished as chapter 12 of Read, *The Philosophy of Modern Art*, pp. 216–25 (p. 220).

29 Henry Moore, in Read, *Unit One*, pp. 29–30. Paraphrased in Herbert Read, 'Introduction', *Henry Moore: Sculpture and Drawings* (London: Lund Humphries/A. Zwemmer, 1944), pp. xvii–xliv (p. xxviii); reproduced as chapter 11 of Read, *Philosophy of Modern Art*, pp. 195–215 (p. 206).

30 Henry Moore, in Read, *Unit One*, p. 30. See *Henry Moore: Sculpture and Drawings*, p. xxix; and Read, *The Philosophy of Modern Art*, p. 207.

31 Herbert Read, 'Henry Moore' (1944), in Read, *The Philosophy of Modern Art*, p. 209.

32 Read, 'Realism and Abstraction in Modern Art', p. 104. The greater part of this essay was written in 1948 as a lecture for various centres throughout the USA, and was published in *Eidos*, no. 1 (1950), pp. 26–37. However, in its republished version in *The Philosophy of Modern Art* an appendix was added which gave emphasis to the idea of 'an inclusive ambivalent attitude, a taking-into-oneself of the complete dialectical process', suggesting that Read decided to give greater weight to this concept as a result of reviewing and reworking his earlier material for republication in this book.

33 Read, 'Realism and Abstraction in Modern Art', p. 97. The bracketed addition to this quotation, changing 'realism' to 'superrealism', is intended to clarify Read's meaning. In the same essay he stated: '... realism will include, not only the attempt to reproduce with fidelity the images given in normal perception, but also those distorted or selected images due to exceptional states of awareness which we call idealism, expressionism, superrealism, etc. In the same way, abstraction will include any form of expression which dispenses with the phenomenal image, and relies on elements of expression that are conceptual, metaphysical, abstruse, and absolute...' (ibid., p. 88).

34 Read, 'Henry Moore', p. 207. The bracketed words are present in Read's handwritten draft of this essay (Blue Notebook, 13/2/3, Read Archive) but appear to have been missed in typesetting, causing ambiguity in the published version.

35 A flavour of their exchange may be indicated in Read's observation to Gabo as follows: 'The ambition to "create reality" seems to me a little self-deceptive. It is an extreme of ego-centrism which I am willing to entertain... but what is essentially a subjective attitude, you turn into a positive activity, and in some sense detach yourself from existence to create essence...' (letter from Herbert Read to Naum Gabo dated 5 October 1947 [Gabo Archive, Yale University Library]). For a summary of the Read-Gabo exchange see 'Appendix to the Essay on Constructivism', chapter 13a, Read, *The Philosophy of Modern Art*. For an extended discussion, including correspondence omitted from this source, see David Thistlewood, *Herbert Read: Formlessness and Form: An Introduction to His Aesthetics* (London: Routledge and Kegan Paul, 1984), pp. 85–94.

36 Herbert Read, 'Realism and Abstraction in Modern Art', p. 99.

231

37 For example, as explicitly as the Museum of Modern Art promoted Barr's scheme. Read was, after all, a consultant to the publishing house Faber and Faber and entirely in command of the publication of his own writings. In the 1950s Barr's Paradigm, which endowed art movements with authenticity to the degree of their descendant relationship to cubism, was widely regarded as an accurate measure of avant-garde significance. However, Barr's Paradigm began to fail when faced with the problem of accommodating abstract expressionism because of the difficulty of reconciling a gestural abstraction with the geometricism of sub-cubist aesthetics. Read's paradigm (second version) not only did not fail at this prospect but was enhanced by the accommodation. As an apparent synthesis of the abstract and the superreal, the supraconscious and the subconscious, abstract expressionism could be regarded as occupying a similar forward staging to Moore's sculpture.

38 As expounded in Read, *Art and Society*.

39 Herbert Read, 'Art and Ethics'(1939), republished in Herbert Read, *A Coat of Many Colours: Occasional Essays* (London: Routledge and Kegan Paul, 1945), pp. 205–07.

40 Herbert Read, 'Art and Crisis' (1944), republished in Herbert Read, *The Grass Roots of Art* (London: Lindsay Drummond, 1947), chapter 4, pp. 77–78.

41 Ibid., p. 78.

42 Herbert Read, 'The Moral Significance of Aesthetic Education' (1949), republished in Herbert Read, *Education for Peace* (London: Routledge and Kegan Paul, 1950), p. 71.

43 Ibid.

44 Herbert Read, *Art and the Evolution of Man* (London: Freedom Press, 1951), p. 39. This was a lecture delivered at Conway Hall, London, 10 April 1951.

Herbert Read's Organic Aesthetic: [II] 1950–1968

DAVID THISTLEWOOD

A T some point between *The Philosophy of Modern Art* (published in 1952 but *written* over the preceding two decades and most accurately representing his position in the late 1940s) and *The Forms of Things Unknown* (1960),[1] Herbert Read ceased to rely mainly on a Freudian model of the creative unconscious and turned instead to Jung. This 'event' is very difficult to locate, and it may be more appropriate to look for a gradual transfer of emphasis. Two things are certain, however. At one important stage in his work Read found Freudian principles particularly useful in explaining a creative individualism associated with surrealism, especially the specifically English derivative he termed 'superrealism'. And at a subsequent stage, when he was conscious of addressing a much broader constituency, he became fascinated with the prospect of creativity as engaging the collective unconscious. In developing this theme he turned decisively to Jungian theory, to the extent of participating regularly in the Eranos Tagung, Jung's annual seminar held at Ascona.

What this indicates is the supplanting of ideas about a *dependency* of art upon nature with ideas about an interpenetration – even an *identity* – of art and nature. To propose that art may be a product of collective unconscious impulses, while believing, as Read did, that it is indispensable to the normal development of humanity, was to endow it with 'ecological' significance. Formerly, Read's exemplary artist was one possessing (among other essential attributes) acute sensitivity towards an abstraction deriving its norms from nature. Latterly, his exemplary artist is driven by purposes which may only be termed 'evolutionary'. It may not be surprising that this change of outlook would stimulate even greater interest in organicist interpretations of art, and especially those which recognized art as having a fundamental role within the general field of evolutionist theory.

Although published prior to *The Philosophy of Modern Art* (which, as noted, is a summation of Read's 1940s thinking), *Art and the Evolution of Man* (1951)[2] clearly signals the new perspective. In its initial passages Read proposes to offer persuasive arguments that art has been not merely a superfluous, but an essential, factor in the evolution of the human species. He adopts the firm position that art *itself* does not evolve, but suggests that what he describes as 'maximum aesthetic sensibility' is evident in the art of all periods from the cave drawings of the palaeolithic culture to the work of Picasso.[3] The subsequent publication of *The Philosophy of Modern Art* would have been a source of potential embarrassment as the latter does in fact privilege an evolving modern art, and especially Henry Moore's command of an advanced condition of creativity. Somewhere between this and the succeeding conception of Moore as one of the most successful of his generation in striving to attain 'maximum aesthetic sensibility' occurs the change from Freudian to Jungian reliance, and it is worthwhile reviewing the principal moments of this transition before exploring its effects in Read's post-1950 theorizing.

It is important to understand that this change entailed sacrifice. Read had regarded the bringing together of his 1940s thinking as the creation of a major work – the definite article in *The Philosophy of Modern Art* brooks no provisionality – and to effect its supersedence before publication was a courageous act. Afterwards he hardly referred to this book (though it had a considerably longer life in print that many of his other works) and the reason may well have been his disaffection for its Freudian content after his Jungian conversion. For the psychological basis of his work in the 1940s (while mixing Freudian and Jungian principles in a way neither authority would have endorsed) had been essentially Freudian in its dynamic. It had featured a system of co-ordinates of which the horizontal scale comprised various Jungian mental types, ranging from introversion to extraversion, and the vertical scale the several layers of a Freudian model of the mind, with extraneous elements at the very base (a Jungian collective unconscious) and at the apex (Read's own idea of the supraconscious, an accessible field *beyond* the range of consciousness).

He developed this model as a succession of experimental diagrams[4] and with considerable licence, for example regarding the Id as an upper region of the collective unconscious, capable of penetrating both repressed consciousness and perceptual consciousness and of linking these with the supraconscious realm. This had conformed to his then-Bergsonian image of the artist as one capable of delving into personal unconsciousness in order to extract forms of potentially *universal* significance. He believed in this construct – it mirrored his own creative experience and it reinforced his original paradigmatic explanation of the English avant-garde.[5] As he gradually became an authority on Jung,[6] however, clearly realizing the essential incompatibility of the two psychological systems he had interfused, he increasingly employed Jungian principles in his higher theory while relegating Freudian ideas to explaining the heroic surrealism they had originally stimulated.

One of the most significant consequences of this change was substantiation of the organic principle, previously regarded as an analogy (a most accurate one, but an analogy nonetheless) but now accepted as the most important formative principle in the structuring of reality. From this standpoint art – a striving for maximum aesthetic sensibility – was to be regarded as the principal means of expanding consciousness in all forms of human endeavour. This signalled a major change for Read, from being principally interested in *how* art functions in its profoundest moments to *why* it does so. Art-making, formerly conceived as ranging between abstraction and superrealism and forming new synthetic percepts – in highly special cases originating

234

increasingly advanced conditions of *art* — crucially now was understood to be extending the capacity and quality of *human consciousness* by the application of constant aesthetic principles to an ever-changing flux of events.

While a Henry Moore sculpture, then, was formerly considered an analogue of a personal vision of nature, it now was recognized as an embodiment of humanity's

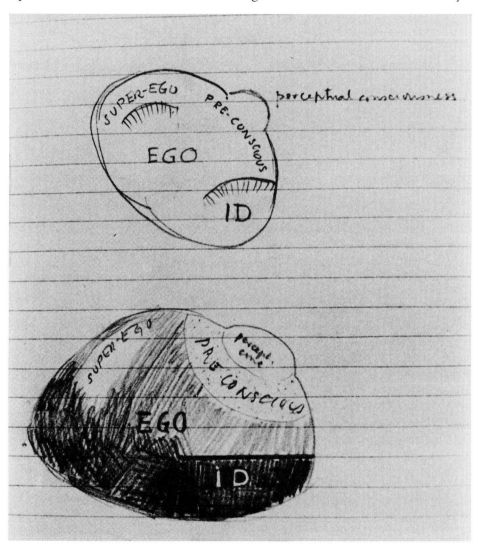

Herbert Read's diagram of the creative unconscious, unpublished, 1943. Two initial stages in the refinement of Read's model. Loosely inserted in his draft chapter 'Unconscious Modes of Integration' (courtesy Read Archive, University of Victoria Library, British Columbia, Canada, © The Trustees of the Herbert Read Estate)

235

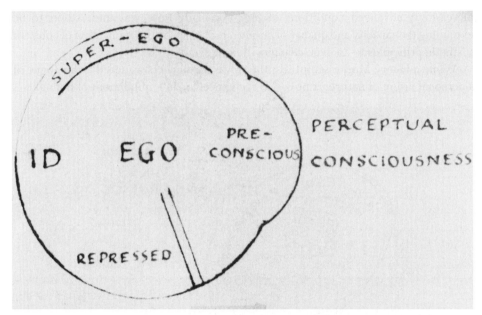

Herbert Read's diagram of the creative unconscious, unpublished, 1943. Third initial stage in the refinement of Read's model. Loosely inserted in his draft chapter 'Unconscious Modes of Integration' (courtesy Read Archive, University of Victoria Library, British Columbia, Canada, © The Trustees of the Herbert Read Estate)

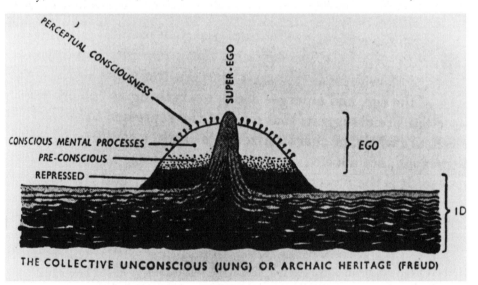

Herbert Read's final version of the diagram of the creative unconscious, 1943. Published in chapter six 'Unconscious Modes of Integration', *Education through Art* (© Faber and Faber and the Trustees of the Herbert Read Estate)

236

collective striving to comprehend the conditions of existence – and not merely as representing this striving but as constituting the vital process of the effective mental evolution.[7] Moore trawled deep *collective* experience, bringing fragments into conjunction with his immediate percepts in order to *know* them and offer them as signifiers to the realm of general consciousness. Thus a Freudian excavation of *new* realities (however significant to the individual artist concerned) was relegated in favour of a Jungian principle of rehearsing *ancient* realities (archetypes), of profound collective significance, in the context of immediate and possibly momentous issues.

This marks a critical point of bifurcation in what Read regarded as his remaining work of prime importance. One strand was to be a progressively more detailed elaboration of his theory of art as identical with developing consciousness. This took *Art and the Evolution of Man* as its starting point – and in particular brief notes on Read's manuscript,[8] indicating his early intention to develop the theme systematically by calling upon historic evidence. Identifiable with this strand of theorizing are the Charles Eliot Norton Lectures, delivered at Harvard in 1953 and published in 1955 as *Icon and Idea: The Function of Art in the Development of Human Consciousness*. Also associated with this theme are the 1954 A. W. Mellon Lectures at the National Gallery of Art in Washington, published as *The Art of Sculpture* in 1956.

The second strand of Read's post-1950 theorizing was to interrogate Jungian theory, with particular attention to the archetype as the unchanging locus of art in the flux of experience and expanding consciousness. Much of this interrogation was conducted in the Eranos Tagung and eventually gave rise to the book Read privately considered his major work,[9] *The Forms of Things Unknown: Essays towards an Aesthetic Philosophy*, mainly written as Eranos papers from 1952 onwards and published in 1960. The two strands eventually recombined – with certain results that were perhaps predictable (confirmation of Moore as exemplary artist; disapproval of the non-organicism evident in pop art) and certain others that were less predictable (recognition of a succession in British sculpture, aesthetically unlike Moore's work but of comparable archetypal potency; and faint praise for American abstract expressionism, which superficially held promise of organicist relevance but failed the acid test of deep cultural significance).

It is clear, therefore, that Jungian theory interrelated with organicist philosophy provided Read's chief inspiration in the 1950s. And just as the Eranos Tagung was to be his platform for Jungian exposition, so the Institute of Contemporary Arts (ICA) in London was to be where he rehearsed organicism. Founded in 1947 by Read, Roland Penrose and a handful of others, the ICA at first modelled a conception of the avant-garde as promoted by the Museum of Modern Art, New York,[10] but within four years its exhibitions[11] and debates were prioritizing philosophies of biological formation, as well as the latest researches in psychology, sociology and anthropology, in close association with organicist abstraction. For a while this became the ICA's special devotion, and it is instructive to sample a little of what its membership would have debated in this regard. Good form is perceptible in all manner of natural organisms at microscopic, normal and macroscopic scales, and exhibits such attributes as structural order, elegance, harmony, economy and dynamic equilibrium. Objectified in art-making, such properties suggest the comparability of growth in nature and composition in art.[12] But their appropriateness is not confined to an art of purely formal relationships. The subjective also respects such principles to the degree that it is *externalized* (objectified) feeling, intuition or emotion; and the subjective may also tend towards formal relationships even when *internalized*, for fantasy and dreaming may be instigated by pathological complexes comparable to force systems, and be subject to intrinsic dramatic unities and patterns of organization.[13] The ICA thus promoted an organicist *identity* of nature, mind and art. At its simplest art-making was to be regarded as an organic event, unfolding in space and time by stages, each stage 'suggesting' to the artist the next 'requirement' of the developing image or form. Eliminating artistic preconception, this model also had the two virtues of conforming to Jung's definition of the artist as a medium or channel for an autonomous creativity,[14] consistent with other vital moments of the universe, and of legitimizing species of 'automatic' creative activity that would convey the possibility of materializing significant form.

Contemporaneously, in *Art and the Evolution of Man*, Read proposed a general theory of the historic identity of art and developing consciousness. This initiated a period of enormous success for Read in the USA – the Norton and Mellon lectureships merely being the most prestigious of a great many he was now to undertake in American universities and art museums. For the essence of his theory was clearly attractive to a culture which considered itself the most advanced in the world – presumably what Read was expected to endorse was that post-war American vanguard art constituted an evolutionary refinement of humanity's grasp on reality. There are no indications that Read was aware of such expectation, and certainly his eventually lukewarm verdict on American abstract expressionism belies compliance. Nevertheless, it is apparent that the two distinct strands of his major work in the 1950s were each conducted in the presence of distinct audiences, one American (the ICA, for this purpose and at this time, is to be regarded as quasi-American) and the other continental Europe. The former effort was geared to confirming the epochal nature of twentieth-century western culture, the other to confirming the modern artist as reviver of contact with ancient wisdom. It is now apparent – it may not have been then – that these positions were equally sustainable only so long as they were distinct, for they were less compatible than Read may have originally thought.

In the Norton Lectures (*Icon and Idea*), then, Read proposed a seven-stage model of historic advances in taking possession of reality by means of art, each the result of an extraordinary application of maximum aesthetic sensibility to prevailing modalities of existence. It is impossible to do justice to Read's argument in summary, but the following may offer a bald outline of his thought. The general style of the imagery

238

of the palaeolithic period is *vitalistic*, serving the need to exert remote influence over animals, the principal means of sustaining life. Here imaging is closely identified with knowing and possessing – maximum aesthetic sensibility is not wasted on human forms, the few depictions of which, because they are not objects of wish projection, are schematic. This observation tempted Read to correlate the vital *need* being exercised and the vitalistic property of *depiction* – the intensity of feeling and the form which adequately symbolizes both condition and degree.[15] This in turn was to suggest to him that vitalism, once attained, becomes a constant if unexercised property of culture – evident in the twentieth century particularly in its lack, which endows great significance on the attempts of an artist like Moore to re-establish contact with its wellspring.[16]

The first stage in Read's scheme of developing consciousness is therefore identification with the vital. He considered this adequate for the general purpose of nomadic cultures dependent on opportunistic forms of sustentation. But as existence became settled and agrarian, modes of interacting with the natural environment necessarily became strategic. This required more than abilities of eidetic depiction – principally capacities to retain images schematically, to compare them, to juxtapose them in new potential relationships, in short to deploy them as instruments of planning and forecasting. 'The vital surrenders to the abstract – the image to the concept.' In this way Read appreciates the less naturalistic art of the neolithic period as a profound heightening of consciousness. Where other theorists and historians find evidence of cultural decline, he perceives a quantum advance into realms of abstract thought – a striving for maximum aesthetic sensibility resulting in considered composition and its concomitant, a sense of *beauty*.[17]

First arising in respect of constructions featuring the *known*, the sense of beauty subsequently transfers into the realm of the unknown as humanity attempts to take possession of the numinous. The instinctive response to challenges from across the threshold of knowledge is to attempt to 'make it evident to the senses, visibly and haptically'. As beauty (of composition, structure, pattern) is already a determinant of value in the known, this criterion transfers into symbolization of the unknown. Imagined realms are constructed, contiguous with the here-and-now,[18] and (as creations of the artist striving for maximum aesthetic sensibility) they are so wonderfully beautiful they are allocated to the gods. Thus a third stage in Read's scheme involves art identifying with nature as extending beyond the immediately perceptible – as a spatial continuum, regions of which must be imaginatively constructed – in the process symbolizing the unknown to such profound effect that it is made divine.

A fourth stage in effect endows divinity on idealizations of the human form, not previously addressed in any real degree in other than schematic representations. Read's difference with other authorities here was to maintain that a conception of beauty had arisen not as an ideal of humanity, but as a means of reducing the chaos of the world of visible appearances to the precision of abstract characteristics:

239

symmetry, balance, harmonic divisions, regulated intervals. Beauty perceptible in such abstractions was *then* recognized as latent in the human form, licensing its idealization. In Greek art this idealization was to be taken to its utmost, but the *genius* of Greek art, evident in the briefest of historical moments, was to temper the conventionalizing of the human form with empathetic vitality – to synthesize the geometry of the general type and the characteristics of individuals.[19] It may not be surprising that such impossibly perfected individuals would be ascribed residence in those idealized realms beyond the limits of known space and time.

A fifth historic advance carried with it the profoundest of corruptions. At its apogee in the Renaissance, artists established an individual clarity of consciousness towards highly particularized circumstances of time and place and percept. A figure by Masaccio, for example, is a real presence standing in a credible, tangible space. Other figures inhabit the same continuum: the physical field which both distinguishes and unites them is palpable. There is no intrusion of stylization such as is evident in Greek art – 'Masaccio's grasp of substance and of space is wholly intuitive'. A vitality of consciousness last witnessed in palaeolithic representations of individual animals is now evident in depictions not only of human subjects but of their personalities, characters and socio-spatial dynamics. The work *samples* an illusory realm comparable in depth and extent with the dimensions of the world of existence. It is a supreme manifestation of consciousness towards physical reality: pregnant with it, however, are major corruptions. One, resulting for example from the codified instructions left by Leonardo, is the subjection of personal vision to 'censorship' by academic conventions. Another is potential contamination with excessive self-consciousness – the prospect of censoring consciousness in the service of effect.[20]

Such corruption led, respectively, to scolasticism and to that extreme condition of romanticism in which the artist conceives of a distinct and personal identity, and regards this as something to be exhibited and valued for its separateness, its distinctiveness, its eccentricity. But a sixth stage in the evolution of consciousness promoted understanding that a personality cannot be reflected on, much less contrived, and can only be more-or-less involuntarily *revealed*. Read used the barometer of self-portraiture as an indicator of artists' gradual revelation of personality, from Rembrandt to Klee, demonstrating the gradual circumvention of the persona, or projected false self, consistent with the symbolization of inner states by means of abstract signs. This tendency, for Read – culminating in the Gestalt-free paintings of the current American avant-garde (action-painting, all-over painting, abstract expressionism) and comparable European work – possessed far less than universal significance, manifesting merely 'some unformulated, some unrealized dimensions of the artist's consciousness'. To his American audience Read suggested that such painting was interesting as involuntary externalization of the fluid nature of the unconscious, as 'an automatic register of the dimensions of the self', and principally as a method for detached introspection. But he resisted ascribing it social significance because of its fundamental incoherence, its lack of cultural unifiers such as only emerge from deeper levels of the unconscious.[21]

For such imperative condensers of new reality, in an American context, Read looked to manifestations of modernism that had crossed the Atlantic, particularly those identifiable with the shifting cultural International – Mies van der Rohe's geometrically formalist architecture and Naum Gabo's dynamically-equilibrate constructions. He regarded these as signifiers of new realities – spatial, plastic, technological (and in view of their pedigree, egalitarian and democratic) – transforming life by 'taking their exact shapes like areas of crystallization in the amorphous fluid of modern consciousness'.[22]

This completed Read's seven stages of the evolution of consciousness: realization of the vital; discovery of beauty through schematic abstraction; symbolization of the unknown; idealization of the human form; apprehension of spatial reality; revelation of the personality; condensation of new consciousness through symbols of constructive potency. He made no bones about its cursory nature, hoping that he had achieved sufficient correspondence between identified moments for others to extend its logic 'to minor and subtler phases of the history of art'.[23] He himself began to attend to this in his Mellon Lectures (*The Art of Sculpture*), in which he surveyed the historic repertoire of sculptural praxis. He was now in effect weaving a fabric of which the stages of evolving consciousness constituted the weft and a number of timeless creative problematics the warp: imaging the human form, organizing space, realizing mass, effecting the illusion of movement and exploiting light. As *constants* these both supported the evolutionary advances in consciousness and, indispensably, connected them back to primordial experience, suggesting a matrix for locating specific sculptural achievements in significant relationship both to deep culture and to advancing conceptions of reality.

It is of course evident that Read's constants in *The Art of Sculpture* were predicated on private convictions about sculptural validity at mid-twentieth century. Evocation of personal fantasy, for example as associated with surrealism, does not figure in his scheme, probably because of irrelevance to socio-cultural objectives. The Duchampian ready-made, ill-fitting the notion of significant form arising from empathetic working of materials, is also absent. Gabo's constructions are privileged, expectedly, for reasons defended in *Icon and Idea* but also because of their *Americanization* of deep cultural problematics – transforming them in the context of American architectonics and by means of synthetic materials, typical products of American industry. And it is inconceivable that any Readian survey of sculpture would not have prefigured Moore.

There is an evident conflict between Read's intellectual commitment to Gabo and his emotional commitment to Moore. In order to suggest their *comparability* Read finds unsuspected properties in Moore's work: his pierced carvings are essays in harmonic exploitation of *light* in the face of age-old difficulties with the form-destroying tendencies of highlight; and piercing the form is also the basis of *linear* expression.[24] It smacks of desperation to identify such attributes of Gabo's in Moore, but Read is on surer ground when, in the concluding passages of *The Art of Sculpture*, he is diverted to an appreciation of Moore he had already rehearsed in the setting of Eranos:

> I myself believe that [Moore's *Reclining Figure*, 1929, in Brown Hornton stone] does suggest, in its magical way, certain chthonic forces – of the earth and of organic growth – and that it is possible that these forces proceed from some deep level of the unconscious, the level Jung calls collective because it is no longer personal. If this belief is true, then the modern artist is once again creating the symbols for our most profound spiritual experiences. He does not create these consciously: the faculties with which he advances beyond the frontiers of existence are exploratory, intuitive. The artist does not seek: he finds.[25]

This may be compared to Read's first proposal to the Eranos Tagung, that Moore exemplified creative access to, and expression of, archetypal experience in what Jung had called 'the chthonic portion of the mind... that portion through which the mind is linked to nature, or in which, at least, its relatedness to the earth and the universe seems most comprehensible'.[26] This definition of the archetype – Read's *preferred* definition – had an obvious affinity with Moore's work: archetypes are the residues of countless ancestral experiences of nature, the earth, cycles of seasonal and climatic change. It accorded with Read's earliest Worringerian image of essential differences of aesthetic disposition conditioned by the Gothic north and the more climatically stable south; and it finally ensured Read's greater allegiance to Moore than to Gabo, who was to be virtually absent from Read's theorizing in its Jungian orientation, most obviously because of the difficulty of associating his constructions with the rehearsal of *ancient* experience.

Also discounted now, and much more decisively, was Picasso, whose work *had* been imbued with ancient mythology. However, Read could no longer accept that Picasso's literal symbolism – for example the horse, bull, light-bearer, and woman with dead child in *Guernica* – constituted a genuine materialization of images from the unknown, for evidence had become available of Picasso's systematic refinement of these symbols in sketches and preparatory studies. The most favourable interpretation was that Picasso had begun with images laden with literal or historical significance, which he had gradually reduced and replaced with new significance deriving from his own powers of formal distortion and exaggerated expression.[27] By indulging in historical and literary allusion he had avoided the prime responsibility to give unmoderated access to archetypal experience. It was a tribute to him that a painting like *Guernica* still communicated profoundly in spite of his strategies for evasion, but what it communicated was due to an extraordinary ability to revivify the cliché rather than to *generate symbolism in living form*.[28]

242

It was this vital ability that distinguished Moore. He worked with very few motifs – most often a coalescence of the female form, the land form and the labyrinth – to reveal essential truths about human existence, mutual dependence and natural sustentation.

> The modern sculptor proceeds from form to image – he discovers (or we discover for him) the significance of his forms *after* he has created them. What we must admire, in the modern artist, is the confidence with which he accepts as a gift from the unconscious, forms of whose significance he is not, at the creative moment, precisely aware.[29]

It is strongly apparent that Read had an abiding preference for this logic of creative origination allied to Moore's characteristically pastoral evocations. However, in debates in the Eranos Tagung he began to argue society's pressing need for a far less comfortable symbolism, 'embracing the shadows that threaten our present civiliza-tion'.[30] Read's rhetoric now – only one year after the publication of *The Art of Sculpture* – reveals his awareness of fascinating and disturbing, yet vitally *necessary*, forms in the work of a younger generation of British sculptors who were blacksmiths. The prototype artist, he said, is Vulcan who forged Achilles's shield of brass, silver, gold and tin, symbolizing respectively, the quaternity of elements, earth, air, fire and water: a culture must rise spontaneously from the collective unconscious through the fiery hands of *our* Vulcans, each beating these constituent metals on his anvil.[31]

This new enthusiasm is a clue to why Read's aesthetic theory was never published definitively. Its dedicated avant-garde had become an old guard. Archetypes evinced by Moore's generation conformed to Jungian staples – symbols of motherhood and the earth, growth and harvest, alternative personalities, mutual aid – in images and forms of relatively clear focus, strong specificity and timeless relevance. A Cold War generation, however, including Reg Butler, Eduardo Paolozzi, Kenneth Armitage, Lynn Chadwick and William Turnbull, materialized ingrained preoccupations that were equally pressing and insistently related to prevailing conditions, such as the instability of world politics. The new sculpture *respected* the organic in its expression of materializing forces: earth, air, fire, water. It harnessed these to a collective psychic anxiety in the presence of the atomic threat, creating restless, linear symbols of energetic nervousness, or casting in the solid state the visual characteristics of molten liquidity. The sculptor exercised 'uncontrol' in rescuing, from the formless flux of molten materials, solidified moments of intense significance.[32] The gentle archetypes of the generation that had matured in the 1930s receded before arche-types shot through with anxiety – the tensed animal; the scuttling insect; the watcher; the stranger flexed for flight – symbolizing a 'geometry of fear'.[33]

This materialization of forms in which primordial and modern existential expe-rience collided, and which condensed collective anxieties without resorting to conventional symbolism, was of immensely greater significance to Read than anything being achieved by the American avant-garde. He felt bound to comment to the Eranos Tagung on the triumphalizing of American art that had accompanied the exhibition New American Painting which had toured Europe in 1958 and 1959. He reviewed American artists' explanations of their creative procedures,[34] noting their concurrence on the importance of circumventing consciousness and precon-ception in order to realize images from the unknown. He had previously referred to their images as instinctive, reflex, instigated by 'internal necessity' but in their moments of expression still unformed. They delivered themselves not so much to the unconscious force of the imagination as to a liberating 'irresponsibility',[35] which to Read signalled no way forward.

> The modern painter has reached the end of his voyage of discovery, and stares into the unknown, the unnamed. To render back to others that sense of vacuity is not to create a work of art, which everywhere and at all times has depended on the presentation of a concrete image…
>
> Our images must be at once universal and concrete, as were the images of past myth and legend… the images of a new mythology, but it must be the mythology of a vision that has explored the physical nature of the universe…[36]

To the Eranos Tagung he said the American example was 'pure gesture' with no concern beyond self-expression. Manifesting only an instinctive self-consciousness – merely a 'bursting shower of selfhood' – it could not hope to condense matters of collectivity or mutuality.[37]

This finally was the fundamental criterion of significance. Certain kinds of avant-garde art were of relatively minor cultural importance because their practitioners were content to fulfil popular expectations of the modern artist (for example, Picasso's distortion and exaggeration of conventional form; the American abstract expressionists' untaxing externalizations of personality). Certain other kinds (Moore's work and that of a succeeding generation in Britain), embodying uncontrived and elusive symbolism of mutuality and not necessarily entertaining to casual inspection, signified nothing less than the conquest of new consciousness. Read's general theory[38] accommodated both kinds but prioritized the latter's sensi-tivity to the immanence of deep cultural phenomena within the newly revealing realm. He respected the nervous arduousness of a life devoted to the apprehension of ungraspable form.

It is not surprising, then, that he reserved his most scathing critique for an idiom that seemed cynically geared to evasion of such effort: pop artists, in succession to the abstract expressionists and partly intending to infuse informal art with signifi-cant form, had settled for a currency of symbolic stereotypes debased by commercial association. Read found it barely acceptable that artists had taken the typical imagery of this 'popular culture' (he considered this term misleading since, largely associated with advertising, it was exploitative) and modified it with some respect for facture, interpretation and transformation – though he doubted whether such remnants of an aesthetic conscience would really redeem it from incoherence and thus irrelevance.[39] He could not tolerate, however, and was compelled to condemn, what he saw as the casual re-presentation of arbitrary forms, a mindless repetition of the clichés of an imposed pictorial regime, a reversal of a culture.

Art would have no history but for the individual artist's efforts to invent new, significant forms in response to some unique, originating intentionality. Culture is a dialectic moving forward, annexing and occupying new experience, an organic event unfolding. In what appeared to summarize not merely this last argument but the whole of his life of theory he wrote:

> I began by asserting that art was a biological phenomenon, closely connected with the development of self-consciousness and intelligence. The relation of individual development to social development is close and intricate: one might say that man evolves as a species but that the decisive steps are taken by individuals. The biologist would, of course, elaborate and qualify such a vague generalization, but the only point I wish to make would not be disputed – namely... we are part of one another and our victories over nature are obtained by mutual aid.
>
> Art is at once an activity that refines the sensibilities and an activity that invents and perfects symbols of discourse – these two aspects of human life are inseparable: self-integration and inter-communication.
>
> The whole process... is infinitely complex, but always at the emergent point of evolution, the bright focus of animal attention, is the discriminating sensibility – that is to say, the aesthetic faculty.[40]

> The genuine arts of today are engaged in a heroic struggle against mediocrity and mass values, and if they lose, then art, in any meaningful sense, is dead. If art dies, then the spirit of man becomes impotent and the world relapses into barbarism.[41]

Notes

1   Herbert Read, *The Philosophy of Modern Art: Collected Essays* (London: Faber and Faber, 1952); Herbert Read, *The Forms of Things Unknown: Essays towards an Aesthetic Philosophy* (London: Faber and Faber, 1960).
2   Herbert Read, *Art and the Evolution of Man* (London: Freedom Press, 1951). This was the Conway Memorial Lecture delivered at Conway Hall, London, 10 April 1951.
3   Ibid., p. 12.
4   Besides the published version in Herbert Read, *Education through Art* (London: Faber and Faber, 1943), p. 175, there are three successive versions of his model in his draft chapter entitled 'Unconscious Modes of Integration'. Two are depicted in the manuscript and one is loosely inserted (13/2, Read Archive, University of Victoria Library, British Columbia). Although devel-

oped in this specifically educational text, this is the model Read consistently applied in his 1940s writings on the English avant-garde.

5 It also clearly illuminated the processes of art education, as the enormous success of his book *Education through Art* continues to bear testimony. This was a standard educational text for over forty years, translated into many languages, and was particularly influential in the United Kingdom throughout the period of effectiveness of the 1944 Education Act. See David Thistlewood, 'Herbert Read (1893–1968)', *Prospects*, vol. 24, nos. 89–90 (Thinkers on Education, vol. 3) (Geneva: UNESCO/Bureau International d'Éducation) 1993, pp. 375–90.

6 Co-editing Jung's collected works: Herbert Read, R. F. C. Hull, M. Fordham and G. Adler (eds), *The Collected Works of C. G. Jung* (London: Routledge and Kegan Paul, 1953 –).

7 Read, *Art and the Evolution of Man*, p. 39.

8 Read identified, in a scribbled memorandum to himself, seven threshold events in art and culture as possible categories of argument ('1. Palaeolithic Art – animalism; 2. Greek humanism; 3. The Romanesque church – holiness; 4. The Gothic cathedral – transcendentalism; 5. Shakespeare and Racine – pure spirit of love – beauty…; 6. Cézanne – realization of the actual; 7. Picasso – dimensions of the unconscious'): Read's holographed MS, 'Art and the Evolution of Man', 29/7, Read Archive, p. 50.

9 According to his son and literary executor, Benedict Read.

10 Its main inaugural exhibitions, Forty Years of Modern Art and Forty Thousand Years of Modern Art, echoed the logic of Museum of Modern Art exhibitions a decade earlier, for example Cubism and Abstract Art (1936), Fantastic Art, Dada, Surrealism (1936), and African Negro Art (1935).

11 For example, Growth and Form, Institute of Contemporary Arts, Dover Street, London, 1951.

12 Herbert Read, 'Preface', in Lancelot Law Whyte (ed.), *Aspects of Form: A Symposium on Form in Nature and Art* (London: Lund Humphries, 1951; 2nd edn, 1968), pp. xxi–xxii. These were the proceedings of the ICA symposium Growth and Form.

13 Read, *Education through Art*, p. 32.

14 '[Jung] says of such a work of art that it is "a force of nature that effects its purpose… quite regardless of the weal or woe of the man who is the vehicle of the creative force"': Herbert Read, 'The Dynamics of Art', *Eranos-Jahrbuch 1952*, Band 21 (Zurich: Rhein-Verlag, 1953). pp. 255–85 (esp. p. 259), quoting C. G. Jung, *Contributions to Analytical Psychology* (London: Kegan Paul, 1928); reproduced in Herbert Read, 'The Creative Process', chapter 3, *The Forms of Things Unknown*, p. 53.

15 Herbert Read, *Icon and Idea: The Function of Art in the Development of Human Consciousness* (London: Faber and Faber, 1955), pp. 21–22.

16 Ibid., p. 34.

17 Ibid., pp. 35–52, esp. pp. 50–51.

18 Ibid., pp. 53–72, esp. p. 71.

19 Ibid., pp. 73–86, esp. pp. 75, 81–82.

20 Ibid., pp. 87–106, esp. pp. 90–91, 96.

21 Ibid., pp. 107–24, esp. pp. 107–08, 121–24.

22 Ibid., pp. 136–37.

23 Ibid., p. 19.

24 Herbert Read, *The Art of Sculpture: The A. W. Mellon Lectures in the Fine Arts, 1954, National Gallery of Art, Washington* (London: Faber and Faber, 1956), p. 113.

25 Ibid., p. 120.

26 Read, 'The Dynamics of Art', pp. 260–61 (quoting Jung, *Contributions to Analytical Psychology*); reproduced in Read, 'The Creative Process', p.54.

27 Read, 'The Dynamics of Art', pp. 272–77; reproduced in Herbert Read, 'The Created Form',

chapter 4, *The Forms of Things Unknown*, pp. 65–69.

28 Read, 'The Dynamics of Art', pp. 277–78; Read, 'The Created Form', pp. 69–70. Jung concurred while delivering an even more devastating critique of Picasso (in a letter to Read dated 2 September 1960, 48/72, Read Archive, in response to Read's gift of a copy of *The Forms of Things Unknown*). Jung defined the modern artist as someone able to dream the future by attending to the images and forms emitting from the unconscious, accepting responsibility to reveal them *without modification*, avoiding temptation to make them conform to the familiar. The creative act was to be regarded as an event *visited upon* the artist (a 'thing that happens to you'). The resulting symbols (unwelcome guests) would be embodiments of primordial experience condensing as reality. 'Who', Jung asked, 'is the awe inspiring guest who knocks at our door portentously? Fear precedes him, showing that ultimate values already flow towards him. Our hitherto believed values decay accordingly and our only certainty is that the new world will be something very different from what we were used to.' Picasso had abdicated the responsibility to come to terms with such visions by *modifying* the results of unconscious formation in order to make them more acceptable by dilution and fragmentation. 'By this regrettable digression he shows how little he understands the primordial urge, which does not mean a field of ever so alluring shards, but a new world, after the old one has crumpled up.'

29 Read, 'The Dynamics of Art', p. 283; Read, 'The Created Form', pp. 74–75.

30 Herbert Read, 'The Creative Nature of Humanism', *Eranos-Jahrbuch 1957*, Band 26 (Zurich: Rhein-Verlag, 1958), p. 334; reproduced in Herbert Read, 'The Reconciling Image', chapter 12, *The Forms of Things Unknown*. p. 191.

31 Read, 'The Creative Nature of Humanism', pp. 346–47, 349; Read, 'The Reconciling Image', pp. 202, 204. My emphasis.

32 See Herbert Read, 'Great Britain', in Marcel Brion *et al.*, *Art since 1945* (London: Thames and Hudson, 1958), pp. 221–50.

33 See Herbert Read, 'Lynn Chadwick' (1958), reproduced in Herbert Read, *A Letter to a Young Painter* (London: Thames and Hudson, 1962), pp. 101–03 (p. 101).

34 In the contributions to the exhibition catalogue by William Baziotes, James Brooks, Adolph Gottlieb, Philip Guston, Grace Hartigan, Robert Motherwell, Barnett Newman, Mark Rothko, Clyfford Still, Jack Tworkov, Willem de Kooning. See Herbert Read, 'Nihilism and Renewal in the Art of our Time', *Eranos-Jahrbuch 1959*, Band 28 (Zurich: Rhein-Verlag, 1960), pp. 372–73; reproduced in Herbert Read, 'The Principle of Speculative Volition', chapter 10, *The Forms of Things Unknown*, pp. 165–66.

35 Referring to such painters as Sam Francis, Mark Tobey and Jackson Pollock. See Herbert Read, 'Blot on the Scutcheon', *Encounter*, vol. 5, no. 1 (July 1955), pp. 54–57.

36 Ibid., p. 55.

37 Read, 'Nihilism and Renewal in the Art of our Time', pp. 374–75; Read, 'The Principle of Speculative Volition', p. 168.

38 The critical, deep-cultural stages of his theory were reprised in a final paper to Eranos: Herbert Read, 'The Origins of Form in Art', *Eranos-Jahrbuch 1960*, Band 29 (Zurich: Rhein-Verlag, 1961), pp. 183–206.

39 Herbert Read, 'The Disintegration of Form in Modern Art', lecture to Documenta III, Kassel, 28 September 1964, published in Herbert Read, *The Origins of Form in Art* (London: Thames and Hudson, 1965), pp. 174–87 (esp. p. 183).

40 Ibid., p. 185.

41 Ibid., p. 187.

Perception and Expression: Read's *A Concise History of Modern Painting*

PAUL STREET

IN recent years there has been a significant renewal of interest in both the life and ideas of Herbert Read, largely occasioned by the centenary of his birth. There was, for example, a lavishly mounted exhibition in Leeds celebrating Read's contribution to the critical acceptance of modernism in Britain, complete with a scholarly catalogue containing critical essays and a detailed, annotated chronology.[1] This present volume itself, of course, will be another contribution to this process of re-evaluation and reassessment. Yet outside this relatively small circle of scholars (and students of modernist debates in Britain in the 1920s and 1930s), it is legitimate to ask how much is Read read today? The answer must surely be 'not very much', with two notable exceptions: *A Concise History of Modern Sculpture* and *A Concise History of Modern Painting*, both published by Thames and Hudson in the ubiquitous World of Art series.[2] One might add *The Meaning of Art* to this short list, but even this is unlikely to be as easily accessible to the casual bookshop browser as the two widely available concise histories.[3] Yet as one looks through the recent scholarship on Read these two books are conspicuous by their absence from the critical commentaries of Read's œuvre. One cannot help but suspect a certain intellectual snobbery at work here. These books were, after all, intended for a general readership, and this might appear to disqualify them from the serious attentions of the Read specialists, despite the fact that they are the books by Read most likely to be encountered by (and thus to influence the thinking of) the intelligent 'general reader' or first-year undergraduate.

A certain amount of personal explanation is necessary, before I proceed further. As a first-year student of History of Art at the University of Essex I bought *A Concise History of Modern Painting* for the same reason as many will doubtless have done both before and after me: I wanted to know about modern painting and this book was both available and affordable. At that time I had little idea who Read was, and to be honest it did not much matter; I wanted to know about modern painting and here was a book which seemed to offer me that knowledge. I suspect that the majority of purchasers today are also in that position.

One final student reminiscence which actually provided the inspiration for me to write this chapter: I still retain my original copy bought fifteen years ago, and it has its original annotations. These, I notice, stop some halfway through, suggesting a

248

book that was left unfinished. This suggests (although I cannot now remember) that I was somehow disappointed by the book, that it failed to live up to my expectations. Perhaps it was too difficult, too full of philosophical ruminations that I did not understand. What I wanted to know about modern art wasn't what Read was telling me, and yet those parts I did read had a lasting influence on my thinking about twentieth-century painting. The great names about whom Read writes with such passion – Cézanne, Matisse, Kandinsky, Picasso, Klee, Pollock – constitute a pantheon of heroic figures, yet the text (I can see now) is also full of anxiety and uncertainty, as though Read was beginning to doubt the modernist project he had spent so much of his life defending. It is this paradox of commitment and enthusiasm in the midst of such unease that makes the book so compelling and worthy of reassessment. If today it seems an unsatisfactory primer of modern painting, as a summation of one man's preoccupations with the potentialities and pitfalls of the modernist project it deserves to be fully reintegrated into the canon of Read's critical writing on art.

The book was first published in 1959, and was reissued in an enlarged and revised second edition in 1968. In 1974 a 'new and augmented' edition was published with new material by Caroline Tisdall and William Feaver and a preface by Benedict Read. The 1968 edition included a brief and profoundly pessimistic survey of developments in art since the first edition, and this section (in which Read seems to have abandoned hope not just for art but for civilization itself) is omitted from the 'new and augmented' edition which contains an unfortunate concluding chapter by Tisdall and Feaver, which not only adds little of interest but jars uncomfortably with the tone of Read's original text. It remains a curiously designed book – the plentiful illustrations rarely coincide with works of art discussed by Read in the text (and it is interesting how rarely Read discusses individual works in any detail). A section (left in place from the original edition) of small black-and-white plates claiming to represent a 'Pictorial Survey of Modern Painting' seems pointless: Read himself admits that it is not, and could not be, comprehensive and there seems to be no particular rationale to justify the inclusion of the pictures chosen: there are few interesting juxtapositions of images and, in any case, the size of reproduction prohibits any useful analysis. The book was last reprinted in 1991 in a print run of 12,000 copies and not only remains in print but is, according to Thames and Hudson, one of their best sellers in the World of Art series. It has recently reappeared in the bookshops with a newly designed cover. It has been translated into sixteen foreign languages including (in addition to French, German, Spanish, etc.) Japanese, Serbo-Croat, Hebrew and Finnish.[4]

At what moment and under what conditions does a history of modern painting begin? One might locate that moment in 1850 when Gustave Courbet showed *The Burial at Ornans* to a bewildered Parisian public, confused as much by the subject as the technique employed; the painting was clearly about something, and its size demanded attention, but it refused to offer up a meaning that could be reconstituted

Gustave Courbet, *Burial at Ornans* 1850. Oil on canvas (courtesy Musée d'Orsay, Paris)

through the available conventions, be they artistic or social.[5] Modernity here is certainly about technique: the painting looks different from anything that had been painted before, but its modernity now seems to reside more in what a contemporary critic called its 'cold image of nothingness', its rejection of any aesthetic or moral comforts for bourgeois viewers as they were 'challenged to try to identify an embarrassing reality'.[6] Perhaps instead one should look for the birth of modern painting in 1863 and in the angular shape of Manet's *Olympia*, that contemporary paradigm of modernity, whether it be for its flatness, its rejection of 400 years of painting as mimetic illusion, or whether it be for its ironic play with the conventions of the nude and its unmasking of a sexual reality (and double standard) beyond the proper concerns of art.[7] One might wish to take the moment forward to 1874 and to a particular place: 35 Boulevard des Capucines, site of the First Impressionist Exhibition, a potent mixture of innovatory technique (the broken brushstroke), novel subject matter (the banalities of bourgeois leisure) and new(ish) institutional structure (the Independent exhibition).

Herbert Read begins his history with none of these, but he is nonetheless certain as to where the genesis of modern art can be found: 'with a father who would have disowned and disinherited his children; it continues by accident and misunderstanding; and can only be given coherence by a philosophy of art that defines art in a very positive and decisive manner'.[8] The father is Cézanne and the philosophy defines art 'as a way of conceiving the world visually'.[9] Naïve art and realistic art are both excluded by Read from his survey, because whilst they are plainly art of this time, they do not exhibit those qualities of 'making visible' that Read defines as the essence of the modern. Read says that there are other ways of conceiving the world: by measurement, by experiment, imaginatively through myth, but the artist is the man (and with one or two exceptions, mentioned in passing, women are absent from

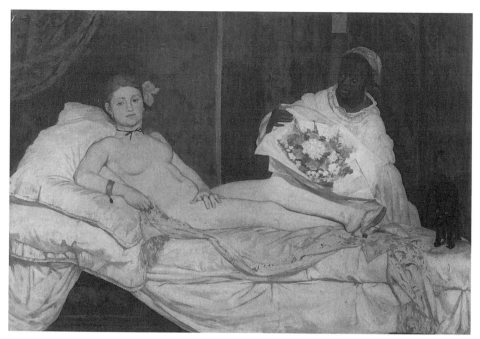

Edouard Manet, *Olympia* 1865. Oil on canvas (courtesy Musée d'Orsay, Paris)

Read's history of modern painting) who 'has the ability and the desire to transform his visual perception into a material form'.[10] This action Read divides into the perceptive and the expressive, although he says that the two cannot be easily separated. Read does not acknowledge Gombrich but it is clear that he draws on ideas that are to be found in *Art and Illusion* for his account of the historical development of art: 'we see what we learn to see, and vision becomes a habit, a convention' and, because we need to make what we see real, 'art becomes the construction of reality'.[11]

Modernity, for Read, has a unity of intention, the desire not to reflect the visible, but to make visible (here he cites Klee). Cézanne is thus crucial as he is the first artist to see the world objectively, without bringing into the process any 'extra-visual faculties' such as imagination or intellect or technical devices like perspective. Cézanne succeeds where all others had failed in 'realizing his sensations in the presence of nature'.[12] Read regards Cézanne's temperament as classical: 'he was for structure at all costs, that is to say, for a style rooted in the nature of things and not the individual's subjective sensations'.[13] Such an approach may seem to be too structured, unless one takes into account the process of *modulation*: the 'adjustment on one area of colour to its neighbouring areas of colour: a continuous process of reconciling multiplicity with an overall unity'.[14]

What is important here is that whilst Read stresses Cézanne's concern for structure, for order, he does so within the context of the romantic paradigm of the artist, engaged in a lonely and heroic struggle, unrecognized until after his death. Cézanne, Read says, attempts to 'pass beyond romanticism (which does not necessarily mean to take a different direction)'.[15] Cézanne is a classical artist with the temperament of a romantic, and his appeal for Read lies precisely in that synthesis. Indeed one could suggest that the two words frequently used by Cézanne and central to Read's understanding of his art — *realization* and *modulation* — represent, artistically, the two sides of the coin. To realize is the activity of a classicist; to modulate, 'to adjust a material (in this case paint) to a certain pitch or intensity',[16] requires the sensibility of a romantic. David Thistlewood, writing about the formation of Read's aesthetics in the 1920s, has shown how Read came to believe that 'reason was... a controlling, harmonizing force rather than a creative one: even in the realm of logic it would be insight that would first arrive at what was new'. Thistlewood suggests that Read's first book of literary criticism could as well have been entitled *Reason and Insight* (as *Reason and Romanticism*), and that it was his declared purpose to reconcile these opposites.[17] *A Concise History of Modern Painting* seems to suggest that Read remained

Paul Cézanne, *Hillside in Provence* probably about 1886–90. Oil on canvas, 63.5 × 79.4 cm (© National Gallery, London)

committed to such a project until late into his life. Andrew Causey cites Read quoting with approval from Gide:

> It is important to remember that the struggle between Classicism and Romanticism also exists inside each mind. And it is from this very struggle that the work is born: the classic work of art relates the triumph of order and measure over an inner Romanticism.[18]

In his Preface Read states that 'the selection I have made, of names and events, will inevitably betray a personal bias, but I have taken some care to correct such bias when it became evident to myself'.[19] In fact Read's personal biases are everywhere apparent, and indeed contribute much to the vitality and interest of the book. Art Nouveau or Jugendstil has the difficult job of following Cézanne in the book and is dismissed as 'not so much a style as a mannerism'.[20] Decorative and symbolic, the art of Gauguin and Toulouse-Lautrec has little to offer Read. Van Gogh is (implicitly) criticized for the decorative qualities to be found in his art, but it is his use of Japanese art for its *expressive* function that makes him important in the evolution of modern painting. Gauguin and his followers are of interest because their art reveals a new will to abstraction that was beginning to emerge in Europe, although its full effects were not to become apparent until later.

Georges Seurat is an important figure in Read's account of modern painting, less because of the technique for which he is most famous, pointillism, but because of his attempt (left incomplete, Read suggests, because of his early death), to produce an 'art of harmony'.[21] Seurat's use of colour theory and optical mixing aimed at a scientific and objective way of rendering the depicted object, but Seurat, claims Read, wanted more than this. Harmonies of line, colour and tone 'can express feelings of gaiety, calm or sadness… the effects are incalculable since they operate on the infinite gamut of human sensibility', and thus, the '*expressive* function of the work of art was recognized and preserved'.[22] For most of his life Read too struggled to resolve this dialectic between the need for art to be based on structure, order and clarity and yet to maintain its expressive potential, and one might suggest that Read is here identifying his own aesthetic journey with that of Seurat. Seurat is certainly more important for Read for his aesthetic theories and personal example than for the art he produced, which is not actually discussed by Read in any detail, and this does indicate one of the difficulties of the book as a primer of modern painting. A (very beautiful) drawing by Seurat and *A Sunday on La Grande Jatte* are illustrated, but readers are left to resolve for themselves the relationship between these two images and Seurat's attempts to resolve his 'dialectical problem'.[23] Certainly it is difficult immediately to detect in the frozen stillness of *La Grande Jatte* the expressive function that Read claims Seurat 'recognized and preserved',[24] whilst the drawing *Place de la Concorde, Winter* is certainly expressive, but any 'scientific basis of aesthetic harmony'[25] is difficult to discern. It may be no bad thing for the reader to be expected

Georges Seurat, *A Sunday on La Grande Jatte* 1884–86. Oil on canvas, 207 × 308 cm (courtesy The Art Institute of Chicago Helen Birch Bartlett Memorial Collection, 1926.224. Photo © 1997 The Art Institute of Chicago, all rights reserved)

to engage in questioning the relationship between text and plates for themselves, but these are complex issues and some guidance from a book clearly marketed as an introduction to the subject might reasonably be expected. With the benefit of hindsight I am beginning to identify where some of my own problems with the book may have arisen.

By the end of the first chapter Read has established the methodology that will inform the remainder of the book: a concern to establish a dialectical relationship between the perceptive and the expressive qualities in art (classical and romantic if you like), which finds expression principally through the work of particular, gifted artists. The implication certainly is that these artists will be isolated, temperamentally 'difficult', obsessive in their pursuit of their aesthetic goals: Cézanne and Seurat are the paradigm models. Running alongside this concept of individual genius pushing art forward, Read posits the *Zeitgeist*, the 'spirit of the age', which in the late nineteenth century is expressed artistically in the 'will to abstraction' discernible beneath the decorative surfaces of art nouveau or the Nabi painters.

The second chapter is entitled 'The Break-Through', and Read's enthusiasm and excitement as he describes this break-through is not hidden:

Georges Seurat, *Place de la Concorde, Winter* 1882. Conté crayon and chalk, 23.5 × 31.1 cm. (Gift, Solomon R. Guggenheim Museum, 19 November, 1941, Solomon R. Guggenheim Museum, New York. Photo Robert E. Mates © Solomon R. Guggenheim Foundation, New York)

> In spite of this apparent arrest in the movement, a position had been established from which there was no retreat: and what had been achieved was so dazzling in glory that every young artist in Europe and America turned towards Paris with unbearable longing.[26]

It is easy to imagine with how much displeasure such a sentence would be met from the austere guardians of contemporary art-historical discourse, where the expression of pleasure in art, never mind enthusiasm, is rigorously discouraged and, of course, it cannot really be defended: *every* young artist? *unbearable* longing? Yet one cannot help but feel that Read's description somehow gets closer towards an understanding of the forces at work in producing the art we call modern, than current concerns with tactical manoeuvres and institutional restructuring and realignments. It is certainly more likely to inspire a reader coming to the text innocent of either modern art or knowledge of Read, and that sentence is one of my own strongest memories of the book.

255

There occurs next a 'concentration of forces'[27] in two centres, Paris and Munich. In Paris it is Matisse and the fauves who take forward the movement, in Munich Kandinsky and the expressionists. The importance of Mattisse for Read is in his discovery (from Cézanne) that colour needs to have a structure, or that structure is given to a painting by the 'considered relationship of its constituent colours'. Read quotes approvingly from Matisse: 'what I am after, above all, is expression... I am unable to distinguish between the feeling I have for life and my way of expressing it'.[28] Matisse wanted an art that was enduring and the product of long consideration which goes further to emphasize his debt to Cézanne. Matisse was seeking 'a higher ideal of beauty'.[29] It is highly symptomatic of the book that Read deals with Matisse almost exclusively through his *writings* on art; none of his paintings are discussed in any detail and, curiously for a book about painting, Read seems happier talking about Matisse's sculpture. Read makes his position clear as to the fundamental importance of the individual genius (a word used frequently) in a passage following his discussion of Matisse:

> All these names, Matisse, Rouault, Vlaminck, Derain, Picasso, refer to human beings in themselves intricately complex, each with a sensibility exposed to an infinite number of sensations, and the movement proceeds, not like an army on the march with one or two commanding officers, but as the gradual establishment of a series of strong-points each occupied by a solitary genius.[30]

David Thistlewood and others have spoken of the crucial importance of the writings (and indeed the friendship) of Wilhelm Worringer in the formation of Read's aesthetic views, particularly in helping him towards an understanding of northern art and of breaking the early spell that classicism held over him. Thistlewood writes that Read was to restate Worringer's philosophy of art for forty years with little modification.[31] For Read German expressionism has some elements in common with French fauvism and an 'exotic' element that derives from Gauguin, but its chief distinction as a style derives from (and here he quotes Worringer directly) 'the transcendentalism of the Gothic world of expression'.[32] Worringer's work, says Read, enabled 'the modern Expressionistic movement [to] advance with a confidence based on historical evidence',[33] although one suspects that the painters themselves were less in need of Worringer's legitimizing philosophy than was Read. There exists a basic urge amongst northern artists towards a 'restless abstraction' which leads to 'emotive distortions of natural forms which seek to express the unease and terror which man may feel in the presence of a nature fundamentally hostile and inhuman'.[34] Nowadays, of course, one may quibble at the extreme generalization inherent in such a definition of the art of the north (which itself needs defining). How useful is it as a way of understanding the art of Dürer, for example, or the clarity and precision of the younger Holbein?

Worringer's thesis does, however, enable Read to locate German expressionism within a dialectical system of development in modern painting. Northern expressionism depicts a 'spectrally heightened and distorted actuality'[35] and Read cites those artists whose art exemplifies this; the list is a familiar one: Van Gogh, Munch, Ensor, Hodler, Nolde, Kandinsky amongst others. Equally important for Read, however, are the individual circumstances within which these expressionist painters worked in their decisive years: all of them, he says, were isolated and lonely figures working in hostile and unsympathetic provincial centres. (This can lead Read into statements of rich, if doubtless unintentional, humour: James Ensor, we are told, 'lived for most of his long life in the extreme isolation of Ostend'.)[36] The need to fit these artists into a particular aesthetic and philosophical argument does go rather seriously awry in the case of Munch, where Read seems to make the mistake of conflating the images with the person who produced them. Munch was 'the most isolated, the most introspective and the most mordant of these melancholy natures... geographically and psychologically he was an "outsider"'.[37] Recent scholarship on Munch has tended to emphasize not only the programmatic and carefully rehearsed nature of Munch's early expressionist work (designer expressionism, one might call it), but also his wide circle of contacts both in Oslo and beyond.[38] Now of course it is not reasonable to expect Read to have been aware of such scholarship, but the case of Munch does illustrate the dangers of constructing a history of modern painting within preset parameters. It is actually very doubtful if Munch's art arose from any existential 'inner necessity'. It is much more likely to be the result of what a highly self-conscious artist thought an art of inner necessity *should* look like.

As one might expect, cubism, whose essential characteristics Read sees exemplified in Picasso's *Les Demoiselles d'Avignon* (the product of 'one individual act of perception'),[39] as a style owes its principal debt to Cézanne, allied to Picasso's discovery of the conceptual element in African art, the fusion being decisive for the entire future of western art. Read quotes from Picasso that cubism is 'an art dealing primarily with forms, and when a form is realized, it is there to live its own life'.[40] One senses, however, a dissatisfaction with cubism, the very success of the style tending towards a 'new form of academicism'.[41] Picasso escapes this charge because of his refusal to remain bound to any stylistic approach.

Gris is important for Read because of his concern for the 'autonomous structure of the picture space... a procedure that profoundly influenced the development of non-figurative art in the post-war years'.[42] Read's belief that modern painting is an evolution towards a particular end (an art of abstraction) makes him regard a 'relatively minor painter' (Read's own words)[43] like Gris as being of more importance than an artist like Léger, whom Read clearly admires whilst being unable fully to integrate into his dialectical model of modernity. Read admires Léger's 'humanity', but one senses a note of regret that Léger's wartime experiences, that led him to reject abstraction, somehow took him away from the true path, an art of 'pure formal order'.[44]

Pablo Picasso, *Les Demoiselles d'Avignon*, Paris June–July 1907. Oil on canvas, 243.9 × 233.7 cm (courtesy The Museum of Modern Art, New York. Acquired through the Lillie P. Bliss Bequest. Photograph © 1998 Museum of Modern Art, New York. © Succession Picasso/DACS 1998)

Read does not deny the importance of 'social and intellectual forces' in the history of art, although he states that 'the history of art… must be written in the terms of art itself – that is to say, as a piecemeal transformation of visual forms'.[45] Nonetheless it is clear that when he comes to consider those developments in modern painting where a concern for social and political action has been central to the rationale of the artists concerned, namely futurism and Dada, the tone of the book changes. What has been a celebratory account of an heroic crusade towards a 'moment of

258

liberation'[46] when the 'free association of images'[47] was accepted, becomes less certain in its judgements. Read talks about the necessity of accepting 'ambiguities and evasions' as the story of modern painting proceeds.[48]

Futurism, Dada and even surrealism are characterized as movements that take 'advantage of the freedom offered by the fragmentation of the perceptual image',[49] and depend for their development as much on poets and 'literary propagandists' as on artists and, although he does not specifically say so, one suspects that Read is wary of artistic movements so founded. Read acknowledges the importance of futurism as helping to develop a new sensibility for the machine age, but the ultimate judgement is damning:

> Futurism was fundamentally a symbolic art, an attempt to illustrate conceptual notions in plastic form. A living art, however, begins with feeling, proceeds to material, and only *incidentally* acquires symbolic significance.[50]

Read, quoting Huelsenbeck, plainly has little time (and less patience) for 'the artists of the Cabaret Voltaire [who] actually had no idea what they wanted – the wisps of "modern art" that… clung to the minds of these individuals were gathered together and called "Dada"'.[51] Read is compelled to acknowledge the political programme of the Berlin Dadaists but sees this as thereby disqualifying them from being considered an art movement. Read's formalist definition of what constitutes the modern – the transformative potential of the dialectic between perception and expression, and the central role it assigns to the sensibility of the individual artist – inevitably makes it difficult for him to deal adequately with those artists and movements which seek to use art for social or political ends. In *A Concise History of Modern Painting* constructivism is dealt with almost exclusively as a phenomenon linked to the 'will to abstraction' identified by Read as having its roots in Jugendstil; significantly, the revolutionary constructivism of Tatlin and Rodchenko in the new Soviet Union merits just one brief paragraph.[52]

As one might expect, Read devotes considerable space to surrealism, but I find the treatment of the movement with which Read is so associated both tentative and unresolved. Read quotes extensively from Breton and others as though reluctant to articulate his own views. He does differentiate between two 'distinct and contradictory tendencies'[53] in surrealism, one a nihilistic continuation of Dadaism, the other more determined by aesthetic considerations. Marcel Duchamp is identified as the movement's link to Dada with his 'disdain for the thesis', and his complete disavowal of the aesthetic category itself. This rejection of aesthetic value, Read sees as a characteristic of much surrealist art: the *Merzbilder* of Schwitters, Ernst's frottages and collages and, of course, Duchamp's own ready-mades. However, says Read, 'beauty would keep breaking in', and he sees in the work of Schwitters, for example, an 'exquisite sensibility'.[54] Read reserves his bitterest words for Salvador

Salvador Dalí, *Metamorphosis of Narcissus* 1937. Oil on canvas (photo Tate Gallery, London. © DACS 1998)

Dalí, citing Breton's charge that Dalí's art sank into *academicism*, a state of affairs made worse by his alignment with Francoism in Spain. Surrealism's principal strength, for Read, is its contribution to the 'emancipation of the visual imagination';[55] yet this is what, for him, characterizes the modern movement in painting anyway and, in the end, one suspects that all that is worth preserving of surrealism for Read is as an 'affirmation of an irreducible freedom'.[56]

Chapter 5 is devoted exclusively to a study of three of the undoubted heroic figures in Read's pantheon of modern painters: Picasso, Kandinsky and Klee. For Read these artists contributed more to modern art than any others, founding movements and influencing movements, but remaining always 'centres of creative energy'.[57] Read clearly admires Picasso, but is concerned about the extent of his influence on other artists ('for an age to be dominated by the idiosyncrasies of a single personality is a sign of weakness'),[58] and is plainly less than happy with certain aspects of Picasso's stylistic variety, particularly the 'archaicizing neo-Classicism' to which he regularly resorted. Read finds in one of Picasso's own quotations – 'I don't work *after* nature, but *before* nature – and with her' – the key to those qualities in Picasso he most admires. *Before* nature is seen as Picasso's 'intuitive awareness of symbolic form', and *with* nature the 'endowment of such symbolic forms with a natural vitality'.[59] Read warns against the danger of attempting to unravel the significance

Pablo Picasso, *Seated Woman in a Chemise* 1923. Oil on canvas (photo Tate Gallery, London. © Succession Picasso/DACS 1998)

of the symbolism in much of Picasso's art, seeing it as archetypal. One suspects here that Read is uncomfortable with the undeniably powerful erotic element in Picasso's work, and indeed even his discussion of *Guernica* reveals an uncertainty about how to deal with the overt political symbolism of the painting. He quotes Picasso's famous statement about painting being an instrument of war, but prefers to see 'the enemy' less as an identifiable external force (Fascism for example), than more generally, '[as those who] threaten the freedom of the imagination'.[60]

Kandinsky's significance for Read's argument I discuss below. The third of this trio of heroic individualists is Paul Klee. Read regards Klee as the 'most significant artist of our epoch', because his art fuses an insistence on the subjective sources of inspiration with a concern for the technical skills necessary to articulate this vision. As we have seen before (with Matisse, for example), it is Klee's writing ('the basic principles of all modern art'), that occupies most of the space allotted to the artist. None of Klee's work is actually discussed by Read, although a number of works are illustrated.[61]

Read's original book concludes with two chapters exploring two divergent paths that artists took towards an art of total abstraction or non-objectivity. One tendency was towards an abstract art of 'clarity, formality and precision', the other towards

Wassily Kandinsky, *Cossacks* 1910–11. Oil on canvas (photo Tate Gallery, London. © ADAGP, Paris and DACS, London 1998)

Paul Klee, *La Belle Jardinière* 1939. Oil and tempera on canvas, 95 × 70 cm (courtesy Paul-Klee-Stiftung Kunstmuseum, Bern. © DACS 1998)

its opposite, or, as Read says, towards 'expressiveness, vitality and flux'.[62] The stylistic labels that are attached to these two tendencies are constructivism and abstract expressionism. Kandinsky and his philosophical mentor Worringer are seen as the origins from whom both pathways proceed. Kandinsky discovered that

> the work of art is a construction of concrete elements of form and colour which become expressive in the process of synthesis or arrangement: the form of the work is in itself the content, and whatever expressiveness there is in the work of art originates with the form.[63]

Abstract forms are inexhaustible in their possible configurations and also in their evocative and aesthetic power. Kandinsky believed that these abstract forms could communicate an 'essence and content of nature lying beneath the surface and more meaningful than appearances'.[64] Read states that Kandinsky was always to remain wedded to an art of subjective inner necessity, but that others developed from Kandinsky's practice an art of *external* necessity in order to create a 'pure art, free from human tragedy, impersonal and universal'.[65]

Piet Mondrian, perhaps not surprisingly, is taken as the leader of this school, with his 'passionate search for the plastic equivalent of a universal truth'.[66] Read's summation of Mondrian's art is both richly poetic and also indicative of the difficulties he plainly has in approving of so much modern art. It is difficult to imagine many artists being able to live up to this encomium:

> A Mondrian painting hung in a house and room designed entirely in the spirit of Mondrian... has a fundamentally different quality and higher stature than any object of material use. It is a most sublime expression of a spiritual idea or attitude, an embodiment of a balance between discipline and freedom, an embodiment of elementary opposition in equilibrium; and these oppositions are no less spiritual than physical. The spiritual energy that Mondrian invested in his art will radiate, both spiritually and sensually, from each of his paintings for all time to come.[67]

Read, of course, either ignores or did not know much that is now considered highly relevant (if not essential) to an understanding of the emergence of non-objective art in the years around 1914: the influence of theosophy on both Mondrian and Kandinsky for example, and the apocalyptic imagery of the great series of Kandinsky 'abstract' paintings of those years. A traditional biblical iconography was reinvented (and reinvigorated) with a new formal language that Kandinsky described as stripping and veiling. Figurative imagery is stripped of most of its clarifying detail and then veiled by the accretion of abstract form. Kandinsky believed that the viewer's response (aesthetically, emotionally *and* religiously) would be heightened by the process of discovering the subject through its veiled and stripped form.[68]

Equally, one feels that Read's discussion of avant-garde art in Russia in the years

Piet Mondrian, *Composition with Grey, Red, Yellow and Blue c.* 1920–26. Oil on canvas
(photo Tate Gallery, London. © Mondrian/Holtzman Trust, c/o Beeldrecht, Amsterdam,
Holland, and DACS, London 1998)

immediately before and after the Revolution is compromised by an unwillingness to
relate the development of non-objectivity to the totality of the situation in which it
emerged. Thus those artists most in sympathy with the revolution, for example
Tatlin and Rodchenko, are barely mentioned (despite the evident importance of
Tatlin to any discussion of non-objective art in this period). It is thus not at all
surprising to find that the Russian artists (apart from Kandinsky) with whom Read
appears most in sympathy are Antoine Pevsner and Naum Gabo, whose manifesto
of 1920 Read quotes from approvingly, particularly Gabo's insistence that 'art has
its absolute, independent value and a function to perform in society, whether

capitalistic, socialistic, or communistic. Art will always be alive as one of the indispensable expressions of human experience…'.[69] As always in the book Read is most comfortable discussing art in these broadly philosophical (or, less charitably, woolly) terms, and least comfortable when having to address the often complex relations that exist between modern art and its political and social context.

To the art of external necessity exemplified by Mondrian, Read contrasts an art of inner necessity, whose roots he traces, citing Worringer again, to northern Gothic art. The general condition of northern man is one of 'metaphysical anxiety', one artistic manifestation of which is expressionism. Read extends Worringer's thesis by asserting that the *universal* condition of man at the present time is one of metaphysical anxiety, and even the apparently rational and objective art of the constructivists is no more than 'an unconscious sublimation of this state of mind'.[70] Read traces this development through the Brücke group, and its successor in Munich, Der Blaue Reiter, of whom, of course, Kandinsky was a leading figure. They were, says Read, the first to show that what matters in art is 'the direct expression of feeling, the form corresponding to the feeling'.[71] This feeling could be expressed either by deformation of the object (the path taken by the Brücke painters and such artists as Kokoschka, Rouault and Soutine) or by the creation of a motif-less painting which used the artist's feelings as the source of the abstraction created.[72] This argument, of course, enables Read to include American abstract expressionism as the artistic culmination of the 'will to abstraction' that characterized the *fin de siècle*. Jackson Pollock is seen as the key figure, his art having links through Masson to the surrealists.

Read's original (1959) edition of the book ends on a note of uncertainty as Tisdall and Feaver point out at the start of their addendum to the 1974 edition. Read laments that the 'notion of an absolute standard, to which all artists should conform, has been lost… An artist's standards become his own sense of release, and whatever aesthetic values may exist in the work of art, of beauty or vitality, are merely incidental, or accidental.' All, however, may not be lost as the 'spontaneous gesture' may be 'guided by archaic instincts'.[73]

The anxiety for the future so palpably expressed in 1959 had become a cry of despair in the brief additions made to the text in 1968. How much more useful the book would be to the contemporary reader (to whom the name Herbert Read, let alone the development of his aesthetic ideas, is likely to be unknown) if the 1968 additions could be returned to the available text, together with a longer introduction that placed both Read and his theory of modern painting in its historiographical context. In 1968 Read argued that the destructive nihilism of Dadaism had returned, and the next step would be 'the systematic destruction of the work of art',[74] which Read regarded as one aspect of the cultural decadence not only of the western world, but of human society generally. Read ended both the 1959 and the 1968 editions of the book (although the passage is not in the currently available text) by invoking, as a sort of talisman against the darkening of the light of civilization, his litany of the 'great leaders of the modern movement' – Cézanne, Matisse, Picasso, Kandinsky, Klee, Mondrian and Pollock. Only an art that returns again to the central concerns of these painters, that is 'to present a clear and distinct visual image of sensuous experience', can hope to contribute to any civilization that may emerge from the wreckage of the present.[75]

Notes

1 Benedict Read and David Thistlewood (eds), *Herbert Read: A British Vision of World Art* (Leeds: Leeds City Art Galleries, 1993).

2 Herbert Read, *A Concise History of Modern Painting* (London: Thames and Hudson, 1959; 2nd edn, 1968; new and augmented edn, 1974); Herbert Read, *A Concise History of Modern Sculpture* (London: Thames and Hudson, 1964; reprinted as *Modern Sculpture: A Concise History*, 1994). The latter book was intended as a companion to the former. In it Read argues that two principal developments have characterized modern sculpture: a concern to 'conceive forms in depth' (the legacy of Rodin) and a concern for the values of pure form (epitomized by Naum Gabo), pp. 14–15. The latter book, perhaps because it lacks much of the philosophical apparatus of the former, remains a more satisfactory primer for the general reader. One also senses that Read was much more relaxed in the writing of the book, and he engages more directly with specific works, something rarely attempted in *A Concise History of Modern Painting*. *A Concise History of Modern Sculpture* is probably of less interest to the Read scholar, whilst remaining a valuable introduction to the field.

3 Herbert Read, *The Meaning of Art* (London: Faber and Faber, 1931; new and revised edn, 1968). This book also shares the distinction of having been continuously in print, along with the two concise histories.

4 Information supplied by Thames and Hudson, summer 1995 and July 1996. According to T. Craker, writing in 1985 a memoir of his time at Thames and Hudson, 'Of all the books in this series [The World of Art] *A Concise History of Modern Painting* has consistently been the biggest seller, year in, year out, since it was first published' (T. Craker, *Opening Accounts and Closing Memories* [London: Thames and Hudson, 1985], p. 46). Benedict Read relates that one museum in Finland displays two rooms of modern art left to them by a collector whose education in modern art was based largely on a reading of the Finnish translation (Benedict Read in conversation with the author, July 1996)! A study of the impact of the book outside Britain would make a fascinating study in its own right.

5 The best account of the painting remains T. J. Clark, *Image of the People: Gustave Courbet and the 1848 Revolution* (London: Thames and Hudson, 1973).

6 Francis Frascina, Nigel Blake *et al.*, *Modernity and Modernism: French Painting in the Nineteenth Century* (New Haven: Yale University Press, 1993), p. 78.

7 T. J. Clark, 'Preliminaries to a Possible Treatment of *Olympia* in 1865', *Screen*, vol. 21, no. 1 (Spring 1980), pp. 18–41.

8 Read, *A Concise History of Modern Painting*, p. 12. Unless otherwise stated all other references to this book are taken from the 1974 new and augmented edition, reprinted in 1991.

9 Ibid., p. 12.

10 Ibid., pp. 12–13.

11 Ibid., p. 16. E. H. Gombrich, *Art and Illusion* (London: Phaidon Press), was not published until 1960, but Gombrich's lectures, on which the book was based, were given in Washington in 1956,

and it is also clear from the Preface that Gombrich had been rehearsing the ideas in public for some time before and after that date. For Gombrich's discussion of the genesis of his ideas, see *Art and Illusion*, pp. vii–x.

12 Read, *A Concise History of Modern Painting*, p. 14.

13 Ibid., p. 16.

14 Ibid., p. 18.

15 Ibid., p. 21.

16 Ibid., p. 16.

17 David Thistlewood, *Herbert Read: Formlessness and Form: An Introduction to His Aesthetics* (London: Routledge and Kegan Paul, 1984), pp. 7–8.

18 Andrew Causey, 'Herbert Read and the North European Tradition 1921–33', in Read and Thistlewood, *Herbert Read*, p. 43.

19 Read, *A Concise History of Modern Painting*, p. 7.

20 Ibid., p. 21.

21 Ibid., p. 28.

22 Ibid.

23 Ibid., p. 29.

24 Ibid., p. 28.

25 Ibid.

26 Ibid., p. 32.

27 Ibid., p. 33.

28 Both quotations from ibid., p. 28.

29 Ibid., p. 40.

30 Ibid., p. 50.

31 Thistlewood, *Herbert Read: Formlessness and Form*, p. 41.

32 Read, *A Concise History of Modern Painting*, p. 52.

33 Ibid., p. 53.

34 Ibid., pp. 53–54.

35 Ibid., p. 54.

36 Ibid., p. 59.

37 Ibid.

38 See, for example, Mara-Helen Wood (ed.), *Edvard Munch: The Frieze of Life* (London: National Gallery, 1992).

39 Read, *A Concise History of Modern Painting*, p. 67.

40 Ibid., p. 78.

41 Ibid., p. 86.

42 Ibid.

43 Ibid., p. 87.

44 Ibid., p. 90.

45 Both quotations from ibid., p. 50.

46 Ibid., p. 96.

47 Ibid., p. 97.

48 Ibid., p. 106.

49 Ibid., p. 108.

50 Ibid., p. 112.

51 Ibid., p. 117.

52 Ibid., p. 205. Read generally has little to say about the emergence of modern painting in Russia both before and after 1917. Much of the burgeoning scholarship on this period post-dates Read's

268

book, but he should have been aware of Camilla Gray's pioneering *The Great Experiment: Russian Art 1863–1922* (London: Thames and Hudson, 1962) when he was preparing the 1968 edition.

53 Read, *A Concise History of Modern Painting*, p. 137.
54 Ibid., p. 139.
55 Ibid., p. 144.
56 Ibid., p. 146.
57 Ibid., p. 147.
58 Ibid., p. 150.
59 Ibid., pp.152–53.
60 Ibid., pp. 160–62.
61 For Read's discussion of Klee, see ibid., pp. 177–87.
62 Ibid., p. 188.
63 Ibid., pp. 194–95.
64 Ibid., p. 189.
65 Ibid., p. 195.
66 Ibid., p. 197.
67 Ibid., p. 203.
68 There is now a large literature on this subject, but see, for example, *Abstraction: Towards a New Art Painting 1910–1920* (London: The Tate Gallery, 1980).
69 Read, *A Concise History of Modern Painting*, p. 209.
70 Ibid., p. 222.
71 Ibid., p. 228.
72 Ibid., pp. 229–30.
73 Ibid., p. 282.
74 Read, *A Concise History of Modern Painting* (1968 edn), p. 290.
75 Read, *A Concise History of Modern Painting* (1959 edn), p.287.

Herbert Read and Englishness

KEVIN DAVEY

> kiss merciful o homily thy keel
> england vesicles of delight
> lost ever ever ever white pyx
> residues of lust ah wax lack[1]

WHILE 'basic black', one of Herbert Read's later poems, contributes to a mood of post-imperial loss, as an experiment in abstract expressionist poetry it simultaneously aspires to transform the way in which the English represent themselves. It is therefore emblematic of the struggle to modernize and renew Englishness which was at the core of Read's work and which remains the major argument for a reconsideration of his œuvre.

The English have long been predominant in the multi-national culture of the islands in which we live. And only recently have they slipped from a position of imperial ascendancy over much of the globe. Citizens and administrators alike have been able to identify themselves as simultaneously English and British in a seamless union which has eclipsed the ever-present and growing diversity of the culture. Everything has its season, however. That Englishness is now a troubled and dissociated identity, bereft of its Empire, increasingly aware of its racial and cultural heterogeneity, and forced to consider the end of formal Union. Stuart Hall has pointed out that 'the issue of cultural identity as a political quest now constitutes one of the most serious global problems as we go into the twenty-first century'.[2] Nowhere is that more true than amongst those who identify themselves as English.

Consequently it is not simply Herbert Read's anglicized modernist aesthetic, his pioneering Jungianism nor his pedagogic innovations that compel a return to his work, but rather his trajectory and achievement as a protagonist in an earlier phase of our contemporary debate about globalization, national culture and identity.

Read was an essayist and reviewer, a thinker who tried to define, transform and mobilize the nation's sense of itself, the Anglo-British national-popular will, through his literary anthologies and surveys of the visual arts, political critique and founding of institutions. Read regularly proposed canons in English poetry, prose and the visual arts, and assembled a number of anthologies to underpin and disseminate his narrative of the nation.

Herbert Read commenced this labour of cultural and political renewal in a period that was formative for contemporary Britain. The years 1880–1920 witnessed what

270

Stuart Hall has called 'the rise of the representative/interventionist state'.[3] The period saw the limited modernization, democratization and collectivization of a number of key institutions and a heavily resisted transformation of many aspects of the nation's imperial culture. Read's outlook was formed by the military adventure and the radical cultural and political ferment of those years and he subsequently found himself at odds with the settlement which emerged and has endured in its fundamentals until the present day.

Read's work challenged key components of the dominant English identity as it existed in early-twentieth-century industrial, cultural and political ideologies. He became a determined modernizer of the English visual aesthetic and canon, a passionate if ineffective critic of a political Englishness based on liberalism and the legitimacy of the British state, and a scourge of British industry's indifference to design. His celebration of the achievement of the Romantics – 'a new extension of the general range of human consciousness'[4] – was also a critique of what he considered an archetypical English masculinity, a gendered form of accommodation to the national culture.

Read fashioned an account of English culture that was designed to help it absorb the challenges thrown up by European modernity: psychoanalysis, aesthetic modernism, Marxism and anarchism. During the inter-war years this account was less susceptible to, but not wholly exempt from, the sense of nostalgia and national loss that characterized the work of contemporaries like Leavis, Eliot and Waugh and to which he also later succumbed.

Read's aesthetic criticism was historical and psychoanalytic, attentive to the *longue durée*, cultural difference and national identity. He constructed and celebrated a transcendent, essentialized Englishness. The cultures of Wales, Scotland and Ireland were marginalized and subsumed in his comments on a subordinate Celtic heritage. In a major essay on English art Read followed Matthew Arnold's strategy in *The Study of Celtic Literature* (1867),[5] and excluded artefacts from Britain's Celtic heritage (and by sleight of hand all Welsh, Scottish, Irish and non-Anglo-Saxon cultures) on the grounds that they 'speak no English to us'.[6] His friend George Woodcock later revealed that Read 'refused to consider himself British and had a healthy resentment of the Scots, whom he accused of stealing the ballad literature of the north country'.[7]

Read celebrated Englishness as 'an ideal, a dynamic vision with which many Irishmen, Welshmen and Scotsmen have identified themselves'. It was summative of the best in Britain and 'that Greater England which includes the whole Empire'.[8] Britishness was simply Englishness writ large. He constructed a Greater English culture that appeared to prefigure and be capable of absorbing modernist challenges at no cost to its own continuity. His confidence in the nation was cultural and circumscribed, however. It did not extend to the political structures of the state.

Their England

What notion of England was Read contesting and seeking to change? The classical reflex of its art galleries and the antiquarianism of its museums; the hollow claim that British political institutions embodied an ideal of liberty; and the cast of the nation's manhood. During the inter-war years Read demonstrated that liberty, reason and creativity were qualities feared and obstructed by the official culture. His critique was comprehensive. It confronted academicism in the art galleries, unresponsive forms of political representation, and forms of English masculinity that diminished sensibility.

As 'a civilization without art', England was distinct from other European nations.[9] A continuing attachment to nineteenth-century classicism and industrialism, 'the peak point of the English cult of culture',[10] was no substitute for contemporary creativity. The Tate Gallery was still denying entry to the French impressionists right into the 1930s. In 1934 the incoming Director Kenneth Clark may have opened the door, belatedly, to Cézanne, but the gallery's walls remained firmly off limits to his modernist successors. London's avant-garde, after the brief but distinctive excursion of the Vorticists, proved little more than a rearguard for post-impressionism. In the 1920s Roger Fry and Bloomsbury obstructed the reception of movements Read sought to assimilate – or as he saw it, welcome back – into the nation's aesthetic culture.

Why were the English so resistant to cultural modernity? Read argued that it was because a combination of puritanism and capitalism had crushed their creative spirit. As the age of capital hadn't precluded great art elsewhere, it was in the psycho-cultural identity of the English that the explanation would be found. Englishmen had two distinctive traits, Read claimed: 'common sense' and 'a sense of humour'. These were usually manifest as an eagerness to defend convention and a tendency to ridicule deviation. The result was a neurotic suppression of instinct which generated hypocrisy, coldness in love, lack of wit and an indifference to the plastic arts.[11] The new romanticism which informed Read's literary, critical, political and educational projects was intended to transform this desensitized national masculinity.

A narrative of the nation

Read refined the broad distinction between southern and northern European cultures that Wilhelm Worringer had developed in *Abstraction and Empathy* (1908) (and which he had come across when editing the *Speculations* of T. E. Hulme in the early 1920s) into a narrative of the origins and defining characteristics of English culture. Worringer's contrast between the geometrical and classical south and the vital, ultimately romantic, north provided Read with a core component of the 'foundational myth' essential to the narrative of a nation.[12]

272

In the inter-war years Read went on to produce an historical, if essentialist, account of English art, emphasizing its north European and Gothic context, and identifying peasant tradition and burlesque, an attention to nature and an emphasis on line, as its key characteristics. These were the essential features that gave the culture its imaginary continuity.

Worringer's distinctions remained basic to the story of Englishness that Read told for half a century. In *The Philosophy of Modern Art* he argued that the attraction of the English Romantic to landscape reflected

> something fundamental in English art, which is only to be understood as the contest between two philosophies of life – one native, indigenous, instinctive, the other imported, imitative, acquired. The native tradition is a Northern tradition, allied to the tradition which stretched right across Scandinavia, Russia, Northern China. The imported tradition is the Mediterranean tradition... In the North the concept of nature may differ from time to time and from place to place; it may be negative, as in Celtic art, transforming natural objects into decorative pattern, or it may be affirmative... striving to reproduce the 'dewy freshness' of the scene. But affirmative or negative, the concept is there all the time, breaking out in the margins of a manuscript, in the tracery of a stained-glass window, in stone capitals and chased silver, above all in poetry.
>
> In Latin countries, however, nature has no existence, except as the unessential background to human activities, as *décor*.[13]

An extended narrative of Englishness appeared in an essay first published in 1933 and reprinted with little amendment twenty years later: 'That style which is the first to be distinct as a style, and to be associated with a racial blend that was henceforth to be distinctively English, was formed during the so-called Anglo-Saxon period – that is to say, during the two centuries which preceded the Conquest'. He cited the Alfred Jewel, the Bayeux Tapestry, the Winchester School of illuminated manuscripts and argued 'this style has for its main characteristic a certain calligraphic or linear freedom', while acknowledging that it appeared to have been inherited from the Celts. This linear style survived the Romanesque period and migrated into the new arts of stained glass and psalter and bible illumination: all share a 'forceful linear rhythm' and all are free of 'Byzantine solemnity'.[14]

A similar tale was told in Read's eulogy for the artist Paul Nash, who died in 1946:

> One returns, for a final emphasis, to Nash's fidelity to a certain nativeness, a quality representing the historical English tradition in English art. I had often characterised this as 'lyricism': it is a quality which we find in the delicate stone tracery of an English cathedral, in the linear lightness and fantasy of English illuminated manuscripts, in the silvery radiance of our stained-glass. It returns, after an eclipse, in our interpretation of classicism – in our domestic architecture, in our

furniture and silver, in Chippendale and Wedgwood. The same quality is expressed, distinctly, in our poetry and our music. It is not a conscious tradition: it is perhaps an emanation of our soil and our climate, as inevitable and as everlastingly vernal as an English meadow.[15]

For Read, Englishness had an additional signature: burlesque. The best English prose writers demonstrated 'a delight in the forms of burlesque' that had offended many of Read's critical predecessors like Ruskin and Arnold. This 'earthy instinct', which could be found in Chaucer and Shakespeare, was destroyed by 'the moral consciousness of puritanism', and did not return until Hogarth.[16]

Read traced this line of descent further in a dismissive review of an authoritative prose anthology by Sir Arthur Quiller-Couch, King Edward VII Professor of English Literature at Cambridge and gentlemanly overseer of the early years of the new discipline:

> ... it is a spirit antithetical to the spirit so fully represented by Sir Arthur Quiller-Couch, which is the spirit of Puritanism and Quietism, of subjective joys and passive aspirations. There is, over against this spirit, sometimes woven in with it, but essentially a part of our national heritage, the spirit of open candour and of active enjoyment, the life of deeds and of zest in the sensuous quality of our flesh. Not the dreamy sensuousness of the South, but the gross *gaillardise* of the North. It might be objected that in its gross state this is not fit matter for literature, though Sir John Falstaff and the Wife of Bath are there to disprove it. But this spirit can be elevated into wit and gaiety; and though Sir Arthur has given us a fair specimen of Sterne, he leaves us aghast at the total omission of Congreve – in whom not only does this spirit attain its highest sublimation but in whom also the English tongue attains its subtlest levity of diction and fine force of aptitude. Other writers, Dryden and Berkeley, Swift and Landor, support the tradition of our national prose; only writers like Congreve and Sterne can be said to adorn it.[17]

If in Read's account the dark age of English prose lay between the fifteenth and eighteenth centuries, the visual and plastic arts underwent an even longer night. After the highpoint of the eleventh and twelfth centuries described above, Englishness was forced underground in its homeland. At first it almost disappeared beneath an imposed European style – standardized Church Gothic – and then the arts themselves were marginalized within the culture as a whole. As the European church homogenized the conventions for architecture, sculpture and other religious artefacts, Read found it difficult to track his linear motif into the sixteenth century. Worse followed: 'What English painting, English poetry, English music and dancing lost by that dreadful and vindictive plague of the spirit known as puritanism even the imagination cannot conceive', he lamented in *The Meaning of Art*.[18]

274

It is ironic that at the very moment Read confronts the British indifference to European modernism in *Art Now*,[19] he was simultaneously mourning the disappearance of the English plastic arts between the fourteenth and eighteenth centuries, a period during which he insists they were superseded by 'a more powerful and an alien mode' from Europe.[20] This ambivalence over non-indigenous prompts to modernization persists in his work, later resurfacing in his response to Americanization and transnational European cultural initiatives in the 1950s.

At one point Read dated the fall of Englishness with precision, to 1530. For the subsequent two centuries, he argues, 'the people at large seem to have maintained a puritanical indifference or even hostility towards all native art'.[21] This account is fully consistent with his more famous assertion that the art of sculpture was dead in England for four centuries, only to return with Henry Moore.[22]

The tale is often retold: 'Between the end of the Middle Ages and the beginning of the Romantic Movement, painting and sculpture in England were almost completely dead: a significant fact. Interest begins again with Gainsborough and Blake.'[23] Blake, who 'embodied consciously and consistently the original characteristics of our art',[24] was followed by a late-eighteenth-century flowering of landscape painting (Girtin, Constable, Turner), the re-emergence of line and the definition of a romantic conception of nature, in which the work of Wordsworth was central.

The English revival was short-lived. All that was recovered is 'lost to France': the initiative passes to Delacroix, the impressionists and Baudelaire while England's puritan stamp and industrial prosperity force a nineteenth-century regression to classicism.[25] Read then found little indigenous cause for celebration until Nazi aggression drove modernist artists to Britain and England became, almost literally, the solitary remnant of a liberal and humane European civilization. From this besieged but receptive English culture springs the mature work of Nash, Moore, Hepworth and Nicholson. Initially ridiculed by the art establishment, in the post-war Venice Bienniales they would represent it: Moore in 1948, Hepworth in 1950, and Nicholson in 1954.

'The poetic sensibility is especially vulnerable, especially in England', Read argued in *Annals of Innocence and Experience*.[26] His poetic canon, at least after an early attachment to Imagism, had similar contours to his account of the plastic and visual arts. In *Form in Modern Poetry* Read had argued that English poetic form was organic, generated and guaranteed by the poet's personality and integrity rather than by pre-existing conventions.

> Historically, I believe that this theory of poetry is illustrated by the main tradition of English poetry which begins with Chaucer and reaches its final culmination in Shakespeare. It is contradicted by most French poetry before Baudelaire, by the so-called classical phase of English poetry culminating in Alexander Pope, and by the late Poet Laureate [Robert Bridges]. It was re-established in England by

Wordsworth and Coleridge, developed in some degree by Browning and Gerard Manley Hopkins, and in our own day by poets like Wilfred Owen, Ezra Pound and T. S. Eliot.[27]

In *Annals of Innocence and Experience* (1940) we are offered as central the work of Blake, Donne, Browning and the Imagists. By the time of *The True Voice of Feeling* (1953) the canon has become Coleridge, Wordsworth, Keats, Hopkins, Hulme, Pound, and Eliot. Always, for Read, the watershed was Wordsworth: 'Wordsworth emancipated himself and the whole tradition of English poetry from the prevailing tyranny of wit-writing, which had lasted for about a century and a half'.[28]

In Read's narrative of the nation, English painting, sculpture, prose and poetry had been engaged in one thousand years of struggle against externally imposed conventions and, later, the indigenous temptations of puritanism and material greed. Romanticism was the moment of decisive breakthrough and national reassertion.

England's anticipatory and universal culture

During the inter-war years, Read's characteristic response to new cultural forms was to identify an English precedent, to claim that each innovation was already prefigured in the national culture, and thereby to offer it a home from home – as refugee Hampstead quite literally became for a large number of European modernists. In marked contrast to the stance he had adopted in his account of an imposed Gothic, in his own time Read dealt with European alterity by claiming that its features were already present, if repressed, within the national culture. The English had nothing to fear for they already encompassed the modern. Read's voice was therefore comforting and challenging at the very same time.

For Read, aesthetic modernity was not a leap into the unknown, but a return to Englishness. Modern art would simply restore to English eyes what 'a dreary waste of commerce, cash values and common sense' had obscured since the nineteenth century.[29]

The strategy was explicit in the way in which Read introduced surrealism to his readers in 1936: 'The evidences on which the claims of Surrealism are based are scattered through the centuries, the partial and incoherent revelations of permanent human characteristics; and nowhere are these evidences so plentiful as in England'.[30]

At different times he claimed English popular ballads, Shakespeare, Swift, Shelley, Swinburne, Lear and Walpole as precursors for surrealism. 'A nation which has produced two such superrealists as William Blake and Lewis Carroll is to the manner born', Read insisted in the catalogue for the pioneering exhibition at the New Burlington Galleries.[31]

On this account, the English had anticipated artistic modernism, and consequently each and every expression of contemporary creativity could be received as a tribute to their cultural pre-eminence. This imperial trope recurred throughout Read's work. Cézanne, after all, had simply intensified Turner's experiments with colour;[32] aspects of the Bauhaus aesthetic had been prefigured in eighteenth-century English furniture and thirteenth-century wrought-iron work;[33] surrealism, most famously, was accommodated as 'a reaffirmation of the Romantic principle';[34] abstract art was not only derived from the Celts[35] but, as 'mathematics translated into plastic material',[36] Isaac Newton also deserved some credit (he was given it in *Art Now*);[37] even existentialist concerns could be presented as a return to Coleridge.[38] What was other became, and was in truth already, ours. What was feared as external and threatening by the state and the academy was rearticulated as an inner strength of the nation's culture; everything was found a place in the anticipatory and universal outlook of the English.

In the introduction to his anthology *The English Vision*, Read's capacious cultural nationalism is at its most explicit. He celebrates 'the universal validity of this our vision. Alone of national ideals, the English ideal transcends nationality.'[39] This confidence that Englishness was not a local particularity but a socially inclusive high point of human achievement – comparable only with Ancient Greece[40] – was the foundation of Read's cultural criticism during the inter-war years.

England's manhood

For Read the crucial resource of this universal English culture was, of course, romanticism. And close to its core was a new practice of manhood.

The historical association of the nation with a vigorous but disciplined masculinity – a public-school athleticism and disdain for ideas, a rigid conventionality which suppressed instinct and feeling[41] – was explored and challenged in Read's account of Wordsworth's poetic development.

Read's identification with Wordsworth blurs culture, politics and biography. A distinctly regional voice, Wordsworth's poetry was nonetheless later enlisted to speak for England as a whole, prefiguring Read's own trajectory in the national culture. Equally, Wordsworth's dismay at the terror which followed the French Revolution prefigured the impact of the Russian Revolution, and later the Hitler–Stalin pact, on the political culture of the British left and Read himself.

In *Annals of Innocence and Experience* Read confessed that Wordsworth was 'a little too near to me. We both spring from the same yeoman stock of the Yorkshire dales, and I think I have a certain "empathetic" understanding of his personality.'[42] Read's account of Wordsworth allowed him to explore, at arm's length, the limits of his own gendered identification, its articulation with the particularities of place, region and nation, and the relationship between public and private spheres of action, the political and the personal.

In the 1929–30 Clark Lectures which formed the basis of his study, Read identified Wordsworth as 'Northern stock', itself a 'recognisable racial type, one of the most distinctive to be formed in the British Isles'. Northern stock was distinguished by 'its hardihood, its pertinacity and its fundamental seriousness'.[43]

An early passage in the book gave simultaneous expression to Read's self-image, regional pride, determinist racial theory and ambivalence about dominant forms of masculinity:

> Yorkshiremen are imaginative, like all northmen, but a matter-of-factness, a strong sense of objectivity, a faculty for vivid visualisation, keep them from being profoundly mystical. The same qualities make them wary in their actions, and canny in their reckonings. But their most extraordinary characteristic, – a characteristic with which in the process of time they have leavened almost the entire English race – is their capacity for masking their emotions. It is not a question of suppression, nor of atrophy; the normal feelings of the human being are present in more than their normal force, but banked up against this impenetrable reserve.[44]

Wordsworth is a key text in Read's exploration of the links between English national identity and restricted masculinity. Read explained that Wordsworth's poetic development closely followed his psychological development. It is no coincidence that this drama takes place at the very time during which Linda Colley has demonstrated that Britishness – predominantly a Francophobe combination of protestantism, monarchism and militarism – was forged.[45] Wordsworth was a great poet for only a decade, Read contended, for the ten years of emotional turbulence that followed a love affair in revolutionary France. In 1792 he had visited the National Assembly, fathered a love child, left its mother and then found himself unable to return to France due to the outbreak of war. The nation's greatest poetry was therefore public and private in origin: the product of the worsening and war-torn relations between the nation states of France and Britain, as they exacerbated the tensions constitutive of a typical English masculinity. 'The outraged feelings sought compensation in memories',[46] Read argued, showing that these were increasingly unconscious recollections of Wordsworth's relations with nature during his rural childhood. The achievements of this period (*The Prelude*) were followed by growing remorse and creative decline (*The Excursion*).

As a poet Wordsworth had managed to exemplify and transcend the limitations of northern-bred Englishness. He certainly had the 'racial capacity for masking the strength of his feelings'[47] that Read recognized and regretted in himself and much of the nation's manhood. But a Romantic dedication to feeling, integrity and sincerity transformed this sensibility. The result, according to Read, was a new and organic form of expression. Read deemed this process to be exemplary for the culture as a whole, and pertinent to the practice of politics as much as to poetry. In this sense Read's celebration of romanticism in general, and Wordsworth in particular, was

278

an indirect but totalizing critique of inter-war Britain and the gendered identities that sustained it.

Political Englishness

Read's notion of English manhood never fully dissociated itself from the gendered sense of glory he experienced in the trenches on the Hindenburg Line. Although the infantry was mired and dying in the French mud, as a young officer Read felt that the British Army's military units provided a better model of community than the society they sought to defend. 'Bombast and swank carry a man nowhere out here', he wrote from the trenches. 'In England they are everything.'[48] The experience was a benchmark against which to measure the political culture back home.

The social upheavals that followed the war resulted in an extension of Britain's liberal democracy, and the partition of Ireland, overseen by a 'capacious liberalism' which gave a new importance to the state.[49] The terms of this settlement embodied a political Englishness with which Read was never able to reconcile himself.

Read took his political bearings from an anti-statist left in Britain (Morris, Carpenter and the Guild Socialists) and the traditions of Continental anarchism (Kropotkin, Proudhon and Bakunin). He quickly realized that the new forms of collectivist liberalism based on the state fell far short of his libertarian aspirations, although it was almost two decades before he spelled this out and declared an anarchist affiliation.[50]

'Political faith and action could not be evoked in England,' he wrote, retrospectively, of the years immediately following the First World War.[51] A later and complementary observation on the stability of the national political culture appeared in the opening pages of *The Green Child*: 'Earthquakes, of course, never occur in England'.[52]

Read was unable to replicate his cultural strategy in the sphere of politics. Despite his belief that liberty, justice and toleration 'had found a firmer embodiment in our customs and institutions than anywhere else',[53] it was virtually impossible to represent political Englishness as accommodatory or prefigurative of political modernity, and it was nowhere near as easy to mobilize opinion against the state as to stage an attack on the nation's aesthetic conservatism. Only rarely did Read attempt to offer a British plinth – such as Edward Carpenter – for the edifice of continental anarchism.[54] Prevented from identifying continuities, he was forced to construct social alterities.

The Green Child offered two imaginary alternatives to Britain's liberal–imperial democracy: the benevolent dictatorship of Roncador, an efficient, non-industrialized and secular republic from which usury had been abolished; and the open hierarchy of a subterranean, Aristotelian Utopia in which sages contemplated rock crystal and order. Although Roncador's citizens suffered none of the deprivations that afflicted depressed inter-war Britain, for Read the nation's 'moral flaccidity'[55] was enough to justify its dismissal and the flight of his protagonist. The underground society in which crystallographers worshipped order was aesthetically attractive but also lifeless and insular.[56] The distance between these two social imaginaries and the British real was immense. Even though they fell short of Read's shifting aspirations, both visions were far without the confines of the British political settlement and unlikely to engage with anything recognizable or feasible in the public sphere.

Read's critique of political Englishness questioned representative democracy itself, but had characteristically little to say about the Union. In Read's eyes, the United Kingdom was managed by 'a select club of old Wykehamists' who ran the Civil Service and dominated the Westminster system.[57] He therefore aspired to remove, not improve, Britain's liberal democratic structures. This required 'federal devolution' to workers' syndicates.[58]

In a wartime reaffirmation of his longstanding Guild Socialist principles, he insisted that there were three conditions for democracy: production for use not profit, giving according to ability and receiving on the basis of need, and workers' control of industry.[59]

Although his views placed him well outside the political mainstream, when the occasion called for it Read accepted the splitting required by his identification as an anarchist and as an Englishman. An indigenous civil libertarian tradition was cited when the editors of *War Commentary* were jailed under the Defence Regulations in 1945. In *Freedom: Is It a Crime?* Read characterized late wartime Britain as a 'fascist plutocracy' and reaffirmed a traditional English radicalism: 'I do not speak to you now as an anarchist: I speak to you as an Englishman, as one proud to follow in the tradition of Milton and Shelley – the tradition of all those poets and philosophers who have given us the proud right to claim freedom of speech and the liberty of unlicensed printing'.[60]

For the second time in his life Read hoped that the impact of a world war would clear the ground for national renewal. Picking his way through the rubble strewn about the institutional pillars of the nation after a bombing raid in 1941, he felt certain that a new beginning was imminent:

> The endless and intricate structures of a civilisation were falling down. It was not merely the jewellers' and furriers' shops, the workmen's tenements and the warehouses which I had passed: it was also the Bank of England and the Royal Academy, the Church of England and the *Times*. These institutions, too, were among the ruins, and if they survived at all, they would have to be rebuilt in a new style.[61]

His hopes came to nothing. Representative democracy endured and with bipartisan consent the scope, the rights and the responsibilities of the state expanded even further. Witnessing the stability of British political institutions for the second time,

Read acknowledged the lifelong political impasse and redirected his attention to educational reform and the founding of new cultural institutions like the ICA (Institute of Contemporary Arts). But he never wholly abandoned the search for alternatives to political Englishness and the particular form taken by British liberal democracy. His continuing quest took him to Mao's China in 1959, where he admired the agricultural communes, and to a Cultural Congress in Cuba in the year of his death.[62] A neo-liberal movement within the British political class began to dismantle the structures he detested only a decade later. If Read had lived, the difference between his libertarianism and theirs would have been only too evident, compelling a return to engaged political discourse.

England and its others

The post-war political settlement unravelled because Britain was being reconfigured by a globalized economy and cultural modernity, a process which has forced modernizing governments in Europe to choose between a replication of the American neo-liberal response or participation in a European trading bloc. In the case of Britain the latter option would have strengthened regional structures and weakened the Westminster government.

During the 1980s Britain took the former course. Invocations of a homogeneous but distinctive British people – a version of Read's 'Greater England' – and the sovereign state were a hallmark of Thatcherism. Their intensity increased as the evidence of their fictionality – the proliferation of national and regional identities, globalized cultural markets, the reduced competence of the state, transnational legislation – has accumulated. As a result, a second aspect of Read's work – his emphasis on decentralization – has new salience.

The identity of the nation has always been defined in relationship to other states, cultures and peoples. During the half century spanned by Read's writings there were radical and significant changes in the way in which he delineated cultures distinct from and thereby constitutive of the boundaries of Anglo-British or 'Greater English' national identity.

The process by which European modernists embraced that which imperial western cultures had differentiated themselves from, the so-called primitivism of non-European and colonial cultures, incorporating their codes, artefacts and images into avant-garde symbolic practices, is now increasingly understood.

> As Western modernity and progress has been made possible through the exploitation of the colonised, so Modernism… developed through disaffection with the societal effects of modernity and turned for creative rejuvenation to the so-called primitive cultures of others. In other words, the non-European has never been outside the modernist enterprise; he and she have always been its invisible and unacknowledged centre.[63]

Read's early historical surveys of art and civilization – *The Meaning of Art*, *Art and Society* – serviced and popularized this process. Both texts are clearly – if unconsciously – colonial. Read's pronounced humanism led him to deny that non-European cultures were in any way outside, subordinated to, or significantly distinct from the English experience. 'Humanity does not change from Ithaca to Yorkshire, from one millennium to another', he insisted.[64]

By constructing Etruscan, Mexican and English art as one and the same activity, as the common creation of a universal humanity whose ideals were best expressed in Greater England's cultural vision, Read both reproduced and obscured the armature of empire.

Acknowledging that Southern European, South American and African artefacts had all had an impact on British cultural practice, he maintained that there was an essential English core which provided continuity to all the hybrid forms which had evolved.

> Such influences are like injections of a drug: they act as a temporary stimulus and restore the body to health. We cannot deny their necessity nor deprecate their usefulness. But they are shocks that should be absorbed into the main blood-stream: they should not persist as a habit or a fashion. The history of art shows that the art of any particular region always tends to revert to a regional norm – to a mode of sensibility and style of expression determined, we must assume, by ethnic and geographic factors... if art's vitality comes from the cross-breeding of styles, its stability comes from roots that grow deep into a native soil.[65]

Although no culture could remain an island, Read was confident that national particularity would never fully dissolve beneath the waves of global change. His stance had a markedly determinist, and ultimately devolutionary, bent. 'We cannot escape our mental climates, for they are in a literal sense the creation of our prevailing winds and the chemistry of our soils', he argued.[66]

Towards the end of the Second World War he urged Britain to draw on this essential strength. 'Regeneration will begin at the bottom, in the family, in the school, in the workshop and in the parish and the borough. Action will be regional rather than national...', he affirmed in *The Politics of the Unpolitical*.[67] During these years, his own focus narrowed to just one of these loci of regeneration. The encouragement of change in the philosophy and practice of education rapidly became Read's principal political strategy.[68]

Between the early 1930s and the late 1950s, there is a related transformation in the tropes that dominate Read's account of the national culture. In the post-war years English – by then usually British – culture is represented as besieged and fragile, and no longer capacious, prefigurative or accommodatory as identified in his earlier work. The Anglo-British are urged to return to their local resources and reject what is being thrust upon them by European politics and transatlantic cultural markets.

282

The political and cultural unity of Europe would not endure, he argued, 'unless it focuses the diversity and multiplicity of local and individual forces'.[69] By the mid-1960s 'Europe is morally bankrupt and mentally exhausted', and Read, dismissive of this 'artificial hegemony of nations', reaffirms the molecular and localized process of renewal that had become his trademark.[70]

When Read wrote these words, the process of European intergration was no more than embryonic. The cultural and political influence of the United States was far more pervasive. Read was not anti-American by instinct, at least not in the sphere of prose. He had never failed to acknowledge – and thereby incorporate – what he called, after Henry James, the 'big Anglo-Saxon total'.[71] He had even argued that Hawthorne and Hemingway were the true legatees of the Bible, Bunyan and Swift, and by far the best exponents of English narrative prose. And as late as 1962 he was still happy to acknowledge that Americans were the better English poets.[72]

Read became assimilated to an older cultural settlement – and alienated a new generation of British artists – as a result of the resistance he mounted to Americanization in the visual arts. After an early burst of enthusiasm for De Kooning, he classified abstract expressionism as a form of 'nihilism'. Pop art he dismissed as 'a highly sophisticated disorganisation of commonplace imagery' that was 'amateurish, flippant, vulgar' and the shadow of European Dada.[73] By 1966, firmly ensconced in the upper tier of the art establishment – a knight and a trustee of the Tate Gallery – Read could be found objecting to the purchase of a Lichtenstein, just as his predecessors had once excluded Cézanne. A national culture wishing to retain its distinction briefly deployed Read – who had made inter-war modernity appear traditional, and whose earlier dissent had a reassuringly patriotic overtone – as a guardian of order and a new orthodoxy based on Moore, Hepworth, Nicholson, Pasmore and Sutherland.

The waves of global exchange were not halted, of course. In a late moment of panic, during what David Gervais has called 'the aftermath of England',[74] Read identified 'incoherence, insensitivity, brutality and privacy' as the most significant features of contemporary culture.[75] Towards the end of his life, Englishness had finally become a fugitive vision.

Herbert Read's work is an early and ambitious attempt to give the diverse subjects of the British post-imperial state a new sense of national identity and worth. But neither the capacious cultural nationalism he fashioned during the inter-war years, nor his later melancholy – the 'vesicles of delight / lost ever ever ever' for which he laments in the poem 'basic black'[76] – represent sustainable responses for our own period. The real legacy is the scope and depth of his enquiry into Englishness, his passionate engagement with a plurality of cultural forms, and his alertness to the gendered nature of national identity and critique of remote but omnipotent forms of government. These investigations prefigure, and help prepare the ground for, the reconsideration compelled today.

Notes

1   'basic black', in Herbert Read, *Collected Poems* (London: Sinclair-Stevenson, n.d.), p. 263.
2   Stuart Hall, 'Negotiating Caribbean Identities', *New Left Review*, no. 209 (January/February 1995), p. 4.
3   Stuart Hall, 'The Rise of the Representative/Interventionist State', in Gregor MacLennan, David Held and Stuart Hall (eds), *State and Society in Contemporary Britain* (Cambridge: Polity Press, 1984), pp. 7–49.
4   Herbert Read, *The True Voice of Feeling: Studies in English Romantic Poetry* (London: Faber and Faber, 1953). p. 151.
5   Which Read quoted at length in *The English Vision: An Anthology* (London: Eyre and Spottiswoode, 1933; repr. London: George Routledge and Sons, 1939). All subsequent references will be to the second edition.
6   Herbert Read, 'English Art', *Burlington Magazine*, vol. 63 (December 1933), pp. 243–76; reprinted in Herbert Read, *The Philosophy of Modern Art: Collected Essays* (London: Faber and Faber, 1952), pp. 249–68.
7   George Woodcock, *Herbert Read: The Stream and the Source* (London: Faber and Faber, 1972), p. 26.
8   Read, *The English Vision*, p. x.
9   Read, *The Philosophy of Modern Art*, p. 69.
10 Herbert Read, *To Hell with Culture: Democratic Values Are New Values* (London: Kegan Paul, Trench Trubner and Co., 1941), p. 12.
11 Herbert Read, 'Why We English Have No Taste', in *Poetry and Anarchism* (London: Faber and Faber, 1938), pp. 31–40.
12 Stuart Hall, 'The Question of Cultural Identity', in Stuart Hall, David Held and Tony McGrew (eds), *Modernity and its Futures* (Cambridge: Polity Press, 1992), p. 294.
13 Read, *The Philosophy of Modern Art*, p. 80.
14 Read, 'English Art', *The Philosophy of Modern Art*, pp. 250–52.
15 Read, *The Philosophy of Modern Art*, p. 194.
16 Read, 'English Art', *The Philosophy of Modern Art*, pp. 252–55.
17 Herbert Read, 'English Prose', in *A Coat of Many Colours: Occasional Essays* (London: George Routledge and Sons, 1945), p. 99.
18 Herbert Read, *The Meaning of Art* (London: Faber and Faber, rev. edn, 1968), p. 128.
19 Herbert Read, *Art Now: An Introduction to the Modern Theory of Painting and Sculpture* (London: Faber and Faber, 1933).
20 Read, 'English Art', *The Philosophy of Modern Art*, p. 254.
21 Herbert Read, *Art and Society* (London: Faber and Faber, rev. edn, 1955), p. 139.
22 Read, *The Meaning of Art*, p. 252.
23 Read, *The Philosophy of Modern Art*, p. 125.
24 Read, 'English Art', *The Philosophy of Modern Art*, p. 260.
25 Ibid., pp. 267–68.
26 Herbert Read, *Annals of Innocence and Experience* (London : Faber and Faber, 1946 edn), p. 92.
27 Herbert Read, *Form in Modern Poetry* (London: Sheed and Ward, 1932), p. 41.
28 Ibid., p. 43.
29 Read, *A Coat of Many Colours*, p. 195.
30 Read, *The Philosophy of Modern Art*, p. 106.
31 Herbert Read, 'Introduction' to *The International Surrealist Exhibition* (London: New Burlington Galleries, 1936), pp. 12–13.

32 Read, 'English Art', *The Philosophy of Modern Art*, p. 267.

33 Herbert Read, *Art and Industry: The Principles of Industrial Design* (London: Faber and Faber, 1934), pp. 60, 84. And see David Thistlewood, 'Herbert Read: A New Vision of Art and Industry', in Benedict Read and David Thistlewood (eds), *Herbert Read: A British Vision of World Art* (Leeds: Leeds City Art Galleries, 1993), pp. 95–101.

34 Read, *The Philosophy of Modern Art*, p. 109.

35 Read, *Art Now*, p. 104.

36 Read, *The Philosophy of Modern Art*, p. 87.

37 Read, *Art Now*, p. 61.

38 Herbert Read, *Existentialism, Marxism and Anarchism* (London: Freedom Press, 1949), p. 5.

39 Read, *The English Vision*, pp. vi–vii.

40 Ibid., p. xi.

41 For the association of English and masculinity, see Philip Dodd, 'Englishness and the National Culture', in Robert Colls and Philip Dodd (eds), *Englishness: Politics and Culture 1880–1920* (London: Croom Helm, 1986), pp. 4–7.

42 Read, *Annals of Innocence and Experience*, p. 217.

43 Herbert Read, *Wordsworth* (London: Faber and Faber, 1949 edn), p. 36.

44 Ibid., pp. 37–38.

45 Linda Colley, *Britons: Forging the Nation, 1701–1837* (New Haven: Yale University Press, 1992).

46 Read, *Wordsworth*, p. 49.

47 Ibid., p. 38.

48 Herbert Read, *The Contrary Experience* (London: Faber and Faber, 1963), p. 97.

49 See Robert Colls, 'Englishness and the Political Culture', in Colls and Dodd, *Englishness*, pp. 29–61.

50 Herbert Read, 'The Necessity of Anarchism', in *Adelphi*, (1937), vol. 13, pp. 458–63, and vol. 14, pp. 12–18, 44–48; reprinted in Read, *Poetry and Anarchism*, pp. 66–98.

51 Read, *The Contrary Experience*, p. 68.

52 Herbert Read, *The Green Child* (London: The Grey Walls Press, 1945), p. 9.

53 Read, *The English Vision*, p. vi.

54 Herbert Read, *The Cult of Sincerity* (London: Faber and Faber, 1968), p. 76.

55 Read, *The Green Child*, p. 105.

56 See Read's comment that 'The realisation of a rational utopia leads to the death of society' in 'The Utopian Mentality' in *Freedom*, 23 December 1950, reprinted in David Goodway (ed.), *Herbert Read: A One Man Manifesto and Other Writings for Freedom Press* (London: Freedom Press, 1994), p. 152.

57 Read, *Poetry and Anarchism*, p. 84.

58 Ibid., p. 86.

59 Read, *To Hell with Culture*, p. 19.

60 Reprinted in Goodway, *Herbert Read: A One Man Manifesto*, pp. 96–99.

61 Herbert Read, *The Politics of the Unpolitical* (London: Routledge, 1943), p. 74–75.

62 Letters written during his trip to China appear in *A Tribute to Herbert Read, 1893–1968* (Bradford: Bradford Art Galleries and Museums, 1975), pp. 43–49.

63 Jean Fisher, 'Editorial', *Third Text*, nos. 8/9 (1989), pp. 3–4.

64 Read, *The Contrary Experience*, p. 328.

65 Herbert Read, *Contemporary British Art* (Harmondsworth: Penguin Books, rev. edn, 1968), p. 50.

66 Ibid., p. 49.

67 Read, *The Politics of the Unpolitical*, p. 143.

68 In *Education through Art* (London: Faber and Faber, 1943), *The Education of Free Men* (London:

Freedom Press, 1944), *Education for Peace* (London: Routledge and Kegan Paul, 1950) and *The Redemption of the Robot: My Encounter with Education through Art* (New York: Trident Press, 1966).

69 Read, *Contemporary British Art*, p. 49.

70 Read, *The Redemption of the Robot*, pp. 207–08 and 228–32.

71 Read, *A Coat of Many Colours*, p. 282.

72 'American Bards and British Reviewers', in Herbert Read, *Selected Writings: Poetry and Criticism* (London: Faber and Faber, 1963), pp. 198–216.

73 Read, *Contemporary British Art*, pp. 47–48.

74 David Gervais, *Literary Englands: Versions of 'Englishness' in Modern Writing* (Cambridge: Cambridge University Press, 1993), pp. 185–219.

75 Herbert Read, *The Origins of Form in Art* (London: Thames and Hudson, 1965), p. 177.

76 Read, 'basic black'.

Herbert Read and Essential Modernism:
Or the Loss of an Image of the World

JERALD ZASLOVE

> Through all the mutations of these years I have relied on a weapon which I found
> in my hand as soon as I was compelled to abandon my innocent vision and fight
> against the despairs of experience. This weapon is adamantine and invincible, like
> the sickle which at the beginning of legendary time Earth gave to Cronus and with
> which he mutilated the divine father. The Furies were born from the drops of
> blood which fell in that fray.[1]

I The loss of modernism

GESTURES of loss. Forces of failed reparations. How do monuments to
modernism fall in England? What is essential in modernism in England? The
reception of the now largely forgotten Herbert Read is paradigmatic of the
failure of classic British literary modernism to develop an historical consciousness
about itself in relation to modernism in art, where the struggle to understand the
culture of capitalism and the destruction of experience is left in the wake of the demi-
urge – the ideal of progress. Our distance from the battles over modernism is too
great. Or too close. Without reflecting upon the politics of those who had moral
authority in the struggle to define the essential in modern experience, the distant
horizon is dominated only by the ruins. A return to the 'political unconscious' of
modernist writers and artists will get us nowhere – if we choose to follow a T. J.
Clark or a Frederic Jameson – unless it is back to the inwardness of a latter-day
Kierkegaardian sacrificial surrender to the world as it is, or to the fantasy that revolutions will change anything but the consumption of more goods.[2]

Inside this story of the twists and turns in modernism is an even older story, of a
cultural criticism in England that became the fellow traveller of art only to betray
classic British romantic radicalism in its anarcho-libertarian turn by the shift to a
broad, almost meaningless use of 'culture' inspired by Matthew Arnold. Arnold's
melancholic fear of industrialism gave cultural authority for a uniquely British anti-
romanticism (Leavis, Orwell, Richards) which endured and tolerated democratic
movements in the 1930s and 1940s without linking romanticism to either populist
movements in the arts or to the emancipatory modernism of figures like Read.
Romantic revolutionaries such as Herbert Read followed the romantics' revolt

against cultural philistinism as far as he could, but then watched, twisting and turning between on the one hand an anarchistic Sancho Panza-like journey of the simple life and on the other a Kierkegaardian existential anarchist vision of the individual who is opposed to all forms of historicism in the arts. As modernist cultural criticism became haunted by the recognition of its own failure to articulate a politics of artistic creation in the world of classical, free-market liberalism that survived the failures of revolutionary movements to change the social structure in England and continental Europe, so Herbert Read's star rose and fell with the incapacity of democratic and socialist movements to link their emancipatory critique of soulless modernity to an aesthetic modernism that would not reify that soullessness. In the face of British welfare culture, the latent humiliations of a class-bound culture, and Bloomsbury legacies, Read's art philosophy would always seem as though he was arguing for progress in the arts while denying any historical legitimacy to progressive social movements.

As modernism slides into mass culture and scholastic dead-ends, one can ask whether Herbert Read predicted its demise, indeed lived its history as a lost cause. Read in this light, we can say that modernism subsumed its own failure because it lived in the epoch of capitalism in which it was grounded, not because it failed to recognize its progressive turn to an emancipatory world view. Even a casual reading of the classics of literary modernism read against the grain of the decline of modernism reminds one of how a sense of irreparable loss marks Read's struggle to understand the furies that haunted his image of the world. In Read's case only an informed anarchism could serve as an adamantine sickle cutting into the new Gothic terror of modernity. But modernism as an artistic depiction of fragmented, traditional belief systems had to go beyond the soullessness of modern culture. It would have to plunge into the depths of the will to self-creation. If art was going to vanish into the aesthetical ash-can of a civilization in decline, the individual would not be far behind. For Read modernism was above all about this extreme separation of the inner world of the creative self from the public world which appropriated the self in the name of social ends beyond the control of the individual. The loss of empathy *and* the inability of the abstract forms of modern art to accommodate the loss of a social vision were represented by the alliance of the industrial bourgeoisie with the state. The bourgeois form of capital just magnified the renunciation of social responsibility by the modern citizen. The deterioration of communal and social responsibility framed Read's ideal world-historical vision: to repair the break inside art's capacity to *re-present* the deepest turmoils in the social. But there was a deeper dialectics in the loss of the will to self-creation which emanated from the *inside* of the art work. This meant that modernism's discomfort with eternal aesthetic essences forced art to retreat from aesthetics as such. So here he had to face a paradox: the struggle both for an aesthetics based on fragmented experience and a philosophy of art that would make that experience conscious in a world locked into reification.

The politics of being modern meant seeking the key to understanding the totality of the modern age which had suffered a radical decentralization since feudalism.

In this respect Read found himself caught between ideals of progress in the use of the arts for social critique and his longing for experiential immediacy and emotional depth revealed in the technics of art styles. He resolved this modernist dilemma by going to the origins of modernist aesthetics. Our repression of that origin is symptomatic of a world that cannot go beyond the hegemonic powers – a kind of pathological 'narcissism' – that has turned industrial labour into a measure of the liberal, laissez-faire, public sphere.

The failure to understand how and why the republican revolutions of the nineteenth century had failed led Read to the obvious conclusion that the ugly ruins of modern life had penetrated to the core of modernity. Modernist art criticism and literary criticism could not fall into forgetfulness about the origins and evolution of capitalism. In this chapter I place Herbert Read's work at the problematic core of any rethinking of the culturally produced aporias and misrecognitions in British modernism's struggle to understand the many-levelled nature of modernity as a rational, and rationalizing, form of enlightenment. I take one principle as the guiding one over the many that can govern discussions of modernism: that the recovery of experience in the face of the grotesque and phantasmagoric face of modernity is the object of Read's quest – namely that the defining objective of modern approaches to art and literature must look toward the recovery of the experiential world commensurable with an ethics of the individual who is lost within the pseudo-public world we live in. No matter what the cultural politics of philosophers of art in the twentieth century – the spectrum from the right Heideggerians to left Habermasians – all have to frame the question of modern art around the question of alienation in modernism. All talk of our living in a post-metaphysical age pales before the actual struggles of humans to define their world. As the attacks on metaphysical thinking have become a riotous babel the critical effort to revive a materialist aesthetics by containing art within the confines of the democracies we live in must recognize the attempt of the older modernism to transcend this form of inner reconciliation with power.[3]

For the now archaic artists and cultural revolutionaries like Herbert Read, capitalism became truly visible after the First World War when the hope for an emancipatory present was appropriated in the name of the mega-state systems and monopoly capital. The new world was a total social process and any thinking about modern art had to confront that foundational totality. The treaties written after the First World War were grand gestures, characterized by Read in his seminal essay 'Essential Communism' (1938) as a 'slow motion farce'.[4] This farce determined for him the loss of a public world expressed in his philosophical anarchism.

Disenfranchised by his lack of residence in any fixed constituency, wandering faithlessly in the no-man's land of his imagination, the poet cannot, without renouncing his essential function, come to rest in the bleak conventicles of a political party. It is not his pride that keeps him outside; it is really his humility, his devotion to the complex wholeness of humanity – in the precise sense of the word, his magnanimity.[5]

This universalism is not a call for liberal humanism nor a plaintive nostalgia for an art disengaged from politics. That would do little more than justify T. S. Eliot's Christian stoicism, or Pound's scornful bullying of anyone who came out for the Spanish anti-fascists. Eliot's anxieties about art and power turned to Christian posturing, and were for Read symptomatic of resistance to the *inevitable* politics inside modernism. This is typified by Eliot's response to a call 'to take sides on the Spanish War', which other writers and poets signed.[6] It is clear that, for Read, the end of the First World War meant the beginning of the Second World War, which he saw emerging from the way British society had turned its back on the Marxist socialist traditions on the continent and Luddite romanticism. His scramble to rescue aesthetic reality after the Second World War was a continuation of his agitational modernism which was embedded in the surrealist radicalism of the 1930s. The aesthetical communism of the 1930s, before it was inundated by a history that reproduced itself in the Second World War, was the basis of his modernism:

> ... the world of history facing a particular generation, which is the world of nature renewed again and again, always without history... When the magical validity of history disappears, as it has done in our time, then the renewal must come from within the self, from this autonomous instinct of origination. That, I believe, is the spiritual and metaphysical significance of the modern movement in art. It is the image, the paradigm, of a new reality. But it does not yet constitute a culture – how could it?[7]

Read's distaste for 'culture' and his rejection of liberalism as an adequate philosophy was based on the failure of the revolutions and the complicitous traditions in art that carried out the legacy of compromise that denied what was happening in reality:

> Only in Russia there was a difference – a withdrawal from the scramble, a struggle for a new order of some sort. But from the depths of imposed ignorance and hopelessness, it seemed impossible to believe in the reality and permanence of that revolution.[8]

Read writes that 'my difficulty then was to find an immediate active role for the intellectual in politics'. His 'only guide', whose authority he later reconsidered, was the conservative, Julien Benda, an ambiguous guide to be sure, who deplored, not the treason of the intellectuals, but their disappearance.[9] In Europe this would mean the entire intelligentsia who conformed to state power, but in England it meant those cultural interpreters and citizen educators who were even afraid to think of them-selves as 'intellectuals', and who would certainly not associate their fate with artists or writers. Not even Trotsky's sympathy toward the artists' and intellectuals' predilection to 'limp after reality' can solve the problem of the avant-garde artist's ignorance of the economic realities and conditions:

> It is another way of saying that the intellectual cannot avoid the economic condi-tions of his time; he cannot ignore them – for they will not ignore him. In one way or another he must compound with circumstances. But to describe the exact nature of the dilemma, a metaphor more elaborate than Trotsky's is necessary. Reality is manifold: a magnetic field with lines of force passing through all points in the compass of human sensibility.[10]

Read's project, which was to dissent from the prevailing culturally sanctioned, decorative illusions about the place of art in England, was very clear: capitalism was social death and class misery; it had taken us to the brink of nothingness; art was a 'form' of legitimation of revolution; a new aesthetics and ethics had to be derived out of the new consciousness-raising cross-breeding of art forms. This meant that all forms of legitimation were brought into question, and it was this tendency that repre-sented the underground tradition in English literature. Genuine art created the terms of its own legitimacy by questioning whether art could be assimilated into culture. Modern art could itself find redemption only in its capacity to repair the damages to the public world. In a world where the self-repair of the subject seemed to be lost in the swamp of ideologies, art as the great destructive refusal could no longer remain simply caught on the problematic horns of 'realism versus romanticism' or of minority art versus élite art. Even literary criticism had to be eschewed for the new cause of the convergence of the arts and the visual literacy implicit in modern art. This new materialism gave the artist a range of powers equal to the powers of liberal democracies.[11] But art could no longer knock on the doors of English 'culture', but would have to exist outside culture. The outsider could never be an insider, unless as a counterfeiter. Later Read would use the arguments against culture against the commodity basis of design and aesthetics: art could not knock on the post-Second-World-War pop-art door without emasculating itself into a cultic movement leading to nowhere – except to self-destruction – and the riskless society that risked nothing less than its own destruction by leaving the welfare state to the culturists who did not understand how the radical roots of aesthetic education would benefit a sick civilization.[12]

II Toward a philosophy of art-making

In *The Forms of Things Unknown* (1960) Read once again found himself grappling with the forms of the imaginary in an effort to correct his failure to link aesthetics to social movements. But where his 1930s deep association with the ideals of 'essential communism' and anarchism had provided the stage for his appropriation of their demiurgic energies and semantic potential to link art to an idea of technical and artistic progression in consciousness, after the war these energies were kept fired by his continuous assault on philistine culture and his advocacy of the unconscious in the creative process. Through his consistent defence of the unconscious in artistic practices in works like *The Art of Sculpture* (1956) or *Art and Alienation* (1967), Read distanced himself from the arguments that made autonomy and engagement in art into false dichotomies. Admitting to himself that his writing could be inconsistently theoretical, he coded his 'essential communism' in world-historical alienation theory that fought against behaviourism in criticism and the commodification of aesthetics in pop hedonism. During the Second World War his sensual and abstract attraction to vanguardism was never abandoned, but informed his disputes over abstract art; references to Marx or anarchism would have to be coded, unsystematic, and based on artists' specific practices.

After the war Read used many sources to extend the semantic-contextual field of 'essential' aesthetic communism of *Art Now* (1933) into modernist art practices of history now.[13] For example, Martin Buber's theories of 'the instinct of origination' reinforced his claims made in *Education through Art* (1943)[14] – a work which annoyed T. S. Eliot – and *The Grass Roots of Art* (1947),[15] namely that human beings make things, *including thing-representations in the unconscious*, and that where creation in religion might arise out of non-being, creation in art arises out of 'intensely experienced action', similar in quality to children's 'intellectual passion in producing speech not as something they have taken over', but – and Read cites Martin Buber –

> '... with the headlong powers of utter newness: sound after sound tumbles out of them, rushing from the vibrating throat past the trembling lips into the world's air, and the whole of the little vital body vibrates and trembles, too, shaken by a bursting shower of selfhood'... This would serve as a description of the new painting, the painting that is a possessing rather than a picturing, a projection of intangible and elusive images that seen to have meaning in terms of feeling. There is an instinct, says Buber, which, 'no matter to what power it is raised, never becomes greed, because it is not directed to "having," but only to doing; which alone among the instincts cannot lead its subject away to invade the realm of other lives. Here is pure gesture which does not snatch the world to itself, but expresses itself to the world.'

For Read this neo-Kantian philosophy of dialogism could become a cornerstone for a politics and aesthetics of international modernism:

> Pure gesture that does not snatch the world to itself, but expresses itself to the world – what a perfect definition of this latest phase of modern art. But gesture

is not enough, Buber goes on to say – and this is the whole point of his address. 'There are two forms, indispensable for the building of true human life, to which the originative instinct, left to itself, does not lead and cannot lead: to sharing in an undertaking and to entering into mutuality.' This raises the whole problem of communication, which is vital to the ethical consciousness; as an originator man is solitary. An education, says Buber: (and by implication an art) based on the instinct of origination would prepare a new human solitariness which would be the most painful of all. Art must lead beyond the arts, to an awareness and a share of mutuality.[16]

The most painful loss of all, the loss of mutuality of community, the forgetting of what was lost, and the overcoming of that immiserated solitariness requires a new sensual aesthetics that overcomes this capitalism of and in the instincts. Here Read's philosophy of artistic convergence is grounded, but not trapped, in the public world of alienated modernity. To those who see modernism and modernity only as a trap, the avant-garde modernist interlude between the wars will be seen as the false or failed materialistic democratic politics. That post-Cold-War democratic politics are lionized now through an optimism of the will (through Gramscian or Althusserean cultural studies) in an effort to build a mass base contributes to the problem of failing adequately to assess Read's vanguardism. Symptomatically, Read's name does not appear in the programmatic *Realism, Rationalism, Surrealism: Art Between the Wars* which is the basis of an Open University course on art in society, even though Read was the champion of non-academic, non-canonical art *practices* and excoriated the art-hating bourgeoisie.[17]

Throughout the 1930s Read recognized that the Marxian dialectic cannot be applied to art without sacrificing the artistic *mind* itself – mind in its Hegelian sense of spirit or consciousness. As evidence for his heretical anarchist and Marxian position, different interpretations of Picasso became touchstones for understanding the will to self-creation in modernism. Read used two examples to show the contradictions within the new Marxist aesthetics as the basis of modern art: Carl Einstein, a radical German anarcho-Marxist, who was associated with Eugene Jolas and Paris- and Berlin-based international movements in art, and who saw in Braque and African art the basis of a new collective sensibility; and Max Raphael, a maverick German art historian, whose Marxist critique of Picasso identified three critical phases in Picasso – negroid, antique and medieval.[18] The modernist search for the objective basis for art in 'primitive' mimesis was couched in Marxist materialist economics. This allowed Raphael to see in Picasso's styles the consummation of phases of bourgeois reaction to art and how devoid the bourgeoisie were of any awareness of how the class struggle forced changes in the styles of art. Later Read came to terms with Raphael's Marxist aesthetics in his preface to Raphael's *The Demands of Art* (1968).[19] He continued to struggle over the significance of Picasso, and provided his own critique of Picasso in *The Forms of Things Unknown*.

While I cannot in this chapter do justice to the arguments which accompanied Read's inner turmoil in his search for a philosophy of art that was also a politics and an aesthetics that could legitimate modernism, arguments he invoked too often in piecemeal fashion,[20] any elucidation of his anarchist aesthetics must come to terms with the immanent totality of his thought, which some critics have located in Read's movement from Freud to Jung. Read's notion of a 'duplex' aesthetic unconscious that is also partisan to a communal public sphere is mediated in particular by his critique of Picasso's monumentalism and exploitative visual genius. Here I will only note that Read's restlessness toward authoritarian monumentality of all kinds is not only connected to his anti-authoritarian personality, but more significantly to a search for the relationship of the 'primitive' to the abstract image. His forays into the ethnographical basis of a social history of art enabled him to see how the elimination of the human image in the unconscious only reflected the struggle *and taboo* that the unconscious directs against the representation of the human subject to which we are erotically – and often violently – attached: *abstraction was part of the dialogical field of representations which could contribute to making art a force in historical change*.[21] Monumentality in Picasso, or in the architecture of industrial capitalism, is suspect because it masks asocial behaviour: 'As for the British Empire... its characteristic architecture is the industrial slum'.[22] Britain is not only the home of nationalism and racial imperialism but its cultural pessimism and philistinism feeds off the narcissisms of monumentalism and heroism. Read's post-war resistance to his earlier Nietzschean, mythopoetic and apocalyptical position of self-construction, based on irrationalism, is itself an important aspect of his critique of the monumental in Picasso. Read's use of psychoanalysis allowed him to hold to an ontology of the creative process and the psychology of the creative unconscious, while at the same time seeing the unconscious as a mimetic representation of an alienated culture's struggle for self-knowledge. Read's early interest in the schizoid nature of our culture as reflected in the artistic processes of Wordsworth and Coleridge – 'the renegade type is a born schizoid'[23] – is carried through into his research on the psychological basis of modern abstract painting.

Picasso's work exposes the neuroses and psychoses of culture but artistically it must carry the burden of that proof. David Thistlewood characterizes Read's struggle over the question of Picasso or Moore as explainable by Read's change to a Jungian model of the unconscious from the Freudian model.[24] While it is appropriate for Freudians to question Read's growing fascination with the inner world of archetypal forms, it is his desexualizing of the *Minotauromachy* that reveals a problem in need of discussion.[25] Read comes back to a Freudian psychoanalysis in the essay 'Psychoanalysis and the Problem of Aesthetic Value' (in *The Forms of Things Unknown*) by continuing to struggle with non-representational symbols as the key to understanding the break with representation and mimesis in the service of the morally conditioned Superego. The reality principle is understood in terms of survival within capitalism's capacity to control the mimetic or the representation of the world. Read returns, as do Herbert Marcuse in *Eros and Civilization* (1955) and T. W. Adorno in *Aesthetic Theory* (1970), to an aesthetics that argues that the unconscious in art can be understood as a reification of capitalist alienation as the bourgeois phase comes into a mass-cultural or fascist phase where culture is assimilated into a consumer economy. However, a pure mimesis of the aesthetic object as the ontological mode of existence of the creative understanding itself, rather than as an abstract and form-obsessed, autonomous image, would present insurmountable problems for any radical aesthetics searching for a social theory. Thus, Read's working aesthetics of semantic experience brings mimesis in by the back door after the work of art has overcome the terror of abstraction and formlessness, and after the taboo against non-representational images is reconciled through its facing the destruction of the public world.[26] This Janus-faced avant-garde semantics of the abstract image becomes intelligible when we see how the elimination of human nature has been surmounted by the 'superrealism', or grotesque second nature, of the artwork. If the construction of fetishes in capitalist reality itself is the subject of the avant-garde's aesthetic reconstructions, then the loss of avant-garde modernism had to be faced as the loss of the heretical powers of expression and dissent.

However, it is important to emphasize that Read is using the avant-garde's concepts of misrecognition and non-identity of art with life in the name of establishing *the ultimate authority of artistic form over culture*. His work in the 1930s, which was so sharply polemical in the tradition of anti-Stalinism and anti-fascism, lost much of the polemical spirit after the war when Read tried to be more systematic in developing a philosophy of art. His post-war apologias for modernism constitute an essential primer or handbook for the cosmopolitan and international, consciously revolutionary art-historical movements – an aesthetic communism which could be coded as liberalism.[27] In this he hoped to create a pragmatics of cultural engagement for a moribund and reactionary English public, weary of war and industrial conflicts, and suffering from the failure of the masses to recognize that their own interests were being eroded with every defeat of socialism. The defeat of labour in the 1930s was just one reason for his advancement of modernism as an integral part of the war on capitalism. The war itself left an irreversible scar on all modernists of the inter-war period. The question changed, however: *was this scar related to the irreversibility of capitalism itself?* Read's own deeply personal project was to indict the blind spot – the iconophobia – in British modernism's inability to construct a comprehensive critique of modernity which would show the Church of Culture's role in constructing national identity and therefore securing barbarism into capitalism as the culture of a new epoch in western civilization.

Read also had to think against the grain of the strong tradition of Christian organicism, which also had an anti-capitalist and anti-modernist side. This side of him was not only directed against Arnoldian forms of anti-modernism, but was specifically articulated against clerisy, myth and authority.[28] Eliot and Leavis might also associate capitalism with greed, power and pandering to the masses, and capitalism is often seen as allied with an abstract and powerful monied 'cosmopolitanism', but – and this is an important departure from Read – they saw Marxism and communism simply as soulless and dehumanizing ethically corrupt political *systems*. Read's distinction from Eliot on this ground is the clarity of his awareness of how corporate nationalism – that is, fascism – communism and capitalism, were similar 'globalizing' economic movements that relied on international capital.[29] The work in the 1930s, which is essentially a critique of modernity, culminates in *To Hell with Culture* with his attack on the 'bourgeois mind' and notion of popular culture that might pass as democratic.[30] Political economy must face bourgeois cultural hegemony. This attack is directed at former avant-garde artists and culture heroes who collaborated with the forces of reaction by using culture as a place from which to attack modernism. Probably having in mind Wyndham Lewis, Read describes the schizoid culture bearer, the destructive character, who seems bent on destroying the memory of art's revolutionary humanist nature.[31]

What did not endear him to many of his contemporaries was his independence, his anarchism and pacifism, his critical dexterity in moving from poetry to painting, to sculpture, to the defence of small syndicalist-inspired groups of artists, which he assumed could be built by constituting Kropotkin-like values of mutual aid, all juxtaposing social theory with an aesthetics of the unconscious influenced both by Freud and idealist philosophers of art like Whitehead. What a provocation to culture!

While Read remained a philosophical anarchist at heart, he always researched alienation theory, centrally in Hegel and Marx, and laterally in ethical anarchists like Simone Weil or Tolstoy, where the sacredness of the personality, the integrity of the person, and a radical defence of human rights as ultimate defences of needs that would include art and fulfilment in education seemed to provide answers to the British tradition's Lockean defence of 'liberty' or citizenship as simply the expansion of legal rights. In philosophical anarchism he found more justification for a synthesis of dialectics and unconscious drives than in having any faith in a revolutionary theory of social transformation. His anarchism was marked by syndicalist forms of social organization, a radical anti-authoritarian ethics, and most of all an ecological-organic sense that the mind and the person were inviolable and could not be coerced into compliance without destroying aesthetic sensibility. He searched among the symbolic philosophers of the unconscious for evidence for semantic idealism, a term which is useful to understand Read's determination to find the clues to the contextual 'nature of the creative mind'.[32] A poignant statement like the following derives from the heat of the culture and class wars of the 1930s:

What in the attitude of our between-war socialists probably repelled me most directly was their incapacity to appreciate the significance of the artist's approach. To me it seemed elementary that a belief in Marx should be accompanied by a belief in, say, Cézanne; and that the development of art since Cézanne should interest the completely revolutionary mind as much as the development of socialist theory since Proudhon. I wanted to discuss, not only Sorel and Lenin, but also Picasso and Joyce. But no one saw the connection. Each isolated on his separate line denied the relevance of the force animating the other lines. No one could see that it was the same force that was transforming the whole of reality – making it possible to give different interpretations of reality. To me it seemed just as important to destroy the established bourgeois ideals in literature, painting and architecture as it was to destroy the established ideals in economics.[33]

His attempt to understand how a modernist public world based on the aesthetics of self-creation within an anarcho-syndicalist tradition could exist under corporate capitalism should have placed him in more regard with the turn toward Marxian cultural studies in England that began to take place after the war. But this was and is not the case; the reverse is true.

Charles Harrison and Paul Wood's thick, 1.3 kilogram *Art in Theory: An Anthology of Changing Ideas*, which is essentially a collection of documents from and about modernism, places Read in the rear-guard battalion that carries the banner 'Freedom, Responsibility and Power'. Harrison, who had in a previous work virtually dismissed Read,[34] now places him in the context of the left critical intelligentsia between the wars:

> What was required was a self-conscious and sceptical representation of modern Western culture itself and of its constitutive values; an analysis made as it were from within, but by reference to concepts from outside – the 'outside' being that imagined world of modern political alternatives for which Communism and Fascism defined opposite poles, the one positive, the other decidedly negative. The methodological instruments for this analysis were largely found within the Marxist intellectual tradition. This was the task variously addressed, at one time or another, by André Breton in France... by Siegfried Kracauer, Walter Benjamin, Theodor Adorno and Ernst Bloch in Germany... and by Meyer Schapiro, Clement Greenberg and Harold Rosenberg in America... *(It is a measure of Britain's relative disengagement from this debate, and of the price that was paid for this disengagement, that Herbert Read's was the strongest native contribution.)* [my italics][35]

However, if modernism became a 'paradigmatic theory and practice in the early 1960s', as Charles Harrison and Paul Wood claim in their survey of the modernist field in *Modernism in Dispute*,[36] it is difficult to understand why a long introductory chapter by Jonathan Harris on the 1930s does not even mention Read's role in the British confrontation with surrealism and Marxist-inspired utopian art. It appears that one must seek answers elsewhere for reasons why the vanguardisms of the 1930s were assimilated into the normative cultural discourses and counter-cultural academicism of the post-war years. Put another way: what is one to make of the turn to cultural studies in England on the one hand and, in American criticism on the other, the turn toward Frankfurt School aesthetics, or the overwhelming influence of French post-structuralism as cornerstones of a new modernism – if the historical line is terminated in the Cold War?

In the 1950s and 1960s, after Read had become an international envoy for a modernist visual literacy, and had supported younger artists while continuing to employ his anarchist affiliations and activism against nuclear weapons and American imperialism, he suffered the critiques of such different polemicists as Clement Greenberg and Wyndham Lewis.[37] Puzzling is his long association with T. S. Eliot, which might appear especially compromising today in the light of the controversies surrounding the relationship of modernism to anti-semitism and fascism in Eliot, Lewis, Yeats and Pound. Even more puzzling is Read's acceptance of the knighthood for literature under Churchill in 1951. In this Cold War atmosphere the aura of the English critic enjoying a certain status and prestige in American New Critical circles both enhanced and confused his image in the public world, since he had already been the main force to divest modernism of Bloomsbury traditionalism and Labour Party illusions without giving up hope for changes in social organization.

In the 1950s he also faced the growing insistence at the ICA that he had become obsolete in the face of new forms of expression being transmitted through pop and minimal art. It seemed that long after he had helped develop an audience for left thoughtfulness about the role of abstract art in regard to social transformation, where his interpretations of Henry Moore, Ben Nicholson, Barbara Hepworth and Paul Nash became touchstones to examine dozens of other artists, many who were not well-known, his influence was waning in the dark light of the anti-leftism and welfare-state bleakness of the 1950s. Since Read saw himself representing not only the spirit but the substance of Marx or Hegel, his politics were doomed to become obsolete in the post-war confusion over the crisis of Marxism and materialism. Modernism's original project of bringing art practices into a direct convergence with literature and philosophy was now desecrated and parodied by pop art and conceptualism. Without his seeing that this vital connection of modernism to the 'other' of emancipatory politics was growing thin, the fate of his reception would be to type him by his 'eclectic' commitment to the fading European movements in art and philosophy. In short, he was typed as a UNESCO-manqué citizen of the art world dominated by élite patronage.

Ironically, this typing finally does separate him from his English modernist counterparts like Eliot or Leavis, Fry or Bell. But this separation only earns him a place in the ruins of modernism where he is interred. Yet it would not be an exaggeration to say that no other British intellectual of the modernist period saw theory and philosophy *inside art production*, and no other British intellectual saw more clearly the dialectical relationship between the empirical demands of the materials of art and the forms of social production that mediated those materials. In short he was the only cultural force in the period who could be compared to the Europeans like Malraux, Benjamin, Valéry, Adorno and Hauser, or in terms of his political outlook, to independent leftists like Silone or Camus. Ultimately this profile would have to see Read alongside the art philosophers like Riegl, Worringer, Raphael, Dvorak or Antal who reconstructed art history around the autonomous art object's capacity to change perceptions about the evolution and costs of civilization.

But if one examines, not just the art world's struggle to define itself in terms of the classical avant-garde, but how the last gasp of the critical bourgeoisie is understood in England, and how Read relates to this lack of self-understanding of the bourgeoisie, we come to the contexts which are important for an understanding of the blind spots in British modernism.[38]

III A helicopter view of modernism or tunnelling under?

By using Read's twists and turns, I hope to have raised some questions which may be instructive about what can be said regarding the reception of his modernism. As a cultural force who worked against the grain of a normative cultural tradition that could not imagine any aesthetic transformation of the public sphere, he stands outside any contemporary tradition.[39] In post-modernism's turn toward cultural studies as the official avant-garde itself we have an example of the social construction of an adversary culture. But adversarial to what? Presumably liberal democracy.

Charles Harrison's claim that 'Read's stress on the essentially non-rational or pre-rational nature of the origins of art was an effective prescription for liberalism in response to the eccentricities of modern art' cannot stand in historical perspective because it eliminates Read's use of Wilhelm Worringer and Marxism, not to say his starting from and going beyond Nietzsche.[40]

To equate anarchism with liberalism is no help at all in clarifying one of the vexing problems about modernism as a set of cultural practices which struggle within liberal institutions in order to frame an indigenous cultural–political plan for dissenting artists. Read's anti-liberalism aside, his anarchism is not equivalent to liberal cultural views of patronage of the arts. Harrison's view does not take us much farther than Wyndham Lewis's invective against Read.[41] This conflating of Read with liberalism may also explain the historical position of neo-'materialist' post-modernism with its 'grass roots' urges in the cultural studies movement. In doing so, cultural studies may be perpetuating the separation of labour and culture by isolating aesthetic culture from experience and from the historical–philosophical contexts of judgement derived from intersubjective relationships and values. One of the vexing problems about post-modernism is the need to set modernism off into the distance as a set of bad feudalistic or élitist cultural practices which struggle against good post-modern pluralistic identities that frame national populism as the unusurpable, political home for dissenting artists.

While this is a subject of another essay, I can indicate the direction of my thought by referring briefly to E. P. Thompson's statement in *The Poverty of Theory* that 'the English experience certainly did not encourage sustained efforts of synthesis: since few intellectuals were thrown into prominence in a conflict with authority, few felt the need to develop a systematic critique'.[42] This inner conflict between a culture of 'intellectuality' that thought of itself 'as exchanging specialized products in a market that was tolerably free, and the sum of whose intellectual commodities made up the sum of "knowledge"',[43] and an aesthetic culture that was divorced from everyday 'knowledge', was Read's very touchstone for seeing how the historiciza-tion of art should be seen in conflict with the authority of culture. Seen in this way, modernism is precisely the linking of aesthetic uncertainty to the crisis of capital – human capital understood humanly. The attempt to make art both expressive of an uncertain reality, without reparation or hope, simply means art is relativized, not in its powerlessness but in the manner of its undermining the hegemony of the bour-geoisie's tolerance of industry, war and Christian imperialism as its self-appointed unique stage in European civilization's perception of itself.

Here we come to something of an impasse regarding the scope of Read's theory of consciousness as grounded in images, symbols, and a reality whose access is primarily through sensual modes of perception. For Read the emptiness of English cultural and aesthetic theory was the reverse image of the despair over the loss of a radical image of the world that could be transformed through aesthetic perception. In this sense, in his studies like *The Meaning of Art* (1931; revised 1959), *Art and Society* (1936; revised 1967) and *Icon and Idea* (1955), Read continually *updated* his pilgrimage through the aestheticized objects that comprise our sensual apprehension of reality. His works form an argument against Christopher Caudwell on the one hand, and T. S. Eliot and Raymond Williams on the other: neither left nor right grasped the constructed image, as enunciated by Gabo, Klee, Schwitters, Pollock, Francis and Moore:

> If anything is communicated by such paintings [as those of Pollock, Tobey, Francis] it can only correspond to some unformulated, some unrealized dimen-sion of the artist's consciousness... What do these Gestalt-free paintings reveal? Is it possible that the artist has now found a method for observing the self which is not at the moment in the act of willing something, or observing other objects – for attaining a direct knowledge of a self which is not at the moment in the act of willing something, or observing other objects? These paintings are not the result of any process of reflection – there did not first exist an external object, or even an internal feeling, for which the artist then found an equivalent symbol.[44]

Yet Read did not just allow this apotheosis of form to remain an ideal. On the contrary he continued to seek anthropological and psychological explanations that would enable him to translate this genetic organicism into a social consciousness whose aesthetic forms would also exercise judgement on society. Historicized as a problem of consciousness within the social matrix, we can see that Read is constantly wanting art to subvert official culture on the one hand, and incorporate the avant-garde movement into a critique of civilization on the other. In order that art is not usurped in the process, art itself has to be continually redefined. In fact, one can summarize Read's entire work as the investigation of how art-making is itself a search for the 'primitive' that co-exists with civilization, as bourgeois civilization is itself an alien 'other' constructed at the frontiers of the self. Here we have to understand how different Read is from those who also look at 'cultural practices' or cultural 'agency' today. Read understood art not only as the 'cultural practices' of an impoverished modernism – what Frederic Jameson obligingly describes for us as 'the other of our society is… no longer Nature at all, as it was in pre-capitalist societies, but something else which we must now identify'[45] – but as an *already* existing struggle against necessity. Jameson's belief that art can be redeemed through a reading of Adorno cannot be fully discussed here, but in order to carry forward Read's modernism as a continuous project of the individual subject struggling against the state and capital in the British context, we would have to look at the reception and influence of Raymond Williams on cultural studies and the recanonization of culture as the intellectual force for a renewed agency-rich non-proletarian public sphere. This helicopter view of culture, to put it mildly, has some severe problems at its very core.

The Readian emphasis was on the aesthetic self or subject that tunnelled under culture. I have in part embraced his project in order to argue that he is a missing part in knowing how we might tunnel back to an emancipatory modernism where the artwork is a building stone for a life-world that includes artistic cognition as a means of coming to terms with historical modernity as a lost and rational, utopian cultural project. This means that a misreading of modernism has consequences for understanding the uses of art as a foundation for philosophical reflection on the nature of the real. The case in point is that a reading of English modernism as a failed historical project has led, as Thompson points out, to the institutionalization of a pseudo-utilitarian cultural attitude that makes out that autonomous art, not experience, is the discursive control panel for both perceptions of change and where change can be located. Thompson's *The Poverty of Theory* opened an attack on the nihilistic or privileged enclave of an already existing post-modernism as the simple reflection of the age when art has become acclimatized to its 'other', mass mindedness and the technicized money economy. It might be argued that cultural studies as a displaced form of social theory has eviscerated any relic of historical, anarcho-communism from theory. This has the effect of limiting historical understanding to either crude identity politics or endowing social movements with a power they do not have in reality. The effect is to assume that the anarcho-modernism of Herbert Read's project is without forebears. The modernism that frames the populism of E. P. Thompson clearly belongs to a tradition that should include Read, but the modernism that haunts the agonies of Raymond Williams's own struggle with modernism, and which appears to define the contemporary traditions, does not.[46]

Williams ignored Read and at the same time bifurcated his own upbringing by describing his self-formation as belonging both to a literate élite and an illiterate majority. In *Writing in Society* Williams poignantly acknowledges that his own educational history separated aesthetic modernism from political modernism, causing him to suffer the fate of 'belonging' to two cultures.[47] Even by using the dichotomy literate/illiterate Williams betrays an attempt to sanction culture that is unknown in Read. On this basis it is understandable that Read's emphasis on an *aesthetic education* would have to be minimized or dismissed, as Williams does in both *Culture and Society* and *Politics and Letters*, where he describes his distaste for Read without much self-reflection or explanation.[48] In *Culture and Society* (he explains in *Politics and Letters*) Read and Godwin were excluded because of the publisher's constrictions, but Williams never corrected this omission in subsequent years and simply allows his conflation of Read's work with Freud or I. A. Richards to stand. Clearly, both Read and Williams come out of the plebeian traditions that make working-class intellectuals into congenital strangers to theory. Williams writes that his 'full social history' estranged him from the critical theories of modernism, that 'the form and language of their systems' is remote from his lived experiences.[49] Read's struggle to find a non-alienated critical vocabulary and to build a modernist theory that was both intellectually penetrating and yet related to libertarian educational movements and workers' self-management, in short to write and speak against the knowledge élites of British institutional culture, should have made Read and Williams bedfellows. But it is Read's Freudianism and, I would say, his aestheticism which Williams finds frustrating; thus Williams continues the school of Eliot, Leavis, and Caudwell that scorns the subjective and individual aspect of the unconscious in modernism and ignores extending the unconscious into consorting with anarcho-syndicalist thought of mutuality and reciprocity in human social organization. Williams dies feeling resigned as an outsider, and so does Read (even though the knighthood gave him pause to think he belonged). Williams tries to escape the library and Cambridge and stumbles over his modernist origins. Read tries to isolate the work of art *from* the museum in order to see it as a dialogue with the world and stumbles back into the museum. Both modernists sense their isolation within British modernism. Starting this chapter with the forgotten Read's sense of how to recover a lost world, we end with Williams's sense of isolation from his own past and the modernism within it.

In the 1955 *Twentieth Century Authors*, the entry states that Read's scope and activities were 'so wide that... some of his admirers hail him as "one of the most notably persuasive influences upon his age"... "a genius too fertile to be constrained with the categories of one art", yet read only by a select intellectual-politico-group'.[50] No longer the case, the reverse is true. There is no group that would extend his work, unless in the schools of art education or industrial design. In this he remains outside contemporary movements, lost in the shadows of modernism.

Notes

1 Herbert Read, *The Contrary Experience: Autobiographies* (New York: Horizon Press, 1963), pp. 352–53.

2 The reference is to Frederic Jameson's *The Political Unconscious* (Ithaca: Cornell University Press, 1981). Jameson interprets Wyndham Lewis as the paradigmatic modern. Lewis's proto-fascist attitudes are associated with modernism as such, and with a specifically futurist, asocial aesthetics of resignation which stands in for fascism. Jameson's claim that Lewis was an 'internationalist, the most European and least insular of all the great contemporary British writers' cannot be substantiated, certainly not in regard to Read's lifelong translation of continental traditions into modernist projects (*Fables of Aggression: Wyndham Lewis, the Modernist as Fascist* [Berkeley: University of California Press, 1979], p. 88). T. J. Clark's criticism of modernism's weak politics is associated with impressionism and the Paris of Baudelaire in *The Painting of Modern Life: Paris in the Art of Manet and his Followers* (New York: Knopf, 1984). This raises questions about the politics of urban modernism that I cannot go into the details of here, just as Read's and Lewis's differences over modernism would be the subject of another essay.

3 See Cornelius Castoriadis, 'The Crisis of Culture and the State', in David Ames Curtis (ed.), *Philosophy, Politics, Autonomy: Essays in Political Philosophy*, (New York: Oxford University Press, 1991), p. 221: 'This is what has been called postmodernism: eclecticism and imitation. In fact, it is a rather cheap version of Alexandrianism. The only really significant contribution of postmodernism is that it has shown how great and creative modernism was.' The struggle against reconciliation with power is already evident in Read's *The Green Child* as it is in his war poems.

4 Herbert Read, 'Essential Communism', *Anarchy and Order: Essays in Politics* (Boston: Beacon Press, 1971), p. 75. This chapter in *Poetry and Anarchism* (London: Faber and Faber, 1938) was first published as a Social Credit pamphlet (London: Stanley Nott, 1935).

5 Read, 'Essential Communism', p. 74. Read was accused by Hugh Gordon Porteus of hiding his communism behind his surrealism. In his defence he linked the surrealist movement to an idea that surrealist principles reside in all of art. Read pointed out that 'If Mr. Porteus had said that I had become a surrealist to save myself becoming a Communist, he might have been near the truth. It is not quite the truth, because if the Communists were anything but abysmally stupid about the subject of art, there would be nothing to prevent me from becoming a member of that political party... in other words, that in spite of all Marx said and did to the contrary, Marxism has become an exclusively rational and anti-aesthetic doctrine... more and more calvinistic... pathetically bourgeois' ('Why I am a Surrealist', *New English Weekly*, 4 March 1937).

6 *Authors Take Sides on the Spanish War* (London: *Left Review*, n.d.). To the question 'Are you for, or against, the legal Government and the people of Republican Spain? Are you for, or against, Franco and Fascism?' Eliot replied: 'While I am naturally sympathetic, I still feel convinced that it is best

that at least a few men of letters should remain isolated and take no part in these collective activities'. In the linking of 'taking sides' to the struggle against fascism this statement would have been confusing and disturbing for Eliot, whose own 'collective activities' did not include criticizing fascism.

7 Herbert Read, *The Forms of Things Unknown: An Essay on the Impact of the Technological Revolution on the Creative Arts* (Cleveland and New York: The World Publishing Company, 1963), pp. 168–69.

8 Read, 'Essential Communism', p. 75.

9 Ibid.

10 Ibid., pp. 75–76.

11 And new obeisances too. Art after the war manifested little social responsibility, could be 'vulgar and moronic' and exhibited itself as pseudo-movements (see Herbert Read, 'The Limits of Permissiveness in Art', in Robin Skelton (ed.), *Herbert Read: A Memorial Symposium* [London: Methuen, 1970], pp. 38–41).

12 Read's understanding of machine production of commodities and the mechanical reproduction of reality can be found in *Art and Industry: The Principles of Industrial Design* (New York: Horizon Press, rev. edn, 1953). In the preface to the 1961 edition he states clearly that there are no national trends in design – the commodity form is universal (p. x). A more philosophical meditation against commodity aesthetics can be found in his essays on art and education, viz. *The Grass Roots of Art: Lectures on the Social Aspects of Art in an Industrial Age* (London: Faber and Faber, 1955). This aspect of his work should be related to Schiller's ideals of aesthetic education as the formative basis of a radically autonomous self. There is no word in English that can adequately convey the notion of *Bildung*, or self-formation, that Read understood from the German tradition.

13 In outlining Read's social symbolism it is not easy to trace his sources, but the aesthetics of Whitehead, Dewey, Worringer, Croce and Coleridge all had their place in his thought, in particular their attempt to face up to science and to construct a modernist cosmology that included science were important to Read. Read's original synthesis of Whitehead's cosmology of beauty within modernist abstract art with many other radical ontological approaches is often so abstract and written so plainly that it is hard to pin Read to a single figure of influence. However, because Read also attacked bourgeois formalist positions it is not possible to frame him within pure objective idealism. But his work can't be understood without being informed by a theory of beauty.

14 T. S. Eliot's comments are marginalia to a copy of *The Education of Free Men*, located in the Read Archive, University of Victoria Library, British Columbia. Read writes: 'Efficiency, progress, success, – these are the aims of a competitive system from which all moral factors are necessarily excluded. In that respect, at least, our schools reflect truly enough our social order.' Eliot sings a rueful and peevish tune in the margins: 'But you cannot have a system which precludes efficiency, progress, success'.

15 Herbert Read, *The Grass Roots of Art: Four Lectures on Social Aspects of Art in an Industrial Age* (New York: George Wittenborn, 1947) were lectures delivered at Yale University in Spring 1946. These lectures contain some of his most controversial utopian thoughts.

16 Herbert Read, 'The Principle of Speculative Volition', in Read, *The Forms of Things Unknown*, pp. 167–68.

17 Edited by Briony Fer, David Batchelor and Paul Wood (New Haven and London: Yale University Press with The Open University, 1993).

18 Read uses Einstein and Raphael as touchstones in 'Essential Communism', pp. 77–78.

19 *The Demands of Art* (Princeton: Princeton University Press, 1968).

20 In *The Forms of Things Unknown* Read argues that he is a 'poet rather than a scientist' (p. 12) and that he is not a systematic thinker (p. 17). He always apologized for the nature of his eclecticism,

but this is a false modesty in the light of his understanding of philosophical issues.

21 In *Art and Society* (1936) Read interprets the 'primitive' as necessary to understanding civilization; civilization needs the primitive to justify why the turn to abstraction continues secular humanism by another name in art styles. Art is a deeper universalism than religion and does not need religion for justification (*Art and Society* [New York: Schocken Books, 1966], p. 8 and *passim*). This view is expanded throughout *Icon and Idea: The Function of Art in the Development of Human Consciousness* (London: Faber and Faber, 1955), whose subject matter might be described as entirely about the movement of art from paleolithic consciousness to modern abstractionism (see pp. 48–52).

22 Read's comment occurs in *The Grass Roots of Art*, 1947 edn, p. 46.

23 See 'The Psychology of Reaction', in Herbert Read, *To Hell with Culture and Other Essays on Art and Society* (New York: Schocken Books, 1963), p. 145.

24 See David Thistlewood, 'Herbert Read's Paradigm: A British Vision of Modernism' in Benedict Read and David Thistlewood (eds), *Herbert Read: A British Vision of World Art* (Leeds: Leeds City Art Galleries, 1993), p. 87. Thistlewood is far more sensitive to aesthetic questions than other commentators on Read, but this view about Read's movement to Jung is also held by George Woodcock in *Herbert Read: The Stream and the Source* (London: Faber and Faber, 1972); and James King, *The Last Modern: A Life of Herbert Read* (New York: St Martin's Press, 1990). My disagreement with these positions that claim his Jungian turn can be explained by a rejection of Freud is taken up in an unpublished essay on Read and T. W. Adorno.

25 In Read, *The Forms of Things Unknown*, particularly the chapters 'The Created Form', 'Psychoanalysis and the Problem of Aesthetic Value', and 'The Reconciling Image'. 'The Reconciling Image' attempts to critique Jungian values as religious-humanist values, without Read's completely falling victim to his penchant to locate the field of representations in modern art within the unconscious forces of organicism. The problem of beauty and ugliness continued to fascinate Read. The struggle between sensual pleasure and sexual representation is never resolved, although, along with Freud and Jung, he turns to Melanie Klein's grim vision in an Eranos lecture, 'Beauty and the Beast', published in a joint volume with A. Hilary Armstrong: *On Beauty* (Dallas: Spring Publications, 1987).

26 Read expounds on this aspect of alienation theory throughout *Art and Alienation: The Role of the Artist in Society* (New York: Horizon Press, 1967), which begins with epigraphs from Marx, Wordsworth and Fromm. See especially, 'Rational Society and Irrational Art', pp. 29–39.

27 Apologias for modernism can be found in *The Philosophy of Modern Art* (London: Faber and Faber, 1964 edn) and particularly in the various prefaces to *Art Now : An Introduction to the Theory of Modern Painting and Sculpture* (1933; 1936; 1948; 1960). The 1960 preface dilutes the 1936 'apologia for modern art' (p. 13) where Read distinguished *modernism as an artistic cause* from *Kulturbolshevism* as an 'invented' label that linked communism to Jewish modernism. The direct reference to the linking of *Kulturbolshevism*, Jews and communism is excised from the 1960 version.

28 See Roger Kojecky, *T. S. Eliot's Social Criticism* (London: Faber and Faber, 1971). Especially important is the role that Karl Mannheim's ideas of the democratization of knowledge may have had for Read, especially since Mannheim came out of the fractured German Marxist tradition which Read admired. Read had no relationship to the Christian Moot group which Eliot attended. The most important group which influenced Read's evolving anarchism was the circle of artists and writers around A. R. Orage, the Leeds Arts Club, and the *New Age*. See the excellent study by Tom Steele, *Alfred Orage and the Leeds Arts Club, 1893–1923* (Aldershot: Gower Press, 1990). Steele correctly points out (p. 235) that Read's latent spiritualism, which emerges in his assessment of Henry Moore, has roots in the socialist humanism and messianism of the Orage years, which provided a 'language' of the local moors that infused Moore's forms with something

mystical and transcendent. Steele remains sceptical about this 'language', especially as it illustrates how Read fails to account for Barbara Hepworth's sculpture. I agree with Steele's assessment that there is a latent mysticism in Read's work, but hope this account of Read's modernism locates this mysticism within his art-philosophical vernacular anarchism.

29 In 'Towards a Duplex Civilization' (*The Grass Roots of Art*, 1955 edn, p. 139), Read clearly identifies how state-controlled styles of art and design – *regardless* of their national origins – are formed through the combination of trade union, managerial, monopolist, and totalitarian pressures that create an 'essential serfdom' for the masses. He understood capitalism as a form of corporatism, anticipating Frankfurt School critiques of capitalism. Read visited China in 1958 and Cuba in 1968 and became enthusiastic about communism as a hybrid of small and large social units. See King, *The Last Modern*, pp. 291–93 and 311–12.

30 In *To Hell With Culture* (1941), reprinted in Read, *To Hell with Culture and Other Essays on Art and Society*, Read searched the streams of surrealism and abstract art for evidence of an aesthetic motive in civilization that would lead to a classless society, that is for 'democratic values as new values'.

31 It is clear that Read thought that modern culture was pathologically schizoid: references to totalitarianism, propaganda, academicism, dilettantism, hieratic art, ornamentalism, monumentalism and consumerism abound in his work, and add up to 'subterfuges to which man resorts in order to preserve his identity. He ends by willingly sacrificing his body in the belief that he will thereby preserve his soul' ('The Creative Nature of Humanism', in Read, *The Forms of Things Unknown*, p. 184). Alex Comfort's *Art and Social Responsibility* (London: Falcon Press, 1946), which carried the metaphor of the pathology of a death-worshipping society almost further than Read, was dedicated to Read.

32 Read, *The Forms of Things Unknown*, p. 11. Read is at pains in this book to divest himself of the new critical tradition of 'textism' by turning to a quasi-scientific exposition of the relationship 'between the symbol to the sign in different stages of human evolution' (p. 65). This involves him in the effort to understand whether Picasso's symbolism can be considered the normative inner artistic style for modernism as a stage of civilization.

33 'Essential Communism', pp. 76–77.

34 Charles Harrison, *English Art and Modernism, 1900–1939* (London: Allen Lane, 1981) p. 99, touts Read as an 'effective prescription for liberalism in response to the eccentricities of modern art'.

35 Charles Harrison and Paul Wood (eds), *Art in Theory* (Oxford, UK and Cambridge, USA: Basil Blackwell, 1992), p. 337. Read is now stuffed between communism and fascism as one of many critics of an 'assumed natural order' (p. 337). This reduction of Read is symptomatic of the careless understanding of his reading of Marxism as a theory of historical loss. Read's sympathetic yet critical understanding of Marxism as a theory of historical decline, not renewal or redemption, is illustrated by his essay 'Existentialism, Marxism, Anarchism' (1949) in Read, *Anarchy and Order*, where he argues that Marxism reifies essences into labour and thus cannot account for artistic essences. But it is important that Harrison at least places Read within the inter-war disputes about aesthetics and politics. However, in Charles Harrison and Paul Wood (eds), *Modernism in Dispute: Art since the Forties* (New Haven and London: Yale University Press and The Open University,1993) Read is missing in action: not even one reference to him by the same editors of *Art in Theory*.

36 Harrison and Wood, *Modernism in Dispute*, p. 170. The chapter inquires mainly into Clement Greenberg's and Michael Fried's different views on aesthetic quality as a measure of the modern in art; but the question of the quality that state-awed citizens demand of culture is not raised in the manner in which a discussion of this kind might have taken place in the 1930s or 1940s. Therefore the attempt to separate cultural agency from classic modernist critiques of culture is directed toward separating modernism from post-modernism (pp. 180–89).

37 Clement Greenberg mounted the harshest attacks on Read. See Clement Greenberg, *The Collected Essays and Criticism*, ed. John O'Brian (Chicago and London: University of Chicago Press, 1993). Greenberg is friendly toward Read's efforts on surrealism and modern poetry in the war period in vol. 1, 1939–1944, but it is very critical of Read's views on naturalism and abstraction in vol. 2, 1945–1949, and maliciously labels his aesthetics 'incompetent' and 'unthought-out' in vol. 3, 1950–1956. Barnett Newman is more supportive but not enthusiastic in *Barnett Newman: Selected Writings and Interviews* (Berkeley: University of California Press, 1992). Neither Greenberg nor Newman are prepared to discuss the problems of left-wing cultural criticism's demise in England, thus leaving Read exposed to similar attacks in England by those who scorned his associations with Peggy Guggenheim, the Bollingen Foundation and his international efforts to advance the causes of modernism at the ICA, or through his writings on Pollock, Miró, Gabo, Ruth Francken, Barbara Hepworth, Sam Francis and Moore. See the chapter 'A Home for Contemporary Art', in King, *The Last Modern*.

38 John Carey, *The Intellectuals and the Masses: Pride and Prejudice Among the Literary Intelligentsia, 1880–1939* (London: Faber and Faber, 1992), is too full of arrogant prejudices and sociological simplicities about artists and intellectuals who are against the popular and the masses to be of much help here. In any case Carey says nothing about the anarcho-socialist tradition represented by Read and prefers to defend mass culture even in its more barbaric forms by claiming to speak for the masses' immunity from élite culture. Hitler's *Mein Kampf* is of the same cloth as 'European intellectual orthodoxy' (p. 208).

39 See Oskar Negt and Alexander Kluge, *Public Sphere and Experience: Toward an Analysis of the Bourgeois and Proletarian Public Sphere* (Minneapolis and London: University of Minnesota Press, 1993). As Miriam Hansen points out in her excellent introduction, Negt and Kluge focus less on patterns of consumption and commodity fetishism and more on productive patterns and the consciousness industries that institutionalize and appropriate reality. This was clearly Read's project, not Raymond Williams's, who was more concerned with rescuing culture as a total form of life than in historicizing art as a problem of the whole culture's self-image.

40 Harrison, *English Art and Modernism*, p. 99. The deep influence of Wilhelm Worringer on Read would have to be examined in this context. *The Philosophy of Modern Art* (1952), arguably Read's most compelling collection of essays, is dedicated to Worringer, '… my esteemed master in the philosophy of art'.

41 See Wyndham Lewis, *The Demon of Progress in the Arts* (Chicago: Henry Regnery Company, 1955), for an archly voiced slam at Read's acceptance of the knighthood and for having turned the ICA into a temple of modernism, or what Lewis calls 'extremism'. Lewis's and Read's different encounters and critiques of fascism and communism are important for understanding Lewis's robotic rages against 'extremism' and leftism, as well as Read's response to fascism and communism. For a discussion of provincial anti-modernism characteristic of English Canadian modernism, see the earlier version of this essay in *Collapse* (Vancouver), no. 1 (1995).

42 E. P. Thompson, *The Poverty of Theory and Other Essays* (London: Merlin Press, 1978), p. 59.

43 Ibid.

44 Read, *Icon and Idea*, p. 122.

45 In *Postmodernism or the Cultural Logic of Late Capitalism* (Durham: Duke University Press, 1991), p. 35.

46 Raymond Williams, *The Politics of Modernism: Against the New Conformists* (London and New York: Verso Books, 1988). In a chapter, 'Beyond Cambridge English' (1983), in Raymond Williams, *Writing in Society* (London: Verso Books, n.d.), Williams sadly, for him, and belatedly for normative British modernism, introduces the framework of immigrant writing, exiles, émigrés and the modernist as an exile in consciousness, who breaks with culture, and is the 'other' of Cambridge

English (pp. 221–22). But Read had negotiated the relationship of modernist Continental philosophy and aesthetics long before.

47 Raymond Williams, 'Beyond Cambridge English', p. 212.

48 Raymond Williams, *Politics and Letters* (London: New Left Books, 1979), p. 99; Raymond Williams, *Culture and Society, 1780–1950* (Garden City New York: Anchor Books, 1959), p. 267.

49 Raymond Williams, *Writing in Society*, p. 223.

50 Stanley J. Kunitz (ed.), *Twentieth Century Authors*, First Supplement (New York: H. H. Wilson, 1955), p. 817.

A Chronological Bibliography of Books and Pamphlets Written, Edited or Translated by Herbert Read

1915
Songs of Chaos (London: Elkin Mathews)

1919
Auguries of Life and Death: Written in Memory of Charles Read, Lieutenant of The Yorkshire Regiment, Born April 24th 1897, Killed in Action at Beaurevoir in France, October 5th 1918 (n.p.: privately published)
Eclogues: A Book of Poems (London: Beaumont Press)
Naked Warriors (London: Art and Letters)

1923
Mutations of the Phoenix (Richmond: Hogarth Press)

1924
(with Bernard Rackham) *English Pottery: Its Development from Early Times to the End of the Eighteenth Century* (London: Ernest Benn)
(ed.) T.E. Hulme, *Speculations: Essays on Humanism and the Philosophy of Art* (London: Kegan Paul)

1925
In Retreat (London: Hogarth Press)

1926
Collected Poems, 1913–25 (London: Faber and Gwyer)
English Stained Glass (London and New York: G.P. Putnam's)
Reason and Romanticism: Essays in Literary Criticism (London: Faber and Gwyer)

1927
(trans. and ed.) Wilhelm Worringer, *Form in Gothic* (London: G.P. Putnam's)

1928
English Prose Style (London: G. Bell)
Phases of English Poetry (London: The Hogarth Press)

1929

The Sense of Glory: Essays in Criticism (Cambridge: Cambridge University Press)

Staffordshire Pottery Figures (London: Duckworth)

(ed.) T.E. Hulme, *Notes on Language and Style* (Seattle: University of Washington Book Store)

(ed.) Laurence Sterne, *A Sentimental Journey* (London: The Scholartis Press)

1930

Ambush (London: Faber and Faber)

Julien Benda and the New Humanism (Seattle: University of Washington Book Store)

Wordsworth: The Clark Lectures, 1929–1930 (London: Jonathan Cape)

1931

The Meaning of Art (London: Faber and Faber)[as *The Anatomy of Art: An Introduction to the Problems of Art and Aesthetics* (New York: Dodd, Mead, 1932)]

The Place of Art in a University: An Inaugural Lecture Given at the University of Edinburgh on 15th October 1931 (Edinburgh and London: Oliver and Boyd)

(ed., with Bonamy Dobrée) *The London Book of English Prose* (London: Eyre and Spottiswoode) [as *The Anthology of English Prose* (New York: Viking)]

1932

Form in Modern Poetry (London: Sheed and Ward)

1933

Art Now: An Introduction to the Theory of Modern Painting and Sculpture (London: Faber and Faber)

The End of a War (London: Faber and Faber)

The Innocent Eye (London: Faber and Faber)

(ed.) *The English Vision: An Anthology* (London: Eyre and Spottiswoode)

1934

Art and Industry: The Principles of Industrial Design (London: Faber and Faber)

Henry Moore, Sculptor: An Appreciation (London: A. Zwemmer)

(ed.) *Unit One: The Modern Movement in English Architecture, Painting and Sculpture* (London: Cassell)

1935

Essential Communism (London: Stanley Nott)

The Green Child: A Romance (London: William Heinemann)

Poems, 1914–1934 (London: Faber and Faber)

(ed., with Denis Saurat) A. R. Orage, *Selected Essays and Critical Writings* (London: Stanley Nott)

1936

In Defence of Shelley and Other Essays (London: William Heinemann)

(ed.) *Essays and Studies by Members of the English Association*, vol. 21 (Oxford :
    Clarendon Press)

(ed.) *Surrealism* (London: Faber and Faber)

(trans., with Margaret Ludwig) Rudolf Arnheim, *Radio* (London: Faber and
    Faber)

1937

Art and Society (London: William Heinemann)

(ed.) *Paul Nash: Ten Coloured Plates and a Critical Appreciation* (London: Soho
    Gallery)

1938

Collected Essays in Literary Criticism (London: Faber and Faber) [as *The Nature of
    Literature* (New York: Horizon Press, 1956)]

Poetry and Anarchism (London: Faber and Faber)

1939

(ed.) *The Knapsack: A Pocket-Book of Prose and Verse* (London: George Routledge)

1940

Annals of Innocence and Experience (London: Faber and Faber) [as *The Innocent Eye*
    (New York: Henry Holt, 1947)]

The Philosophy of Anarchism (London: Freedom Press)

Thirty-Five Poems (London: Faber and Faber)

1941

To Hell with Culture: Democratic Values Are New Values (London: Kegan Paul)

1942

The Weathering of Art (Stoke-on-Trent: Society of Staffordshire Artists)

(ed.) *Kropotkin: Selections from his Writings* (London: Freedom Press)

1943

Education through Art (London: Faber and Faber)

(with Henry Strauss, Francis Meynell and Tom Harrison) *Four Lectures on Design:
    Delivered at Meetings of the Design and Industries Association* (London: Hutchinson)

The Politics of the Unpolitical (London: George Routledge)

1944

The Education of Free Men (London: Freedom Press)

(with Toni del Renzio and R.S.O. Poole) *Flicker* (Croydon: R.S.O. Poole [for the Oxford University Film Society])

Paul Nash (Harmondsworth: Penguin Books)

A World within a War: Poems (London: Faber and Faber)

(ed.) *Henry Moore: Sculpture and Drawings* (London: Lund Humphries and A. Zwemmer)

1945

A Coat of Many Colours: Occasional Essays (London: George Routledge)

Freedom: Is It a Crime? The Strange Case of the Three Anarchists Jailed at the Old Bailey, April 1945: Two Speeches (London: Freedom Press Defence Committee)

1946

Collected Poems (London: Faber and Faber)

The Future of Industrial Design (London: Design and Industries Association)

(ed.) *The Practice of Design* (London: Lund Humphries)

1947

The Grass Roots of Art (London: Lindsay Drummond)

Youth and Leisure: An Inaugural Address (Peterborough: Peterborough Joint Education Board)

1948

Culture and Education in World Order (New York: Museum of Modern Art [for the Committee on Art Education])

Klee (1879–1940) (London: Faber and Faber)

(ed., with Ben Nicholson) *Ben Nicholson: Paintings, Reliefs, Drawings* (London: Lund Humphries)

1949

Coleridge as Critic (London: Faber and Faber)

Education for Peace (New York: Charles Scribner's) [London: Routledge and Kegan Paul, 1950]

Existentialism, Marxism and Anarchism; Chains of Freedom (London: Freedom Press)

Gauguin (1848–1903) (London: Faber and Faber)

(ed., with Bonamy Dobrée) *The London Book of English Verse* (London: Eyre and Spottiswoode)

(ed.) Paul Nash, *Outline: An Autobiography; and Other Writings* (London: Faber and Faber)

1951

Art and the Evolution of Man: Lecture Delivered at Conway Hall, London, on April 10th, 1951 (London: Freedom Press)

Byron (London: Longmans, Green [for the British Council and the National Book League])

Contemporary British Art (Harmondsworth: Penguin Books)

The Helmsley Festival Play (Helmsley: privately published)

1952

The Philosophy of Modern Art: Collected Essays (London: Faber and Faber)

(ed., with Barbara Hepworth) *Barbara Hepworth: Carvings and Drawings* (London: Lund Humphries)

1953

Conflicts in Contemporary Art: The Third Annual Foundation Lecture Delivered at Bretton Hall, Wakefield, 25th May 1953 (Wakefield: County Council of the West Riding of Yorkshire Education Committee)

The True Voice of Feeling: Studies in English Romantic Poetry (London: Faber and Faber)

1954

Anarchy and Order: Essays in Politics (London: Faber and Faber)

1955

Education through Art: A Revolutionary Policy (London: Society of Education through Art)

Icon and Idea: The Function of Art in the Development of Human Consciousness (London: Faber and Faber)

Moon's Farm and Poems Mostly Elegiac (London: Faber and Faber)

The Psychopathology of Reaction in the Arts (London: Institute of Contemporary Arts)

1956

The Art of Sculpture: The A.W. Mellon Lectures in the Fine Arts, 1954, National Gallery of Art, Washington (London: Faber and Faber)

(ed.) *This Way Delight: A Book of Poetry for the Young* (New York: Pantheon) [London: Faber and Faber, 1957]

1957

The Significance of Children's Art: Art as Symbolic Language (Vancouver: University of British Columbia)

The Tenth Muse: Essays in Criticism (London: Routledge and Kegan Paul) (ed., with Leslie Martin) *Gabo: Constructions, Sculpture, Paintings, Drawings, Engravings* (London: Lund Humphries)

1958

(with Marcel Brion and others) *Art since 1945* (London: Thames and Hudson)
Lynn Chadwick (Amriswil: Bodensee-Verlag)

1959

A Concise History of Modern Painting (London: Thames and Hudson)
(ed.) *Kandinsky (1866–1944)* (London: Faber and Faber)

1960

The Ambiguity of Modern Sculpture (Stockholm: Kungl. Akademien för de Fria Konsterna)
(with Thomas Munro) *The Creative Arts in American Education* (Cambridge, Mass.: Harvard University Press)
The Forms of Things Unknown: Essays towards an Aesthetic Philosophy (London: Faber and Faber)
The Parliament of Women: A Drama in Three Acts (Hemingford Grey, Huntingdon: Vine Press)

1961

Aristotle's Mother: An Imaginary Conversation (North Harrow: Philip Ward)
(with Edward Dahlberg) *Truth is More Sacred: A Critical Exchange on Modern Literature: James Joyce, D.H. Lawrence, Henry James, Robert Graves, T.S. Eliot, Ezra Pound* (London: Routledge and Kegan Paul)

1962

Ben Nicholson: Paintings (London: Methuen)
Design and Tradition: The Design Oration (1961) of the Society of Industrial Artists (Hemingford Grey, Huntingdon: Vine Press)
A Letter to a Young Painter (London: Thames and Hudson)
A Short History and Description of the Church of Holy Trinity, Stonegrave (Stonegrave: privately published) [c.1962]
vocal avowals: worte sagen aus (St Gallen: Tschudy-Verlag)

1963

The Contrary Experience: Autobiographies (London: Faber and Faber)
Lord Byron at the Opera: A Play for Broadcasting (North Harrow: Philip Ward)
Selected Writings: Poetry and Criticism (London: Faber and Faber)
To Hell with Culture: and Other Essays on Art and Society (London: Routledge and Kegan Paul)

1964

Art and Education (Auckland: Paul's Book Arcade)/(Melbourne: F.W. Cheshire)

A Concise History of Modern Sculpture (London: Thames and Hudson)

High Noon and Darkest Night: Some Observations on Ortega y Gasset's Philosophy of Art
    (Middletown, Conn.: Center for Advanced Studies, Wesleyan University)

1965

Henry Moore: A Study of his Life and Work (London: Thames and Hudson)

Johannes Vermeer (London: Knowledge Publications)

The Modern Art Book (Middletown, Conn.: Columbiad Club)

The Origins of Form in Art (London: Thames and Hudson)

1966

Collected Poems (London: Faber and Faber) [revised edition]

(with Jean Leymarie and William S. Liebermann) *Henri Matisse* (Berkeley and Los
    Angeles: University of California Press)

The Redemption of the Robot: My Encounter with Education through Art (New York:
    Trident Press) [London: Faber and Faber, 1970]

T.S.E.: A Memoir (Middletown, Conn.: Center for Advanced Studies, Wesleyan
    University)

(ed.) *Henry Moore: Mother and Child* (London: Collins in association with
    UNESCO)

(consulting editor) *The Thames and Hudson Encyclopaedia of the Arts* (London:
    Thames and Hudson)

1967

Art and Alienation: The Role of the Artist in Society (London: Thames and Hudson)

Hieronymous Bosch (London: Knowledge Publications)

Poetry and Experience (London: Vision Press)

1968

Arp (London: Thames and Hudson) [as *The Art of Jean Arp* (New York: Abrams)]

The Cult of Sincerity (London: Faber and Faber)

1969

Essays in Literary Criticism: Particular Studies (London: Faber and Faber) [reprint of
    Part II of *Collected Essays in Literary Criticism* (1938)]

1971

(with Jean Cassou and John Smith) *Jan Le Witt* (London: Routledge and Kegan
    Paul)

* * *

1982

George Woodcock (ed.), *Letters from Sooke: A Correspondence between Sir Herbert Read and George Woodcock* (Victoria, B.C.: Victoria Book Arts Club)

1983

Herbert Read, *Pursuits & Verdicts* (Edinburgh: The Tragara Press)

1987

Herbert Read and A. Hilary Armstrong, *On Beauty* (Dallas: Spring Publications)

1994

David Goodway (ed.), *A One-Man Manifesto and Other Writings for Freedom Press* (London: Freedom Press)

316

Notes on Contributors

Peter Abbs is Reader in Education at the University of Sussex. His books on education and culture include *Living Powers* (1987), *A is for Aesthetic* (1988), *The Symbolic Order* (1989), *The Educational Imperative* (1994) and *The Polemics of Imagination* (1995). He has a special interest in the history and use of autobiography, his doctorate being on 'The Development of Autobiography in Western Culture: From Augustine to Rousseau' (University of Sussex, 1986). He is also the author of five volumes of poetry, most recently *Angelic Imagination* (1996).

Bob Barker, FRSA, is Adult Education Lecturer in Philosophy and Curriculum Team Leader, Access and Continuing Education, Bromley College of Further and Higher Education. He has published articles on *The Green Child* in *Notes and Queries* (1977 and 1980). His PhD thesis was 'A Critical Study of Herbert Read's *The Green Child* in the Light of its Cultural Milieu' (Royal Holloway and Bedford New College, London, 1988).

Andrew Causey is Professor of Modern Art History, University of Manchester. He is the author of monographs on Paul Nash (1980) and Edward Burra (1986), and many other publications on twentieth-century British art. He has organized exhibitions and was chair of the selection committee of British Art in the Twentieth Century, Royal Academy, 1986. His *Sculpture since 1945* was published by Oxford University Press in 1998.

Hugh Cecil is Senior Lecturer in Modern British History, University of Leeds. He is the author of *The Flower of Battle: How Britain Wrote the Great War* (US edition, 1996) and co-editor of *Facing Armageddon: The First World War Experienced* (1996). His *Clever Hearts: A Life of Desmond and Molly MacCarthy* (1990; jointly with Mirabel Cecil) won both the Duff Cooper Memorial Prize and the Marsh Biography Award.

Kevin Davey works in a community college in Inner London. He is convenor of the Signs of the Times seminar and conference group, and a former chair of the Socialist Society and the Socialist Movement. A regular contributor to the *New Statesman*, a columnist and feature writer for *New Times*, he has recently completed *English Imaginaries* (Lawrence and Wishart, forthcoming).

John R. Doheny retired in December 1992 after 33 years of teaching in the Department of English, University of British Columbia, Vancouver, Canada. He has published several articles on Thomas Hardy and two monographs (*The Youth of*

Thomas Hardy [1984] and *Thomas Hardy's Relatives and Their Times* [1989]), as well as articles on D. H. Lawrence, the Brontës, George Eliot, education, and anarchism.

David Goodway is Lecturer in History, School of Continuing Education, University of Leeds, and specializes in nineteenth- and twentieth-century British social and cultural history. His doctoral thesis was published as *London Chartism, 1838–1848* (1982). He has edited *For Anarchism* (1989) for the History Workshop Series, and also volumes of the anarchist writings of Alex Comfort (*Against Power and Death*) and Herbert Read (*A One-Man Manifesto*), both 1994.

Robin Kinross works as a typographer and editor in London. He has written many articles for the design press in Britain, a book *Modern Typography* (1992) and a pamphlet *Fellow Readers* (1994). His imprint, Hyphen Press, has published two books by Norman Potter.

Norman Potter was happy to design anything, from a book to a BA (Hons) course, but worked chiefly in furniture, interior and exhibition design. He sidestepped any continuous academic involvement, but taught influentially in art, design and architectural schools, and at every level from foundation to postgraduate work. His books included *What is a Designer* (1969) and *Models & Constructs* (1990). He died, at the age of 72, on 22 November 1995.

Malcolm Ross taught English and Drama in schools and teacher training, 1956–1967, before moving to the University of Exeter, where he was, until his recent retirement, Reader in Arts Education. His publications include *The Creative Arts* (1978), *The Aesthetic Impulse* (1984), *The Claims of Feeling* (1989), *Assessing Achievement in the Arts* (1993) and *State of the Arts in Five English Secondary Schools* (1997).

Paul Street is Lecturer in History of Art, School of Continuing Education, University of Leeds. He studied History of Art as a mature student at the University of Essex, and completed his PhD at Leeds on familial imagery in eighteenth-century British painting. His research interests are now principally concerned with aspects of Victorian art and society, including the landscapes of John Linnell and the social realism of Frank Holl.

David Thistlewood was Professor in the School of Architecture, University of Liverpool. He published extensively on Herbert Read, notably *Herbert Read: Formlessness and Form* (1984) and, as co-editor with Benedict Read, *Herbert Read: A British Vision of World Art* (1993). He was editor of the Tate Gallery Liverpool Critical Forum Series, for which he produced *American Abstract Expressionism* (1993), *Joseph*

Beuys: Diverging Critiques (1995), *Barbara Hepworth Reconsidered* (1996) and *Sigma Polke: Back to Postmodernity* (1996). He died as this book was going to press.

Kieron Winn read English, 1987–90, at Christ Church, Oxford, where he was a Scholar. After graduating he taught English and Drama at his old school, Tonbridge. Now back at Christ Church, he is writing a doctoral thesis on the literary work of Herbert Read.

Jerald Zaslove is Director of the Institute for the Humanities, Simon Fraser University, Burnaby, British Columbia, where he teaches European literature and modernism, aesthetics and politics, and interdisciplinary approaches to the arts. Recent articles are on the artist Jeff Wall, Kafka, literary hybridism, human rights and constitutions as literary values, Siegfried Kracauer, and propaganda. He is completing a study of Herbert Read as well as a book on the relationship of anarchism to modernism and the problem of the loss of historical consciousness.

Index